$3.50

JOHN MARSH, PIONEER

ONE AFTERNOON on a California hillside the author listened while a wizened old woman, one of the earliest settlers, pointed with a crooked, bony finger toward Mount Diablo and said:

"Over there, in an adobe at the base of that mountain, lived the most mysterious of California's pioneers. His name was John Marsh. He was a doctor, a hermit, a misanthrope."

The mystery of the man Marsh struck the author's imagination. For five years he searched out the past of this man. Then he put a full, vibrant portrait of John Marsh and his time into this book.

John Marsh graduated from Harvard in 1823. He was the first schoolmaster in Minnesota. He wrote a dictionary and a grammar of the Sioux language. He married a beautiful half-breed—French and Indian—and by her had a son whom he believed dead for many years, ultimately to find him begging at his door unaware that he besought his own father.

John Marsh was an Indian agent; some of his acts incited Indian wars; some of them terminated such wars. He traded furs, ran a store into bankruptcy, and then started on the long trek over the Santa Fé trail to California. Without having studied medicine he acted as a doctor in Los Angeles in 1836—the first in California. He became a cattle baron, participating in the revolutions which preceded California's entrance into the Union, which he helped to effect. He discovered gold. He was finally murdered, leaving a vast fortune hidden, undiscovered to this day.

John Marsh's life story is better than fiction. So also is the story of his time, of the life on our Western frontier, and in California before the days of '49.

Recovering the Glamourous Facts of John Marsh's Life

THE AUTHOR begins the very extensive and valuable bibliography appended to this biography with this statement:

"This biography of John Marsh is based entirely on source material: on old diaries, journals, faded letters, statements, reminiscences and memoirs found in many quarters: the library at Harvard University; the Minnesota, Wisconsin, and Illinois Historical Society Collections; the Historical, Memorial, and Art Department of Iowa at Des Moines; the Michigan Historical Commission at Lansing; the Jefferson Memorial at St. Louis, Mo.; the files in the Indian Office of the War Department at Washington, D. C.; the Bancroft Library at the University of California; and the California State Library at Sacramento. All these sources have been culled in the interests of John Marsh. All of them have yielded up valuable and, in many instances, hitherto unused material regarding some phase of his career.

"It has taken five years to locate, assemble, and piece together the material thus collected."

Dust jacket, front and back flaps, first edition, 1930

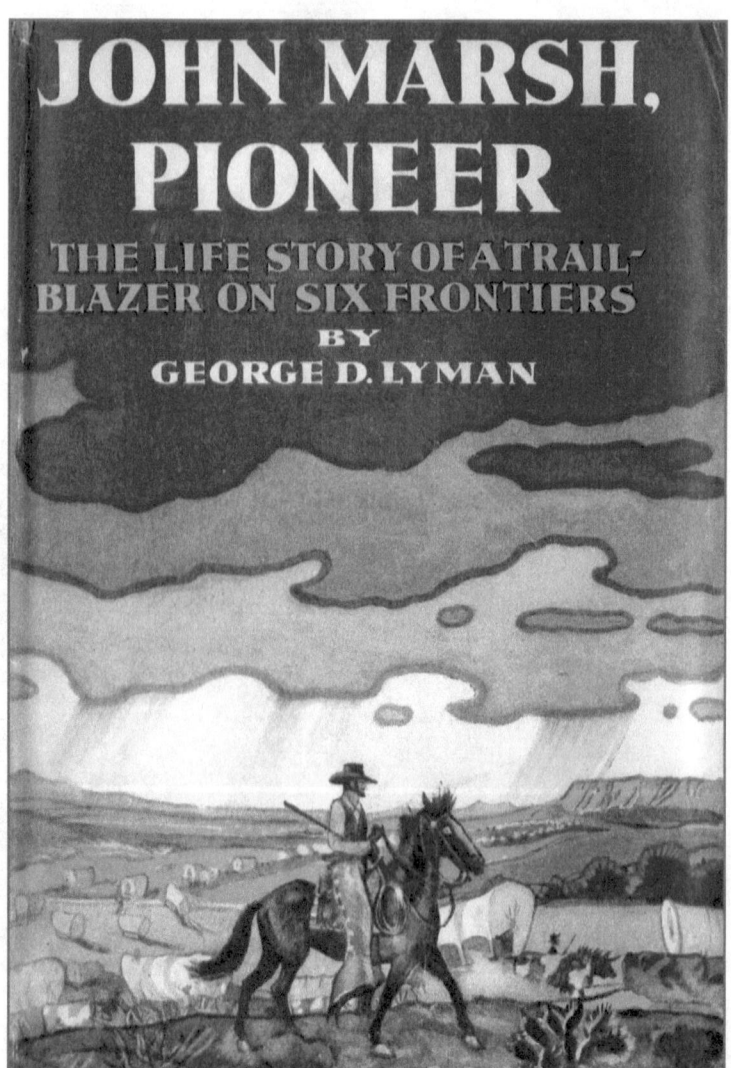

Front of dust jacket, first edition, 1933

John Marsh, Pioneer

*John Marsh, Abigail Marsh, and daughter Alice Francis.
Daguerreotype, BANC PIC 1963.004:123—CASE. Courtesy
of The Bancroft Library, University of California, Berkeley*

Original daguerreotype of the 1856 John Marsh house. 1963.007:001—CASE. Courtesy of The Bancroft Library, University of California, Berkeley

John Marsh, Pioneer
The Life Story of a Trail-blazer on Six Frontiers

By
GEORGE D. LYMAN

ILLUSTRATED

A complete facsimile edition
of the original work of 1930

with an Introduction and Apologia by Carol A. Jensen

Byron Hot Springs

Copyright © 2012 by Carol A. Jensen
First Printing: 2012
All rights reserved
ISBN: 978-0-615-65369-3
Published by Byron Hot Springs, San Francisco, California
Printed in the United States of America
For all general information, please contact:
Historian@ByronHotSprings.com
or visit the website at: http://ByronHotSprings.com

Disclaimer: All errors, additions, and omissions
are the responsibility of the publisher.

Cover photo: The John Marsh Stone House, built by John and Abigail Marsh in 1856, as photographed circa 1870 by Eadweard Muybridge (b 1830, d. 1904). The house still stands and is located west of Brentwood, eastern Contra Costa County, California. Courtesy of the Library of Congress, Historic American Building Survey, Gleason Collection, San Francisco College for Women

Spine photo: John Marsh, Abigail Marsh, and daughter Alice Francis. Daguerreotype, BANC PIC 1963.004:123—CASE. Courtesy of The Bancroft Library, University of California, Berkeley

Cover, new text design and composition: Leigh McLellan Design

"The names of the Indian fighters, the treaty makers, the wilderness wanderers, who took the lead in winning and exploring the West, are memorable."
—Roosevelt's *The Winning of the West.* vol. IV, p. 5

*Dedicated to Elizabeth Lyman Potter,
daughter of George D. Lyman, whose dedication to
restoring Marsh's Great Stone House is unflagging.
Thank you.*

Rancho de los Polpones cattle brand

INTRODUCTION TO THE NEW EDITION

THE "MEANEST MAN IN CALIFORNIA"[1] receives his chance at redemption thanks to this reprint of *John Marsh, Pioneer* by George Lyman. Few today recognize the importance of Marsh in western frontier history due to this famous epitaph by early California Pioneer John Bidwell (b.1819, d.1900). Thanks to this facsimile reprint of the 1930 edition we can rediscover the story of an 18th-century Massachusetts native, the son of English immigrants, as he moves west to explore the frontier. How many of us could name those six American frontiers today? They are the Atlantic/Colonial East, the Trans-Allegheny West (Ohio Valley), the Trans-Appalachian West (Mississippi Valley), the Rocky Mountains (Dakota Territory), the Southwest (New Mexico/Arizona), and the Pacific. John Marsh left a legacy at each step.

John Marsh (b.1799, d.1856) was a colorful man and influenced people and events throughout his life. Marsh knew Abraham Lincoln when the future president was a soldier in the Black Hawk War. Some even allege Marsh may have helped start the war by selling guns to the Native Americans. El Pueblo de Nuestra Señora la Reina de los Ángeles might not have become the Los Angeles known today had "Doctor" John Marsh not provided small pox immunizations. John Fremont and Kit Carson were guests at Marsh's Rancho Los Megaños. Marsh Landing, located at present-day Antioch along the Sacramento and San Joaquin River Delta, was established seven years before Captain John Sutter became lost in the tule rushes sailing to present-day

---

1. Bidwell, John, and John Henry Nash. *A Journey to California: with Observations About the Country, Climate and the Route to This Country.* San Francisco: J. H. Nash, printer, 1937.

Sacramento. The first overland emigrants from within the United States, including Benjamin and Nancy Kelsey with their infant daughter, came to California specifically with Marsh's adobe home in mind as their destination. Marsh knew mountain men, scouts, and members of the ill-fated Donner Party from his Illinois and Wisconsin days. The list of coincidental and "six degrees of separation" connecting John Marsh with historic figures and places in United States history is surprising.

Marsh was an early and important proponent of California settlement and peaceful inclusion into the United States a full twenty years before the Gold Rush. He justifiably expected party nomination for Governor of California in 1857. After Marsh's untimely death on September 24, 1856, Democrat John B. Welter secured the political party's nomination in September 1857 and served as governor from 1858 to 1860.[2] Marsh leaves no personal memoir of his experiences in the West.

John Bidwell felt sorely used by Marsh in 1841 and never forgave him. Bidwell's reminiscences as captured by Hubert Howe Bancroft's history machine in 1877[3] relegate Marsh to a footnote on the California Trail. Bidwell recalled arriving at Marsh's Rancho de los Polpones with the first overland group of 32 emigrants to California in November 1841. The party was half-starved, lost, and guided into today's eastern Contra Costa County by one of Marsh's Native American Polpone tribe vaqueros. Marsh fed the relieved Bartleson-Bidwell party pork and tortillas. The emigrants helped themselves even more. Appreciation and pay-

---

2. *Our Campaigns—CA Governor Race—Sep 02, 1857*. Our Campaigns: A Collaborative Political Resource, n.d. Web. 25 Sept. 2012. http://ourcampaigns.com/RaceDetail.html?RaceID=122004.
3. Leek, Nancy. *John Bidwell: The Adventurous Life of a California Pioneer*. Chico, CA: ANCHR, 2010. Print.

ment were expressed with gunpowder, lead, and a surgical instrument kit.[4] The price for Mexican government passports and visas for California residency were negotiated, Marsh's prize bull shot, and seed corn consumed; all to the personal travail and building animosity between Marsh and Bidwell.

The secret to securing your place in history is living long enough to tell your part. Young John Bidwell went on to settle in the northern Sacramento Valley, gain military title and fame, compose his memoirs, and live to see the 20th century. John Marsh however, lived just long enough to experience the Gold Rush and California statehood, only to be murdered. Twenty-two year old Bidwell's 1842 letters home to Missouri branding Marsh as the "meanest man in California" stuck to Marsh's reputation. Marsh died unheralded; Bidwell lived.

Historians, book lovers, California Emigrant Trail enthusiasts, and those seeking a real-life adventure story will enjoy this biography. The exploits of Dr. John Marsh are as absorbing as those of legendary bandits Joaquin Murrieta and Three-Finger Jack, or the fictionalized Don Diego de la Vega as Señor Zorro. Marsh's feats are real! Modern scholarship contradicts some of the original narrative and literary license taken by George Lyman in creating his "Larger than the West" hero. Marsh as an historic figure is full of contradictions, temperament, fallibilities, exasperation, and strength. Lyman captures that spirit within his sometimes embellished facts. A scholarly, well-researched, modern biography of John Marsh is overdue. Marsh is an American pioneer who moved west and lived in bounty at the end of his life

---

4. Bidwell, John. *Echoes of the Past: an Account of the First Emigrant Train to California, Fremont in the Conquest of California, the Discovery of Gold and Early Reminiscences,* by the Late General John Bidwell. Chico, Calif: Chico advertiser, 1900. Print.

in California; he recaptures his rightful place in history thanks to this reprint.

Readers interested in learning more about John Marsh, his great stone house, and his legacy should visit Brentwood, in eastern Contra Costa County, located 50 miles east of San Francisco, California. Here you will find the terminus of the first overland California Trail, located at the Marsh Creek State Historic Park as administered by the California State Parks and Recreation Department. The John Marsh Historic Trust is dedicated to the restoration of the three-story stone home built by John and Abigail Marsh in 1856. For more information about this architectural gem and efforts to restore it for public use, please visit http://JohnMarshHouse.com.

Carol A. Jensen
Brentwood, California
September 24, 2012
John Marsh Murder Remembrance Day

APOLOGIA

apo-lo-gia (noun) An apology or formal defense of an idea, religion, etc., esp. such a defense of one's own beliefs or conduct.

GEORGE LYMAN wrote in the genre of the 1930s with romantic hindsight of life in Mexican California and early California statehood. Frederick Jackson Turner declared in 1893 that unlimited free land was at an end and with it came the end of the American frontier. However, the psychological frontier tradition continued with a robust life in literature, pride in the past, and development of the uniquely American "can do" ethos. Along with the idealized 19th century historical view came less savory relics of pioneer life: racism, marginalization, and defamatory lexicon.

This reprint in facsimile of *John Marsh, Pioneer*, refers to "Indians," and at times marginalizes and defames Native Americans in terms that, we hope, are extinct in the 21st century. No effort has been made by the editor to sanitize the text to modern, politically correct vocabulary. As Mark Twain's *The Adventures of Huckleberry Finn (1884)* captures 19th century American idiom, so too does *John Marsh, Pioneer (1933)* mark that vocabulary continuing into the 20th century.

The editor asks the reader to focus on the life and impact made by one great man as he follows the routes of western expansion across the United States. Individual folly and success are all part of the Western experience, along with dominance and imperialism. Herein the reader will find a model of life containing elements both to emulate and to avoid.

Carol A. Jensen

Variant jacket decoration, 1930

John Marsh, Pioneer
The Life Story of a Trail-blazer on Six Frontiers

"The names of the Indian fighters, the treaty-makers, the wilderness wanderers, who took the lead in winning and exploring the West, are memorable."
—Roosevelt's *The Winning of the West.*
Vol. IV, p. 5.

JOHN MARSH.

John Marsh, Pioneer

The Life Story of a Trail-blazer on
Six Frontiers

By
GEORGE D. LYMAN

ILLUSTRATED

NEW YORK
CHARLES SCRIBNER'S SONS
1930

COPYRIGHT, 1930, BY
CHARLES SCRIBNER'S SONS

Printed in the United States of America

A

TO

MY MOTHER AND FATHER

ANNA LOUISE DUNLAP
DEAN BRIGGS LYMAN

AND

MY FOSTER PARENT

ADELAIDE HAUGH

IN REMEMBRANCE

PREFACE

I can almost recall the day and hour that I first heard the name John Marsh.

It was at a little hillside town in California. I was talking to a neighbor, an old wizened woman, one of the earliest settlers. We were standing on the brow of a hill, looking across the Santa Clara Valley, and discussing the pioneers and the reasons that brought them to California when that country was still a Mexican province.

"At that time California was a place for hunted men," she said. "They came here to hide and be forgotten." She pointed a bony finger over in the distance toward Mount Diablo.

"Over there," said she, "in an adobe at the base of that mountain, lived the most mysterious of California's pioneers. His name was John Marsh. He was a doctor, a hermit, a misanthrope. He hated men."

After that, I couldn't forget him, the mysterious John Marsh—a doctor in Mexican California as early as 1836! In those days Mount Diablo was a semi-savage wilderness!

"Most of the early settlers in these parts were fugitives," the old woman continued. "They were hiding from themselves or from some one else. Many of them were outlaws: forgers, deserters from the sea. Even murderers hid in these redwoods. Practically all of them had been driven out of some more settled community. They

PREFACE

were all afraid of something or somebody. Fear brought them here. Fear kept them hiding. But no one ever found out why Marsh hid in the shadow of Mount Diablo."

That talk haunted me. Question after question popped into my head.

What was a highly educated American doing in California before the conquest?

What did he fear?

What made him a hermit?

Why did he avoid his fellows?

To all these questions, the old woman replied: "Don't know."

I could not get Marsh nor the circumstances connected with him out of my mind.

None of my other neighbors knew as much about him.

To the oldest settler he was a mystery.

That fact spurred me on. That fact started me on a search for John Marsh's past. The quest lasted for more than five years and led me from the Pacific to the Atlantic, from California to Massachusetts, and then through the files of many of the great State libraries of the country. For it was in these historical collections that I first picked up John Marsh's trail and followed it into exile. It was in them that I eventually solved his problem. Disappointment and disillusionment made him a hermit. Or was it a conscience? In vagous mood, fate led him on and on.

I located Marsh in many places: in Massachusetts, where he was born; at Phillips Academy, Andover, in his prep days; at Harvard, where he graduated; at Fort Snelling, Minnesota, where he taught the first school; at Prairie du Chien, Wisconsin; at Davenport, Iowa; at New Salem, Illinois; at St. Louis and Independence, Missouri; at

PREFACE

Santa Fé, New Mexico, and finally on a rancho in California.

When I had run down the clews, collected my data, and pieced together my information, what a history it disclosed! What a man! I had found a hero neglected by the historians!

For John Marsh was one of the greatest of our early adventurers. He was a pioneer on six American frontiers, a founder of commonwealths, a power in every community in which he lived. What other frontiersman, I ask, can equal that record? What other man figured as largely in the pioneer annals of the frontier as he?

John Marsh was a Harvard graduate. How many others, of our wilderness wanderers, boasted an Alma Mater? That diploma made him unique as a frontiersman. He carried the intellectual traditions of New England from the Atlantic to the Pacific. The faded and dusty records show that he made them revered. He helped to bind Massachusetts, the Mississippi, and the Pacific with one indissoluble bond. Therein lies John Marsh's chief claim to fame. Not only did he blaze a trail; he carried a torch.

One of John Marsh's acts is quoted as a cause leading up to the Black Hawk War. He was a witness of the treaty that terminated that struggle, and that transferred an immense tract of land from the possession of the red men into the hands of the whites.

Another of his acts started the prairie schooners rolling across the continent. Still another freed California from the last of her Mexican governors. Both those accomplishments paved the way to California's ultimate acquisition by the United States.

Many of Marsh's deeds were greater than the man himself. Many fell far short. Sometimes he destroyed. Mostly

PREFACE

he builded. He was strong. He was weak. He was great. He was small. He loved. He hated. But always he was human. On every occasion but one he was master of circumstances. Even then, in defeat, he was heroic.

Wherever John Marsh went, there was romance and adventure. His life reads like a volume of fiction. It was as thrilling as a cinema! The name of Marsh should be a household word. Yet Fate, for some inscrutable reason, denied him a place among the immortals.

To all those interested in the bold and daring lives of our wilderness wanderers, I offer this biography as a belated tribute to John Marsh, whose stride westward was marked by Sheepskin, Redskin, and Cowhide.

GEORGE D. LYMAN.

SAN FRANCISCO,
May, 1930.

CONTENTS

BOOK ONE: SHEEPSKIN

CHAPTER		PAGE
I.	John Marsh of Salem	3
II.	Danvers and Franklin Academy	7
III.	Lancaster Academy	14
IV.	Annual Training and Drilling	22
V.	"Brimstone Hill," Phillips Academy—Andover, Massachusetts	25
VI.	Harvard	34

BOOK TWO: REDSKIN

VII.	Massachusetts to Fort St. Anthony	49
VIII.	Fort St. Anthony, the Snellings and Taliaferro. Indian Agent of St. Peters	55
IX.	Minnesota's First School, Its Master and Pupils	61
X.	Mail-Carrier	68
XI.	Sioux Indian Agent	72
XII.	Departure and Return	81
XIII.	Taliaferro's Revenge	89
XIV.	Marguerite	98
XV.	Prairie du Chien	101
XVI.	Justice of the Peace, Michigan Territory	112
XVII.	Red Bird. The Sioux Warning	115
XVIII.	Marsh Commands Fort Crawford. Red Bird Appeals to Marsh. Surrender	122
XIX.	Gagnier's Scalp	133
XX.	Marsh, Henry Dodge, and the Treaty of Green Bay	139
XXI.	Partiality for the Sioux	145
XXII.	Marsh Betrays the Foxes to the Sioux. Black Hawk Retaliates	152
XXIII.	Marguerite's Flight to the New Salem and Sandridge Settlements of Illinois	161

CONTENTS

CHAPTER		PAGE
XXIV.	The Black Hawk War. Marsh Commands the Sioux	169

BOOK THREE: COWHIDE

XXV.	Escape to the Rocky Mountains	183
XXVI.	Merchandising; Independence, Missouri	189
XXVII.	Flight Down the Santa Fé Trail	195
XXVIII.	First American Doctor in California. El Pueblo de Nuestra Señora, La Reina de Los Angeles	200
XXIX.	Explorations. Yerba Buena	206
XXX.	Cattle Ranching, Los Meganos	212
XXXI.	The Doctor and the Horse Thieves	224
XXXII.	Treachery. The Graham Affair	231
XXXIII.	Inaugurates California Immigration	237
XXXIV.	First Emigrants Arrive at Marsh's Rancho	243
XXXV.	Betrays Micheltorena	250
XXXVI.	Treachery. Battle of Cahuenga	258
XXXVII.	Marsh Calls the Americans to Arms. The Republic of California	262
XXXVIII.	Frémont. Coup d'État Fails	268
XXXIX.	Park's Bar	276
XL.	Women	283
XLI.	Abby	290
XLII.	Vigilantes	298
XLIII.	Robbers	304
XLIV.	Harvest Time	314
XLV.	By the Laws of France	324
XLVI.	Marsh's Light	333
	Appendix—	
	Acknowledgments	339
	Bibliography	343
	Index	385

ILLUSTRATIONS

John Marsh	*Frontispiece*
	FACING PAGE
The Opening Scene of the "Great Rebellion"	42
Fort Snelling	58
Major Laurence Taliaferro	82
Dr. Edward Purcell	82
Wabashaw	108
Red Bird	130
James Pantier	166
Susanna Murphy Pantier	166
Interior of the Pantier Home	166
Black Hawk	176
A Bull Fight at Mission Dolores	208
Californians Throwing the Lasso	218
Californians Branding Cattle	218
Marsh's Cattle Brand	226
Isaac Graham	234
Manuel Micheltorena	252
Pio Pico	262
The Call to Arms, 1845	264
San Francisco in 1848	280
Los Angeles in 1853	280
The Stone House Built by Marsh	294
Proclamation Regarding Capture of Morena	325
Charles Marsh	334

BOOK ONE
SHEEPSKIN

CHAPTER I

JOHN MARSH OF SALEM

1633

ONE late afternoon of an early summer day in 1633 there was great excitement along the beach at Salem. On top of a high hill the beacon was signalling the approach of a vessel. Soon a sail was seen off Marblehead's outward point. The news flew swiftly through the few streets, that an English ship filled with colonists and bringing letters from England was in the offing. The men left the sawpits, the women deserted their thatched log-cabins and with their children congregated on the shore.

Among those awaiting the oncoming vessel was the village minister, the Reverend Samuel Skelton, in black small-clothes, high-heeled buckled shoes, and large white ruff.

By his side was his daughter, Susanna—a fair, blue-eyed young woman in tight waist, flowing gown, and inevitable ruff. Both watched the incoming vessel eagerly. Her countenance was lit with mingled joy and anxiety.

As the ship drew nearer, the onlookers could read her name, *Mary and John*. There being no wharves in old Salem, the anchor was cast off. The bow and side-rail of the ship filled with passengers! The minister and his daughter scanned their ranks and finally singled out a man standing on the deck.

"That is he; that is he!" said the happy young lady, as she wiped away her tears.

JOHN MARSH, PIONEER

"That is your John; I mean our John," replied the Reverend Skelton.[1] *

On the quarter-deck stood the stalwart figure of a splendid-looking youth, hat in hand, bowing and smiling. Soon one of the ship's small boats neared the shore, and the stranger leaped upon the beach, ran along the strand to the little group that moved to the water's edge to meet him, and grasped the old clergyman's hand in a firm and tender clasp. Then turning, in one rapturous moment he took the fair Susanna in his arms.

Thus, picturesquely, the family genealogist described the landing of John Marsh, his English ancestor, on the shores of New England in 1633. He is pictured as being six feet of British manhood, distinguished by a broad forehead, steady eyes that showed he was not to be trifled with, and a firm, decisive step.

Shortly after John Marsh's arrival, the Reverend Samuel Skelton, who had graduated at Cambridge University in 1611 and had organized the first church of the Puritans at Salem, died. One year later, John Marsh led the minister's beloved daughter, Susanna, to the altar her father had consecrated, and made her his wife.

On Sunday, April 30, 1637, at the proper stage of the services and in the church hallowed by the memory of his grandsire, John and Susanna Marsh presented at the baptismal font, a baby boy. The minister took the child in his arms. As the congregation rose to their feet, he sprinkled water on the little bald head, and said: "Brethren, this is Zachariah Marsh, the grandson of our late beloved Pastor Skelton."[2]

Again the same scene was repeated in the same little

---

* Numerals in the text refer, chapter for chapter, to corresponding numerals in Bibliography at close of book.

JOHN MARSH OF SALEM

church, in the same impressive way, March 16, 1639, when the second child, John Marsh, was baptized. During the next twenty years, John and Susanna presented nine more of their babies at the font to receive the benediction of the church. Thus were the children of John Marsh of Salem descended from the Reverend Samuel Skelton, the first minister of the first Christian church in Massachusetts.

During these years the roots of the Marshes were growing deep into the soil of Salem. They loved the land which they had reclaimed. When Ezekiel, the great-grandson of "John Marsh of Salem," was born, on May 27, 1710, scarcely a descendant had migrated more than a hundred miles from the original rooftree.[3] Salem was their stronghold. They remained, upholding and transmitting its Puritan traditions. As Ezekiel grew into manhood, this love of home and of family was so marked that not even war could disrupt the tie. When the Revolution began, he became an ensign in Captain Larnard Epes' company of thirty-nine men and marched away to Lexington and Concord. In the same company were his two sons, Lieutenant Ezekiel Marsh, Jr., and John Marsh.[4]

After the Revolution, the ensign and his sons marched back over the Ipswich road to the lands of their forbears. Lieutenant Ezekiel returned to the "old homestead," which his father had deeded to him; it was built in 1692. The ensign with his other son, John Marsh, retired to the new house on the Ipswich road, which he had built in 1766. Here father and son planted and reaped, and John Marsh waxed prosperous enough to own a slave.[5]

Two years after the War of Independence, John Marsh sickened and died. Four months later, at the end of a wintry November day of 1778, his widow gave birth to a

JOHN MARSH, PIONEER

posthumous son. He received his father's name and helped to mend the broken heart of his old grandsire. For twenty years more they sowed and reaped. When John grew to man's estate—tall, blue-eyed and muscular—he married Polly Brown.

Barely a year later, Polly added another blue-eyed, fair-haired man-child to the long line of Marshes. She, too, gave him the name of John. He was the seventh in descent from his God-fearing ancestor of Salem. Like that progenitor, he was an adventurer; like his grandsire Skelton, faith was early manifest; and like Ezekiel, the love of his own flesh and blood was strong within him.

CHAPTER II

DANVERS AND FRANKLIN ACADEMY

1807–1817

JOHN MARSH grew to boyhood in the old homestead which his great-grandfather, the Ensign Ezekiel, had built in 1766. It was a typical New England farmhouse, with much white paint, green blinds, cobblestones and numerous ells and sheds in its makeup. It was situated on the old Ipswich road to Boston, the first highway in the town, originally an Indian trail, but used by the settlers since 1630. Governor John Winthrop traversed it in 1634 when he went to visit his son, John Winthrop, Jr., in Ipswich; Justices Hawthorne and Curwen travelled it in witchcraft days, and Rebecca Nourse followed it on her way to the Salem jail. Benedict Arnold and his troops took it on their memorable march from Cambridge to Quebec in 1775. Over it the bodies of the Danvers men slain in the battle of Lexington were returned to their desolate homes. Along it young John's grandfather and great-grandfather marched triumphantly on their way to and from the war.

All these traditions of Indians, witchcraft and revolution appealed strongly to the susceptible mind of the growing lad and left an indelible impression upon him. To him the old Ipswich pike was the road to adventure, and he longed to travel it. Often he looked longingly down it, first in the direction of Salem and its wharves and then to where it disappeared toward Boston and the Unknown.

But explorations in either direction were forbidden,

JOHN MARSH, PIONEER

and John gave himself up to trapping and hunting in the immediate vicinity. The groves and brooks nearby abounded in fox, squirrel, and muskrat. He spent his spare time capturing them and was rated as an adroit and clever trapper.[1] Occasionally there was a visit to his Aunt Williams in Salem and an opportunity to go to the quays along the waterfront. On such excursions he would sit watching the harbor life and the sailing vessels coming and going to the Orient and distant Pacific ports.

One wild night, while he was in Salem, the *Union Osgood* from India ran ashore on Baker's Island. The crew were saved, and a cargo of pepper and block-tin salvaged, but the ship itself was a total loss. The first thing in the morning John hastened to the island. The wreck was thrilling.

About this time another fascinating thing occurred. A serpent of enormous size was seen in the harbor of Gloucester. Enchanting descriptions of the monster filled the papers. Every time John got a chance, he ran away to the wharves. The old sailors pictured it as enormous—some said 60, others 140 feet—but the most authentic reports stated that it was in the neighborhood of 70 feet long, about the breadth of a barrel and covered with hard scales.

One night some men in a small boat came within reach of the serpent with their oars. They were upon it before they saw it and were so terrified that they made a hasty retreat. Finally one of the young of the serpent was killed on an island in Gloucester harbor and was exhibited at the Essex Coffee House. Here John saw it. It was three feet long, brown in color, and had thirty-two humps upon its back. Exciting!

In the fall of 1818 a steamboat made an appearance in the harbor. John went all through her. She was about

DANVERS AND FRANKLIN ACADEMY

eighty-five feet long, with elegant accommodations in the stern and bow. The machinery was large and occupied the centre part, but it was so intricate that the youth was unable to comprehend its mechanism. She was going to the Pacific. There was also in the harbor, at this time, a brig bound for a South American revolution. John saw the sailors loading her with cannon balls. The sight filled him with a desire to go too. He would have liked to follow up that cannon fodder! When he reached home, he threw his arms around his mother's neck and said: "Mother, when I grow up, I shall make my home beyond the Rockies."[2]

John was not an only child; he was the eldest of seven. To the mother, her first-born was especially dear. All her life she recalled this period when he filled the house with gay laughter and told stories of wrecks, serpents, cannon balls and revolutions. Such things he liked, but the work on the farm palled upon him. "Poverty, ignorance and the soil," he once noted, "go hand in hand." To avoid these, he discovered, one must have an education. Early in life he made up his mind to get one and escape, perhaps into the ministry. That was what his mother wanted him to be—a minister. Once she told him it would make her very happy if he gave himself to God. After that, in the home circle, it was tacitly understood that John was destined for the pulpit. Thus do mothers consecrate their sons!

In the meantime John and his brother Caleb went to the village school. One of their first teachers was Mary Felton, who received two dollars and thirty-four cents for schooling them—thirteen weeks at nine cents per week.[3] At a later period, when he was eleven years old, he had John Hastings for a schoolmaster. The latter received three dollars and fifty cents each quarter.[4]

On Sundays John went to church, often twice a day,

JOHN MARSH, PIONEER

and most frequently to the old South Church of Danvers. But he was not always listening to the words of prayer; instead, he developed a critical attitude and spent his time analyzing the minister, the Reverend M. Walker, noting his appearance, delivery, choice of text and composition. Once, when he came home, he horrified his father by remarking: "Walker is insipid. I could preach a better sermon myself." For that heretical remark he was sent to his room to reflect on the enormity of his criticism and to write from memory a synopsis of the sermon of the morning. In spite of having dedicated his future to the church, there were moments when his allegiance was divided between divinity and cannon balls. Strange as it may seem, cannon balls played a conspicuous rôle in his career.

When he was fifteen, John decided the time had come to insure his escape from the soil. During the fall of 1815 he persuaded his father to send him to boarding school. In November he left home for Franklin Academy in North Andover, of which Rufus P. Hovey of Haverhill was preceptor.[5] Here he took a room in Mrs. Abbot's boarding house, where he was required to furnish his own candles and wood for the fireplace. One of his instructors made his home in the same place.

The winters were bitterly cold in North Andover. It was not easy to find wood at hand or to carry enough to his room. He was properly very much disgusted when he discovered that some one had been rifling his woodbox during his absence at classes.

At first he lay in wait for the thief and tried to catch him red-handed, but this proved impossible, so he laid a trap for him. Carefully piling the logs in his woodbox, he bored holes in several, which he filled with gunpowder, then went about his classes. When he returned, his wood-

DANVERS AND FRANKLIN ACADEMY

box had been almost emptied. He waited in fear and trembling for the dénouement, which was not long delayed.

That night there was a terrible explosion in the young instructor's room. The horrified boarders ran to his rescue. They found that while the young instructor was safe, his room was wrecked. When John discovered who the thief was, he fled the wrath to come, and packing his clothes, returned to Danvers. His father was disgusted and put his son to work on the farm.

Hateful as chores were, John declared they were preferable to being imposed upon. The harder he worked, the greater became his thirst for knowledge. For the rest of the winter he made a study of crime, attending all the murder trials for miles around and filling his journals with grewsome details drawn from the evidence.

The fate of one, Henry Phillips, who murdered Gaspard Dennegri in the Roebuck Tavern in Boston, was engaging the general attention and John's in particular. Gaspard, an ignorant Italian, was one night ejected from the Tavern, but returned and while looking through the window was mysteriously struck down from behind by an iron loggerhead. Phillips was suspected, arrested and brought before the supreme judicial court sitting in Boston, Chief Justice Parker presiding, and was eventually found guilty and sentenced.

The scene in the court-room was indelibly impressed on John's mind, and he described minutely the scene there, the prisoner at the bar, the Judge delivering the sentence, transcribing his exact words in his Journal, writing them in capitals: *"That you be carried from here to the prison from whence you came and from thence to the place of execution on the thirteenth day of February next, and there be hanged by the neck until you are dead!"*

JOHN MARSH, PIONEER

After his experience at Franklin Academy, John's father would not give him any more money for schooling, so John decided to earn some. During the winter of 1816–1817 he taught the village school at Danvers. Among his pupils were David Newhall, D. Stone, Thomas Williams and Jonathan Nourse. David was fifteen and Nourse seventeen. John was not yet eighteen. Young as he was, he allowed none of his pupils to subvert his authority and chastised Thomas Williams for playing truant and severely ferruled young Stone for telling a lie.

One bitterly cold February day both Newhall and Nourse refused to remain in their seats and insisted on coming to the fire, thus upsetting the morale of the school. Marsh ordered them to return to their places. Nourse, who was as tall and brawny as Marsh, was particularly defiant and refused to go. "Father said I should go to the fire when I had a mind to, and I'm going," he said.

Marsh replied, "I am master here; you must either obey orders or leave the school." Suiting action to his words, he took his recreant pupil by the throat and shoved him toward the door.

Nourse struggled in his grip and gasped, "If you try to put me out-of-doors in the snow, my father will put you out of the school."

But before that threat was fully uttered, Marsh had pushed him into the entry, saying, "You can't return until you obey orders," and closed the door behind him.

When Newhall, whose father was a trustee, discovered how his classmate had fared at the hands of the young schoolmaster, he took his seat, but with poor grace and acted vexed and angry, showing signs of continued disobedience. Marsh then went to him and upbraided him roundly: "There is no one in the school that I have spent

DANVERS AND FRANKLIN ACADEMY

so much time instructing as you in your studies. Is this the return? Is this the way you reward my extra exertions? If it is, it is poor encouragement."

To this plea Newhall made no reply, but hung his head. About this time the door opened, and Nourse reappeared, took his seat and was ever after obedient.

Toward the close of the winter term, the school committee, composed of the Reverend Mr. Walker, pastor of the first church of Danvers, Doctor Andrew Nichols, a Harvard graduate who had practised in Danvers for upwards of fifty years, and whose motto was "to live for man and work for humanity,"[6] and Captain J. Proctor, came to examine Marsh's students. At the conclusion, they reported themselves well satisfied with their progress, commended him for his efforts and promised him a certificate recommending him as schoolmaster. The term ended successfully on February 19.[7] John was jubilant. He had earned enough to go to Lancaster Academy at Lancaster, where his friend and fellow townsman John W. Proctor, Harvard 1816, was preceptor. At last, chores would be behind him.

CHAPTER III

LANCASTER ACADEMY
1817–1818

On April 7 John arose at sunrise. With Mr. Proctor he departed for Lancaster, passing en route through Lynn, Chelsea, Malden, and Charlestown. From the latter place he had a distant view of Boston. He was thrilled at the sight of its lofty spires, magnificent State House and several large ships-of-war lying at anchor in the harbor.

From Charlestown the road passed the memorable battleground of Bunker Hill. John viewed with feeling the inscription "Commemorating the death of the brave and accomplished General Warren." Soon after, crossing the mouth of the Middlesex Canal, they came into Cambridge, passing some old entrenchments which the American army had thrown up while the British were in possession of Boston.

At an inn near Harvard University, they put up for the night. John was greatly interested in the college "yard," containing at that time five large edifices built of brick and one of white stone. He felt they were delightfully situated and presented an inviting appearance, and added prophetically, "Some day I shall go there."

Next morning they passed through West Cambridge, then Lexington, and John carefully noted the spot where the first blood was shed; the gray granite shaft with its inscription: "Sacred to the liberty and right of Mankind: The Freedom and Independence of America! Sealed and defended by the blood of her sons!" thrilling him to the core.

LANCASTER ACADEMY

From Lexington they passed through Concord, Stow, and Bolton, arriving at Lancaster late Saturday evening. Greatly fatigued, John spent the night with Mr. Proctor at Major Carter's home, and from there went to board with the Whiting family. Here there were two daughters, an older of some thirty summers with a dogmatic disposition, and a younger in whom nature had blended the charm and mysteries of sixteen. Beside himself, there were a number of other boarders, among whom he mentioned: C. C. Tucker, a Southerner; Luther Wheelock; Isaac Davis of Northborough; Fletcher, Haven, and Burridge, all of whom attended the Academy, and one young lady, Maria Lincoln of Leominster, who taught a neighboring school. All interested him immensely. Before long he was analyzing them and confiding their whims and foibles to his Journal.

At first Marsh roomed with Davis and was greatly impressed with him. He was preparing for Yale. John felt he had a sincere heart, some wit, singular manners and many talents. On closer acquaintance he concluded that his wit was low and frequently vulgar; that his singularity was affected to hide his want of knowledge of propriety; that he was vain of his abilities and sought praise by pretending to think himself ignorant, particularly in those things in which he was most thorough.

C. C. Tucker was preparing for Harvard, and John summed him up as a "person of much affability who attached an undue importance to what concerned himself or his connections and entertained an exalted opinion of himself and of his knowledge and attainments. He disliked very much to be contradicted and was possessed of what he calls 'fine feelings' and a delicate sense of honor. The slightest hint of anything contrary irritated him very

JOHN MARSH, PIONEER

much. With a confidence and pleasing address mixed with a little abstruse flattery, he soon ingratiated himself into female society. A native of the South, his disposition partook of the ardour of his native clime."

The day following his arrival, John explored his new surroundings and was delighted with the beauty of Lancaster's setting. The lovely valley of the Nashua, the rich meadows, the river winding through them, the elm-shaded streets and river, the academy on the Old Common and the picturesque outlines of Wachusett, Watatic and the Grand Monadnock in the distance were not lost upon him.

The day being Sunday, his explorations ended at the meeting-house. He felt it was the most elegant structure of its type he had ever seen. The Reverend Nathaniel Thayer was in the pulpit that day, and John was pleased with the congregation and formed a good opinion of the society of the place from their appearance.

On Monday morning he hurried to the Common and began the classics that were going to shatter the shackles that bound him to the soil. The first day he construed several chapters in Historia Sacra and wrestled with the first book of the Æneid. In four months he finished the Latin grammar, went twice through the Epitome Historiæ Sacræ, twice through the first book of Virgil's Æneid, once through the second book and had progressed 150 lines in the third. In addition, he did some rhetorical work and wrote several compositions on such subjects as "Fame," "Pride," "Calumny and Slander" and "Solitude." These subjects were apparently suggested by daily occurrences.

It was not all study. Once several of his classmates, accompanied by an equal number of fair ladies, went on a picnic to the summit of the Wachusett Mountain. John was anxious to go, but feeling he was only a scholar

LANCASTER ACADEMY

upon the lowest steps of Minerva's Temple, he stayed at home and wrote a paper on "Solitude" and studied, for study meant emancipation.[1]

It was a practice at the school to declaim every Saturday. Marsh was of such a self-conscious nature that he dreaded these occasions more than any others and saw the fatal day approach with considerable inward trepidation and suffered untold qualms during the delivery of his parts. On one occasion he spoke the lines of Goliath in the dialogue of "David and Goliath." C. Thayer took the opposing part. Again John argued against spirituous liquors, while Isaac Davis spoke in the affirmative. Apparently on both occasions he acquitted himself well.

All of this study and declaiming was not accomplished without considerable physical strain. He suffered almost continually from headaches. Having little time for exercise, his spirits were often depressed and his attitude toward life dejected. Outside the classroom the main diversion he allowed himself was the services in the meeting house. To them he went two or three times every Sunday and listened intently and critically to the sermons, noting the delivery, the choice of words, the piety and orthodoxy of the preacher. More and more the church and his classical studies claimed him. Closer and closer he was drawn to a life of piety. Finally he set aside one hour of each day for reflection and consideration of his faults. But sometimes another side of his nature burst through.

One Saturday, John and ten of his classmates went to an orchard in the vicinity to help themselves to some fruit. To prevent discovery, they blackened their faces with berry juices and armed themselves with clubs. The owner and his family were a shiftless lot, noted about the countryside for their slovenly habits—cats, dogs, lambs,

JOHN MARSH, PIONEER

fowl and pigs occupied the living quarters with them. In the midst of their pilfering, the old farmer discovered them and started in pursuit. John organized his gang, and, as the old man approached, they bombarded him with apples and then fled, but in his flight John stumbled and fell. Before he could get to his feet, the old man was upon him and in a trice had him bound to a tree with ropes. Leaving him, he took his basket away and went in pursuit of the others. While John was trying to escape, a vicious hog attacked and bit him several times, but frightening him more than hurting him. At last he succeeded in loosening one of his hands, when an old hag pounced upon him and tried to bind him again. Shoving her off, he extricated himself, armed himself with a club, walked boldly into the house, demanded his basket, recovered it and fled.

It was at Lancaster that John had his first love affair. The girl was Maria Lincoln of Leominster, a fellow-boarder. He was so fascinated by her charms that he made a careful study of her personality. "Her appearance," he confided in his Journal, "is that of modesty and diffidence. At first acquaintance one would think her mental powers or attainments were not of the first order, but upon a more thorough knowledge, she improves very much. Her feelings easily wrought upon, her mind naturally quick and penetrating, she observes and judges with more than common accuracy. She is very studious not to offend and very ready to make acknowledgment when she fears she has. Her disposition is frank, open and sincere. I think her one of those persons who participate in the sentiment and sympathize in the feelings of those around her. She is very fearful of danger at a distance, yet when it comes, meets it with firmness."[2]

LANCASTER ACADEMY

There was at this time a rich man in Lancaster named Emerson. John did not like him; especially as Emerson liked Maria. He set him down as a "brutal, malicious, detracting wretch." Emerson tried to force his attentions on Maria, but she spurned his advances. Afterwards he endeavored to injure her reputation by some false and ungrounded slander concerning her conduct. Like a real woman, she ignored him as well as his remarks, but when they went unnoticed, he adopted more insulting measures, sending her a package containing a small fish, with an insulting note.

Then Maria appealed to John, and John came to the rescue. He organized a band of twenty of the most respectable young men of the town for the purpose of teaching the old villain a lesson. One night at ten o'clock they assembled and, providing themselves with bells, horns, trumpets, conch-shells, or any instrument that could contribute a noise, they went to Emerson's house and gave him a serenade.

"It was certainly," wrote Marsh, "the most horrid noise I ever heard with the most discordant yells and hallooing, the old animal soon came out of his house in a great rage to know what it meant, when he was insulted by the most irritating language it was possible to invent. He bore it with many bitter imprecations as long as he was able and then turned to go in, when some one hurled a large club, hitting him squarely in the back. The noise was continued until all the parties were weary and was so tremendous it was heard miles around." Thus was Maria avenged.

At the same period, there was another young girl in Lancaster, Caroline Lee Whiting, who took Marsh's eye. Her mother was the widow of General John Whiting.

JOHN MARSH, PIONEER

Caroline taught the district school on the old Common, and was noted in the village not only for her charm, but for her literary accomplishments. Her poems and stories and readings from them enlivened many an evening's gathering. So clever were her compositions that they were eagerly solicited by the periodicals of the day and were eventually collected into several volumes. Among these may be mentioned: "The Planter's Northern Bride," "Marcus Warland," "Rena or the Snow Bird," "Linda," and "Ernest Lenwood."

John first met Caroline on May 27, 1817. Under that date he recorded that it was a warm spring day with the apple trees in blossom and flying pigeons in the air. He spoke of her as a young poetess, "engaging in disposition and elegant in person with a mind enriched by much reading and an acquaintance with the most celebrated poets and writers of the age and uniting with all so many agreeable qualities as to render her company very agreeable." In his diary he alluded to her as "Pulcherrima C. L. W." The day after their first meeting he bought a pair of gloves and a new hat and towards evening called at her home. Together they walked to the Laurel grounds and along the banks of the Nashua. "The weather was very fine and the surrounding scenery most delightful, and the company being of the finest and most interesting, all conspired to make this much the pleasantest walk I ever had." Once she asked him to tea, and John took his copy of Johnson's "Lives of the English Poets." Together over their teacups they read and discussed the writers and their poetry. Later in the evening they went for a walk around the waterfalls at the dam.

In the midst of all these new impressions, June 5 dawned, and John celebrated his eighteenth birthday. "I

LANCASTER ACADEMY

look back on the past year and think what change there is in my affairs," he writes. "A year ago I was unfixed in my determination as to my employment for life, but now I am determined, with the assistance of Providence, to fit myself with all possible expedition to enter Harvard University and the Ministry."

The term closed the end of August, and John went home. Soon after, in a letter, he received an amazing piece of news from Lancaster. A bond had been issued by the authorities against one of his fellow-boarders of the Whiting household. It appeared that a neighboring farmer's daughter was in trouble, and that she had implicated his classmate as the father of her unborn babe. Marsh was greatly upset and astounded when he received this news. He admired the youth in question highly and held him as one of the most brilliant and polished of his friends there. In fact, he had quite envied him his ease and success with the village girls. The accused was just entering the Harvard Divinity School. John feared the disgrace would ruin his career and saddle him with a burden he could never carry. Unborn, fatherless babes did not fit into the traditional background of Danvers or Salem. Late that night he wrote in his Journal that he never would have believed it of ——! But there came a time when he scoffed at this point of view of his youth.

CHAPTER IV

ANNUAL TRAINING AND DRILLING

1817–1818

JOHN's father had another piece of news for him that upset his home-coming far more than the Lancaster letter.

The annual training and drilling time had arrived. That very day the sergeant had called to warn John that he was enrolled and to report for duty. That was a blow indeed. Above everything, he hated drilling, orders, martial affairs, and marching around with a gun; but he knew that if it were discovered that he was at home after being warned, a heavy fine would be imposed upon him. Thus he fled to his aunt's home in Salem, where he arrived long after midnight, determined to hide until all military manœuvres were passed.

By Thanksgiving Day drilling was over. He returned to Danvers and went to hear the Reverend Mr. Walker preach, but found his sermon "a very inferior thing." Besides making several blunders, the minister excited John's wrath by claiming that those who give to the poor lend to the rich. When he reached home he tried to recall some passages worthy of his Journal, but found he could not recollect a single sentence and blamed the minister for not having energy enough to arouse the inattentive to attention.

But if John's church had failed him on this great New England day, not so his heart. He was full of thanksgiving and confided to his Journal that the season had

ANNUAL TRAINING AND DRILLING

been most abundant; that nature had smiled in an unusual manner upon the labors of the husbandman and that he had never known a time when he had greater cause to offer thanks to the Giver of every good and perfect gift. Soon thereafter he persuaded his father to let him go to Boxford to study Latin and Greek with the Reverend Mr. Eaton. He did not want to go back to Lancaster. He longed for new fields. He could make more rapid progress toward Harvard with a private tutor, he said, and his father allowed him to go.

Twice a day, immediately after breakfast and at 3 P. M., he presented himself at the vicarage and recited for an hour to Mr. Eaton. The time between was required to prepare for the next session. One day it was Virgil; another, Cicero or Greek Minora; sometimes it was Greek grammar and the verbs in Omega, or seven chapters from the Greek testament.

Thus another year rolled around before he realized it was again fall and training time. On September 18, 1818, he received a warrant to drill in the militia at Andover and to report the 22d instant. On the day specified, much against his will, he presented himself for duty but without equipment, as he had discovered the law did not require it. At the roll call, he answered to his name, and the presiding officers compelled him to take up a long birch stake and carry it like a gun. With this staff over his shoulder, he marched up and down for about half an hour. It was very fatiguing. He loathed it. Finally he came into the rear section, and finding an opportunity, unperceived by any but the two who stood next to him, he slipped out of the ranks and went home.

So much did he despise drilling that he determined to get out of it by hook or crook, so that day he intentionally sprained his ankle and sought out the surgeon, Doctor Osgood. Exhibiting his swollen foot, he asked for a certificate to excuse him from further training. The doctor made an examination, wrote out a certificate, and John spent a happy evening talking to the surgeon's daughter and drove home, much elated over his success.

That night he could not sleep; his conscience would not let him. Although excused, his neglect of duty prevented him from resting. In the afternoon his guilty feelings drove him back to the parade ground. From behind a covert he watched the training, sham fight and manœuvring, complaining bitterly that he hated and despised it all!

The next morning he was still conscience-stricken; had not slept, and was afraid of being fined. He made up his mind to go to Doctor Osgood, confess what he had done and ask him to cure his foot so that he could drill again. He arose with the dawn, hired a horse to drive to Osgood's, but by the time he reached the doctor's office he had changed his mind and drove on home—that was the easiest way! His father seemed to sense the trouble. Being short of hands, he put his son to work in the hay fields. That was a blow. Farm-work was more distasteful than drilling. John worked at it against his will, glad enough when he could escape.

Had he only known then what the future held in store, how he would have drilled and drilled and drilled! But his only argument at that time was, "Ministers are for peace, not for war."[1]

CHAPTER V

"BRIMSTONE HILL," PHILLIPS ACADEMY—
ANDOVER, MASSACHUSETTS
1818–1819

JOHN was a rolling stone, always changing schools. He always found some good reason to move on. That was characteristic of his life. He must always move on. Late in August of 1818, he persuaded himself as well as his father that Phillips Academy, Andover, was the place for him. It was the best school in New England to get religion, he told his father. Religion was what he wanted. Accordingly, he went there and interviewed first Mr. Newhall, the assistant, and finally Doctor John Adams, the preceptor. With the latter he spent some time and was greatly impressed, feeling that he was in the presence of a master of his profession. After some questioning on his part, Doctor Adams assigned him to the senior class, instructed him to provide himself with a Bible, a prayer-book, and Mason "On Self-Knowledge" and to use them daily. Thus admonished, he sent him to the treasurer to pay his entrance fee of five dollars, and directed him to prepare a lesson in Greek Minora and to report next morning with the seniors.

Later John found a temporary abode at Mrs. Corn's; agreeing to share rooms with a youth named Niles, paying two dollars a week in advance for board. However, John did not go to Andover for religion alone. His great-

JOHN MARSH, PIONEER

est requirement was Greek—Greek enough to get into Harvard.

Even in 1818 when John Marsh ascended Andover Hill, the Academy enjoyed traditions of a glorious past. Wherever he walked, wherever he studied, he was on ground hallowed by generations of illustrious men who had preceded him, nine out of ten of whom became doctors of divinity or pillars of theology, for Andover Hill, with its Theological Seminary close by, was the stronghold of the Calvinists whose tenets were delivered with threats of sulphur and "everlasting bonfire." So noted was it for its gloomy bigotry and fiery epithets that in derision it was sometimes called "Brimstone Hill." Passengers, on frosty mornings, as they jolted by on the Boston stage, used jokingly to hold out their hands toward it for warmth.[1]

Doctor John Adams was a staunch upholder of these doctrines; but there had been a time when he was more worldly and his thoughts centred on mundane affairs. When he graduated from Yale, his high scholarship entitled him to deliver a commencement address and he chose as a subject—"The Benefits of Theatrical Amusements." He was conceded the best dancer in the class and because of his efficiency in terpsichorean matters, he was the leader of the annual student ball; but by the time John came under his influence his attitude toward such harmless and human frivolity had hardened into intolerance and the recollection of these follies of his youth was a haunting memory.[2] His avowed desire at Andover was not to foster social leaders, but to lay as securely as possible, in the character of every pupil, the foundation of Christian manhood.

No one of our generation can appreciate the religious

"BRIMSTONE HILL," PHILLIPS ACADEMY

fervor of those days. Men believed in a covenant-keeping God, in conversion; and in an agony of spirit they prayed for divine assurance of salvation or strove for rich spiritual experiences. The Lord was an absorbing topic; conversation hinged on his love, and death was hailed by the devout as a triumph.

From the moment of Adams' arrival he did his utmost to fulfill the stipulations of the constitution regarding the influence of the principal on the religious tone of the school. If anything, he overdid that side of schoolboy life. The pious were his favorites and he did his best to stimulate revivals. Practically every one of his classes underwent one, and he was never so happy as when he saw one budding or his graduates heading for the ministry. In his eyes the "promotion of true piety and virtue" was the primary object of the institution. Instruction in English, Latin and Greek was of only secondary importance. He was always proselyting.

One summer's day, after a session of four hours, he dismissed the school in the usual form. No sooner had he done so than he added: "There will now be a prayer meeting; those who wish to lie down in everlasting burning may go, the rest will stay." Two, only, had the audacity to rise and leave the room and one of them lived to become a great doctor of divinity.[3]

Such was the atmosphere of Phillips Andover, when John began his senior year there. Adams impressed John very forcibly. "The principal is an excellent instructor," he wrote, "very strict in recitation, very pleasant in his manners and very instructive in his observations and a perfect master of his business."

On his first Sabbath, John attended public worship in the chapel of the Theological Seminary. Doctor Ebenezer Porter, Bartlet Professor of Sacred Rhetoric, performed the exercises and delivered the sermon in a masterly and impressive manner, and John found his style of eloquence very affecting. At the afternoon services, Mr. Stewart, another professor, delivered the sermon and young Marsh "hardly knew which to consider the superior"; either of them was far ahead of anything he had ever heard.

In the evening he attended worship in the chapel and noted that "the prayers offered up to the Supreme Being were awfully solemn and the address calculated to arouse the most stupid conscience of fallen, unregenerate man to a sense of his perishing state." The next morning being Monday, before proceeding with recitations, his class was called upon to give abstracts of the sermons of the previous day and to recite a moral lesson in Greek and Latin from Porteus' "Evidence of the Truth of the Christian Religion."

During the winter before Marsh entered Andover, the Academy building had burned to the ground. A new "Classic Hall" was in process of construction and there were hopes that it would be finished before the winter began in earnest. In the meantime his classes were held elsewhere, and he complained bitterly of the cold and of running back and forth from classroom to bedroom. He gives the schedule of his days as follows:

"Arise at five in the morning, review our lessons and take breakfast—be at school at half past eight where we are detained until about eleven—home again—study Virgil. Begin to recite at half past one, which takes until half past three. Home again—study Greek until half past four. Up to school again to attend religious exer-

"BRIMSTONE HILL," PHILLIPS ACADEMY

cises—home again, study until half past eleven and then to bed. So busy cannot write letters. Too tired to sleep. Suffer from headaches."

In addition to home work, he was frequently required to attend religious meetings at night, over which different members of the Senior Class officiated. On one occasion, the passage of scripture on which they dilated was: "And the herd of swine ran violently down a steep place into the sea and were choked in the waves." It was stated during the discussion that "the race of mankind by nature run headlong to their own ruin, and unless they repent in time, they will end in utter destruction."

Sometimes one of the theological students from the Seminary addressed these meetings. On such an occasion a Mr. Dewey preached, stating and proving that the angels and blessed spirits look down on earth and take an interest in the good or bad conduct of mortals. "This idea of continual espionage is terrible," wrote John. "It induces one to future circumspection and an earnest endeavor to walk in the path of duty."

On December 9, after a brief vacation, the new term began. John moved to a Mrs. Chandler's and roomed with a man named Doan, from Maryland. As usual, they had to supply their own means of heat. On this occasion they divided between them the cost of a cord of wood, amounting to five dollars; a saw, four cents, and a bellows fifty cents. The weather was very cold. Marsh was much disgruntled that the new Academy building was not finished as had been promised, especially as he suffered intensely in the chilly classrooms and could scarcely keep himself warm. "While one side burns before a great fire," he complains, "the other freezes by the intenseness of the cold and I thus suffer what I recollect to have heard is the kind of punishment which the Icelander imagines that the souls of the wicked suffer after death,—first roasted in the volcano and then frozen among the mountains of ice on the seacoast." Although the texts of the Academy sermons dealt with terms tending to suggest warmth and heat, there was nothing material about them. The chapel was even colder than the classrooms. Even in a heavy coat with muffler drawn about his ears, John sat and shivered.

The Reverend Doctor Porter opened the new term with a sermon suggested by a person who asked our Savior if in the ultimate accounting, only a few should be saved, and the Lord replied: "And ye shall see them sit down with Abraham and Isaac and Jacob in the Kingdom of Heaven and ye yourselves cast out." John listened to this discourse; back in his room, he wrote that it was "evident that some will be finally rejected from the Kingdom of Heaven and it is probable that it will be a part of their punishment to see those who were their former companions enjoying that blessed state from which they are excluded by their own folly and sin. The punishment and tortures of condemned spirits will be increasing to all eternity. How tremendous and overwhelming is the thought that the suffering of one soul will be greater than the united suffering of all in the universe for millions of ages."[4]

On Monday, December 21, 1818, the asperity of the weather had moderated. John attended classes in the new Academy for the first time. He was now compelled to study all day in the classroom under the direct surveillance of an instructor and deprived of the privilege of studying in his own room. John did not like the new system. The noise and confusion the first day were so dis-

"BRIMSTONE HILL," PHILLIPS ACADEMY

turbing that it gave him a headache and he could not sleep that night or attend his classes the following day.

As the term progressed, his lessons in Greek and Latin increased in length and difficulty. It required the utmost diligence to learn them. He studied late every night, arose before dawn every morning, but his Cicero, Virgil, Odes of Anacreon, Xenophon and Greek prosody were never finished. The translations were so long and difficult that he was forced to neglect his arithmetic but comforted himself that Greek was far more important than that science to his future career. A minister doesn't have to know anything about mathematics! It was nonsense!

In addition to Latin gymnastics, Saturdays always required a recitation, ten pages at a clip, in Mason's "Self-Knowledge." After lunch came declamation before the whole school. Marsh still dreaded these ordeals. Once on a flimsy pretext he asked to be excused, but when his request was granted his conscience began to prick and the next week, realizing the importance of public speaking, he determined to make an attempt. According to his Journal of December 23, 1818, he quailed in his seat in "durance vile" until his turn came. Then he mounted the rostrum and made a beginning, at first agitated and excited beyond measure; his legs trembled and his knees smote against each other like those of Belshazzar at the feast. But by exerting all his will-power he gradually recovered himself a little, and finally made out better than he expected. He grieved mightily over this failing. It was a flaw in his character. "This diffidence or excitement is a failing that I cannot possibly avoid," he noted, "but feel confident that by practice I shall overcome it."

In spite of all this Greek and religion, John could not escape the fascination of a good murder trial. Once,

JOHN MARSH, PIONEER

when a man named Phillips, accused of murdering his wife, was on trial at Salem, John stole away from the Academy and made his way to the court-house. By the time he arrived, the courtroom was crowded but he slipped in and found a seat. The testimony of the witnesses proved that Phillips was insane, or acting so, and he was sent back to his cell to remain there until he again came into possession of his faculties. Disgusted at the brevity of the proceedings, John returned to school.

Without any apparent festivities, Christmas day dawned. "This is the day which is kept as a holy one in commemoration of the advent of the Messiah into the world," wrote John on December 25, 1818, "with what great propriety is this event celebrated, an event of infinitely more importance to mankind than any other that ever occurred. How strangely blind and inconsistent are men. When the celebration of the birth of the Glorious Redeemer of the world is neglected it appears as if the same spirit which caused men to reject the Saviour when on earth still operates in this neglect. It is objected by some that the day of Christ's nativity is not precisely known but that I conceive to be no excuse."

On New Year's Eve John was alone in his room, nursing a violent headache and cold. He had not been in school all day and was feeling miserable. Rain was falling in torrents, beating against his windows and contributing to his depression. He picked up a Greek book but felt too sick to study and, laying it aside, took up his Journal. "I have for this year been pushing forward towards the hill of science and have made some progress," he wrote, "but it is remembered with regret that every portion of the past year has not been improved

"BRIMSTONE HILL," PHILLIPS ACADEMY

to the best advantage which, by Divine blessing, I hope to amend in the improvement of the next year. It is but just to acknowledge that I have been singularly blessed and prospered through the whole course of my life, and particularly through the last year, that I have met with fewer of the evils and less of the troubles of life than usually fall to the lot of man. I am indulged with advantages and opportunities of acquiring knowledge which but comparatively few of the human race enjoy. May a merciful God, who gives me these privileges in his mercy, grant me grace to improve them for his glory and the benefits of mankind!"

CHAPTER VI

HARVARD

1819-1823

JOHN graduated from Phillips Academy, Andover, in the summer of 1819, and almost immediately entered Harvard University, becoming one of the eighty odd members of the class of 1823. Late in August he arrived at Cambridge and presented himself to the authorities to take his admission examinations. These were oral in nature, and lasted for several days, beginning daily at six A. M. and continuing until dark, with only a half-hour intermission for lunch.

John's greatest ordeal of the series was in Virgil's "Georgics." That part of the entrance test was conducted by the President, Doctor John Thornton Kirkland, who availed himself of this opportunity to study the character and countenance of the applicant before him. John dreaded that test the most, but it was unnecessary. The president was magnetic and drew John to him by his fatherly attitude.

The president was always on the watch for occasions when he could be of assistance to his boys. Although a strict disciplinarian, he inflicted punishment with a due regard to the self-respect of the offenders—always endeavoring to preserve it. Hence they remembered their wounds with kindness and not with rancor. As a result, he had the love and respect of the student body. Some idea of the position he occupied among them may be deduced from one of the old class-songs:

HARVARD

"To jolly old Kirkland, Let's drink the first glass
Whom a bottle did ne'er with impunity pass,
Let's pray to the gods to protect him from har.n
And to send him a wife to tuck him up warm.
Health to Kirkland! Blow it out, Kirkland! Stick to the bottle
Gee up and Gee Ho!"[1]

Doctor Kirkland took a particular interest in John, not alone on account of his scholarship, but because of his family. He did not have to be reminded that his ancestor, the Reverend Samuel Skelton, was the first ordained minister of the first church in Salem; nor that a less remote one, the Reverend John Marsh, was the last Harvard graduate to wear a wig at commencement.[2]

As John faced his inquisitor during the "Georgics" ordeal, he could not realize that the kindly dignified divine was to have more to do in directing his destiny than any other human being; and in a way least suspected by the august president or the candidate for admission. Marsh passed satisfactorily and matriculated in a class with youths from all over New England as well as the South; it included in its ranks such names as William P. Lunt, Henderson Inches, George Ripley, John P. Robinson, James Trask Woodbury and Samuel H. Stevens—many of them destined to be noted New England divines—to say nothing of Thomas W. Dorr, of Rhode Island Rebellion fame; John Adams, son and grandson of a President of the United States; Charles Carroll of Carrollton, a grandson of the Signer; Stephen Webb, Mayor of Salem and later a lawyer in San Francisco; Charles Calvert, a descendant of Lord Baltimore, a Tayloe of Maryland; and Charles Pickering—destined to be a physician as well as an explorer.

JOHN MARSH, PIONEER

At the time Marsh began his college career, there were no luxurious dormitories, marble-lined and steam-heated, no tiled baths or glass-enclosed showers. Instead, he shared a meagre, bare room with a classmate; neither was there an excess of expensive furniture, nor any evident extravagance at all, for that matter. Ten dollars would have covered the entire expenditure. No carpet or rug covered the floor; no curtain floated in and out of the small-paned window. There was a pine bedstead in one corner, a washstand in another, a table, a desk, and a few chairs—the sort of furnishings that nowadays the average servant would despise.

Neither were there electric bulbs, matches, hot water nor instantaneous heat, at easy reach. Instead there were dipped candles, flint and steel and tinder box; and in winter, a fireplace that must be fed, coals that must be banked and nursed; flickering lights that required continual snuffing, and, worst of all, in the cold gray of many a winter's dawn, ice in the wash-pitcher that must be broken before scurrying to prayers in a cold chapel. A student's life was hard in John Marsh's day—hard and uncompromising. But the class of 1823 did not submit to the latter without a struggle or receive the stamp of their alma mater until they had "degraded" the class, as John Quincy Adams expressed it,[3] blasted the career of their president and decimated their own ranks to less than half their original number. It included many revolutionary spirits, but, strange as it may seem, two of its greatest rebels, Ripley and Dorr, did not develop their rebellious proclivities until long years later.

The class of 1823 was a rollicking, turbulent set. A large majority of Marsh's classmates, like himself, were headed for the ministry. They were the serious-minded

HARVARD

element—over-zealous, solemn and anxious to uphold the college laws. These qualities earned them a place on the "Black List." From the beginning, John was against them. They rubbed him the wrong way. He, therefore, aligned himself with the belligerent element, who were in the ascendency and against the college government. This number included many of the most promising members of his class.

John had more to do with University Hall than any of the other academic buildings. In summer he was there daily at six A. M. for morning prayers, and in winter in the bitter cold dawn, an hour before sunrise. From the chapel he went into an adjoining classroom and recited for two periods, before breakfast was served in Commons. Reinforced with coffee, hot rolls and butter, he attended lectures until dinner-time. The afternoons, except Saturday, he devoted to "gym" or study. At six P. M. he was at evening prayers in the chapel. From devotions he went to tea and cold "woolleny" bread in Commons. At eight in winter and nine in summer, the curfew rang. After that there was enforced silence until the heralds of a new day started the machinery of repression in action again.

The Sabbath was a sort of religious nightmare—a gloomy round of services, sermons, expositions and catechisms, from morning until night. From these soul-cramping regulations and their deadly monotony and with practically no athletics or competitive games to work off excess energy, there were bound to be frequent explosions.[4]

John's freshman year passed quickly. There was plenty of Greek. That was what he wanted. It was manna to his starved intellect. He loved it!—the Greek Testament, Greek *Collectanea* with just a spicing of Latin: Livy and Horace. As for geometry and algebra, they hardly counted. He wanted the classics.

JOHN MARSH, PIONEER

All went peacefully that first year until the time for the annual freshman dinner rolled around. It was scheduled for the latter part of the third term, the night of the annual examinations. It was an old tradition. From time immemorial it was customary for the class to sup together that night. It was eagerly anticipated. Almost on the eve of the celebration, the college government forbade John's class to hold their meeting. The dinners had become too convivial, they said. The president decided to put an end to them, but the class, oblivious to orders, decided to uphold the ancient tradition.

At sunset of August 16, 1820, John and his classmates joined forces at the Neponset Hotel, ten miles from Cambridge. After amusing themselves with billiards, bowling, etc., they seated themselves at the banquet table at eleven o'clock. Everything was conducted in the finest style. A full band of music increased the merriment of the night. Charles T. Haskell of Charleston, South Carolina, presided as toastmaster. Speeches were required of each individual, which did not at all please John. Then a class song, composed for the occasion, was sung to the chorus of "Derry Down," and received with great acclaim.[5]

CLASS SUPPER SONG

In council one night, as report now will have it,
When the Government members consulting were met:
While every one "dicere sententiam amavit,"
And the scrapings of Freshmen were themes of debate—

First the Præses rose up, and in anger began:
"These Freshmen—'twere best that we scatter them all,
"Ere our laws they shall trample, suspend every man,
"And the breezes alone better sigh through our hall."

HARVARD

But the sound of his voice had so bristled his hair,
So fell was his menace—his gesture so tragic:
"Mrs. Hedge and myself" thought "the nail was hit fair,"
And lik'd the proposal because he lik'd Logick.

The Præses continued: "these upstarts we'll tame,
"Or send them all off in a quintuple ratio;
"Et nunc quantum sufficit, your judgment I claim,
"And Pop's[6] expectatur imprimis opinio"—

The Doctor looked wild as is always his custom,
When made adhortare on matters of moment:
Where extracts of Greek non vacanter in question
As those ignorare qui aliter volent.

"Μοι δοκει," sayd he, "if 'tis actively used
"That a scrape is το ηχος a noise of the feet,
" 'Tis a play which δοκαζειν seems greatly abused
"Αξιος και ζημιασ—to speak in plain Greek.

"Πολλακισ τον τροπον, according to custom,
"All the scrapes which they give me I sometimes review
"And now μετρεσαντας by just calculation,
"I find they are πεντε και δεκα and two.

"Νυν εστιν κρατιστον, I think it most proper,
"That ταχιστα τι ισκμος should quickly be shewn,
"Or by Jove it will happen δικαιος και οπερ
"Του Διαβολου εκειν before we have done."

Ira Blanchard then spoke with unusual vim,
"I've dealt them dead setts, tho they've scrap'd till I'm sore,
"And I'll stay here no longer unless you begin,
"Ad docendum profanos to scrape me no more."

But Dr. Sykes rose at this perilous moment,
The *whole scope* of his motions he *stated* had fines,
"For 'tis mete that by letting them off so at present,
"We shall get a fresh wine butt and bag of long nines."

39

JOHN MARSH, PIONEER

The weighty proposal was sanctioned with joy,
"Συμβουλειν τοκαλεις," says Popkin "you call,
"Παρα το βελτιον Χοειςθαι—Ωποποι—
"Δαιμονιον αλιςκε, the Devil take all—"⁷

At half-past four the following morning the banquet terminated. John and his classmates returned to Cambridge in a heavy shower of rain, attended prayers, and took "dead setts" ("complete failure" in the slang of the day) at the morning exercises. Two days later, three of his classmates, including the toastmaster and the committee of arrangements, were suspended for six months for being "prodigal and dissipated." They left college amidst the cheers of their classmates. Order was then restored.

John's sophomore year began on September 28, 1820. There was more Latin and Greek, but too much geometry, analytics, trigonometry and topography to suit him. Mathematics was still the bane of his life. A few weeks after he matriculated, Nichols of Boston died, and John, along with the rest of his classmates, wore a crêpe badge on his left arm for thirty days.

One Sunday evening toward the end of October, there was a "rush," in Commons Hall, between the freshmen and the sophomores. It was just the sort of thing John liked. The door between the dining-halls was smashed. All the windows were broken. John distinguished himself by hurling cups, saucers, plates and food through them. A few days later the blow fell—three of John's classmates were called up and suspended. The rest were left in a rebellious mood. That night, they kindled a fire in front of University Hall, feeding valuable papers taken from the library, to the flames. During the confusion, James Hayward, later Hollis professor of mathematics, received a bucketful of ink on the head, and Professor Downing was

HARVARD

almost killed by a falling cannon ball which, landing, split one of the stone steps of Hollis, as may be seen to this day.

The next day, Dunbar, a ringleader in the disturbance, was suspended, and his classmates were in open rebellion. At midnight they met at the "Sign of the Golden Eagle," on the Commons, and arming themselves with clubs and stones, broke all of Hayward's windows and threw bricks through those of the president's study.

John revelled in it. It was just to his liking. At the height of the excitement, he and one, Greenough, seized several cannon balls, climbed to the upper story of one of the college buildings, wrote out insulting messages to several of the professors they did not like, attached them to the balls and hurled them into the yard below. The next day John was called before the college government. His letters had been recovered, his handwriting recognized. He had no adequate excuse. On November 4, 1820, he was dismissed from college.[8]

John was popular. The whole class was up in arms when it was learned that both he and Greenough were dismissed. Cutting prayers, they held a meeting and circulated a petition requesting that their punishment be mitigated. The college government replied by suspending two of the petitioners.

Thus, in the middle of his second year, still unprepared for his religious career, John was expelled from Harvard and returned to Danvers in disgrace. Again cannon balls marked a turning place in his career. John's father was disgusted with him for his part in the disturbance. He pointed out the sacrifices he had made to send and keep him in college. Now, he said, he could go to work on the farm; he was through with him. John was disheartened. Back to chores! He would never get away from them now.

JOHN MARSH, PIONEER

He became silent and morose. The gay laughter that delighted his mother died out of him. The more he dwelled on the ministry, the more his spirit rebelled. He could not make it; Harvard had taken such thoughts out of his mind; he was unsuited for a life in the pulpit. He wanted action, not peace.

In the meantime he performed his menial work with a heavy heart and drifted like a rudderless ship. He was hopeless. His mother still had faith in him, though she was sore distressed. She would go to his room at night and weep over him. Once John awoke to find her kneeling by his side. She said she could not endure having him a failure; that she wanted him to devote his life to some good. Taking him in her arms, she said: "Be a good boy, for your mother's sake."

Shortly after that, he announced his intention of going back to college and becoming a physician and surgeon. The fountains of hope were renewed. With rejuvenated spirit he worked at his tasks. That winter he taught the village school. By spring, he had earned enough money to return to college.

On September 28, 1821, the Harvard government reinstated him on condition that in the future he refrain from all college disturbances. Joyfully he returned to Cambridge and entered on his junior year—logic, moral philosophy, Hebrew, Tacitus and Homer—with enthusiasm. Determination ran high. He would become a physician and make his old mother proud of him. He worked hard, and his junior year ended peacefully. During the long winter vacation he went back to Danvers and the village school, earning sufficient money to carry him through his senior year. He was very ambitious that term; in addition to the prescribed subjects, he took courses in anatomy in

THE OPENING SCENE OF THE "GREAT REBELLION."
Courtesy of Harvard University.

HARVARD

Holden Chapel and some medical work with Doctor John Dixwell, in Boston. Even in those days Harvard required a bachelor's degree before a candidate could work for a medical one, and John decided to have a head start.

Doctor Kirkland was much pleased with John's scholarship, and the effort he was making—not only to redeem himself, but to become a physician. Knowing of his meagre means, he made every effort to assist him. When Colonel Josiah Snelling, Commander in Chief of the great fortress of St. Anthony, situated at the junction of the Mississippi and Minnesota rivers in Michigan territory, wrote him to recommend and send a tutor for his boys, Doctor Kirkland's choice fell upon Marsh. Calling him to his office, he offered him the appointment. For such a tutor, the colonel promised to provide fare, board and lodging in his own home and a salary far in excess of anything John had earned previously. Here was the means to continue his medical course. Two years in the wilderness, he told himself, would enable him to earn enough to graduate in medicine. He jumped at the opportunity.

John's mother discouraged him. She wanted to keep her first-born near her. She said she would find a way for him to continue his medical training without going so far West. But John was restless. It was time to move on. To her arguments he pointed out that he could continue his medical studies, under the tutelage of the regimental surgeon on the Mississippi, just as well as he could at home, and with the added advantage that during his absence he would earn and save enough money to come back to Harvard and take his M.D. degree. Only half-convinced, she was persuaded to let him go. John made ready to depart. He was elated—the unknown, adventure, romance awaited!

JOHN MARSH, PIONEER

Commencement approached. Before it dawned, the friction between the faculty and the seniors engendered so much heat that a rebellion—called the Great One—broke out. Those in charge were unable to handle it. The college was shaken to its foundations.[9]

It was well that John had promised at the time of his reinstatement to refrain from all college disturbances; otherwise, he would have been drawn into the maelstrom, and have broken his mother's heart. During this final upheaval, over half his class were expelled, and on the eve of graduation. His subsequent career proved that intrigue and revolution were the salt of his life, but John remained true to his promise.

When Commencement Day arrived on August 27, his name, written in Latin as *Johannes Marsh*, was included among the candidates for the Degree of Bachelor of Arts. There should have been over seventy candidates, but the expulsions left only thirty-six of the original number to receive their diplomas and take a part in the exercises. The programme with its elaborate Latin inscription was dedicated to the Governor of Massachusetts, the Vice-Governor, and the president, etc., and read as follows:

Illustrissimo GULIELMO EUSTIS, Arm° LL.D.
Gubernatori;

Honoratissimo LEVI LINCOLN, Armigero,
Vice-Gubernatori;

Consiliariis et Senatoribus

Republicae Massachusettensis;
Cæterisque Universitatis Harvardiannae Curatoribus
Honorandis atque Reverendis;

Reverendo JOHANNI THORNTON KIRKLAND,
S.T.D. LL.D. Praesidi: etc.

HARVARD

It embraced fourteen different items, orations, conferences, discussions, disputations and dissertations. It included an oration by George Ripley, subsequently the great Transcendentalist. He received first honors, and his subject was "Genius, as Affected by Moral Feeling."[10]

Thomas W. Dorr of Rhode Island received second honors and delivered an English oration on "Improvement." The Salutatory and the Valedictory were both delivered in Latin.[11]

BOOK TWO

REDSKIN

CHAPTER VII

MASSACHUSETTS TO FORT ST. ANTHONY

1823

JUST before Class Day, John received word that a detachment of the Fifth United States Infantry, then stationed at Boston, had been ordered to join its commander and regiment at Fort St. Anthony, and was to concentrate at Buffalo, preparatory to sailing in a government-chartered boat for Green Bay, Wisconsin, the ancient French trading settlement of La Baye. He was advised to join them. He had fulfilled all the requirements, President Kirkland gave him his bachelor's degree, and he took his diploma with him into the wilderness. No sheepskin ever experienced more varied adventures than that little roll of parchment! Among the very first Harvard degrees on the banks of the Minnesota, the Wisconsin, the Mississippi and the Missouri Rivers; wherever John went, whatever position he occupied—and the vicissitudes of his fortune were many[1]—that Harvard diploma went with him. While it was often the only link with his past, it also formed his introduction to the West, securing him a teaching position in a remote fortress, where he was to win a niche in Minnesota's scholastic history as her first American schoolmaster. That Harvard degree and all it implied made Marsh a man of parts, a power in every territory in which he lived; it lent tradition to a wilderness that had none, supplied a background that his contemporaries admired, feared and envied; and to-day it still throws a glamour

JOHN MARSH, PIONEER

about a man who would have become a figure in any community where education and talent count, and who did so in surroundings where, to all intent and purpose, they did not. It made him for thirty years one of the most unusual adventurers on the frontier. Without that degree it would have been impossible to trace his footsteps—they would have been lost with many others on the trails he helped to blaze. Paradoxical as it may seem, his education supplied the stepping-stones of his wilderness career. It is not his self-reliance, his heroism, his endurance of hardships, or his feats of valor, and they are many, which distinguish him among his fellow adventurers, not his strength of heart or brawn, although they contributed their quota, that set him apart. The imprint that he has left is not so much of a physical as of an intellectual quality.

Early in August he left Harvard, went to Danvers and bade the old folks good-bye. He deeply loved his mother, there was a tender tie between them, and the last words he said as he took her in his strong, young arms were, "Don't worry, mother. I'll be back in two years." Then he was gone, down the ancient Ipswich pike. On Thursday, August 7, 1823, he was at Albany, New York, and at five o'clock in the morning was writing to his father.

"I arrived here at eight o'clock last evening, safe and sound without accident or delay, after a very pleasant journey. Last Monday I spent in Boston and with some difficulty succeeded in buying $100.00 in gold at 1½ per cent, which I have since worn in my girdle. Mr. Dixwell had all things ready; I called on him as soon as I arrived and ascertained this. Took tea and spent the evening in his very charming family.[2] I have a letter to Colonel Snelling and one to Colonel Hunt at Detroit from Dixwell, and Colonel Snelling's own letter, and, from President Kirk-

MASSACHUSETTS TO FORT ST. ANTHONY

land, one to Colonel Snelling, and two to his friends in Utica. The night I spent in Boston, I slept none at all. I started at one o'clock, breakfasted at Sudbury, passed through Worcester, Leicester, etc., and dined at Brookfield and arrived at Springfield at eight. In travelling the last fifty miles you will readily believe that I was thoroughly fatigued and sleepy and a little sick. I retired at nine and slept till twelve, when I awoke in perfect health and spirits and in the delight of yesterday, I felt no fatigue nor any other inconvenience. I have not lacked for company. Mr. Childs, of Boston, and his two sons (with all of whom I am acquainted) rode with me all the way and I have met about twenty other acquaintances. I shall go no further than Schenectady today."[3]

On August 17, 1823, he wrote to his father from Buffalo, after having passed through Utica and Palmyra and visited the Falls of Niagara. He did not undertake to describe them, though he wrote of finding them "grand, magnificent, sublime beyond anything you can conceive. I send you a branch of cedar from the American and Canadian sides of the Falls. I shall embark tomorrow morning in the steamboat for Green Bay. She is chartered by the government to carry a detachment of troops to that place. They are on their march to Council Bluffs. I am already acquainted with many officers.[4] The steamboat is a splendid vessel of 250 tons. I think myself particularly fortunate to meet with the opportunity. I shall now probably travel with an escort of 250 to the mouth of the Wisconsin and perhaps further.[5] My journey thus far has been truly delightful. I have met with no accident or misfortune. My health is better than when I left home. I have had very agreeable company all the way. I expect to be at Detroit on Wednesday (August 20). I wish you to send

JOHN MARSH, PIONEER

me a letter directed to Fort St. Anthony as soon as you receive this, that I may get it soon after my arrival."[6]

Next he was at Detroit, thrilled with the new sights and sounds around him, "too excited to sleep," he wrote. Green Bay was his next stop. On he sailed, with elation in his heart, on through the St. Clair river and down Lake Huron. One day he found himself in the straits of Mackinac and near the island of that name, in the very midst of the Indian country. Mackinac meant adventure. It was the heart of the wilderness. Green Bay and Prairie du Chien were but points on its distant arteries. Mackinac was at this time in its prime as the headquarters of the American Fur Company, which had inherited the traditions of those autocratic privateers of commerce, the Hudson's Bay and the Northwest Companies of Canada. From the deck of his boat John could see the Company's quaint, irregular buildings and primitive magazines, the white walls of the fort, and the wigwams and scattered canoes of the Ottawa, Chippewa, Potowatomi, Menominee and Winnebago, drawn up on the sloping beach. For it was to this place these tribes brought their furs,—beaver and otter, mink and marten—and received in return blankets and guns, looking-glasses and combs. Here they exchanged the treasures of the forest for the gewgaws of civilization. John was enchanted with this view of an unknown world.

When he emerged from Lake Michigan and landed at Green Bay he could have believed he was in France. Even the Indians hailed him with a hearty *"Bon-jour."* The *fleur-de-lis* had not floated over this country for the better part of two centuries for nothing. Even Prince Rupert and all the hard-drinking emissaries of the Hudson Bay and Northwest Companies had not been able to eradicate the stamp of Versailles. What most dumfounded John was

MASSACHUSETTS TO FORT ST. ANTHONY

that even the Indians bore French names. The Winnebago were *"les Puans,"* and the foxes were *"les Renards."* He thanked his lucky stars that he could speak French and speak it well.

Green Bay had been, for almost 200 years, the *"entrepôt"* of the fur trade, and was manned entirely by the French. The *"voyageurs"* who covered the waterways in birch-bark canoes; the *"coureurs des bois,"* the outlaws of the bush; and the athletic *"bois-brûlés"* or half-breeds all attested that the roots of France were deep in the soil of this wilderness.[7]

From Green Bay John had still some 500 miles of waterway to cover before he reached Fort St. Anthony. After a day or two of delay, he set out with the troops in a keelboat, over the Fox-Wisconsin River route to the Mississippi. He was following in the wake of Joliet and Marquette: that fact alone stimulated him. It was a long tedious pull, ascending the sluggish stretches of the Fox. Time and time again they were forced to disembark while the boat was hauled over some swampy area. It took them ten days to reach the rice bog at the Portage. By then the worst part of the voyage was over. A mile brought them to the gloomy reaches of the Wisconsin. Soon they were afloat on its swift current, and shooting through deep ravines and open prairies studded with Indian villages, to the Mississippi. As they struck the "Father of Waters" Marsh was thrilled, but sobered by the stillness and solitude about him.

Five miles to the north of the mouth of the Wisconsin they came to Prairie du Chien, and John walked through the straggling street to the old fort. It was a lonely, dilapidated-looking hamlet. The houses were falling to decay. The people he saw were half-breeds. The words he

JOHN MARSH, PIONEER

heard were French. There was something amiss with his adventure. The sun was clouded and his excitement was dimmed. As he started on the last lap of his journey he was dejected. The strangeness of his surroundings and the isolation were appalling. As the boat threaded its way by the wooded bluffs and barren cliffs his depression gave place to awe. Not one white man's habitation along the whole route.[8] "Sublime," he wrote, "but too lonely." Here and there were Sioux and Winnebago villages, and once a rock painted with Indian hieroglyphics, but mostly—solitude. "Man seems too insignificant here," he wrote.[9]

On turning a point of the Mississippi, there suddenly appeared before him a sight he never afterward forgot,—imposing limestone cliffs surmounted by the gray walls, towers and battlements of Fort St. Anthony, holding as though by magic force its position on a high, precipitous bluff, and proudly floating the Stars and Stripes. The flag struck him the most forcibly. The flag and the utter wilderness around it.

On October 8, 1823, he disembarked and climbed the roadway, white as loaf sugar, along the cliffs to the Fort.[10] The air was hazy. Cob-webs floated across his vision, for it was Indian summer when he climbed that roadway and passed the garrison garden—the cattle grazing on the uplands,—the Sioux agency of St. Peters, and entered the iron gates of St. Anthony.

CHAPTER VIII

FORT ST. ANTHONY, THE SNELLINGS AND TALIA-
FERRO. INDIAN AGENT OF ST. PETERS

1823

THE world that John found when he entered was different from anything he had previously known. No familiar village green or college yard greeted his eye. Instead, he entered upon a strange world of stone, soldiers and sentries, of ordnance, magazines, barracks and bastions. Everything was stern and unrelenting. How he had hated such things! Now, here he was in the midst of them. The parade ground where he found himself was diamond-shaped, to conform to the contour of the land at the confluence of the rivers he could hear surging below. At its four corners were stone block-houses, some pierced for forty guns. He felt that he was in a prison and would never escape. Two walls hemmed him in—one of gray stone, ten feet high, and a green one of impenetrable trees.

As John walked toward the commander's quarters the colonel saw him, and came out to meet him. Only a day before, an express had arrived from Prairie du Chien notifying him of the arrival there of the detachment.[1] Thus he was expected and we can picture the commander meeting the young tutor, clasping his hand, drawing him into the house which was to be his home for the next two years, and summoning his household, consisting of his wife, Abigail Hunt Snelling, and their children, Mary, Henry and the infant James—the latter probably in the arms of his nurse, Barbara Ann Shadecker, a Swiss refugee of the

JOHN MARSH, PIONEER

Selkirk colony—and "Joe," the colonel's son by a previous marriage.

They saw a man in the flush of youth, untamed, unbroken, slightly stooped of shoulder, straight of limb and powerful of build. They noted that his hair was fair, his color ruddy, his features well-defined; that his eyes were blue-gray, like an eagle's, with an expression both direct and fearless; that his mouth, the most tell-tale part of his countenance, was cruel, and that his chin was square and determined. Perhaps they noted that his linen was spotless, that his clothes fitted him well; that his general appearance was manly, and that his manner, though courteous, was bold and brusque, testifying that he was not to be trifled with. Perhaps Marsh, as he looked from one figure to another, wondered where Mrs. Snelling was going to tuck him, for the colonel's quarters contained but four living-rooms. But if he did not know it then, he learned later that, in the wilderness, the line where the stranger on retiring hung his clothes, constituted a partition that no man transcended; that wives and daughters slept in the same room with wanderers, and yet the amenities of virtue were preserved and the honor of households maintained.

To the Snellings, who had lived the two previous years in the cabin of a Mackinaw boat and a house of logs, these quarters were a palace.[2] After living in a wide, rambling New England farmhouse, Marsh found them crowded and complained that he had to room with the boys. There was a barred window in his room. The view from it was magnificent and pleased him, but the isolation never ceased to pall upon his spirits. "The silence here is terrible," he wrote home—"not a sound but the wind through a crack in the door, the chirping of birds and the croaking of odious frogs."

A hundred feet below him, at the base of precipitous

FORT ST. ANTHONY, THE SNELLINGS

cliffs, were two great rivers, the one he had just ascended and the Minnesota. To his right, the latter stream approached through an open vale of hills and forest. Across the Minnesota, where Mendota now stands, was a cluster of trading houses, the ware and store establishment of the American Fur Company, where the skins of buffalo and beaver, otter and mink, were sorted, weighed, and divided into packs to be shipped to Mackinaw, en route to London, St. Petersburg, Berlin and China.[3] But beyond these few trading houses and the conical tepees of the Sioux surrounding them, was the wilderness, intangible but complete. To John, it was a wall.

Mrs. Snelling had been the prime mover in importing John to tutor her children. She was anxious to equip them as completely as possible to meet the world. Up to his coming she had done the best she could, herself.[4] She was still little more than a girl—but a few years older than Marsh.[5] When barely fifteen, in the eventful days preceding the ignominious surrender of Detroit, she had married Josiah Snelling, a gallant captain in General Hull's army. Even as she stood before the chaplain who made her Snelling's bride, the initial stages of the siege began.

The brave and impetuous commander, Colonel Snelling, appealed greatly to Marsh. He, too, was a native of Massachusetts, and about ten years Marsh's senior. He was a high-spirited, red-haired, bald-headed gentleman, whom the garrison affectionately dubbed the "Prairie Hen." He was a great favorite with his troops, even though he wielded a vicious "cat," with nine knotted tails, over the bare backs of the garrison drunkards. Aware of his own failing in that direction, he was very severe with those who drank too freely and strapped them until they yelled

JOHN MARSH, PIONEER

for mercy.[6] He was the "Lord of the North," but a kindly one, for his was the only law that 300 miles of wilderness knew. But his power was confined to the whites.

Over the red men Major Laurence Taliaferro, Sioux Indian agent, exerted a similar sway.[7] He was very jealous of his prerogatives and brooked no interference, a stickler for right and wrong, for duty and its performance.[8] Because of the impartiality of his actions to all nationalities —American, Scotch, French and Sioux, they called him "Four Hearts";[9] but the Indians honored him with the name of "Mah-sa-busca"—iron-cutter—a Sioux translation of his Italian name.

By birth, Taliaferro was a Virginian of ancient lineage and of Italian extraction, a man so proud of his ancestry and breeding that it would have been impossible for him to do anything ignoble, at least in his own estimation. When John arrived, the major's brother, Muscoe, was assisting him in the agency and the closest bond existed between them. No matter how testy the major was with any one else about the Fort, he was always solicitous of his younger brother.[10]

In addition to these two officers, there were eighteen to twenty others and about 250 troops. They were all young, from drummer boy to commander,[11] and all full of life and vigor. The officers were well educated. Most of them were representatives of the first and most aristocratic families of the East and South, and the majority were West Pointers, although a few had received their commands by way of Tippecanoe, Brownstone, and the Indian wars. John enjoyed these virile young sons of Mars, especially as winter approached and it was impossible to explore the prairies. Often he joined them at night in their quarters, played a hand of cards with them or drank a cup of their

FORT SNELLING.
From an engraving in the possession of the Minnesota Historical Society.

FORT ST. ANTHONY, THE SNELLINGS

hot toddy. Sometimes these parties lasted into the night and occasionally degenerated into quarrels, which led to duels and the spilling of blood.

They liked their fun, these young blades—their cards, their wine, their smokes, but they missed their women, missed them sorely. Especially was this true of John— men he liked, but women he loved. He liked to talk with them, read to them, walk with them. He needed them, needed their society. From the first he had little chance for their companionship. All the women were married, and remote. In the beginning, there were but four women at the Fort; even after the arrival of the Marsh detachment there were not more than ten, and among them was only one, a beautiful girl of fifteen, unmarried, and she, in the winter preceding John's arrival, hied herself off by sleigh to Prairie du Chien with a dashing young lieutenant, St. Clair Denny, and married him, there being no chaplain at the Fort.[12]

If there was a dearth of womankind within those stern barriers, without, in the virgin, unbroken wilderness, they were plentiful. Why worry about color when youth, romance and adventure were calling? And the young blades of the Fort responded heartily to the charms of the comely squaws and handsome half-breeds in the neighboring wigwams. Be it to their credit, many of them held these ties with the tepees as sacred as they could have courtships under the elms of New England. They were just as ready to defend them in the lists as any knight of old. One chivalric West Pointer, Lieutenant James McClure, had a sweetheart in a neighboring wigwam, the daughter of a Sioux chief, Manza-ku-to, the "Walking Shooting Iron," or "Gun."[13] Once a brother officer spoke disparagingly of her, which so incensed the lieutenant that he challenged

JOHN MARSH, PIONEER

him on the spot and in defending her honor and his, severely wounded his antagonist.[14] After that, McClure and his Sioux sweetheart were married and in due course of time she presented him with a daughter, Nancy.[15]

This was not the only romance with the wigwams. Practically all the young officers had mistresses in them and became the fathers of numerous brown-bellied babies. Some had two women—a mistress in the wigwam and a wife in the Fort.[16] Before the removal of the last troops, there were but two officers who did not have a squaw, and many had half-breed children.[17]

In spite of all these allurements, never for a moment did John forget his purpose at Fort Snelling. Soon after his arrival he made the acquaintance of Doctor Edward Purcell, the post surgeon, and began reading medicine in his office and under his supervision.[18] Sometimes he borrowed his medical books and often, while the wolves prowled about the walls and the winds moaned through the bastions and the snowdrifts obliterated the prairies, John lay on the floor of his quarters, reading medicine by the firelight. Sometimes he read all night—his thirst was avid. For two years he kept up the study under Doctor Purcell's tutelage and had almost finished the course mapped out, when Purcell suddenly died.[19] The tragedy of this was that Purcell had not written him a certificate, but John never lacked for expedient.

CHAPTER IX

MINNESOTA'S FIRST SCHOOL, ITS MASTER AND PUPILS

1823–1825

Soon after his arrival, John opened the post school— the first school in the state of Minnesota.[1] It assembled in a building to the right and just beyond the main entrance of the Fort, and under the same roof with the offices of the commander, paymaster, quartermaster and commissary.[2] His pupils were less than ten in number and ranged in age from four to twenty. His youngest was a baby, and his eldest had seen as much or more of life than the master.

From what we know of it, the curriculum was not particularly varied. At that period, reading, writing and figuring to the rule of three, constituted a liberal wilderness education, while those who delved into the mysteries of geography, grammar and rhetoric had reached the realms of higher education. At least part of the instruction was very primary in character, for it was John who taught Charlotte Ouisconsin Clark, his youngest pupil, only four years old, to spell in Webster's spelling book and to read, in that time-honored volume, of the "boy who stole the apples"; of the conceited "country milkmaid" who spilled her milk with a toss of her head; and of the good "dog Tray," who fell into bad company and suffered the consequences.[3]

School began somewhere around nine o'clock. At that hour the drum beat for breakfast. After that event, the school bell rang, and Marsh's pupils filed into the class-

JOHN MARSH, PIONEER

room.[4] Besides the Snellings, Joe, Henry and Mary, John had several other pupils, Malcolm Clark, his sister Charlotte, James W. Hamilton and John and Andrew Tully.

Charlotte Ouisconsin Clark, the baby of his classroom, was born at Fort Crawford, in the French and half-breed settlement of Prairie du Chien, near the mouth of the Wisconsin, or "Ouisconsin," as the French traders then called it, when her parents were on their way to the military post at the mouth of the St. Peters. The officers were so delighted with the event that they hailed her as the daughter of the regiment, and gave her the name of "Ouisconsin."[5]

The only other girl in the school was Mary Snelling, the eldest child and daughter of the commandant. She was ten years old, lovely and frail, but shy. She remained under Marsh's tutelage for the two years he maintained the garrison school. Then she was sent to Washington for finishing touches, where she contracted brain-fever and died.[6]

With the boys in his school, Marsh had his hands full and frequently lost his temper.[7] Three of them, Henry Snelling, Malcolm Clark and John Tully, were about the same age and full of mischief. Sometimes they played at being drunk and did it so realistically that the commander was horrified.[8] Again they took turns at the whipping post, beating one another on the bare back with a knotted rope until "enough," was cried, the idea being to see which could stand the most punishment without giving up.

Malcolm Clark was the leader of this group, a brave, handsome, venturesome lad, given to riding over the prairie without saddle or bridle.[9] Once, during a wolf hunt, he held the jaws of that savage little animal until one of the soldiers was able to muzzle him.[10] He was passionate,

MINNESOTA'S FIRST SCHOOL

quick with words, quick with blows, and left many black eyes and bloody noses in his wake.[11]

Henry Hunt Snelling, another member of his school, was a lad of seven years, brave and daring, and the hero of many adventures.[12] At the grand review of the troops during the visit of General Winfield Scott, he climbed to the top of a high stump to get a better view of the parade. It was partially hollow and apparently filled with dry leaves. Childlike, Henry stirred the leaves with a stick, and they instantly came to life, and he found himself covered with bees and stung in so many places that he was frantic with pain. For a few tragic moments he danced upon the edge of the stump like a showman's monkey under the whip, then fell to the ground, still pursued by the insects. Cries of agony brought a squad of soldiers, who drove off the bees with much difficulty. The boy was then carried home, entirely blind, hands and other portions of his body swollen enormously, and for several days he lay in great danger of death.[13]

On another day he fell into the river, and had it not been for Lipkap, a discharged soldier, who was in a garden near by, he would have drowned. Just in time he was fished out with a pole. When he came to his senses, Henry told a marvellous tale of catching an immense catfish on his line, which was so strong that it dragged him into the river and beneath the surface.[14]

Probably Marsh's eldest pupil was Joe Snelling, the colonel's son by an earlier marriage—a wayward, red-haired, slightly bald-headed lad of nineteen, given to drink. Born at Boston, December 26, 1804, he was almost as old as his teacher. When he was fourteen years old, he entered West Point, but was dismissed shortly before graduation.[15] His stepmother had no fondness or respect for him, perhaps because of his intemperance. But his father adored him. Once, when his father became involved in a duel with Lieutenant Hunter, Joe wielded the weapon against his father's antagonist and thereby lost a finger.[16]

One day late in the fall of 1823, Marsh dismissed his school for the noon recess, and the children raced across the parade ground, Charlotte and Malcolm Clark in the lead. Suddenly, Charlotte saw a little fair-haired stranger on the porch of her father's quarters and called to her brother: "Oh! Malcolm, look at that little boy on the steps; who can he be? Where did he come from?"

"Do you think he can be the little brother we have been praying God to send us?" asked Malcolm. "Let's run home and ask mother about it."

So Charlotte and Malcolm ran home. There on their doorstep stood Andrew Tully, a light-haired, smiling, blue-eyed, seven-year-old boy, who gazed back at them with wonder.[17]

If at this moment they could have looked in on the Snelling household, they would have found in their midst another light-haired, blue-eyed stranger, John Tully, nine years old. Thus Marsh acquired two more students, both of whom had to be instructed in the French tongue, for they were refugees from the Swiss colony at Pembina, where their father, John Tully, had been one of the leaders.

The boys had had a pitiful history. In the early spring of 1823, their father had become disgusted and disheartened with the colony's outlook. As soon as spring permitted, he set out with his family, John and Andrew on foot, and his wife and daughter in a Red River cart. At first all went well. But somewhere around Lake Traverse they met a horde of bloodthirsty Sisseton, flushed with the

MINNESOTA'S FIRST SCHOOL

"white man's milk," as well as with the spoils and trophies of a recent victory over the Chippewa. The Indians stopped the travellers and insolently demanded provisions. Tully resisted. In the struggle that followed, he and his wife and baby were tomahawked and scalped.[18] Then, with a yell of exultation, the Indians seized the two children, John and Andrew, and disappeared in the wilderness, making their way toward their village, where the orphan boys, as is the practice among them, were adopted into the tribe.

John, who was nine years old, felt keenly the tragic death of his parents and little sister and gave way to frequent lamentations, which so incensed the Indians that they subjected both to harsh treatment. This developed John's spirit of resistance to such an extent that he tried to escape. One fine day he took Andrew by the hand and disappeared in the forest surrounding the village. All day long they hid in the bushes. At night they forged ahead, but at the end of three days, they were discovered. John resisted recapture so doggedly that his captors scalped him on the spot, removing an area about two inches in diameter. In this state they returned him to the village, no attempt being made to dress the wound.

Not long after this, Colonel Snelling, through some traders, heard of the two white boys with the Sisseton, and sent a detachment of soldiers to bring them to the Fort. Poor little John was in a deplorable state. The wound in his head had become a festering, running sore, and it was feared he could not be saved, but Doctor Purcell, the Fort surgeon, treated it skilfully. In a few weeks an ugly scar was the only outward evidence of this brutality, but his experiences left him depressed with gloomy thoughts and recollections.[19]

JOHN MARSH, PIONEER

One day in school John was caught whispering to a boy at a neighboring desk. They were both called up for punishment. The master came down from his pulpit-like desk and seated himself upon a chair, the boys standing before him with long faces and sheepish looks while he administered to them a pedantic reproof upon the enormity of their offense. He then bid the youngest to hold out his hand while he inflicted the punishment due. After a few raps of the ferrule, he sent him to his seat. John, being the elder, was reserved for a more serious application of the rule. When the command came, he held out his hand boldly. The teacher raised the ruler above his head and brought it down with full force, but instead of encountering the resistance of John's hand, it came in contact with his own knee, John having turned his hand dexterously to one side.

The master lost his temper. Blood mounted to his face. He snatched the extended hand, seized it firmly by the fingers and pressed them back so as to leave the palm free to receive the blow. Then he laid the ruler on heavily. John never winced; not a tear appeared in his eye, although the angry teacher continued to apply the ferrule until the hand was blistered, and fatigue compelled him to stop.[20]

Such were the children whom Marsh taught in Minnesota's first school.[21] Just what effect, if any, he had on their lives is problematical, but he instructed them for two years—the terms of 1823–24 and 1824–25. "He was considered very competent for his work," writes Charlotte Clark, "but he was a violent-tempered man and only maintained his position a few years, but what we learned then, we know now, and the thorough drill we received each day, turned out correct spellers and good readers; with all the improvements in the way of textbooks and methods, I do

MINNESOTA'S FIRST SCHOOL

not think the results, as far as fundamental education goes, are more satisfactory now than then."[22] That is Minnesota's memorial to her first schoolmaster.

CHAPTER X

MAIL-CARRIER

1825

THE lack of mail was a sore trial. Sometimes John did not hear from Danvers for six months or even longer. Then he would receive a bundle but the feast would be followed by a famine. In summer, mail came every three or four months—in winter not at all. Once, during February of 1825, Colonel Snelling offered John forty dollars to carry the mail from Fort St. Anthony to Prairie du Chien and return.[1] It was a dangerous and hazardous undertaking, through a trackless wilderness, ice-blocked rivers, snow-drifts and tempestuous weather, to say nothing of hungry timber-wolves, coyotes and hostile red men.[2] It meant many nights' lodgings in the lee of the snow-drifts, the mail-bag for a pillow and only half-closed eyes, for the fire must be kept smouldering and the wolves frightened away.[3] There was not one civilized dwelling along the entire route.

If the Indians were hunting, as they usually were in winter, there was little chance of meeting a single person during the entire distance. But John did not hesitate; he would do anything to earn sufficient money to take him back to Cambridge. One February day, with no other guide than an old Sioux called Okh-pee, he started out. We can picture him in fringed buckskins, elk-hide moccasins, wolf-skin hat with the animal's tail hanging down his back, knife, pistol and hatchet plunged into the belt about his waist, and the mail strapped to his back, leaving

MAIL-CARRIER

the Fort and turning his steps toward Prairie du Chien.

When he reached there, he wrote the old folks at Danvers, mentioning the object of his journey. Ten days later he was back at Fort St. Anthony and, under date of February 22, 1825, again addressed them:

"I arrived here in health and safety in ten days, after having performed a journey of 600 miles on foot,[4] through an uninhabited country, in which I waded through several rivers, slept on the snow in the open air with only a single blanket when the thermometer stood at eighteen degrees below zero, and for six days had next to nothing to eat, but my health did not suffer in the least and the journey on the whole was a pleasant one.

"I once thought myself tender and unable to endure hardship, but I now know by experience that in this respect I excel most men, and those even who have been inured to it from infancy. Okh-pee, the Indian who accompanied me, declared on our return that I was as 'tough as an old he-bear.' On my journey back, having one day outwalked the rest of my party, I found that they would not be able to overtake me and I determined to spend the night at a Sioux camp, which I knew was not far off, and where I arrived about sunset. I was immediately invited in the lodge of the Red Wing, a Chief whom I have before mentioned and by whom I was treated with the greatest hospitality and kindness. A huge piece of venison was roasting at the fire, with which they desired me to stay my appetite till supper was ready. The old man's pretty granddaughter took off my wet moccasins and stockings, which she dried and mended. A comfortable bed was made for me and the good old man before he retired himself came and 'tucked me up warm,' as my own dear Mother has done so many times and which I never expected from any other person.

JOHN MARSH, PIONEER

"I wrote to you some time ago that I was Acting Indian Agent at this post which office I still retain and shall till May, perhaps longer.

"I live in Colonel Snelling's family where I am quite at home. I am on terms of the closest intimacy and friendship with the Colonel. Of this friendship, I have had many assurances and what is better, substantial proofs.

"It is probable I shall go to Washington on business next spring or summer and of course I shall come home.

"It gives me sincere pleasure to hear that you all enjoy health and prosperity and as soon as I can possibly make my duty coincide with my inclination, I shall hasten to revisit the 'home of my Fathers.'

"I do not believe there is a spot on earth more healthy than Ft. St. Anthony. I have enjoyed better health than I ever did in Massachusetts.

"I have not had so much as a cold or the headache since I came here. You have probably seen many monstrous stories in the public print of Indian outrages in this quarter. They all belong to the 'humbug family' and originated in trifles. It is true that two Canadians and two discharged soldiers set out from P. du Chien last summer with a barrel of whiskey in a canoe which they intended to sell to the Indians, contrary to law. They met with a war party of Chippeways near L. Pepin who came from L. Superior to 'strike' the Sioux, having intoxicated the Indians, a quarrel ensued in which the four smugglers were killed.

"This affair will cost the U. S. an immense sum to punish the Indians, who rather deserve a bounty for ridding the world of four worthless scoundrels.

"The people of Missouri have been in the habit of driving large herds of cattle a distance of sixteen hundred miles through the Indian country to the British settlement at Ft. Douglass. One of these drovers in passing the

MAIL-CARRIER

St. Peters about 200 miles above this place lost five horses which he says were taken by the Sissetons (a band of Sioux). The Indians say the men were frightened and ran away and left them. The Chief of this band came to the Agency House a few days ago to receive his—present of tobacco and whiskey, and was seized by the Col and confined as a hostage for the recovery of the horses. He attempted to escape and was shot by the sentinel. The ball broke and shockingly lacerated his arm above the elbow, which has since been amputated. It is not improbable that this affair will incite the Indians to acts of violence on the traders, for which they will suffer severely. You may form a just opinion of Indian ferocity, of which you have heard so much, when I assure you that I went a few days ago with only the Interpreter, a Sergeant and four men into an Indian camp of 200 persons at the hour of midnight to seize two of the warriors.

"The express which carried this will be the last till the ice breaks up and it is therefore probable you will not receive another letter for nearly two months, but I shall not fail to write often.

"I have only room to say, give my love to all the family. . . ."[5]

Okh-pee could never be induced to guide the courier or to carry the mail again to Prairie du Chien. On his return to the Fort, John received the forty dollars, pocketed it, and gave the old Sioux nothing.[6] Marsh was now in the throes of his great ambition—to get a medical degree, and every dollar counted. Okh-pee was entirely forgotten.

CHAPTER XI
SIOUX INDIAN AGENT
1824–1825

SCHOOL-TEACHING was not enough to keep John busy. As soon as he had dismissed his classes he hied himself off to the prairies and explored the Sioux villages near the Fort. Many of them were within a stone's throw and they fascinated him. Black Dog's village was two or three miles up the Minnesota. The village of Little Six was further up on the present site of Shakopee; the village of L'Arc, (The Bow) was still higher on the Minnesota but the extensive village of Cloudman was near by on the shores of Lake Calhoun. These villages were all very much alike, bark lodges swarming with children, squaws, painted warriors and yelping dogs. But they interested John and he spent long, happy hours with the inhabitants. He played ball and games with the boys and that won the hearts of the squaws. He filled the pipes of the old bucks from his own pouch and thus gained their approval.

About the villages were cornfields and the scaffolds, where, wrapped in buffalo skins, reposed the bones of their hunters who had followed the Milky Way to the "Land of the Ghosts." In all these wigwams John became a welcome guest. He would squat by the tepee fire, eat their maple sugar and venison, and engage the old chiefs and warriors in conversation. He had a natural flair for languages and before long mastered their tongue—so successfully that it would have required an expert to know that he had not always lived among them.

SIOUX INDIAN AGENT

Then he commenced to write a book on the customs, language and traditions of the Sioux and daily jotted down his observations and impressions, which kept him busy. The old chiefs grew fond of him, and often on stormy nights he never left their warm, comfortable wigwams, but, wrapping himself in their great buffalo robes, would throw himself down beside them and sleep with a feeling of perfect security.

During October of 1824, Laurence Taliaferro departed for St. Louis and left the agency in charge of his brother Muscoe.[1] After that, John, who was devoted to the latter, spent many hours in the agency with him. It was a fascinating place. Delegations of Indians came and went all day long, and John improved every opportunity in "trying out his Sioux" on them and getting material for his book. One day Marsh and Muscoe had a quarrel. The argument waxed hotter and hotter. Marsh was furious. Taliaferro struck him. John lost his temper completely and whipping out a cane beat his adversary unmercifully —almost into insensibility; although it was Taliaferro's fault, Muscoe never forgave him the humiliation of that thrashing. His liking turned to hatred, and he thirsted for revenge. John was banished from the agency.

The story of the fight came to Colonel Snelling's attention, and he wrote to the major: "Mr. Marsh had an unfortunate affair with your brother, but Muscoe was so decidedly in the wrong that I am sure your liberality of feeling will prevent you harboring any prejudice against him on that account."[2] On top of that, and before his brother's return, Muscoe resigned the sub-agency and returned to his father's home in Virginia, leaving a letter for his brother Laurence charging him above all things to take vengeance on Marsh "in my behalf."[3]

73

JOHN MARSH, PIONEER

With Muscoe's departure, the Sioux agency of St. Peter's was left with no official head except Colonel Snelling, and the arduous duties fell upon his shoulders, leaving him little time to carry on his other work. One day, when he was particularly rushed with business, he sent for Marsh and asked him how he would like to take over the agency until Major Taliaferro's return from St. Louis. John was still tutoring the colonel's children, but he felt he could carry on the agency as well, especially as the added work meant added pay and so an increase in the hoard he was saving against the day he returned to New England and resumed his medical work. To be absolutely certain regarding the latter, John inquired of the colonel what the salary would be. Snelling allowed him to believe that it would be equal to a sub-agent's pay, or $500 a year. This was a great sum in those days. John jumped at the chance of earning it, or even a part, with alacrity, and accepted the agency. Now his return to the medical school was assured. The colonel immediately reported the result of this interview to Taliaferro at St. Louis.

"I have been compelled to grant eight licenses (traders') before having received your authority to do so," he wrote, "and for the last week my quarters have scarcely for an hour been free from Indians; finding it impossible to do justice to my command and attend to the affairs of the agency, I have engaged Mr. John Marsh, the gentleman who came here as a tutor, to reside at the council house and attend to their calls, with instructions to keep me informed of all important events. I have given him no assurance of compensation for his service, but have encouraged him to believe that while he does the duty you will allow him the pay of a sub-agent ($500.00 a year). I consider him fully competent to fill that office and beg

SIOUX INDIAN AGENT

leave to recommend him for the appointment."[4] The colonel's course at the time met Taliaferro's approbation. Fortunately he had not as yet read his brother's letter, and he replied to the colonel that if Marsh would conduct the affairs of the agency during his absence, he would remunerate him, not with the salary of a sub-agent from the government, as he could not promise that, but he would see that he was adequately compensated for all his trouble, out of his own private funds.[5]

Immediately after his talk with the major, John left his comfortable berth in the Snelling household and moved into the council house, to be nearer the Indians. Thus began that close connection with the Sioux that was never afterward severed.[6]

That he was considered by the commander capable of taking over an agency of its consequence, at once the most important and influential civil office on the upper Mississippi, reveals how rapidly he had acquired the ways of the wilderness and just how high he was held in the colonel's esteem. With his school, the carrying of the mail, some trading enterprises, and the agency, he spent an active winter. The Harvard fund grew apace. John wrote home that he would enter medical school that fall.

The Indians had great respect and fondness for their new agent. So adept had he become in their tongue that he dealt with them without the services of an interpreter.

The agency consisted of three buildings—the council house, the agent's house and an armorer's shop. John moved into the former,—a very unique structure built of stone and logs.[7] Within, the council house boasted of six rooms, lined with pine planking and separated from each other by panel doors.[8] John took possession of one of these rooms. The main part of the building was occupied by the council chamber, a great hall built of trunks of trees, with pipes, calumets and medals, presented by the Indians as a pledge of friendship and a proof that they abjured all alliance with the English, hanging on the walls. Altogether, they gave a remarkable and characteristic air to the room. Here, seated at a table, Marsh held his councils, all in the Sioux tongue, the visiting chiefs and delegations squatted on the floor before him.

St. Peter's was established primarily for the Sioux, 7,000 of whom, subdivided into seven tribes, or "fires," occupied the great prairies between the Mississippi and the Missouri rivers. Five of these centred about the fort: the Mdewakanton, or "people of the Spirit's Lake"; the Wahpekute, or People of the "Plucked Leaf"; the Wahpeton, or "People of the Leaf"; the Sisseton; and the Yankton, the "People of the Fern Leaves." The Tetons or the "Braggers" seem to have had little connection with St. Peter's.

The Sioux were a splendid race, tall, well set up, of lofty mien and noble bearing. Their chiefs comported themselves with dignity, wore their buffalo robes with the majesty of the Roman clamis and carried their bows and arrows with the pride of sceptered kings.[9] John appreciated them keenly. They were real men. In all matters concerning lands, hunting treaties, and annuities, they looked to Marsh for advice or explanation. He supervised and regulated all these contracts, and if there were complaints he listened to both sides. If trespassers were unlawfully present in the Indian country, or redmen accused of committing a crime, or a distillery to be broken up, he had to attend to it, although he could call upon Colonel Snelling for assistance if the necessity arose.[10]

Scarcely a day passed but delegations from the differ-

SIOUX INDIAN AGENT

ent villages came to consult him or dropped in to chat. In one month there were 1400 Indian visitors from all sections of the region, all with grievances of some sort, and to all of them he had to lend a sympathetic ear, give a satisfactory answer, and present a personal gift.[11]

In addition to the Sioux, Marsh had much to do with the traders, and it was his duty to safeguard the Indians' interests from the nefarious among them. By the time Marsh reached the wilderness much of the romance had been lost from the fur trade. The good old traders of the Northwest, and the Hudson's Bay Company, were gone. The American Fur Company, with headquarters at Prairie du Chien and a Minnesota River *entrepôt* among the "Frogs" at Mendota, had inherited the traditions of these privateers of commerce. There were no more silks and satins, French chefs, and baskets of champagne. All that had faded with the French and British dreams of empire. The traders with whom John came into contact were a remarkable set of men, recruited from the ranks of many races.[12] These *"Gens Libres"* took their fun where they found it, spent the winter in the Indian villages, danced Chippewa mazurkas at the medicine balls at trading houses, picked out handsome squaws for mistresses or wives, and left in their wake a myriad of half-breeds, with complexions like burnt wood, the *bois-brûlé*—the tragedy and problem of every frontier.

One day a delegation of Wahpetons came to the agency with a grievance. Among the number was a young girl whom Marsh could never forget—a half-breed, dark, petite and lithe. She was quick of movement and quick of speech—as graceful and slender as a reed. Marsh could not keep his eyes off her, and his fascinated gaze took her in, from the feather in her hair to the fringed deerskin that skirted her ankles. Not an iota escaped his attention. The impression she created was an indelible one. She looked more French than Indian and spoke that language as well as Sioux.[13] When she smiled—and she smiled often, she displayed a row of beautiful, even teeth. They were the most remarkable thing about her—those white teeth when she smiled. To his dying day Marsh declared her the prettiest creature he had ever seen.[14]

Their mission accomplished, John detained her as long as possible and before she departed learned that her name was Marguerite Decouteaux, that her father had been a red-haired French-Canadian, an independent trader on the Minnesota as early as 1804. When the Northwest Company sent Jean Baptiste Faribault to Little Rapids, a post forty miles above the mouth of the Minnesota, he found Decouteaux trading with the Wahpetons. He had enlisted as a *commis* and had married into the tribe and was living there with his wife and his daughter Marguerite. Shortly after his daughter's birth, Decouteaux had an unfortunate altercation with his wife, upbraiding her severely for some breach of conduct. In anger her father shot him,[15] and Marguerite and her mother returned to the Wahpetons.

After she left the agency that day, John could not get her out of his mind, and shortly after, he mounted his horse and sought out her tribe up the Minnesota.

"She was the gentlest creature," he was ever after wont to say—"the gentlest creature I ever knew, just like a fawn, clinging and affectionate."

Perhaps this was what appealed most to John, for with all his learning, he was brusque and rough in his manner. She was unlike Marsh in another particular—she was wholly uneducated and could neither read nor write.[16] Instead of being a barrier, her lack of education drew them together. Her intelligence and aptitude astonished John. Before long he discovered that she could help him in his Sioux investigations. In his leisure hours, she piloted him over the prairies, telling him the legends of this or that stream, lake and cliff. When he left her, he wrote down the legends just as she told them. He would use them in the book he was still writing.

Once she told him the story of Winona, who ended her blighted romance in the Lake of Tears. Again she took him to the Falls of St. Anthony and told him the story of Ampata Sapa (The Dark Day), a Sioux maiden who, discarded by her lover, committed suicide by going over the falls in her canoe. Sometimes, she told him, Ampata Sapa's ghostly form came back, and her people could hear her death-song mingling with the roar of falling waters and see her wraith descending the deceitful current; for the passions that agitated the hearts of the young Sioux maidens were not at all different from those that rent the bosoms of other heroines of romance. Little did Marsh realize the kind of fire he was playing with. Like a furnace, the wilderness tested the metal of which he was made. The veneer disappeared. The real John Marsh stood forth.

There was no Sioux dictionary, and realizing this need, John began the compilation of one and found Marguerite invaluable in the task of helping him collect the words and work out their meaning. As was inevitable, with one so apt and clever, John began to take an interest in her own intellectual development. In order that she might be of greater assistance, he gave up temporarily his Sioux investigations to teach her words in his own tongue, showing her how to write them down and study them. Then he was lost.

JOHN MARSH, PIONEER

Marguerite learned so rapidly that he marvelled at her progress and devoted all his leisure to her education.[17] His pride in her intellectual development knew no bounds and ripened rapidly into love. He had the same feeling for her as inspires an artist when he sees a great painting materialize under his brush—the same feeling that filled Pygmalion when he became enamored of the beautiful statue he had chiselled from stone.

On her side, Marguerite responded with all her heart to the efforts of her lover. She worked hard to please and delight him.[18] She was thrilled with his stories of the world beyond her land of many waters. Soon she was reading his French Bible and became familiar with that favorite book of his—the "English Poets," which he sometimes read aloud. Almost before he knew it, she was approaching the standards that Danvers and the Nashua had once demanded. He afterward claimed that he was never so happy as when he suddenly discovered that he had created a companion for himself in a wilderness where to all intent and purpose they were few. She was his, his work. His accomplishment swept him off his feet. Its demands outweighed the traditions of the Marshes, Salem and Brimstone Hill. For the time, he forgot his medical career in New England. He loved her. He told her so. She loved him. That was enough. Held in the toils of a passion from which he did not wish to escape, he succumbed to it, revelled in it, unmindful of past or future.

Before the summer began, he took Marguerite under his protection. She came to live with him at the council house.

CHAPTER XII

DEPARTURE AND RETURN

1825–1826

MARSH's romance had a rude awakening. Early in April, 1825, after six months' absence at St. Louis, Major Taliaferro returned to the fort, apparently very much out of sorts. During the winter he had had an unfortunate love affair with a St. Louis belle, Miss Pratte, who had broken her engagement with him. According to Colonel Snelling, report had it that a Miss Choteau (a mischievous jade) had been busy in the affair and had told the young lady some tales to his disadvantage,[1] perhaps the romance of his Sioux sweetheart and their half-breed daughter Mary, or rumors of his reputation for a testy disposition. At any rate, the engagement was off. Perhaps that had something to do with the major's disposition. But when he found his brother's letter, learned of the thrashing Marsh had given Muscoe, and read the latter's plea for revenge, there was more than rancor in his breast —there was hate.[2]

He sought Marsh out, discharged him from the agency, put him and Marguerite out of the council house, accused him of neglect of duty, of unwarranted absence from the post, of stealing a letter concerning himself from Colonel Snelling's files,[3] threatened to prefer charges against him with the Secretary of War at Washington, and, as a final insult, refused to pay him more than $50.00 for his services during his absence. John was furious. That was the money that was to take him back to Harvard. His future depended on it. He wouldn't be cheated out of it. The pay of a sub-agent for that period would have been $250.00. Marsh told Taliaferro that Colonel Snelling, when he engaged him, had led him to believe that he would receive the pay of a sub-agent. The duties of the agency had been arduous.[4] He had, according to many advices, carried them on satisfactorily.[5] Taliaferro persisted in his offer of $50.00. He said that was ample compensation for services such as his had been. Marsh scoffed at the offer, flatly refusing to accept it, and went to Colonel Snelling's office with his difficulties. There he found the commander surrounded by the confusion coincidental to departure; for that morning, May 17, 1825, he was leaving with his family for Detroit.[6]

Marsh reminded him of their conversation regarding his pay when he took over the agency, and asked him if the major had not, in a letter from St. Louis, promised to compensate him for his services out of his own funds. The colonel replied that he had and, at Marsh's request, produced Taliaferro's letter and read aloud the passage bearing upon the salary question. After reading the letter he replaced it in the right-hand corner on the top of the file. He then hurried out of the office, leaving Marsh still there.[7] That day the letter disappeared.

After the colonel's departure John revisited Taliaferro and repeated his demands for the pay of a sub-agent, bolstering up his argument with quotations from the major's letter written from St. Louis.

Taliaferro still persisted in his refusal and immediately wrote to Snelling in Detroit, telling him that Marsh was in possession of his letter written from St. Louis, in which he had promised him a salary out of his own funds. The colonel replied as quickly that he was at a loss to con-

MAJOR LAURENCE TALIAFERRO.
From a photograph taken about 1865, in the Museum of the Minnesota Historical Society.

DR. EDWARD PURCELL, THE FIRST PHYSICIAN IN MINNESOTA.
Courtesy of Miss M. C. Purcell, Manhattan, Kansas.

DEPARTURE AND RETURN

ceive how Marsh had come into possession of this letter; that Marsh had never received it from him, and that if he had it, it had been clandestinely taken from his files. "No person but Mr. Marsh," he concluded, "was left alone in the office afterwards until my departure."[8]

John's ire was up. He did not propose to be imposed upon. He had calculated upon that money to see himself through medical school, and he intended to get it. Since the Snellings had gone to Detroit he was no longer needed as a tutor, so he determined to go to Detroit himself, seek out Governor Cass, who was also Superintendent of Indian Affairs and the major's immediate superior, and appeal directly to him. Further, he determined, should the latter appeal prove futile, to go to Washington and appeal directly to the Secretary of War. He would "show" Taliaferro. He wrote his father, "I am determined to leave nothing undone for want of exertion. I feel extremely anxious to see you and all the family and shall hasten home as soon as I can do it consistently with my duty, and I know you would not wish to see me sooner."[9]

With this determined attitude he put Marguerite in a canoe and paddled down the river to Prairie du Chien, where they arrived early in June. On arriving, he discovered that the grand conference to determine the boundary between the Chippewa and the Sioux was scheduled at the Prairie for August and that Governor Cass was expected at the conference as one of the two United States Government Commissioners.

John decided not to wait for the governor's arrival. Every hour counted if he was to get the money. In the meantime, too, some derogatory statements might reach the governor about him. He would seek him out as quickly as possible—would meet him en route if necessary, but he must go. Accordingly he made plans for immediate departure. In the meantime he would leave Marguerite at Prairie du Chien.

Marguerite knew only too well what that might mean. If John received the money from the governor he would return to Harvard, and she would never see him again. If his efforts with the governor failed, she knew he was determined to go to Washington and appeal to the Secretary of War. That was equally bad. In either case he would be lost to her. She would have to return to her tribe. This was the history of the pretty Sioux maidens in these cases. They lived for a time with the white man, bore his burdens, did his work, and, when he went back to his world, they either went over the falls or returned to their tribe.

But Marguerite was different. She was half French; she loved John; she wanted her man; she would not give him up. She watched his preparations for departure with dismay; he who had taught her and opened a new world to her was going. He would forget. She would go back to her tribe and remember. Before he could bid her good-bye, she went to him in tears. She had a secret—half-surmised, which she told him—of a baby—his baby.

John was stunned. Such a possibility for some reason had never entered his mind. His baby! A Marsh—and its mother a Sioux. His people at Danvers! What would they think? They must never know of this affair, and how about Harvard? Could he leave his own flesh and blood in the wilderness among the Indians, go back to school and be content? A Marsh—among the Sioux? No! No! His conscience would not let him. It was against the code of his fathers, against his own. They had loved their children; that was a family trait. They had all kept them close. He was the only one who had wandered away from

DEPARTURE AND RETURN

Danvers. He could never be happy in New England if he deserted his unborn child now. Besides, he was fond of Marguerite. He had educated her, made her what she was. He could not think. His mind was a confusion. Thoughts were jumbled together like the pieces of a puzzle. He was dumb. His career, Harvard, the governor, Danvers, his mother, Marguerite, a baby, were one incoherent thought. Out of chaos one idea resolved itself. He must get away, find the governor and tell him of Taliaferro's injustice. After that perhaps he could think—perhaps he could choose between a medical career and his code. Accordingly, he pacified Marguerite and departed for Green Bay.

By good luck John met the governor at the latter place en route to the conference at Fort Crawford. At once he made a great impression on Michigan's chief executive and lost no time in telling him the story of his difficulties at Fort Snelling, how Taliaferro was attempting to impose upon him, and that he was returning to his New England home because of it. The governor lent a sympathetic ear. He had no intention of allowing this intelligent, highly educated man to leave the wilderness. He could make due consideration for the quarrelsome disposition of the Indian agent at St. Peters. Moreover, he needed just such a man as Marsh. At this time he was endeavoring to obtain all the authentic information possible regarding the Indian tribes in his vast domain. Here it was, ready at hand. Marsh had much of it at his finger-tips; he was an acknowledged Indian linguist of unusual ability, could speak all of the Sioux dialects, and but one man—the great Schoolcraft—had a greater knowledge of the Indian customs than he. The governor was delighted to find one so well versed in the very subject that was uppermost in his mind. Straightway he settled his difficulties.

JOHN MARSH, PIONEER

The influence he exerted on John's career at this critical juncture may be judged from the letter which John long years later penned to his benefactor:

"You will, I think, remember a youth whom you met at Green Bay 1825, who having left his Alma Mater, had spent a year or two in the 'far, far West,' and was then returning to his New England home, and whom you induced to turn his face again toward the setting sun; that youth who, but for your influence, would probably now have been administering pills in some quiet Yankee village, is now a gray-haired man. Your benevolence prompted you to take an interest in the fortunes of that youth, and it is therefore presumed you may not be unwilling to hear from him again."[10]

On the spot, the Governor offered to have him appointed sub-agent of Indian Affairs at Prairie du Chien for the special purpose of gathering information on the traditions, customs and linguistic tendencies of the tribes centering about that place, and he promised to pay him a monthly salary[11] out of his own pocket in addition to the one he would receive from the government.

Cass also proposed that for the time Marsh forget the money Taliaferro owed him and suggested that in the fall he accompany him and Schoolcraft to Washington, as his guest. There, he explained, he would be in better position to intercede with President Adams and Secretary Barbour regarding Taliaferro's charges, to collect his unpaid salary as sub-agent at St. Peters, and to obtain official sanction of his appointment as sub-agent at Prairie du Chien.[12] Thus Marsh faced about and triumphantly returned to Prairie du Chien. Had the governor or Marguerite decided his future? At any rate, long afterward he

DEPARTURE AND RETURN

stated that the governor "left him at peace with himself."

Marguerite was overjoyed when her stalwart young lover appeared again on the Prairie. He was her man. She fluttered around him like a bird. Always proud of him, there was about him now the added lustre of the governor's patronage. In addition he had worsted his enemies. During the next few weeks she helped him to acquire information of the Sioux, Winnebago, and other Prairie tribes, for Governor Cass. But their Arcadian romance approached an interruption.

One day late in the fall of 1825 John received a letter from Governor Cass directing him to proceed to St. Louis, where he and Schoolcraft would meet him and together continue to Washington.

There were many reasons now why John dreaded leaving. Marguerite filled his mind. She was approaching her period of travail. Too, there were many reasons why he must go—the money, his appointment as an agent, Taliaferro's charges, his mother—and Cambridge. Everything lay with the governor.

About the middle of November he departed down the river, leaving Marguerite with the Boilvins at the agency. On November 22 he wrote his father from St. Louis:

"Arrived yesterday at this place on my way to the east, and shall leave here for Washington in two or three days. In the last letter which I wrote you from P. du Chien I informed you that I had entered into an engagement with Gov. Cass. I am to meet him in Washington on the 1st of January and shall then proceed directly to Massachusetts, but it is impossible to say at present how long I shall be detained at Washington—when I arrive there I shall write to you again. I have not heard from home since last July and how to account for it I do not know, except that you did not know where to direct me— You may perhaps have heard of the great sickness that has prevailed on the Upper Mississippi and particularly at Prairie du Chien this season and felt some anxiety on my account. I have been indeed a little sick, but never enjoyed better health in my life than at present. I have reserved all my stock of news till I reach home, which I hope to do in February if not before."[13]

CHAPTER XIII
TALIAFERRO'S REVENGE
1825

FROM St. Louis to Washington on horseback was a long, tedious journey. Marsh left the former place over the old National Road, November 25 or 26, 1825, and arrived at the capital, December 26, and a few days later, December 29, 1825, wrote his father:

"In my last letter which I wrote from St. Louis, I promised to write to you again when I arrived here. I now fulfill my promise, although I have little to communicate that cannot be done better when I come home. I came here three days since with Governor Cass and am now living with him; he is as much disposed to assist me now as he professed to be when I met him in the wilds of the west.

"I shall finish my business here in a few days and shall leave this place as soon as possible as I am tired of it already. Congress are doing nothing of consequence.—The great men of the nation who make such an imposing figure when at a distance are mere common mortals when once you are near them.

"I have not heard from home since last May which I do not know how to account for, except that you did not know where to direct me. I shall probably stay here about six days longer, it will take about six days to travel hence to Boston and I shall stop three or four days in N. York you may therefore expect me at home between the fifteenth and twentieth of January."[1]

When Taliaferro discovered that he had been unsuccessful in driving Marsh out of the Indian country, he

JOHN MARSH, PIONEER

was furious. He was still more agitated when he found that he was at Prairie du Chien, reinstated, and stronger than ever with the powerful backing of the governor behind him. His chagrin knew no bounds when he found he was actually in the employ of Cass; that the governor had promised to have him appointed Indian sub-agent at Prairie du Chien, and that he was already en route with him to Washington in order that his appointment might be ratified by the President and his St. Peter's difficulties adjusted. These facts so enraged Taliaferro that he immediately filed the charges he had prepared against his erstwhile sub-agent, dating them from the Indian agency, St. Peter's, December 10, 1825, and addressing them to James Barbour, Secretary of War:

"I am induced, from recent advices, to trouble the Department of War with this communication, and it is hoped that the statements hereinafter made and the object thereof, may be considered my information and to the end that a man of unstable character and penurious views may be unmasked.

"I allude to a Mr John Marsh, who was for some time employed as public tutor at this Post, and on losing his Station, was requested by the Commanding officer (Colonel Snelling) to attend to the duties of this Agency after the departure of the Sub-Agent in the Month of October, 1824—who resigned his Appointment shortly after, and during my unavoidable absence at St Louis, in the same *fall*.—

"Colonel Snelling informed me by letter of the course he had adopted, which at *the time*, met my approbation, but stated to him in my answer that Mr Marsh could not receive the salary of a Sub-Agent from the Government, but that I would compensate him for any trouble he might

TALIAFERRO'S REVENGE

be at, in the discharge of my duties, out of my own private funds.—On my return to this Post the 2d. of April last, I had every reason not to be satisfied with the general course which had been pursued by this Gentleman, for instead of bestowing his undivided attention to the duties of the Office—he performed but little, in fact so little, that he was absent some *thirty* or forty days, under a contract to convey the Express Mail from this Post, to Prairie des-Chiens—for which service he received *forty dollars*—At the same time was under an engagement to instruct the children of a private family and received therefor, his *board* and *seventy-five dollars*—

"Also, in February last, did receive of Daniel Whitney, Merchant of Green Bay, an Invoice of Merchandise to be disposed of, on Commission or *Salary* and stored the same, in the Agency house and traded by him to the Soldiers, Citizens and *Indians*, indiscriminately.—

"On my taking his whole course into consideration—he was proffered the sum of Fifty dollars—which was deemed to be ample compensation, by a number of the Gentlemen of Fort Snelling.—Now it appears, after declining to accept of the sum before stated, he as I understand is determined to apply to the Dept. of War, to the end that he may if possible obtain the Salery of a Sub-Agent, for *any time, he may* think proper to charge the Government.—

"I have also been led to believe that it is his intention if aided by Governor Cass, to apply for an Appointment in the Indian Department. Now, Sir, to show that he is not entitled to either attention or Notice, independently of what has already been stated Mr Marsh did clandestinely take, a letter of mine off the *file* in the Office of the *Commanding Officer*—which had been addressed to *him* by me from St. Louis—Of this *fact* there is no doubt as I have it both by *letter* and personally from Colonel Snelling."[2]

Marsh was in Washington when these charges arrived

JOHN MARSH, PIONEER

and Cass not only helped him refute them but addressed the following letter to the Secretary of War:

"Washington, January 3, 1825 (1826)

Sir:

"The situation of the Indian Department at Prairie du Chien, requires that a Sub Agent should be appointed, and permanently stationed there. This measure is rendered necessary, as well by the importance of the post, and by the number of Indians who resort there, as by the circumstances in which the Agent is placed.

"I recommend for this appointment, Mr John Marsh, who has resided at Prairie du Chien and St. Peters, and has been employed in the Indian Department at both places—He is well acquainted with the Indians and has a competent knowledge of the Sioux language—I am enabled to say, from my own personal observation, that he would discharge the duties of that office, with fidelity and ability, and I am confident the public interest would be essentially promoted by his appointment.

Very respectfully,
I have the honor to be Sir
Your obt. servt,
LEW CASS"

"Hon James Barbour
Secretary of War
Endorsed: Washington Jan. 3, 1826. Gov. Cass Recommends John Marsh for sub agent at Prairie du Chien
Recommended for the Secty's approval
T. L. McKENNEY, Approved."[3]

Shortly after this, President Adams approving Governor Cass' recommendation, Marsh received the following official communication:

"To Mr. John Marsh;
"You are hereby, with approbation of the President of

92

TALIAFERRO'S REVENGE

the United States, appointed Subagent for Indian Affairs, at Prairie du Chien.

"You will report yourself for duty to Mr Boilvin, the Indian Agent at that place, under whose direction you will act.

"Your compensation will be at the rate of $500. per annum, in full for your services, which will be paid to you thro' the agent aforesaid, quarter yearly.

"Given under my hand and the Seal of the War office of the United States this twenty day of January 1826.

JAMES BARBOUR"[4]

On January 11, 1826, the Department of War forwarded Marsh his commission as Sub-Agent to Mr. Boilvin, at Prairie du Chien, and notified him his compensation would commence coincidental with his arrival at the agency.[5] Marsh did not stay in Washington as long a period as his correspondence suggests, but he remained long enough to attain several of the goals he set out to accomplish. He had an opportunity to meet the President of the United States, John Quincy Adams, as well as Mrs. Adams and other government dignitaries, as his letter dated Washington, D. C., January 12, 1826, indicates:

"I wrote to you when I first arrived here that I should be at home in a very short time, but I have met with so many delays in transacting my business that I cannot expect to finish it for some time to come. I have not been idle, as I have accomplished two of the five objects for which I came here—to wit I have received two hundred and thirty two dollars from Govt. for past services which I considered at best as a bad debt, and I have received an appointment which will give me 500 dollars per annum, the commission of which has just been sent me—I wish I could tell you when I shall leave this place, of which I am heartily tired—it will be in two weeks—perhaps sooner. I could give you a description of this famous city and the many splendid things to be seen here, but it can be done so much better when I come home that I shall defer it. I will only say, I have been at the President's levee,—been introduced to Mr. and Mrs. Adams the heads of departments and other great dignitaries—mere common mortals when you are near them and only look great at a distance."[6]

It must have afforded him no little pleasure to have received $232.00 from the government for his services at the St. Peter's agency during the winter previous, a sum far in excess of the amount the major had offered him. In addition he had bested his enemy at St. Peter's in two other respects. In spite of the latter's active animosity and the charges filed against him, he had received the appointment at Prairie du Chien, and best of all, he had in his possession the charges filed against him. "It seems," the commander of Fort Snelling wrote Taliaferro, "that Mr. Secretary Barbour took no other notice of your letter than to send it to Governor Cass and he gave it to Marsh, 'and so we go.' "[7]

After leaving Washington, Marsh hastened eastward and spent the remainder of the winter with his parents in the old homestead at Danvers, Massachusetts. But never in his conversation with them did he mention Marguerite or the grandchild so soon expected on the distant Mississippi. Yet his mind reverted more than once to that gentle girl quickening into maternity. They would not have understood that alliance in Puritanical Danvers, but, had he told them then, how different the future might have been! When the snows lay deep on the Massachusetts landscape he must have wondered how Marguerite was faring. During the bleak, fleeting days of late February, the time of

TALIAFERRO'S REVENGE

her accouchement, he must have suffered, wondering whether she lived or died; whether he was the father of a son or a daughter; whether his child survived or perished; and whether he had given up his career in vain. That hurt the most—his medical career! He longed to stay in New England, to settle down near his people. He belonged there—but the thought of Marguerite and his child. That decided him. He could not desert them.

Long afterward his family recalled his distraught condition during this period. Then they put it down as the natural sadness attending his approaching departure. How they hated to have him go! He had promised to come back in two years. The time was up and now he was going back. Home had a just claim on him but the West had a greater. To all their pleas he replied that he must go; that he had promised to do some work for Governor Cass and could not disappoint him. He was his benefactor. Then spring came and he was gone.

Only four months at home after many months' absence! Perhaps this time he was going forever. But he had something to look forward to. The wilderness had lost its menace.

Caleb, his brother, went with him. He was going to settle in the West. Caleb intuitively knew that there was something amiss with John—but what? On April 28 they were at Buffalo and John wrote:

"Agreeable to my promise I hasten to inform you that Caleb and I arrived at this place last evening—We expected you know, to arrive here sooner but we have met with several delays on account of the badness of the roads —We were three days in getting to Albany—we arrived at Schenectady just in time to come in on the first packet[8] —and in it we were detained some time by obstructions in

JOHN MARSH, PIONEER

the Canal—The ice still remains in this harbor and we shall probably be detained here a week or more unless we conclude to go on by land—on this we have not yet determined—Our journey thus far has been very pleasant we have traveled in company with several persons from Mass. who are going to Michigan—particularly a Mr Fay with his wife & children with whom we are much pleased—Caleb is in high spirits & has acquired more confidence already than he would by staying at home twenty years—

"There is a considerable body of U. S. troops who are going to Green Bay—& those at that place are to move to the Mississippi, so that I can if I choose go in military company this time also all the way—I shall write again from Detroit."[9]

Not until May 9, 1826, did the steamboat, *Henry Clay*, with Marsh aboard, reach Detroit. They had been detained ten days at Buffalo; the passage had been a stormy one and John had been sick. He was hardly able to travel. Caleb wrote home that he acted worried and was irritable.

Already twenty-one days had passed since John had left Boston and many more must elapse before he could reach Prairie du Chien and Marguerite.

At Detroit John found Governor Cass. The governor was very kind and took him home to tea with his family. The country about was a perfect paradise and John was thrilled with its beauty. The fruit trees on both sides of the river were in full blossom, filling the air with a delightful perfume which subtly affected him.[10]

John left Caleb at Detroit,—he would not let him go on. He told Caleb that he would find greater opportunities there than at Prairie du Chien. John seemed so sick and irritable Caleb was loath to leave him but John would not listen to him and sailed for Green Bay, alone.

TALIAFERRO'S REVENGE

There were five hundred passengers aboard, the trip was tedious and uncomfortable and they ran short of provisions. Ten days later, during the night, they landed at Green Bay.[11] John was weak and fatigued. The boat for Prairie du Chien left at day-break; the noise and bustle confused him; he could not sleep. When dawn came he was too sick to rise. He had a raging fever—worry and fatigue took their toll and he despaired of ever seeing Marguerite or Prairie du Chien again.[12]

CHAPTER XIV

MARGUERITE

1825–1826

IT had been a terrible winter for Marguerite, the worst the Upper Mississippi had ever known.[1] The oldest inhabitant could not recall such blizzards, such cold and snow. Thirty lodges of Sioux starved in their tepees. Marguerite would have shared the same fate had it not been for old Boilvin, who treated her like a father. In February, in the midst of a terrible tempest, Marguerite's baby was born. Almost before she was about again the ice on the Mississippi broke. Great cakes began to move down the current, sweeping everything before them. Suddenly the river began to rise, reached flood proportions and overflowed its banks. It deluged the Prairie. Fort Crawford was flooded. Tightly clutching her baby, Marguerite fled with the Boilvins to higher ground beyond the devastating waters.

Ere the flood had subsided the horror of Indian massacre was added to the portion Marguerite endured that winter. One of her neighbors, M. Methode a half-breed, and his wife, five children and pet dog were killed at Painted Rock, twelve miles above the Prairie, where they had gone to make maple sugar. There was no clue to the murderers beyond a mouthful of red cloth tightly locked in the jaws of the dead dog.[2] Little did Marguerite realize the effects that mouthful of red cloth could have on her life. The Prairie was in a panic. Everyone feared an uprising. Shortly afterward Wa-man-goos-ga-ra-ha, a

MARGUERITE

Winnebago of evil reputation, appeared at the agency. He came to tell Nicolas Boilvin how much he loved the Americans and that he suspected the Sioux of the murders that had been committed. It was noticed at the time that a large piece of cloth was missing from the back of one of his leggins. He demanded a bottle of whiskey and a blanket as a reward for his confidence and friendship. Old Boilvin looked at the leggins and realized that the part that was missing was just about the size of the piece they had found in the jaws of M. Methode's dog. He promptly arrested the Indian and put him in jail. The murderer forthwith called up his Indian spirit and confessed his guilt. Subsequently two others implicated in the outrage were caught and confined in the guard-house at Fort Crawford.[3]

This act was a final blow to the Winnebago. Already angered by the white men trespassing on their lead lands on the Fever River, they now took up arms and threatened to attack Fort Crawford and kill the inhabitants of the Prairie unless the prisoners were released.[4] They enlisted the aid of Wabashaw and Red Wing, two of the most powerful Sioux chiefs on the Mississippi. The reports of impending attack were of such terrifying character that the inhabitants were greatly alarmed. Colonel Snelling reinforced Fort Crawford. Companies A, B, and I were detached from his command and dispatched post haste, under command of Captain Wilcox. Marguerite was distracted. No news from her man; she thought she was deserted. She was on the point of returning to her tribe for protection. In the midst of her grief and desolation John returned; it was on July 14, three months after he had left Danvers. He was wasted and worn and she hardly knew him. For four weeks, he said, he had lain violently

JOHN MARSH, PIONEER

ill with a fever; everyone thought he would die. He looked sick and old.

Marguerite's joy knew no bounds. She ran to the cradle and held her baby aloft in her arms. His baby,—a splendid four-months-old man-child. A tiny replica of its father, sturdy of frame, blond of hair and blue of eyes,— the Marsh type again. Marguerite exhibited him proudly, her perfect little flaxen-headed Anglo-Saxon. John thrilled with pride. He took the child in his big arms and looked him over with professional and parental interest, rejoicing in the diminutive features so closely resembling his own. Not a blemish marred their perfection. He toyed with his hands, straightened the little fingers; inspected the chubby little legs and feet. What was this? The toes betrayed the stigmata of degeneration, for those of the right foot were webbed—webbed from joint to tip of nail.

CHAPTER XV
PRAIRIE DU CHIEN
1826

MARGUERITE wanted to name their baby "John." He would have been the eighth in line, but Marsh would not hear of it. He named him "Charles." Four days after his return, Marsh wrote his father but not a word did he say of his son or of the boy's mother. He wrote:

"I am now in tolerable health, this place has suffered much from inundation this spring but the water has long since subsided & the inhabitants have returned to their houses.

"The place is as healthy as usual. You have probably seen in the newspapers an account of the murder of a family near this place in March last. The horrid deed, it is supposed, was committed by the Winnebagoes, six of whom are now in prison here. They were peaceably given up by the Chiefs and no further trouble is apprehended—

"I have not been here long enough to tell you much of affairs all I can say is that everything looks favourable. Old Mr. Boilvin received me very kindly and announced to the Indians that I was appointed by the President to assist him & that whatever I said to them was the same as if he said it &c.

"You do not know how often my mind returns to my dear native home, how often I contemplate the looks and features of every one of the family. Ezekiel I am particularly anxious for his success—pray let some one write to me frequently & let me know all the family concerns—give my best love to all the family——"[1]

JOHN MARSH, PIONEER

John did not appear greatly alarmed over the Winnebago disturbance, threatening as it was. In its midst he went through the back country to Fort Snelling. He said he felt he could not be happy until he had faced Taliaferro and made him retract his charges. Unfortunately, when he arrived the major was absent and he had to content himself with a letter of refutation from Colonel Snelling, which contradicted the most material portion of the charges.[2]

"Head Quarters, 5th. Infy.
Fort Snelling August 18th. 1826

Dr. Sir

"In reference to our conversation of yesterday relative to a letter written by Mr. Taliaferro to the Secretary of War, I have to say that I am not aware of any injury to the public service by your visit to Prairie des Chiens in the winter of 1825, nor do I think that the sum received by you for taking the express mail was more than sufficient to pay your guide, & other necessary expenses.

"The merchandise mentioned by Maj. Taliaferro was stored at the agency house, by my order, & I have no knowledge nor did I ever hear of any part of it ever having been sold to Indians.

"On the morning of my departure for Detroit (May 17th 1825) I well remember your asking me for the letter which is alleged to have been clandestinely taken, I took it from my files and handed it to you, in the hurry of preparation I forgot it, & have no recollection of it afterward. I did not think it of any consequence except to your self as it treated generally on trifling subjects.

    Respectfully
     your obt servant
      J. SNELLING
      Col. 5th. U.S. Reg. of Inf.[3]

"Mr. John Marsh
S. Agent Pr. du Chien"

PRAIRIE DU CHIEN

Marsh felt the colonel should have written a much more forceful letter but the commander "candidly declared as his reason that he did not wish to involve himself with Mr. T. or his connections."[4] Nor did Marsh let the matter rest there. Taliaferro was in St. Louis at the time of his visit to St. Peter's, but Marsh left a threatening letter, condemning him for filing his malicious charges. To this Taliaferro replied characteristically:

"I never had in all my life a disposition to injure any man—but the duty I owe my country is paramount with me to every personal consideration. The extremity of mortal daring is nothing to me, being well acquainted with faces both rough and smooth."[5]

Prairie du Chien, when John went there to live, was entirely different from his former home at Fort Snelling. Only in its proximity to Fort Crawford, with the familiar bugle-calls at *reveille* and the plaintive strains of taps, was there the least resemblance. "Fort Snelling was a fortified oasis in a desert of barbarism." Prairie du Chien, on the other hand, was an old settled French community, so ancient that the stories of its foundation were lost in a legendary past.

Marguerite was absolutely at home at the Prairie, the majority of the inhabitants being like herself,—half-breed—of French and Indian extraction. Even the queenly wife of "King Rolette," Astor's partner in the American Fur Company, was closely connected with the Ottawa. However, in spite of this free dilution of the original French blood, the sentiment of the village was French to the core. They still sang their French songs and preserved the gay and debonair air of La Belle France. John might as well have been in France.

JOHN MARSH, PIONEER

At the time of his arrival, in the summer of 1826, Prairie du Chien was still within the bounds of Michigan Territory, and Cass was still the governor. Measured as a village, it was a small, shabby hamlet. Measured by its influence as a fur depot, it was the centre of a tremendous trading district, now comprising four commonwealths,— Minnesota, Wisconsin, Illinois and Iowa. It was the capital of the upper Mississippi. Every fall a flotilla of its voyageurs sadly departed for their winter hunting-grounds. Every spring they blithely returned, singing their *chanson de retour*, with the boats loaded to the gunwales with muskrat, beaver and racoon skins. These were sorted, packed and stored in the warehouse of the American Fur Company. Eventually they reached St. Louis and were re-shipped to London, St. Petersburg and Pekin, where they were destined to upholster the gilded coach of a British earl, to embellish the imperial mantle of a Russian Czar, or to line the damask coat of a Mongolian mandarin. Around the traffic in these furs revolved the economic machinery of the Prairie, the garrison and the Indian Agency.

Marsh was delighted with his new home, and wrote to his father, telling him to think of him as 2,000 miles due west from Danvers, in "one of the most beautiful places and in one of the most delightful countries under heaven. This is a country of vast, grassy plains and long sloping hills without trees. The whole appearance is as different as possible from anything east of the Alleghenies. The country is certainly beautiful, and to a stranger it seems very romantic. Everything is on a grand and ample scale—man seems to be too small and insignificant to occupy it. The hills and valleys of New England afford many snug nooks and corners that a man seems fully com-

PRAIRIE DU CHIEN

petent to occupy. There, if anywhere, he can be happy, and in some one of them I intend to end my days, if the Supreme Being shall give to me length of them."

Probably the history of Prairie du Chien, which Marsh wrote to his father at this time, is about as correct as anything that has been written.

"About two hundred years ago," he wrote, "and not very long after the French had begun to settle in Canada, those enterprising people had penetrated through all the Great Lakes, and established trading forts and Jesuit religious schools at Mackinaw and Green Bay. From their establishments at the latter place, six daring Frenchmen ascended the Fox River to near its source, and then across the Portage and down the Wisconsin to the Great River as it was then called. This was thought an immense undertaking in those days; but both those rivers are now as familiar to me as Goldthwait's Brook or Rocky Run. Near the mouth of the Wisconsin were several large bands of Indians, and the Frenchmen found no difficulty in loading their bark canoe with beaver skins for a few small articles of merchandise. These traders, as may be supposed, returned the next season, and some established themselves in the Indian village on the Prairie just above the mouth of the river, and where this village now stands. These men took them wives of the daughters of the land, and their descendants now are the inhabitants of this place. Many more Canadians soon established themselves here, and as there were no white women they commonly married Indian women. The Indian trade was much more attended to than anything else, and they cultivated only as much land as would just support them. About one fourth part of the inhabitants are pure French, and the others have more or less a mixture of Indian blood. These people are generally remarkably handsome, and in point of capacity and conduct fully equal to the others. Many of the Prairie's principal inhabitants are of this class. These people are but poor farmers, but in general they are not ambitious of wealth—there are however, some exceptions. They have heretofore considered Canada as the best place in the world, next to old France.

"What surprises the people here most is the miners. Five years ago, some Americans discovered a lead mine at Fever River about eighty miles below this place, and now there are four or five thousand men employed in working the mines in that place and the adjacent country. Some thousands of tons of lead have been mined, and many poor men have suddenly become rich. The mining business has been much retarded the past season by the difficulties with the Indians, but they are now advancing with astonishing rapidity. Multitudes of men are now flocking here from every part of America and Europe. One drunken Irishman, a few weeks ago, discovered a mine of lead ore, for which he was offered thirty thousand dollars, but he laughed at the proposal. This man came into the country about two years ago, a common bog trotter without a sixpence.

"I returned two or three days ago from the new town of Cassville about thirty miles below this place. There are at present only about a dozen log huts, but there are thirty or forty men at work, and I doubt not before twelve months there will be a large town. The country abounds in lead ore—every hill is full of it. It is found in masses from the size of a bullet to a barrel, and even larger. It is truly surprising to witness the labour of these people. They penetrated into the earth from twenty to eighty feet, and often through the solid rock. You may easily believe that men, stimulated by such prospects of gain, would not pay much regard to the rights of the Indians who own the most valuable part of the mineral country.

PRAIRIE DU CHIEN

The agents of the Government have not been able to govern the miners, and nothing but a strong force can control them. A treaty will be held with the Indians next spring, to attempt to purchase the land. There is no doubt that the murders committed by the Indians last summer were partly caused by the aggressions of the whites. Eight of the Indians are now in irons at the fort, and will be tried and probably hanged next May. I expect that this and the treaty together will breed a war in which the Winnebagoes will be exterminated. This is now, has been, and I fear ever will be, the fate of the redman when he comes in contact with the white strangers.

"There is a great demand for all sorts of men at the mines. A common labourer gets twenty dollars per month, and can hardly be obtained at any price, since everyone can obtain a grant of a small piece of ground and dig for himself, and there are plenty of merchants and traders of all sorts who will advance tools, provisions, and clothing on credit, to be paid in mineral when it is found. The ore, when raised to the top of the ground, is as current as silver at about sixteen dollars per thousand."[6]

One of the oldest pioneers, Mme. Cardinal, was still living at the Prairie at the time John arrived. Indeed, she lived for some time after his advent, dying in 1827 at an advanced age. Some accounts place her age as high as one hundred and thirty-seven years. She is said to have accompanied her husband, Jean Marie, and an Indian slave, Colas, to the Prairie in a canoe early in the preceding century. By the time Marsh arrived, Jean Marie had died; the widow had married her slave, Colas. When he, in turn, had succumbed, she was ready for further matrimonial ventures. Women were very scarce in this wilderness and in demand at any age, and as she was

JOHN MARSH, PIONEER

seemingly endowed with perennial youth, the change from widow's weeds to bridal raiment went on swiftly and almost without interruption.[7]

Marsh was already a resident of the Prairie the last time this virile woman, well over the century mark, took unto herself a mate half her age. But this marriage was not successful, and after a honeymoon of some two or three days, she was still energetic enough to kick the bridegroom from her bed and board.

Ever since 1669, when the French founded Fort Nicholas,[8] Prairie du Chien could boast a fort, but when Marsh arrived, the fortification was known as Fort Crawford. It did not compare in point of construction, or romance of setting, with the one he had so recently quitted. Fort Snelling, on its river-girt cliff, had all the grandeur of a Rhenish stronghold. Fort Crawford, on the other hand, was built on the flat flood lands of the Mississippi; and although gray, quaint and interesting, it had the squat appearance of the block forts that once dotted our fur-trading frontier. With the exception of the magazine, there was little of stone in its construction. Wooden palisades twenty feet high enclosed its gravelled parade ground. Barracks, quarters, stores, and warehouses for a garrison of five companies were banked against the walls. It was fortified at opposite corners by two square bastions of two stories each, surmounted with artillery, as well as loopholes for muskets, and apertures for field pieces.

Since its construction in 1816, it had known many commanders, perhaps none more picturesque than that convivial tyrant, Lieutenant-Colonel Talbot Chambers, who was cashiered for ordering the ears of one of his soldiers cut off for infraction of duties; and for behaving like a frenzied satyr while chasing a helpless female

108

WABASHAW.
From a painting by J. O. Lewis made at the Treaty of Prairie du Chien, 1825.
Courtesy of the Wisconsin Historical Association.

PRAIRIE DU CHIEN

through the village streets. But mostly they were a very decorous set, these officers with whom Marsh came into contact. He rubbed elbows with many of the most noted military men of his time, notably Colonel Willoughby Morgan, Brevet-Major Stephen Watts Kearney, Lieutenant Jefferson Davis, Colonel Zachary Taylor, Lieutenant Albert Sidney Johnston, and Surgeon William Beaumont.[9]

Just outside the walls of the fort was the Indian Agency, where Marsh and Marguerite lived, with Colonel Boilvin.[10] Marsh greatly respected the bluff old colonel, who juggled his French and English into a humorous polyglot. He was a French-Canadian, jovial, genial and well met,[11] and was very popular with the garrison. His quarters were a favorite rendezvous with the officers. It was much the fashion among them to lounge in his office of a morning, and to spend an idle hour chaffing and joking, and quaffing with him a bumper of brandy and water, which he kept on tap at all hours and designated quaintly as taking a little "*quelque-chose*." Soon after Marsh's arrival Boilvin started for St. Louis to spend the winter, and left the former in charge.

Prairie du Chien had always been considered neutral ground and all the tribes in the neighborhood frequented it.[12] However, it was the Winnebago who congregated there, especially, and who looked on Marsh as their particular father. Probably of all these chiefs Marsh loved and respected the Red Bird most. His band lived on the Black River, not far from Prairie du Chien, and he was a frequent guest at the agency and a favorite one with Marguerite. His advent was the signal to produce the best that her larder provided. Marsh always felt that he could trust him implicitly, even with Marguerite and

JOHN MARSH, PIONEER

his son, should the circumstances require it. To one and all Red Bird represented the perfect type of Indian manhood.

Of the Sioux, L'Arc and Wabashaw were frequent visitors at the agency. The latter's village was one hundred and twenty miles above the Prairie, on the site of the present town of Winona, Minnesota. Wabashaw was an influential and powerful chief and devoted to John and Marguerite, and they were equally devoted to his cause. He was distinguished by a black silk handkerchief that he always wore across half his face to hide the empty socket of an eye, accidentally destroyed while whittling a willow stick.[13]

Then there was the united tribe of Sauk and Fox. They had their own agent at Rock Island, but they made frequent visits to Marsh's agency. John did not like them, —perhaps because of Marguerite. She hated them. In fact all the Sioux disliked them. They were ancestral enemies and never missed an opportunity of expressing their hatred, but they were the most powerful tribe on the Mississippi.[14] Of these chiefs John respected Morgan, the supreme warrior of the Fox, the most. He lived near Du Buque's mine and in plain view of the cross on that old trapper's tomb.[15]

Near the Iowa River was Keokuk, the principal chief of the Sauk. John liked him too, but he disliked Black Sparrow Hawk, commonly called Black Hawk, who lived on Rock River. He was an Indian of great pretension, neither a hereditary nor elected chief, but by acknowledgment of superior prowess, the leader of his village. He hated the whites and he hated the Sioux.[16] Any one who was unfriendly to the latter, John abhorred. The Sioux were his friends and it was notorious on the border that he stuck to them through thick and thin. Their enemies were his enemies.

Thus it will be seen that Prairie du Chien was almost completely surrounded with Indians. In the village, with the exception of Lockwood, Dousman, Brisbois, McNair, Brunet and Marsh, all the others were half-breeds or quarter-breeds. A pitiful handful of whites, in case of an Indian uprising, with but one garrison at hand, and Fort Snelling and St. Louis miles away.[17] But Marsh did not fear, or in fact, even think of it. He had Marguerite, Wabashaw, L'Arc and his friends the Sioux, behind him.

CHAPTER XVI

JUSTICE OF THE PEACE, MICHIGAN TERRITORY
1826

Soon after his arrival Governor Cass further exemplified his admiration for Marsh by appointing him Justice of the Peace of Crawford County, with headquarters at Prairie du Chien. After that, John was hailed as "Judge Marsh." Writing home of this new distinction conferred upon him, John concluded:

"To let you know how fast I am acquiring honors and dignities I must tell you that I have received a commission of a Justice of the Peace and all the honors and emoluments appertaining thereto."[1]

Crawford County was created by Governor Cass by running a line from north to south through the Portage of the Wisconsin to the Illinois line and extending it to the Missouri. All the country west and south of this imaginary line, including now the States of Iowa and Minnesota, as well as part of Wisconsin, was Crawford County. Over this great area, as big as a European principality, the sub-agent was known and quoted as "Judge Marsh." Just what he knew of law and its codes is problematical. Perhaps the closest he had come to it was the study of Say's "Political Economy" during his senior year at Harvard; but he did not need to have much knowledge of the law to compete with his immediate predecessors. He inherited three law-books from Nicolas Boilvin: one

JUSTICE OF THE PEACE

a volume of the statutes of the Northwestern Territory, another of Illinois, and a third of Missouri Territory. They probably constituted the first law library in Wisconsin. But whether he had recourse to them is problematical, for some of his decisions as justice of the peace were as arbitrary as those of his forerunners, Charles Reaume of Green Bay,[2] and Boilvin.

Marsh was in the habit of taking notes for collection, and of issuing processes on them. Some person sent him from Green Bay a note to collect against Benjamin Roy. At this time there were two men in the country, of that name; one resided at the Portage of the Wisconsin, and the other was in the employ of the American Fur Company at Prairie du Chien. Neither of them could write his name. The note was signed with a mark, and witnessed by a man who wrote his name, who since had gone into the Black River country to winter. Marsh, believing that the Roy who was at home was the man, issued process and had him brought before him—but the latter denied any knowledge of the note. Marsh, satisfied that he was the person who had given it, rendered judgment against him and said he would examine the witness when he came down in the spring. Colonel Dousman, hearing of this decision, went to Marsh and told him that if he proceeded any farther in the case, he would report him to Governor Cass. That ended the proceedings.[3]

There were frequent conflicts between Marsh as Indian agent and Marsh as justice of the peace, as these pages will subsequently show.

By 1828 the lumber interests of Wisconsin were coming to the fore and, in spite of laws concerning trespassing on Indian lands, the whites were accustomed to help themselves to valuable timber. Often in the dead of night

JOHN MARSH, PIONEER

they would steal into the Indian country and cut down the trees.

Once, under cover of darkness, Jean Brunet, the tavern-keeper, managed somewhat surreptitiously to reach an island below the mouth of the Wisconsin, where he helped himself to some walnut timber. But before he could haul it away, Street, then Indian agent, and Marsh's superior, heard of what was going on and, with a military escort, followed him for the purpose of arresting him and confiscating the lumber.[4] Before his arrival Brunet made his escape, minus the timber he had cut. Street seized the lumber, and Major Stephen Watts Kearney, then commander at Fort Crawford, had it hauled into the fort and commenced to use it in the construction of the new Fort Crawford. At the time this occurred, Marsh was at Fort Winnebago on another lumber mission. During his absence a writ of replevin was issued and served by the sheriff. Major Kearney resisted and retained the lumber until the pleasure of the government could be ascertained regarding the matter. At the same time he directed the sheriff to let it alone.

When Marsh returned from the Portage, Brunet appeared before him and complained against the commander. Judge Marsh immediately issued a warrant against Major Kearney and the latter was arrested and held to bail in the sum of $400.00 with a surety to appear at the next court to answer for resisting the civil authority. This action caused considerable commotion at Prairie du Chien. Street accused Marsh of being pecuniarily interested in the transaction and it did not endear the judge either to the military or to his superior in office in the agency.[5]

CHAPTER XVII

RED BIRD. THE SIOUX WARNING
1827

WHEN John returned to the Prairie, the two Winnebago, charged with the murder of the Methodes, were still in the guardhouse at Fort Crawford awaiting their trial. Before their imprisonment the tribe were agitated beyond endurance by the squatters on their lead lands. With their confinement, the last blow was struck, and they threatened to sack Fort Crawford.[1]

In the midst of these alarming rumors, the War Department suddenly ordered that Fort Crawford be evacuated, and that the entire Fifth Infantry be concentrated at Fort Snelling. Under the circumstances, this news was horrifying to John, but General Snelling had had personal difficulties with some of the traders, notably Rolette, and had decided to leave them, threats or no threats, to shift for themselves. The order went into effect in October, 1826, and the commandant, his troops, and the two Winnebago murderers, proceeded at once up the Mississippi. The tribe, knowing nothing of Snelling's quarrels with the traders, were impressed quite differently. To them the abandonment of Fort Crawford, in the face of their threats, amounted to a confession of weakness. As soon as they learned that their two warriors had also been transported to Fort Snelling and put in the jail there, they girded themselves for war. In this they were abetted by the British traders.

JOHN MARSH, PIONEER

Soon after the garrison had departed, Marsh wrote to Cass:

"The Fort at this place has been abandoned about a month. The troops have gone to St. Peters and carried the two Winnebago prisoners with them. Several families have removed from this place to the mines, and if the Post is not re-established in the spring, it is probable the settlement will be nearly deserted. The miners at Fever River have been very successful and the prospects are better than ever. It is said by well informed persons that there are now 1500 Sauks at the mines and that the number will be at least doubled next season. Some of the most important discoveries of ore are on the lands of the Winnebagos, and some difficulty has occurred in consequence. The Indians are actively engaged in working their own mines and are jealous of the intruders. I think some interference on the part of the government will be necessary."[2]

Cass realized more than any one else, that government interference was going to be necessary, and he determined to hold a treaty during July of 1827 at Green Bay to settle the difficulty. To this end he had Marsh appointed as a delegate[3] with instructions to accompany the Winnebago and Menominee of his agency there the next summer.[4]

Fort Crawford having been abandoned, Prairie du Chien was left to the mercy of the Winnebago. "All the buildings, and public property, amounting to about one hundred and fifty thousand dollars," were put in Marsh's possession, and, as the latter wrote, it was "rather a heavy responsibility for a man who is worth nothing! However, I hope to make four or five hundred dollars by it, and with this I shall be satisfied. It is supposed a new fort will

RED BIRD. THE SIOUX WARNING

be built in the spring. For my own part, although I have to work rather hard, I am very happy and contented, because I think I have a good prospect before me, and I find others think so too."[5]

Winter was fast approaching, and there was little activity in the agency. The trappers and voyageurs had departed to the hunting grounds, and the Prairie was virtually deserted. Except for Lockwood, McNair and Marsh—the only Americans in the village—a few traders and old decrepit voyageurs, and the women and children, the village was empty. But all about them the Winnebago were gathering, six to seven hundred strong.

Just as the Winnebago were feeling the bitterest about the squatters and the imprisonment of their two warriors, a band of Sioux went to Red Bird's village and told him the two prisoners had been put to death. "They have cut their bodies into pieces no bigger than the spots in a bead garter," said the Sioux. It was a lie, but how could Red Bird and the Winnebago know that? They believed that their tribesmen had been put to death without the trial that had been promised them. A cry for vengeance arose. Revenge was a sacred duty among the Winnebago —more sacred than among other tribes. They demanded, not "an eye for an eye, or a tooth for a tooth," but two lives for one. "Two for one," was now the cry that went up from many throats.

It was a notorious fact on the border that none of their blood was shed unavenged. The leading Winnebago chiefs decided to enforce the law of retaliation, and Red Wing was called upon to go out, and as they phrased it, "take meat!"

Not wishing to appear a coward, he undertook the enterprise, secretly rejoicing that the business had been entrusted to him, for he had resolved, whatever the consequences, to make a circuit of the white settlements and return, saying he could find no "meat." This he did, and after several days reappeared without any white scalps. This failure was too much. His fellow braves upbraided and taunted him unmercifully, called him a "coward," and pointing out that if he had the spirit to avenge the wrongs of his people, he could, by going to Prairie du Chien, get as much "meat" as he could bring home. Their jibes and jeers outweighed his friendship for the whites and he resolved, at any cost, to redeem his character as a warrior and a chief.

Late in May, the Sioux told Marguerite that Red Bird was planning to attack Prairie du Chien, scalp her husband, burn the fort and steal the cattle. Marguerite would not believe it. Red Bird was their friend. Then the old Sioux chief, "Elazeph"-L'Arc, or The Bow, who was very fond of Marsh, sent him an express notifying him that the fort was to be attacked at "the full of the present moon," or a little before; that Lockwood,[6] McNair and himself were to be killed; that the fort and houses were to be sacked and burned, the cattle stolen; that he sent the warning to give him a chance to escape. He further told him that previous to the attack on the Prairie, St. Peter's was to be visited, and Taliaferro killed. Then, and only then, would the Winnebago be avenged.

When he heard the threatened fate for his old archenemy, Taliaferro, perhaps Marsh was tempted to let matters take their course. That would have been a most natural impulse, considering the enmity Taliaferro had shown him. But in spite of Taliaferro's bad treatment, Marsh was too magnanimous to allow such a fate to overtake him. As soon as he received the threatening news, he

RED BIRD. THE SIOUX WARNING

sent an express to the major, with a message bearing these words: "I send an express to convey you news which both my duty and inclination forbid me to neglect. . . . Previous to the attack on this place, a party of Sioux from the lower band and about thirty Winnebagoes are going to St. Peters to kill *you* and any American that they can find at a distance from the Fort. The above news is corroborated by so many circumstances that I think they deserve more credit than common Indian stories. It is said and believed by the Sioux and Winnebagoes that the two Winnebago prisoners have been given up to the Chippewas and killed by them—this, though I cannot believe it, has all the effect of truth with the Indians."[7]

Marsh was convinced from all these circumstances that an attack was imminent. He warned Colonel Snelling to take steps for the defense of Prairie du Chien.[8] Marsh was right. There were not only rumors of war, but war itself was at hand.

The Winnebagoes, suspecting that their intentions were discovered, began hostilities ten days earlier than they had planned. On June 26 some twenty of them stopped at the agency and asked for Marsh. Had the moment come? John was on guard, but saw nothing to excite his alarm. The Winnebagoes asked him what news he had received from the upper Sioux. They behaved in a very dignified manner and departed, declaring they had no intention to do mischief.[9]

On the 27th, Red Bird, We-Kau and two other Winnebagoes called at the agency to confer with Marsh.[10] They acted in the same friendly manner. They begged to be regarded as the staunchest friends of the Americans and asked for liquor. Marsh admittted their claims, but absolutely refused, on account of it, to give them any whiskey. Red Bird left.

JOHN MARSH, PIONEER

Even if the Winnebagoes had, as he suspected, come to the conclusion that the honor of their race demanded the blood of four Americans, Red Bird's visit at the agency did not excite any alarm in Marsh's breast. He knew Red Bird and We-Kau to be men of great influence in their nation. They were leaders. Both were remarkable for their good characters. In Red Bird, especially, he had great confidence. He was a noble red man—the last to be suspected of a violent deed.[11] He trusted him, liked him.

However, Marsh never came closer to losing his scalp than he did on that 27th day of June, 1827, for Red Bird was at last looking for "meat." He was the martyr of a cause. If he could not get Marsh's scalp, he must find others. He must be redeemed! His tribesmen avenged!

From the agency, Red Bird went to a trader and obtained an eight-gallon keg of whiskey. Then he visited Judge Lockwood's house. The judge was absent, but Mrs. Lockwood was at home. His menacing attitude sent her scurrying from the room. The chance presence of an old trader aborted the Indian's plans and saved her from death.

Not to be thwarted, Red Bird and his accomplices crossed the prairie to McNair's Coulee. Some three miles from the lower extremity of the town, they reached the farm of Registre Gagnier. Gagnier was living there with his wife, a half-breed of French and Sioux extraction, and their two children—one a lad of three years, and the other an infant of eleven months—and a hired man, Solomon Lipcap, an old American soldier.[12] The Gagniers were delighted to see Red Bird, for he was a great favorite with them. Then, while Mme. Gagnier busied herself preparing food for him, the chief deliberately lifted his gun to his shoulder, aimed and shot her husband through the breast.

RED BIRD. THE SIOUX WARNING

At the same time We-Kau dispatched the old soldier, Lipcap.

Then We-Kau turned his gun upon Mme. Gagnier. She would have shared the same fate as her husband, had she not run toward the murderer, grappled with him and wrested the gun from his grasp. Lifting it to her shoulder, she pointed the barrel at his breast, but found she could not pull the trigger. Like one in a dream, her finger refused to obey the command of her brain. She dropped the gun, caught up her three-year old, threw him on her back and ran for the village.

CHAPTER XVIII

MARSH COMMANDS FORT CRAWFORD. RED BIRD
APPEALS TO MARSH. SURRENDER

1827

IT was about noon. Marsh was at the agency. A woman with a child on her back rushed panic-stricken through the village street. She was giving an alarm. Murder had been committed! Red Bird! Marsh heard what had happened. It had come then? The uprising! L'Arc was right! He rushed out. There was the wildest confusion. Fear. Panic.

Marsh was the only man in Prairie du Chien with authority. He took charge, raised a posse and hastened to the coulee. Registre Gagnier was dead, a bullet hole in his chest, his head nearly cut off and scalped. Under the bed lay the baby. She, too, was scalped, her neck gashed to the bone, but she was still breathing.[1] Outside in a field near the house lay Solomon Lipcap—face down in the grass, butchered and scalped in a fiendish manner.[2]

Marsh could not find the murderers. They had escaped to the mouth of the Bad Axe River, where Black Sparrow Hawk joined them and helped them attack two keel-boats, killing two and wounding four of the boats' crews.[3] The Winnebagoes were avenged! Five for two!

Meanwhile the inhabitants of Prairie du Chien were in a frenzy. Their consternation knew no bounds. An uprising—they all knew the horror of Indian warfare! A general alarm was sounded. The outlying farms were abandoned. Their inmates crowded fear-stricken into the

MARSH COMMANDS FORT CRAWFORD

dismantled fort. The Indians threatened to burn it. Marsh took command.

With the exception of Thomas McNair and Judge Lockwood, who was then on the *Wisconsin* en route to New York, Marsh was the only American in the village. By virtue of his position as Indian agent, and owing to the fact that the fort had been left in his charge, he became a figure of authority in this emergency, and the defense of Prairie du Chien devolved upon him. Some idea of the horror of the situation and his mental condition at the time may be reflected in the urgent message, "For God's sake return," which he dispatched by a Menominee express in pursuit of Lockwood.[4]

At the same time he sent warnings to the various garrisons up and down the Mississippi, telling them what had happened, and that he feared a general uprising and needed reinforcements. Two men on horseback he sent express through the back country of Iowa to Fort Snelling. Others he dispatched to General Clark at St. Louis and to Governor Cass, who was then en route to Green Bay to attend the council scheduled for July first at Butte des Morts.

Then Marsh rallied the cowed inhabitants. Under his leadership, they showed considerable spirit and made preparations to defend themselves. Although there were no troops at Fort Crawford, and the fort itself was dismantled except for a few damaged arms and an old brass swivel which had been left in his charge, he quickly set the people to work repairing the walls and blockhouses, and raising an earthwork two or three feet high around the bottom logs, which were rotten and dry and would easily ignite.

Marsh had the old brass swivel and wall pieces re-

JOHN MARSH, PIONEER

mounted in the blockhouses and stationed a crew of picked men who were trained to operate them. To guard against fire, barrels filled with water were placed against the walls. All the blacksmiths in the village were put to work repairing muskets.[5]

As soon as Lockwood returned, he obtained an abundant supply of powder and lead. Marsh manned the fort with women as well as men; in all, some ninety people. Any one capable of handling a musket, in case of attack, was pressed into service. Even Marguerite, with her boy to protect, shouldered a gun.

Marsh also enlisted the help of a hundred Menominee. They were useful as messengers and as express riders, for they could pass where white men dared not.[6] So great were his exertions and anxiety that for forty-eight hours he went without sleep or rest.[7] On July 1 a feeling that he should separate the friendly from the hostile Winnebagoes seized him. He rounded up all who were available, loaded them into canoes and attempted to reach the council at Green Bay by way of the Wisconsin. On the fourth day after his departure, he met Governor Cass coming down the river. The latter had been at Butte des Morts when he received Marsh's urgent message. The governor now persuaded Marsh to turn about, return with him and help him to perfect measures for the defense of the Prairie. He feared a general uprising in which Sioux, Fox and Sauk would join the Winnebagoes against the whites.[8]

On the morning of July 4, they reached the Prairie and found the inhabitants still beleaguered in Fort Crawford. The people were terrified beyond measure, momentarily expecting another attack, with a general slaughter and the burning of the fort. To add to their fears, famine was staring them in the face. Owing to the fort's

MARSH COMMANDS FORT CRAWFORD

dismantled condition, there were few supplies, and those were about exhausted.[9] After a general inspection of conditions, Governor Cass pacified the terrified inhabitants, commended Marsh for his prompt and energetic measures in defense of the people, and then prepared to move on.

The governor knew enough of the Indian country to realize that conditions were critical and that he must be swift and sure in his measures if he wished to save the situation and quell a general uprising. Having accomplished all that was possible in the brief time allotted to Fort Crawford, he ordered Marsh to accompany him to Fever River and Galena and aid in recruiting volunteers and in obtaining ammunition for the defense of the Prairie. On the way they stopped at a neighboring Fox village, where Cass made a speech, requesting the Indians to keep out of the hostilities and encouraging as many of them as were prepared to return that evening with Marsh and assist him in the defense.

They found the lead regions in an uproar. The miners were thoroughly frightened. The roads were filled with them, and the little village of Galena was overwhelmed with disorder and filled with panic-stricken settlers fleeing from the outlying districts.

While the governor exhorted the horror-stricken miners to defensive measures, John was rounding up powder and lead and loading it into canoes. On departing, the governor gave him $600 to use for emergencies.[10] That night, with his ammunition and several boatloads of volunteers, John started up the Mississippi. The darkness, the silence, the wildness of the scenery, the intense excitement and anxiety lest his efforts should be too late, made the deepest impression upon his memory.

JOHN MARSH, PIONEER

In a brief period he reached the Prairie. In the meantime, Colonel Snelling, in response to his express, was hastening down the river in two keel-boats.[11] In an incredibly short time, troops from all over the Mississippi frontier converged at Prairie du Chien. The swift gathering of this overwhelming military force, all under the command of Brigadier General Atkinson, struck terror to the breast of the red men.

As soon as possible after he reached the Prairie, John collected as many Winnebagoes as he could and made an appeal to them, promising that if they would cease their hostilities, the United States government would redress instantly and fully any injury they had received at the hands of the Americans. Then he invited the whole nation to the council scheduled at Butte des Morts and promised to lead them there himself and to provide them with provisions and presents if they would go at once. In this way he hoped to separate the hostile from the friendly bands. At the same time, he visited the neighboring Sioux and asked their assistance.[12]

Late in July, with the Indians he had won to his cause, he left for Butte des Morts. The Winnebagoes learned of his departure and vowed that he would never reach there alive. Nevertheless, he set out in a canoe with seventeen good rifles[13] and forced his way to the Portage. There he was stopped by an overwhelming force of Winnebagoes, and in spite of his escort, was forced to flee for his life, barely escaping their vengeance.[14] Later, he made a third attempt to reach the council grounds, and this time succeeded.[15]

During these attempts, he learned that Red Bird and his tribesmen were concentrating near the Portage,[16] and that the chief, realizing his desperate condition, had sent

MARSH COMMANDS FORT CRAWFORD

an express to his tribesmen on the Rock River, in which he said, "Now we have begun the war, we must carry it on—if we stop, the Americans will hang us, and it is better to die bravely with our arms in our hands." From a knowledge of his character, Marsh felt that he would persevere, and that as soon as his force was sufficiently strong, he would attempt to accomplish his original purpose— the entire destruction of Prairie du Chien and Fort Crawford.[17]

Marsh's reaction to the danger and anxiety about him may be deduced from a letter he wrote his father about this time—"An Indian war has just commenced in this country, and I write to tell you I am safe and likely to be so. You may perhaps be alarmed for the accounts in the newspapers. Only four or five of the people in this place have been killed and about twice that number of Indians. As soon as I have a little leisure, I will write you all the particulars of the horrid murders that have been committed. Mr. Boilvin is dead, and I have the whole direction of affairs. I have a fine chance for exertion, and that is all I want. This war tho' terrible to some, brings good luck to me."[18]

The council at Butte des Morts opened on August 6. One thousand Indians, mainly Chippewa, Menominee and Winnebago, were present. Many of them Marsh had been instrumental in bringing together.[19] Cass opened the council with an address in which he warned the Winnebagoes to surrender the perpetrators of the outrage at Prairie du Chien and thus save their people from the consequences of war. He threatened that if they did not surrender the murderers, he would cut a path through their territory, not with axes, but with guns. Cass feared that if he procrastinated the Winnebagoes would attack the lead miners

JOHN MARSH, PIONEER

in the Galena district, and he urged Atkinson and the troops to concentrate at the Portage. As soon as the treaty was signed, Major William Whistler, accompanied by Marsh, McKenney, 101 regulars and 23 militia, and a band of friendly Menominees, started through the Indian country to make a show of force. On September 1 they reached the Portage and were met by an express with orders from General Atkinson to halt, fortify their position and await his arrival. He announced his approach with the regulars and with Henry Dodge with the Galena Rangers. Accordingly, they pitched their tents on a high bluff which commanded a wide sweep of the country.

The Winnebagoes had now reached a desperate pass. They were dumfounded at the rapid movement of troops which hemmed them in on all sides, and they faced the dire alternative of Whistler's guns or the surrender of Red Bird and We-Kau. The latter they were loath to do. According to their viewpoint, their chief had not perpetrated a wanton crime. Instead, he had performed a meritorious act in retaliation for the wrongs the whites had visited upon his people. Although the Gagniers, Lipcap and the murdered voyageurs were innocent of the outrages of which the Winnebagoes complained, yet Red Bird, in scalp-taking, abided by the stern ethics of his people and acted impersonally as the avenger of his tribe. He had to have two lives for one. In the eyes of Prairie du Chien he was a murderer. In the eyes of his people he was a popular hero—a martyr of a forlorn hope.[20] Yet, with the white man's armies close at hand, the band must surrender their hero to save their tribesmen from further punishment.[21] And they looked upon it as nothing less than a tribal sacrifice.

MARSH COMMANDS FORT CRAWFORD

On the second afternoon following their arrival, a Winnebago emissary suddenly appeared before the tent of McKenney. When the object of this visit was questioned, the Indian replied: "Do not strike. When the sun is there to-morrow,"—he looked up and pointed to the spot where it would be at about 3 P. M.—"they will come in."

"Who will come in?" was asked.

"Red Bird and We-Kau will come in," was the answer. Then, wrapping his blanket about him, the emissary disappeared as quickly and as silently as he had come. This performance was repeated three times that same day, in precisely the same way.

Probably that information was a relief to Marsh, for the next day, September 2, 1827—the day of the promised surrender—he wrote to his father:

"I arrived at this place yesterday for the third time this summer in company with a large body of troops and some hundreds of Indian warriors for the purpose of compelling the Winnebago to give up the murderers who were implicated in the late horrid affair at P. du Chien. They have promised to surrender five of the murderers, and two are expected today.

"There is a prospect that that business will soon be finished without fighting, but nothing certain is known. Whatever may be the result, be assured that I am not in any danger. I shall probably return to the Prairie in a few days, from which place I shall probably write to you again as soon as there are news."[22]

It could not have been long after he had finished writing that letter that there was seen descending a mound of the Portage in the direction of Whistler's camp, a body of Indians. If Marsh had had a glass, he could have seen that they bore no arms. Some were mounted, others were on foot. In advance walked three Indians, two of whom, the one in front and the one behind, bore American flags. The man in the middle was Red Bird, and he held aloft a white flag. Had Marsh listened, he might have heard the chief singing his death song.

Closer and closer they advanced. Nearer and nearer sounded the chant of death. Barges were sent across the river to receive them, and an escort was dispatched to accompany them within the lines. In the meantime the soldiers were drawn up on dress parade. The stage seemed set for some great ceremony, and immediately there swept across it the opening scenes of the most dramatic incident enacted on the Mississippi frontier. An Indian delegation approached with slow and solemn steps. Martial honors were accorded them. To the left were the friendly Menominees, squatted upon their haunches. On the right was a military band playing softly Pleyel's hymn. Major Whistler, Marsh and McKenney stood near the troops. In front of the centre, at a distance of a few paces, walked the murderers, Red Bird and We-Kau. On their right and left, forming a semicircular group, were the Winnebagoes who had accompanied them. All eyes were fixed on the magnificent figure of Red Bird—six feet in height, erect and perfectly proportioned. His every movement seemed to be imbued with grace and stateliness. He was dressed in barbaric splendor, in a suit of white deerskin appropriately fringed and decorated. Around his neck hung a collar of blue and white wampum, and over his breast and back lay a fold of scarlet cloth. Both shoulders were decorated with the preserved feathers of a redbird. It is not to be wondered at that he seemed to the spectators, even of a hostile tribe, "a prince born to command and worthy to be obeyed."[23]

RED BIRD IN FULL REGALIA.
From McKenney and Hall's "History of the Indian Tribes of North America," Philadelphia, 1849.

MARSH COMMANDS FORT CRAWFORD

The effect of his magnificence was heightened by contrast with his miserable accomplice, We-Kau. "Meagre, cold and dirty in his person and dress—crooked in form, like a starved wolf, gaunt and hungry and bloodthirsty" —his entire appearance accorded with that of a fiend who could scalp a babe in the cradle.

Some paces in front of the place where Major Whistler, McKenney and Marsh were standing, Red Bird came to a halt. Not a muscle moved, nor did the expression on his face alter. He was the embodiment of dignity, decision, stoicism and purity.

He appeared aware that, according to his code, he had committed no wrong. His conscience, according to Indian law, was clear. As to death, his lofty demeanor proved he despised it.

The music having ceased, all seated themselves except Caramaunee, a distinguished Winnebago chief, who now advanced toward McKenney and Marsh and, addressing the former, said: "They are here, like braves they have come in—treat them as braves—do not put them in irons."

McKenney replied that he was not the big captain, and that he must appeal to Major Whistler. Caramaunee hesitated. There was an aversion to being given up to the military. He advanced to Marsh and pleaded that Red Bird might be turned over to him, thus showing the confidence of the chiefs of the Winnebagoes in their sub-agent. Seeing their fondness and faith in him, McKenney intervened, saying that Marsh should go with them. This comforted and composed them.[24]

At the conclusion of the ceremony, Red Bird stood up, facing Major Whistler. Two more perfect specimens of manhood never faced one another than this noble red man of the forest and this splendid type of the military frontiersman. There was a momentary pause, during which the chief's eyes swept the troops with a cursory survey and observed his own people composedly. Then they came to rest on Major Whistler and Red Bird spoke, "I am ready." Advancing a step or two, he again paused and continued: "I do not wish to be put in irons. Let me be free. I have given away my life—it is gone—" stooping and taking some dust between his finger and thumb, he blew it away, "like that." Eyeing the dust as it fell and vanished from sight, he concluded: "I would not take it back—it is gone." Having thus spoken, he threw his arms behind him, to indicate that he was leaving all things behind him, and marched briskly up to Major Whistler until they stood breast to breast. A platoon was wheeled backwards from the centre of the line. Major Whistler stepped aside. Red Bird, the magnificent, and We-Kau, the miserable, marched down the line and were handed over to Marsh, as they had desired.

Thus ended the Winnebago War. The Indians were cowed, not conquered. The squatters, like thorns, still festered in their flesh. Nothing was settled, nothing could be settled, least of all their boundary lines, which gave like a rubber-band against the ever-increasing pressure of the whites. The original cause of their dissatisfaction remained; in fact, it had come to stay, and the aggressions of the lead miners continued. They were fighting a losing fight, and, confronted with the spectre of white domination, they continued fighting, falling and retreating. To harness and harass them further, Fort Winnebago emerged from the bogs of the Portage. Red Bird could read "the writing on the wall" and, before he could be tried, he sickened and died of a broken heart.[25]

CHAPTER XIX

GAGNIER'S SCALP

1827–1828

FOLLOWING the surrender, Marsh had a brief respite at the agency with Marguerite and his little son. Charley was now crawling about the floor. Sometimes he rolled down the stoop, but Marguerite let him roll. She wanted him to learn for himself. Sometimes he burned his fingers in the hot coals of the open fire, but Marguerite trained him never to cry. Now John was content. He seldom thought of his medical ambition. The exciting conditions in the agency absorbed him. Life slipped quickly by.

Whenever there came a lull in the activities, he and Marguerite worked on the Sioux dictionary. Once John wrote to Cass and promised to give him an account of his work in the spring.[1]

Finally the dictionary was completed. Then, with Marguerite's assistance, he wrote a grammar, entitling it "Rudiments of the Grammar of the Sioux Language." When Caleb Atwater came to the Prairie, John presented it to him, and he included it in his "Remarks made On a Tour to Prairie du Chien, etc." It covers twenty-three pages of that work, and Atwater gives full credit of its authorship to Marsh.[2]

In the fall of 1827, John had to go to St. Louis to give General Clark a quarterly report of Indian affairs. By September 30 he was there.

"Since all the difficulties with the Indians are settled," he wrote his father, "I came down to the city to adjust the

JOHN MARSH, PIONEER

account of the agency with General Clark, the Superintendent. I have been here about ten days and expect to return to the Prairie tomorrow in the steam packet.

"This place, although it is commonly called sickly, is at present quite healthy. My own health is excellent, and has been so the whole season. I have reason to be abundantly thankful for this, when I remember how much I suffered last year. There is a strong military force at the Prairie, and a new Fort is to be built there next year. When you think of the Prairie, remember, it is due west two thousand miles, one of the most beautiful places, and in one of the most delightful countries under heaven— this place [St. Louis] is due west from Washington, yet I came down here in four days, and expect to go back in eight. Since the trouble with the Winnebagoes began, I have had no rest, and have been constantly traveling through the Indian country in every direction. I begin to grow tired of this, and long for rest. I have nothing in particular to tell you, but that I enjoy health and happiness. What more does anyone want? I answer: A single man wants a wife. A single woman wants a husband. I, for my part, expect to want something to the end of my life, and never expect to be more contented than I am at present."[3]

But even at this time, there was something Marsh wanted, and wanted very keenly. He was content as Indian sub-agent, but would have been more so as agent. Boilvin was dead and his desire was to succeed him, and Cass was equally anxious to have him receive the appointment. The latter was at St. Louis when he learned of the colonel's accidental death, and immediately wrote James Barbour, then Secretary of War: "As Mr. Marsh, the sub-agent of Indian affairs at Prairie du Chien, is fully competent to discharge the duties of agent, there is perhaps

GAGNIER'S SCALP

no necessity that the vacancy caused by the death of Mr. Boilvin should be immediately filled. If there is none, permit me to suggest the expediency of delaying the appointment until the return of Colonel McKenney. He is acquainted with facts which he would report to you, and which would perhaps have some influence upon the selection to be made."[4] This recommendation shows the confidence his superiors placed in his attainments and capabilities, but even the patronage of the governor of Michigan Territory was unavailing. He was doomed to disappointment. That very summer, in spite of Marsh's heroic efforts during the Winnebago upheaval, in spite of his knowledge of Indian languages and the tribes about Prairie du Chien, a Kentucky editor, Joseph Montfort Street, totally ignorant of the red man and his affairs, received the appointment. He arrived at the Prairie November 1, 1827,[5] and Marsh was continued as sub-agent, on the same salary of $500 per annum, for the next two years.

Street arrived at the Prairie soon after Marsh's return from St. Louis, and in order to accommodate him at the agency, it was necessary to partition off the council room.

When he failed to receive the appointment Marsh did not seem to be particularly disturbed, anticipating that he would have more time to devote to his Sioux studies, and to Marguerite and his boy.

Soon after his return he wrote to his father:

"My last letter to you was written from St. Louis, but I have been traveling so much, and so rapidly for the last five or six months that I can hardly recollect where any particular occurrence took place.

"After transacting a great deal of business at St. Louis, I returned home to this place, and shall now endeavor to rest for the season. The Indian wars are all over for the present at least. They have been of no disadvantage to me, although I have been obliged to make great exertions, but this is exactly what I want—an opportunity for action.

"My health is excellent, and has not suffered from fatigue or exposure, or from a climate hot or cold. A treaty is to be held here next summer, in which I expect an appointment, and hope to be sent to Washington next Fall. If so, I shall not neglect to come to Massachusetts when I am so near. There is no news in this part of the country that would be interesting to you, except that I am enjoying health and happiness, and plenty of future anticipations, which, if they are never realized, are at least pleasant to contemplate."[6]

But Marsh knew no rest that summer. His superior officer was a pompous, garrulous individual who let his subordinate do all the work while he took the credit and did the resting.[7] In the beginning, Street was greatly impressed with Marsh, and commended him on the faithful records he had kept since Boilvin's death, the only ones he could find in the agency, and for his activities and useful service in behalf of the Indians. "I am highly gratified," he wrote, "to find him a man of collegiate education and possessed of an active, discriminating mind."[8]

Marsh endeavored to please the general, and offered, soon after his arrival, to take him on a winter trip to Fort Snelling, holding out as an inducement some four or five nights of "pleasant lodgings" in the wilderness. But Street refused to be coaxed from the warmth of the agency.[9]

As for the Indians, there was no rest or tranquillity in their country. The peace following the Red Bird distur-

GAGNIER'S SCALP

bance was transitory. While the war was at its height, the Winnebago lead lands about Fever River and Galena were deserted. With its cessation, a veritable stampede to those districts followed, and they were overrun with adventurers and speculators from Missouri, Kentucky, Tennessee, and Southern Illinois,—a lawless, independent element, who neither feared nor respected the laws of God or man. The excitement and furore were intense. Lead fever in the Northwest in 1828-29 was analogous to the gold malady which raged in California in 1849. Scenes and conditions in both localities were similar. Shanties and stockades for protection sprang up like mushrooms over night, and unruly prospectors picked holes all over Wisconsin and Illinois and pushed the Winnebago, Sauk and Foxes rudely aside. They operated their shafts and smelters in such a way that the red men could no longer work them with their crude tools. Cheated, maltreated and abused, the Indians were driven out of their country, and only waited an opportunity to repeat the scenes of the summer. This attitude did not at all surprise Marsh. In fact, he had been anticipating it. The war had not borne in its wake the tranquillity for which he hoped. "The effect," he wrote, "supposed to have been produced by the movement of General Atkinson, although doubtless considerable, I think has been overrated. I am far from believing the nation [Winnebago] has been humbled, and should not be surprised if more white men were killed before next spring. God grant that the horrid scenes of last summer may not be repeated!"[10]

He knew that they were on the verge of repetition when he learned that Registre Gagnier's scalp was hanging on a pole over the graves of the Winnebago who had been killed during that summer at Prairie La Crosse, in the

JOHN MARSH, PIONEER

fight with the keel-boats. He recognized in this act that they were nursing ill feeling, and were not hesitating to express it boldly. Early in December, 1827, Street, too, learned of this and was informed that it was a hostile demonstration. Although he knew its recovery was a dangerous mission, he determined to regain it, not by himself, but by sending his sub-agent. At the time snow was on the ground and the Mississippi and Wisconsin were full of floating ice. The weather was cold, but not yet cold enough to close the channel. As soon as the river was frozen over, he ordered Marsh to go secretly to Prairie La Crosse, recover Gagnier's scalp, and bring it back to Prairie du Chien.

One night, without a guide, Marsh ascended the river and located the hostile village. Waiting until all activities about the wigwams had ceased, he made his way through the drifts to their cemetery, which crowned a little hill. The dead warriors were lying on rude scaffolds, the snow banked high against them. On one of the uprights he could see Gagnier's scalp, the long hair flapping in the wind. Marsh afterwards claimed he would never forget his feelings that night as he climbed the rickety scaffold for the trophy. The fear of making a noise and being detected, the eery hour,—starry though it was, the snow, the feel of the wet robes wrapped about the dead warriors, and the sensation that went through him as he pocketed the scalp, left an indelible impression.

CHAPTER XX

MARSH, HENRY DODGE, AND THE TREATY OF GREEN BAY

1828

THE rescue of Registre Gagnier's scalp had hardly been accomplished before Christmas arrived; but Marsh had little opportunity to enjoy the holiday with Marguerite and his little boy, who was approaching his second birthday.

The New Year had scarcely dawned before mutterings of discontent in the Winnebago country reached such a pitch that Street became greatly alarmed, especially when he learned that General Dodge and about fifty men armed with rifles and prepared for any emergency had squatted on the Winnebago lead lands and were working their mines. "Many are flocking to him from Fever River," wrote Street, "and he permits them to join upon paying certain stipulated portions of the original purchase. The ore is more abundant, nearer the surface, and obtained with greater facility than ever known in this country. It is said that he has raised about half a million of mineral, smelted from 900 to 1,000 bars, and is smelting 50 bars a day. With two negro men in one place he raised about 2,000 pounds per day. What will be the effect of these high-handed measures I am at a loss to say."[1] Street was not at a loss for many days. On January 26, 1828, a Winnebago chief, Corumna the Lame, came to the agency and complained that a large camp of whites had gone far into his country and were taking lead. "We did not expect this," he complained, "and we want to know when this will stop. The hills are covered, more are coming and shoving us off our lands to make the lead. We want our Father to stop this before blood may be shed. . . ."

Street was so alarmed over these covert threats that he ordered Marsh to go to Dodge Diggings on the Wisconsin and to notify the general to move off instantly if he did not wish to be removed by force.[2]

It was the dead of winter, while Street remained snug and warm in the agency, "writing freely, perhaps not wisely,"[3] that Marsh set out on snow-shoes over the frozen prairies and rivers and through a trackless forest to the present village of Dodgeville (Iowa County, Wisconsin), but then the hunting ground of the Winnebago. In summer it was a land of babbling brooks and crystal springs, of beautiful oak openings and rolling prairies. In January it was no-man's land, a frozen waste beset by harsh weather[4] and hostile red men, and it took more than an ordinary amount of courage and stamina to enter so frostbitten a region.

In obedience to Street's instructions, Marsh ascended the Wisconsin to English Prairie,[5] some sixty-five miles from Prairie du Chien. There he left the river and travelled due south fifteen miles, until he came to several high ridges running parallel with the Wisconsin. He then climbed until he reached an undulating divide, devoid of trees, from which the waters on the west side fell into the Mississippi, while those on the east emptied into the "Pikitolika" (Pecatonica), a tributary of Rock River. Travelling along this broad ridge in a southeasterly direction, he eventually located Dodge's establishment three miles from the Pecatonica, some thirty miles from the Wisconsin, and about ninety-five from the agency.[6]

DODGE AND THE TREATY OF GREEN BAY

On the evening of the fifth day following his departure, he entered the stockade and searched out the general:

"Your letter to General Dodge I delivered immediately," he wrote to Street, "and I informed him and others who were located in that vicinity that I had a communication to read to them from the Indian agent at Prairie du Chien. The next morning I read your notice—to all the principal miners. Not being able to discover any indications of an intention to remove out of the Indian country, your address was also read and the extracts from the treaty therein referred to.

"General Dodge addressed the people and explained to them his views of the subject. He insisted principally that there was no definite line of demarcation between the lands of the Winnebago Indians and those of the Chippewas, Pottawottamies and Ottaways of the Illinois, on which the citizens of the United States had a right to dig for lead ore, and that until such line should be definitely marked and established it was by no means certain that the place where they were was on the lands of the Winnebago.

"The remainder of the day was spent in examining the country. Ore is found in great abundance near the surface, and in large masses. Few of the excavations are more than ten feet deep. The whole country appears to be literally full of lead ore, and the labor of obtaining it is trifling. Traces of old Indian diggings are found throughout the country for several miles. There are also furnaces where the Indians smelted the ore.

"General Dodge resides in a small stockade fort near the principal mine. There are about twenty log houses in the immediate vicinity, besides several more remote. He has a double furnace in constant operation, and a large quantity of lead in bars and in the crude state. From the best information I have been able to obtain, there are about two hundred and thirty men engaged in mining at this place, and completely armed with rifles and pistols. I was also informed that there are about fifteen Winnebago ten or twelve miles distant who frequently visit the mines, and who have been presented by General Dodge with several hundred dollars worth of provisions and merchandise. When about to return I was desired by General Dodge to inform you that he should leave the country as soon as he conveniently could."[7]

Whatever his intentions were, with Marsh's departure the general threw up a stockade fort, provided himself and his neighbors with several hundred guns and announced that if the officers and soldiers of the regular army had more guns than he had they could come and try them.[8] And he meant what he said, as Marsh could testify. His cabin bristled with guns and ammunition, and what was more, he had a man for every gun.

Immediately upon receipt of this communication, Street called upon the commanding officer at Fort Crawford for a detachment of 180 troops to remove the trespassers by force. Major Fowle replied that he had only 147 men in his command, and but 130 of them were fit for duty, and it would be out of his power to comply with his request. Street was forced to bow to the inevitable and, in a very short time, under the terms of the treaty of August 25, 1828, the Indians were expelled from their hunting grounds and their titles extinguished. Thus Dodge held his ground unmolested and waxed wealthy on the land of the Bear,[9] shipping his lead from Helena on the Wisconsin direct to New Orleans, in privately owned steamers so constructed that the cargoes did not have to be transferred at St. Louis. After the treaty was ratified, he be-

DODGE AND THE TREATY OF GREEN BAY

came proprietor of more than a thousand acres and upon this Winnebago principality, for more than four decades, made his home, fame and fortune. From there he sallied forth on three successive occasions to become governor of the Territory of Wisconsin as well as territorial delegate to Congress and, finally, as United States Senator, thus becoming an upholder of the law he had once defied.

Of such mettle was the frontiersman whom Marsh commanded to leave the Winnebago lands that winter day of January, 1828.

The threatening attitude of the Winnebago lasted all winter and continued until the council convened at Green Bay during that summer. Street was very anxious to be appointed commissioner, but Governor Lewis Cass and Colonel Pierre Ménard received the appointments, much to his chagrin.

It must have made him still more mortified when Cass requested that Marsh should be present and that he should accompany the principal chiefs of the Winnebago nation to the council grounds.

On July 29, 1828, Marsh dropped his venerable father a line:

"I shall set out tomorrow for Green Bay to meet Governor Cass with all the principal chiefs of the Winnebago nation. The aggression of the whites on the Indian lands has been the cause of much trouble and some bloodshed and it is to endeavor to settle their difficulties that I am about to undertake this journey. The country immediately below this is one of the richest mining districts in the world. It belongs to the Indians but there are now about 10,000 white men intruders upon it. The mineral riches of the country have caused people to flock into it

JOHN MARSH, PIONEER

with a rapidity altogether unparalleled. There is, at present, some probability that after I arrive at Green Bay, I shall be ordered to proceed on to Washington as the Indian chiefs have declared that they will not go unless I accompany them. If I should go to the east, I shall endeavor if possible to visit you."[10]

An agreement was reached by August 25, 1828, and Marsh signed his name to the treaty as a witness, where it may be read along with the names and subjoined marks and seals of the Winnebago chiefs whom he led to Green Bay, as well as with many a man distinguished on the Mississippi frontier, including John H. Kinzie, C. Chouteau, Henry Gratiot, Pierre Paquette and R. A. Forsyth.[11] By it he saw transferred to the whites some 8,000,000 acres of the choicest Winnebago lands.

CHAPTER XXI

PARTIALITY FOR THE SIOUX

WINTER 1828-29

REGARDLESS of the fact that Marsh was the Winnebago agent, his sympathy was entirely with the Sioux, and he never missed an opportunity of proving it.

In November, 1828, Morgan, the war chief of the Fox Indians, who lived on the Mississippi sixty miles below the Prairie, made an excursion into Sioux territory and fell upon a small hunting party of Sioux. One of his braves killed a resisting squaw with a hatchet and they captured and abducted two others,—the wife and child of an influential chief, and carried them away to their village.[1]

Late in December, news of this murder and abduction reached the Prairie du Chien agency. Street was in a panic and feared that the Sioux would retaliate and drench the frontiers with blood before he could act to prevent it. Hastily summoning Marsh he ordered him to go express into the Fox country, find Morgan's camp, rescue the squaw and child and, at the same time, threaten the Fox chief and his followers for making war on the frontiers of the United States.

Just before Christmas Marsh set out in the snow to find Morgan and his village. After a six-day search he located them, rescued the captives, and threatened their abductors with the vengeance of their Great Father, the President. Then, with the captives and Morgan himself

JOHN MARSH, PIONEER

in tow, he started out for Prairie du Chien, arriving about New Year's Day of 1829.

By this time Street was in a frenzy. Owing to the delay while Marsh was on his mission, he feared that the Sioux, still ignorant of the fate of the chief's squaw and son, would strike a retaliatory blow.

Allowing John but one day of rest, Street ordered him to start for the Sioux country and to travel as rapidly as possible to the captured squaw's home, a Wahpacoota village on the Cannon River.

The next day John started out, his pack animal stacked with presents to placate the Sioux. In addition, he carried a few provisions, but for the main part he had to depend on his rifle. The squaw was in an advanced state of pregnancy,—another reason for speed. It was impossible for her to walk, so she and her son rode the horse and Marsh trudged along in the snow at their side. Every night they bivouacked in the drifts. Every day Marsh's trusty rifle brought down game for the party and together they cooked it over the camp-fire.

There is something peculiarly reminiscent of the Nativity, in that expectant mother mounted on a horse, with Marsh walking alongside in the snow, as they turned their faces that January day into a wintry wilderness. Luckily he did not have an added papoose to attend on that memorable journey.

Marsh had proceeded through the Sioux country in a northwesterly direction and finally reached the Red Cedar River and delivered the squaw to her tribe. Then he turned nearly north, crossed the Des Moines near its source, and struck the Terre Blue (Blue Earth) River one or two days from its mouth, and passed down the St. Peters (Minnesota River) to Fort Snelling,[2] where he arrived on

PARTIALITY FOR THE SIOUX

February 5, 1829.[3] In a little more than a month he had covered some three hundred miles, not a bad accomplishment in winter, with a trackless wilderness, inclement weather, and hostile surroundings to contend with. Taliaferro greatly appreciated Marsh's accomplishment and warmly commended him, and wrote to Street recommending him for extra compensation.[4]

On his return to Prairie du Chien, along the east bank of the Mississippi, Marsh encountered a Chippewa band on Black River. One of their chiefs gave him a pipe with a bullet attached at each end of the stem, and a wampum belt, with directions to give them to the Sioux. It was a hostile message—a challenge. This Marsh well knew but he felt it was his duty to warn the Sioux. On arriving at the Prairie, he turned them over to Marguerite with instructions to give them to her people. Sinister, or insignificant, it was impossible to live on the Mississippi frontier and not take sides with one or the other belligerent tribes. Every one knew that Marsh was a warm partisan of the Sioux.[5] He was proud of their confidence.

As soon as the Sioux received the pipe they prepared for trouble and sent runners to their winter hunting grounds with word to their warriors to return immediately to their villages. The traders were greatly perturbed.

Street heard of the episode through one of them and he was terribly exasperated with his sub-agent for serving as Sioux ambassador, and with Marguerite for bearing a message which she knew would cause trouble.

He berated Marsh roundly and immediately wrote to General Clark, at St. Louis, a letter of complaint. "The whole of Marsh's attention," he said, "is absorbed in an erroneous view of the Indian differences among themselves, enlisting his feelings with the Sioux and becoming a partisan in their differences with the Foxes. The unfortunate connection between the sub-agent and a Sioux woman has biased his mind and made him the apologist for their cause."[6]

Shortly after Marsh returned from his long journey into the Sioux country, two Winnebago presented themselves at the agency complaining bitterly that a white man and several Indians from Green Bay were cutting shingles on their lands a hundred miles north of the Portage.[7] The Winnebago threatened that unless Street kept these poachers off their lands they would take measures into their own hands. This frightened Street. Although it involved another perilous journey into a country where men were notoriously careless of human life, he determined to send Marsh there to arrest the offenders and deliver them to the civil authorities.

When he ordered Marsh to go, the latter was not at all enthusiastic. He reminded his superior that he had but just returned from an exhausting trip into the Sioux country and needed rest. But his objections were of no avail. Street instructed him to proceed at once to Fort Winnebago, providing him with a requisition on Major Twiggs for a military escort, guide, and necessary provisions.

About March 2 he started, much against his will and judgment,[8] and he freely declared that he went only because he was compelled, and that he disliked the duty.[9] However, he accomplished his task.

About a hundred miles above the Portage and just off the river, he came upon a white man, Pliney Sabins, and several Stockbridge Indians, cutting timber and making shingles. Marsh arrested them all and forced them to return with him to Fort Winnebago where he turned them over to the Commandant.

PARTIALITY FOR THE SIOUX

Having delivered over the thieves, Marsh now searched the Indian lands adjacent to the Portage to make sure there were no other trespassers engaged there. Having assured himself, he sought out the chiefs of the neighboring bands, pacified them, and entreated them to keep the peace and not to resort to hostilities.[10]

During his absence from Prairie du Chien, an unfortunate incident occurred for Marsh. On March 7, 1829, an article appeared in the *Miner's Journal* of Galena, entitled "Sioux Indians," which claimed to have been inspired by him. In fact it made use of his name as the authority for its statements. The article declared that there was a good deal of discontent among the northwest tribes in consequence of misunderstanding between them and the whites; that because of it, 4,000 Sioux intended to descend the Mississippi in the spring and that their object was unknown. The appearance of this article caused consternation and panic on the Fever River; the squatters in the lead mines were badly frightened, their guilty consciences pictured an avenging host descending upon them and regaining their lost lands.

Street, in his dramatic way, wrote to Clark, "here is a Pandora Box, filled to the brim and ready to fly open at the least unskillful handling and deluge[11] our frontiers in blood and sweep from its surfaces with the besom of war the busy myriads who are quietly procuring their fortunes in the mining district!"[12]

As soon as Marsh returned from Fort Winnebago, Street upbraided him for such unguarded remarks. John just as promptly denied their authorship and contradicted them in the Galena *Journal*, under date of Saturday, April 11, 1829:[13] "I have observed with surprise," he wrote, "an article in your paper of the 7th instant under the head of 'Sioux Indians,' in which an unauthorized use has been made of my name. It would have been sooner noticed but for my absence in the interior of the Winnebago country, and I now hasten to correct a statement so erroneous in point of fact, and so liable to make a false impression at a distance. After my late journey through the Sioux country, the principal object of which was to compose the difficulties then existing between them and the 'Sacs' and Foxes, I have in several cursory conversations stated my belief that if a general war should take place the Sioux would send a body of 3,000 or 4,000 men against them. The Sioux nation by the latest intelligence is entirely tranquil, and I have no knowledge of any unusual collection of Indians in any part of the country, and never for a moment entertained the idea that they had contemplated descending the Mississippi. As respects the Sioux in particular, it is a fact well known to all who have even a slight knowledge of the Indians on this frontier, that while they are the most numerous and powerful, they are, and always have been the most friendly and well-disposed towards the whites."[14]

But, the damage had been done. Street claimed that Marsh was biased by the Sioux and had written the article with the idea of upsetting the peace and quiet of the frontier. Without giving him the benefit of the doubt, he filed charges against him and dispatched them to General Clark, the superintendent at St. Louis.

"The man is absolutely mad," he wrote, "or his ideas have been deranged by entering into the feelings and views of some border, savage warriors. I rather think that his strong party Sioux feelings have induced him to make this publication to scare the Foxes. How shallow this is even in relation to Indians you know better than I do!

PARTIALITY FOR THE SIOUX

Morgan has more sense than he imagines. He knows that Indians cannot do without food—and that if 4,000 Indians were ever collected they could not remain together without starving for more than a few days unless subsisted by white men."[15]

He berated Marguerite and Marsh's relationship with her and laid his sympathy and partiality for the Sioux directly at her door.[16] His complaints bristled with charges and ran the gamut from the trivial to the serious. Among others, he charged that during the early days of the Winnebago outbreak Marsh had dispatched an express on his own horse to Fort Snelling, begging for assistance; that subsequently the steed was lost in the public service and Marsh received the price of him from the government;[17] that later the horse was found; that Marsh laid claim to him, recovered him and kept the money as well.

In all, he filed two letters of complaint.[18] In the course of time they reached General Clark at St. Louis and subsequently the Honorable John H. Eaton—then Secretary of War at Washington,[19] and John lost his office.

Thus, mainly because of his partiality for the Sioux, John was removed from the agency.[20]

Shortly thereafter he, Marguerite and the boy, Charles, moved into a house which he had recently bought from John Brunet.[21] It fronted on the Mississippi and here he opened a store, stocking it with merchandise, guns, rifles, ammunition, and articles of appeal to the Indian eye. The law sternly forbade the selling of arms to the red men, but what was a law like that to John if he could turn a neat penny?

CHAPTER XXII

MARSH BETRAYS THE FOXES TO THE SIOUX.
BLACK HAWK RETALIATES

1830

By the spring of 1830 the situation between the Sauk and Foxes and Sioux reached the breaking point and everything pointed to another Indian uprising. Street decided to stop it by arranging a conference at Prairie du Chien between representative chiefs of his agency and those of the Sauk and Foxes—hoping that they would meet and settle their difficulties in a friendly council. He arranged a date early in May and carried out the details more or less secretly.

Somehow Marsh got wind of the approaching meeting, learned the date set for it, and that a large party of Sauk and Foxes were expected. Being a Sioux man he lost no time in telling Marguerite and passing on his information[1] to several Sioux chiefs, telling them the exact date on which the Sauk and Foxes were expected at the Prairie.[2] Here was an opportunity for which Sioux braves thirsted.

On the afternoon of the appointed day, a war party of Sioux and Menominee joined forces at Prairie du Chien. Together they slipped down the Mississippi to the lower end of Prairie du Pierreaux, some twelve or fifteen miles below Prairie du Chien, where a narrow channel of the Mississippi ran close to the end of the prairie.

Arriving at the spot where they knew their intended victims would encamp, they drew their canoes on land and

BETRAYS THE FOXES TO THE SIOUX

carefully secreted them in the underbrush. Then, with true Indian cunning, they hid themselves among the trees and grass but within gunshot of the landing place and lay in ambush for their prey. No fire was made. The stillness of death pervaded the forest. Nor had they long to wait for their foes. Between sunset and dark the Foxes in three or four canoes arrived, landed, and started preparing the evening meal. The party consisted of eighteen persons, led by the distinguished old Fox chief, Kettle. With him were one squaw, a boy of fourteen years, and fifteen warriors, including two of his own brothers and two minor chiefs—Broken Face and Piermosky—all from a village near Dubuque's mines.

Upon landing, the party commenced unloading the canoes, leaving in them only their guns and war clubs. All this was carefully noted by the ambushed war party, but they remained perfectly quiet, scarcely breathing, so as to take their victims completely by surprise. When all the Foxes had landed, the Sioux and Menominee bounded to their feet and, with a horrible yell, fired a murderous volley into their midst. All the Foxes fell except one brave and the boy. The former reached a canoe, seized a loaded gun and discharged it, mortally wounding one of the Sioux, but was immediately dispatched by the rest of the band. Now, out of the original party of eighteen, only the boy survived. Before he could escape he was captured and both his arms were broken. Then placing him in a canoe, they pushed him off from shore and told him to go to his home at Dubuque's mine and tell the news of the massacre to the village.

Then the Sioux and Menominee turned their attention again to their victims. All who still breathed were horribly mutilated and then killed. Hands, feet, fingers, ears and scalps were lopped off, and more horrible still, the heart of the aged chief was cut from his breast; all were carried away by the victors as trophies of the bloody fight.

On the day following, the victorious Sioux and Menominee assembled and, accompanied by a few squaws, paraded the streets of Prairie du Chien with the monotonous sounding drum and rattle, displaying on poles the scalps, the dismembered human fragments taken from the bodies of their victims. All were painted for war and had smeared their faces with the blood of their enemies. They wore feathers, carried tomahawks, war clubs and scalping knives.

Thus equipped, they marched up and down the main streets of Prairie du Chien, passing *en route* the home of Rolette and other settlers. When the procession passed the house of Marsh, what thoughts must have filled his mind? Some carried limbs, freshly hacked and gory, one bore aloft a dismembered head with a stick thrust through the throttle.[3] One old squaw held overhead an entire hand with a long strip of pendant skin attached and swaying in the wind. The latter flapped against her hair and face, but she did not care and kept up the scalp song and joined in the scalp dance, yelling like an incarnate devil.

After this exhibition, which lasted for two or three hours, they went to a small mound, made a fire and roasted the heart of the old murdered chief—Kettle. It was then divided into small pieces and distributed among the warriors, who devoured it—to inspire them with courage and "make their hearts glad."

In the afternoon, following this bloody debauch, they embarked in their canoes and ascended the river, taking their mangled trophies with them, around which to frolic and dance again and again. On the minds of Marsh and

BETRAYS THE FOXES TO THE SIOUX

Marguerite and all those others who witnessed this frantic orgy, what recollections and haunting memories did it leave in its wake![4] Marsh was harshly criticised for his part in the massacre. Although it was retaliatory, *lex talionis*, and although he was a Sioux partisan, it was felt that he had made a great mistake, and had entered too intimately into an Indian affair. His act had not only lasting consequences on his own life, but is frequently quoted as being one of the causes leading up to the Black Hawk war.[5]

The Fox massacre caused such a commotion in the Indian country that a council was immediately called at Prairie du Chien, and the Sauk, Foxes, Sioux and Menominees were prevailed upon to attend and to settle their difficulties amicably.[6]

The sessions began on July 7, 1830, and by the 15th, the Sioux on the north and the Sauk and Foxes on the south had ceded a strip of territory twenty miles wide, on each side of the boundary line between their lands established by the Treaty of 1825.[7] For these cessions the government, among other annuities, monetary in nature, promised to furnish them with blacksmith shops, iron and farm implements, etc.[8]—in other words, a modern social-service centre.

During the treaty Marsh obtained a contract to erect a blacksmith shop for the lower Sioux at the Kettles[9] near the village of Wabashaw, about 120 miles above Prairie du Chien.[10]

John was glad to get this contract and to remove Marguerite and his son from Prairie du Chien. He wanted to get them among the friendly Sioux. Ever since he had betrayed the Foxes, his position at the Prairie had been a difficult one. He was unmercifully criticised by the whites for his Sioux connections and worse by the sympathizers of the butchered red men. The Foxes threatened to retaliate against him. His friends warned him to be watchful of Marguerite and Charley on account of their Sioux blood. That thought filled him with dread and foreboding. He complained bitterly of the attitude of the whites and the Indians toward him.[11] He was happy to go up the river and he departed for Wabashaw's village without regrets. He decided to stay as long as possible.

After his arrival at the Kettles, John wrote home: "I should have written to you more frequently but I have been in the upper country almost a year, superintending my business in that quarter, which has been very extensive and which has occupied my time." But, yet, not a word did he say of Marguerite and his boy. In spite of his loyalty to the latter, he was far more loyal to the traditions of New England. Salem could not have appreciated his liaison with the wilderness. What would they have thought had they known that his devotion to the Sioux had cost the Foxes seventeen scalps!

Neither did John find the happiness he had hoped for at Wabashaw's village. The trouble was his boy. He was devoted to the five-year-old youngster—but he saw him growing into a young savage—a blue-eyed, blond-haired Sioux. The old chief taught the boy how to draw the bow and speed the arrow. His marksmanship was remarkable, but when one old fellow gave Charley a tomahawk John rebelled.

Some whisperings regarding his domestic affairs evidently penetrated to the Danvers fireside, emanating from Ann Crowninshield, an acquaintance of the Marsh family, who at that time was teaching school at one of the military reservations on the Mississippi. In reply to a letter, he de-

BETRAYS THE FOXES TO THE SIOUX

nied the existence of a wife and family. Poor John,—life was becoming more and more complicated every day! What a snarl he was creating for the future to unravel. "In your last letter," he wrote, "you inquire if I am married and a number of other questions which seem to have been suggested by some report of Ann Crowninshield. I have to answer that I am not married and am sorry to say that I can see no prospect of it, nor has any material alteration taken place in my affairs. Ann Crowninshield has not to my knowledge been within 500 miles of me and knows about as much of my affairs as her brother who was hanged some time ago."[12]

At last the blacksmith shop was finished. Whether he would or not, Marsh and his family had to return to Prairie du Chien. The place was far from tranquil. The threat of the Foxes destroyed his peace of mind. As time went on he became more and more apprehensive for the safety of Marguerite and his son. Murder, butchery and reprisal went merrily on, day and night, on every side. Although the Indians made and signed many treaties and smoked the pipe of peace with one another innumerable times, it was but an outward camouflage, complied with at the whites' insistence. Treaty or no treaty, they reserved the privilege of exacting their own dues, in their own way, at their own time, and the Foxes gave evidence that they had not forgotten the ambuscade of their tribesmen by the Sioux, nor the part Marsh had played in its execution. In fear and apprehension he looked eagerly about for a safe retreat for Marguerite and the boy until the trouble blew over.

Marsh knew that revenge would come swiftly and silently and the very thought filled him with fear. He could see the uprising coming, every day the situation between the Sauk and the Foxes on one side, and the Sioux and Menominee on the other, became more tense and in the approaching conflict he felt that Marguerite's and Charley's doom would be sealed unless he could do something and do it quickly. In addition, the squatters were driving Black Hawk, the Sauk leader, to desperation.

During the winter of 1831, they had completely wrecked Saukenuk, his ancient village, plowed up the graves of his ancestors, scattered their bones and desecrated their graves with crops. When Black Hawk returned from his winter's hunt and found what they had done, he was so enraged that he and his band threw down the fences the settlers had built, tramped down their corn and dug up their potatoes, saying the land was Sauk and that they had not sold it. Then the Hawk told them that they must and should leave his village, and gave them a definite time in which to vacate. The squatters construed his statement as a threat against their lives and showered Governor Reynolds of Illinois with messages and petitions cloaked in exaggerated terms. The governor caught the general excitement of the situation and issued a fiery proclamation asking for volunteers. By so doing he ushered in the darkest tragedy that blots the annals of the Mississippi frontier.

Marsh happened to be at Fort Armstrong at this time, and he realized that the uprising he had feared was at hand. "The Kickapoos—Iowas—Ottawas, and Pottawatomies are assembling at Rock Island to join the Sacs and Foxes against the whites," he wrote. "General Edmund P. Gaines is on Rock Island with some regular troops and the Governor of Illinois, John Reynolds, is advancing with 700 or 800 militia to join him."[13] These combined white forces staged a demonstration before Black Hawk's village on the 25th of July. Realizing they intended to show

BETRAYS THE FOXES TO THE SIOUX

him no mercy, the Hawk stealthily withdrew his entire band to the Iowa shore during the night. On discovering this, Governor Reynolds went in pursuit and brought him back, forcing him to sign drastic articles of capitulation, solemnly agreeing never, without the express permission of the U. S. government, to return to the east side of the river.

On the night of July 31, a little more than a year after Marsh had betrayed the Foxes to the scalping knives of the Sioux and Menominee, he was reminded that Black Hawk had not forgotten that slaughter. He was also forcibly reminded of Marguerite's and Charley's situation.

On the evening of that day a party of twenty-eight Menominee, consisting of warriors, their squaws and children, encamped on an island almost directly opposite old Fort Crawford. They brought with them the Fox scalps they had taken the year previous[14] and, feeling in perfect security, danced around them, drank freely of whiskey and gloated over their victory. Marsh must have gone to sleep with the sounds of that celebration in his ears. The pow-wow lasted until the late watches of that night. Then the participants threw themselves down and sank into a drunken slumber, unaware that their foes had been watching the whole affair from the Iowa shore.

Some two or three hours before daybreak, Black Hawk and a Fox force, numbering about one hundred, slipped quietly across the Mississippi, crept silently upon the sleeping camp and fell upon them as they slept. Then began an orgy of blood that beggars description. The Menominee were slaughtered where they lay, almost without resistance, for during the night's debauch, the squaws for safety had hidden their guns. So silently did the Foxes approach and so swiftly did they execute their victims that the garrison, almost directly opposite, heard nothing. Yet when dawn broke over the Mississippi, it revealed a ghastly sight. All the Menominee were dead—men, women and children, scalped, butchered, and weltering in blood.[15] Thus were the Fox scalps of the previous year avenged and thus the ball Marsh had set in motion the previous May continued to roll.

CHAPTER XXIII

MARGUERITE'S FLIGHT TO THE NEW SALEM AND SANDRIDGE SETTLEMENTS OF ILLINOIS

1831

THE murder of the Menominee was a final blow to John. It filled him with terror. The same horrible fate, he argued, awaited Marguerite and his boy unless he could get them out of Prairie du Chien and hide them where no Fox would know of their Sioux blood.

Once, during one of his trips down the frontier, Marsh had come to Sangamon County, Illinois, and had visited New Salem and Sandridge,[1] settlements made by frontiersmen of English and Scotch descent, who mostly hailed from the clearings in Kentucky, Tennessee, Georgia and Missouri. They had not intermarried with the natives. There were no half-breeds among them. That fact impressed Marsh forcibly. Here, he had argued, would be an ideal place to wean Charley from his Indian environment. There, he now determined, would be the place to take them. No Fox would ever look for them in such a community.

One day he put Marguerite and Charley in a canoe, and with a faithful old Sioux named Antoine they started for the Illinois clearing. The most direct route was by the Mississippi and Illinois Rivers. It was also, at this period, the most dangerous, for the Sauk and Fox villages occupied sites on both banks of the former. On this account, Marsh was forced to direct his passage by the longest way around—the Wisconsin and Fox Rivers to Green Bay and

JOHN MARSH, PIONEER

Lake Michigan, then by the Chicago and Illinois Rivers to their destination.

When they arrived at New Salem, they went to Cameron's tavern. John M. Cameron, the owner, was a Cumberland Presbyterian, a millwright by trade—a preacher by ordination.[2] He had come to New Salem with his uncle, James Rutledge. Ann Rutledge, the beloved of Abraham Lincoln, was his cousin. At this very period, Lincoln, rough and illiterate, his coat sleeves too short and his trousers too brief, was boarding with Cameron and working in the village store. Lincoln, in his big-hearted way, took a great interest in Charley, whittled out toys for him by the hour and gave him his first knife—a never-to-be-forgotten gift.

Cameron and John became great friends and laid the foundation of a relationship that was destined to play an imporant part in Marsh's affairs.[3]

There was another among the pseudo-professional men of the neighborhood to whom Marsh was particularly drawn—"Uncle Jimmie" Pantier—a doctor.[4] He lived near by in the Concord settlement on Sandridge. "Uncle Jimmie," as he was affectionately known on this part of the frontier, enjoyed a great reputation as a physician. By the right of man, he was not a licensed "M. D.," but by the grace of God he boasted that he was a healer and was alternately known as a faith doctor or "yarb" doctor.[5]

He was a mystic, and it was acknowledged near and far that he possessed great medical skill. He liked to wander in the woods, to sit and reflect and to study the habits of the wild things. Wild animals and birds seemed to know him as a friend and allowed him to approach them without fear.

This led people to attribute to him mystical powers

MARGUERITE'S FLIGHT TO NEW SALEM

over them. He was acquainted with the different wild plants and their medicinal qualities, and these he used successfully in his "yarb" drinks.

It was thought that he could cure certain human ailments by the laying on of his hands or by blowing his breath in the face of the victim. Thus warts disappeared when he breathed upon them, and the lame arose and walked when he laid on his hands. Many were the calls upon him for these purposes, and many were the grateful patients who profited by his powers. Some very remarkable cures were laid at his door, and his reputation extended far beyond the narrow confines of Sandridge. The afflicted made long trips from far within and without the frontier to consult him.

He never attempted to explain his gift of healing. It was evident to him, as well as his patients, that he possessed it. Being a gift, he claimed that it was something he could neither question nor talk about, and being of divine origin, it was, he thought, something for which no man could pay, feeling that if he did charge for its application, the grace of healing would be denied him.[6]

Just what it was about "Uncle Jimmie" that appealed so strongly to Marsh, it is difficult to say. But the more John saw of him, the more he liked him and the more he felt he was just the person to whom he could intrust Marguerite and his son. He went to Pantier and told him of Charley and his mother, of their Sioux blood, of the threat against their lives, and of the fear he felt for their safety. The upshot of their conversation prompted "Uncle Jimmie" to take them into his cabin and to promise, should the occasion arise, to protect them.

Thoroughly satisfied with this arrangement, John returned to Prairie du Chien.

JOHN MARSH, PIONEER

It was a hard wrench to tear himself away from Marguerite and his boy. Long afterward, Charley recalled that parting, the stoical behavior of his mother, the grief of his father, as he held him in his arms for a last embrace while the tears rained down his cheeks.

Charley was now six years old, and up to this time his only playmates had been Indian boys and half-breeds. In spite of all his father could do to the contrary, he was more savage than civilized. Although he spoke French like all the villagers, he talked Sioux like a native, and with increasing solicitude his father watched him growing up more a Sioux than a Marsh.

The older the boy grew, the fonder Marsh became of him. He was proud of his straight, slim body and pleased that his webbed toes made no difference in his fleetness of foot. To look at his fair hair, blue eyes and ruddy coloring, no one would have dreamed that he was other than a young Anglo-Saxon. To all outward appearances the rich strain of Sioux was lost. John had great ambitions for him.

To further these ends, "Uncle Jimmie" was particularly instructed to wean his young charge from Indian companions and confine his contacts to the young Americans in the settlement. It was further agreed that as soon as all danger from the Foxes was past, Marguerite was to return to Prairie du Chien and leave Charley to "Uncle Jimmie's" upbringing. Marguerite did not like that plan—she wanted her boy. Such a prospect made her sick at heart.

Marguerite was a person of considerable curiosity to the Pantier family. For her, the change of environment was not easily accomplished. Living in the free and easy French-Indian community of Prairie du Chien was one thing, while life in the raw-boned Illinois clearing was

MARGUERITE'S FLIGHT TO NEW SALEM

another. She pined for her old life, for Marsh and her people, and she grew melancholy and unhappy. Her stoicism deserted her, and she wept most of the time. The Pantiers did the best they could. They were kind and solicitous, especially when they learned that she was on the verge of maternity for the second time.[7]

Although their hospitality was all that it should be, their quarters were crowded. The Pantier house was a log-cabin affair, divided by a wooden partition into two apartments. Upstairs was a loft reached by a ladder. It had one window and holes in the roof, through which the stars peeped and the snow drifted in winter. These quarters were assigned to Marguerite and her boy, and "Granny" Pantier made them comfortable with her best feather mattress and her only two hickory chairs. Downstairs the appointments were equally meagre. The living quarters centred about a great open stone fireplace.

Marguerite could not adjust herself to her new surroundings, and as time went on, she became more and more unhappy. She pined for Marsh. Finally she begged, danger or no danger, to be allowed to return to Prairie du Chien, but "Uncle Jimmie" would not listen. Then one fine day, he found that both she and Charley were missing.

With the help of others, he tracked her and overtook her at Miller's Ferry,[8] a ford on the Sangamon River about seven or eight miles from Petersburg. In her flight she had decided to reach an Indian village in Mason County, with which she had affiliations, feeling that if she could reach them, they would help her to return to Prairie du Chien and Marsh. The latter had instructed Pantier to keep his boy from just such an environment, and Uncle Jimmie brought the reluctant mother and son back to his home. But Marguerite was more unhappy than ever and made up her mind to escape again when the opportunity offered.

Among Mrs. Pantier's choicest possessions were several China cups. They were used only on state occasions and were carefully guarded. One day Charley asked for a drink, and Marguerite, unaware of their value, took one of them, filled it with water and passed it to her son. Inadvertently he dropped it on the floor, and it flew into a thousand pieces. "Granny" lost her temper, seized Charley and gave him a sound trouncing.

Marguerite's eyes blazed with anger when she saw the other woman slapping her child, but she remained quiet and bided her time until she found a hatchet. Then, mounting the ladder, she disappeared in the loft. A few minutes later those below heard a terrible racket of splintering wood, interspersed with yells. They knew that the hickory chairs were being reduced to splinters, but no one dared go aloft. Then they heard her drag the feather bed across the floor, heard her rip it open and shake the contents out of the window, with every shake yelling, "Whoopee! Whoopee!" When the feathers were flying the thickest, Marguerite lowered herself to the ground and disappeared in the forest. In spite of every effort "Uncle Jimmie" and the neighbors made, they failed to track her.

Many days later she arrived at Prairie du Chien; whether by canoe or by foot, by river, or through the trackless forest, no one ever knew. She was too far spent and exhausted ever to tell the story of her escape. Fortunately for her, Marsh was at home when she dragged herself across the threshold. There was no time to lose. The tremendous effort of the past days had been too much for a woman in her delicate condition. Exhausted, she had nothing left with which to meet the ordeal that was upon

JAMES PANTIER.
1779–1859.
Courtesy of Robert S. Torrey, Los Angeles.

SUSANNA MURPHY PANTIER.
1781–1870.
Courtesy of Robert S. Torrey, Los Angeles.

INTERIOR OF THE PANTIER HOME.
Courtesy of Thomas P. Reep, Petersburg, Illinois.

MARGUERITE'S FLIGHT TO NEW SALEM

her. Shortly after, she gave birth to an infant daughter, too weak and feeble to live, just as she was too depleted and worn out to rally. That day both she and her baby died. She had been loyal and loving. John was brokenhearted. For seven years they had lived together as man and wife.

Coming suddenly out of a clear sky his loss was a bitter blow. It had a terrible effect upon him.[9] He was conscience-stricken. Then he regretted most that he had betrayed the Foxes. Had he not done so, Marguerite would never have had to leave the Prairie. Thus he argued until life was a torment. He was borne down with a grief he could not throw off. He became dispirited and melancholy. It was all his fault. He began to avoid his fellows. They condemned him. He wandered about the woods and by the banks of the river, but could find no comfort. He did not eat or sleep. His friends feared for his reason, or that he would destroy himself. They advised him to pack up and go away.

Once he went back to Concord Settlement to see his little motherless boy and spent several days with "Uncle Jimmie," but it did not ease the pain in his heart. During this time he had the Reverend John Berry baptize his boy into the Presbyterian Church. When he was leaving he put $300, a large sum in those days, into the possession of "Uncle Jimmie," with instructions that it was to be used for the education and care of Charley, and told him that he was going back to Prairie du Chien to wind up his affairs, that then he was going further west, and that when he found another home, he would come back to Sangamon County and take Charley away with him.[10]

This would have been the opportune time to have taken Charley and returned to New England and to have begun

JOHN MARSH, PIONEER

his career as a physician. But it was impossible. His family had expected much from him. He had accomplished little. They did not know they had a grandson with Sioux blood, on the Mississippi. In spite of his grief at Marguerite's death, he could not face his fireside with that story. It was sacred to the wilderness. The frontier understood. Salem never could. Besides, he had been too long on the borderlands of civilization to restrict himself to the confines of a New England village. The only road lay westward. Gloomy and unhappy, he returned to Prairie du Chien, and became so melancholy that his friends were alarmed for his safety.[11]

Just as he was on the point of wandering off into the West, word reached Prairie du Chien that Black Hawk had crossed the Mississippi; that General Atkinson and a force of regulars were in pursuit, demanding the surrender of the murderers of Menominee; that the Rock River border was in a panic, and that war was inevitable. Then Atkinson called on Marsh for help. Thoroughly aroused, John gave up his plan for immediate departure and threw himself heart and soul into the struggle against the enemies of the Sioux. He hated them.

CHAPTER XXIV

THE BLACK HAWK WAR. MARSH COMMANDS THE SIOUX

1832

ATKINSON's messengers overtook Black Hawk at Prophetstown with the demand that he surrender the murderers and retire to the Iowa shore.[1] But the Hawk sent back word that "his heart was bad,"[2] that he was determined not to turn back, and that if Atkinson wished to fight he might come on,[3] and Major Isaiah Stillman, with 350 troops, took up the pursuit.

Near Sycamore Creek, a tributary of the Rock, Black Hawk attacked and completely routed him and Stillman's men fled in an agony of fear.[4] Their blood-curdling cry: "The Indians, the Indians," played havoc in the settlements through which they retreated. Terror gripped the border in their wake. "The howl of a wolf in the Prairie; the fall of a forest bough; the report of a hunter's gun, were sufficient in this time of panic to blanch the cheeks of the bravest men."[5] The border press reflected the general atmosphere: "To arms! To arms! Blood and carnage mark Black Hawk's path."[6]

Humiliated by the rout at Stillman's Run, Governor Reynolds on May 15, 1832, penned a second call for 2,000 more volunteers,[7] and General Atkinson wrote to General Street for help.[8] "Send me at this place with as little delay as possible," he demanded, "as many Menominee and Sioux Indians as can be collected within striking distance

JOHN MARSH, PIONEER

of Prairie du Chien. I want to employ them in conjunction with the troops against the Sauks and Foxes, who are now some fifty miles above us in a state of war against the whites. . . . Colonel Hamilton [9] will hand you this letter. I have to desire that Mr. Marsh may be sent with Colonel Hamilton and the Indians." As soon as he received this appeal, General Street summoned Marsh and ordered him to recruit the Sioux and Menominee and march with them under his command to the relief of Atkinson.[10]

The nearest Sioux village, Wabashaw's, was 120 miles up the river from Prairie du Chien. On May 30, Marsh, with the sub-agent Burnett, set out for there in a canoe manned with eight men. En route it occurred to them that the Winnebago of the upper Mississippi, being in sympathy with the Sauk and Foxes, might engage in hostilities with them. The next night when they reached their village on the river La Crosse, they stopped, and, around their council fires, Marsh told them about the war and invited them to march under his command and join General Atkinson. Their chief, Winnieshiek,[11] opposed the measure and refused to have anything to do with it, saying the Sauk had twice during this year presented red wampum to the Winnebago at the Portage; that as often they had washed it white and handed it back to them; that he did not like that red thing and was afraid of it. Waugh-ha-ta-kau took the wampum and said that he, with all the young men of his village, was anxious to go on the expedition and promised to join Marsh as soon as he returned from the Sioux village above.

On June 1, Marsh and Burnett reached Prairie Aux Ailes—where Winona, Minn., now stands. Here Marsh was on the familiar ground of Wabashaw's Prairie. The old chief was still a devoted friend of his and here too, he

THE BLACK HAWK WAR

found the Sioux chief, L'Arc—The Bow—whose warning during the Winnebago war had probably preserved his life. Both Sioux chiefs and their tribesmen were enthusiastic about the prospects, and were anxious to march against their old enemies.

Marsh accomplished some very successful recruiting, especially as he was authorized, during the duration of the war, to promise the Sioux subsistence and pay and support for their families, and it did not require much persuasion on his part to urge them to march with him, as their commander, against the Sauk. Even if he had not come, they told him, they were intending on their own score to make a descent upon their ancient enemies.

Encouraged and heartened by Marsh, they engaged with alacrity in their preparations, which were so extensive that he had to grant them two extra days to complete their plans. At last all was ready, and one forenoon at nine o'clock Marsh and Burnett with the chiefs, Wabashaw and L'Arc, and eighty of the Sioux warriors, left the Sioux village.

At Prairie La Crosse they stopped and were joined by twenty Winnebago warriors. On June 5, after six days of recruiting, Marsh and Burnett, with the combined fleet of Sioux and Winnebago canoes, drew up on the quays of Prairie du Chien.[12] Here they were delayed two days longer being outfitted and were augmented by other Indians who arrived hourly. When fully recruited, Marsh had a command of 225 Indians, of whom about a hundred were Sioux and the remainder Fort Menominee and Winnebago from the Upper Mississippi.

Burnett recorded that as a recruiting officer, Marsh displayed great zeal and energy in effecting the Sioux and Winnebago alliances, and that his exertions had brought

JOHN MARSH, PIONEER

out the greatest possible force from the bands called upon.[13]

Most of the Indians had no firearms, for the traders who were in the country with them had withdrawn the guns allotted them when they found that the Indians were resolved on war. Consequently, Street was compelled to purchase firearms from the American Fur Company at the Prairie for more than half Marsh's command, as none would go unarmed, nor did he wish them to.

In all, he supplied twenty with rifles and handed them over with the admonition: "These guns are your Father's. He puts them into your hands to fight the Sacs and the Foxes. They are now yours if you employ them well. Go and be revenged of the murders of your friends. . . . If you desire revenge you have permission to take it. I will furnish you arms, ammunition and provisions and here is the man who is sent to conduct you to the enemy. Follow him, and he will lead you to the murderers of the Winnebagoes, the Menominee and the Sioux."

"I am much indebted to Mr. Marsh and to the sub-agent, Mr. Burnett," Street wrote, "for their extraordinary exertions in enabling me to assemble and equip the Indian forces. Mr. Marsh appears to have devoted his whole soul to the cause and gives by his example great spirit to the Indians, who seem impatient to meet the foe."[14]

On June 7 all was ready, and, with banners flying, feathers waving, blood-curdling war-whoops and monotonous beat of Indian drums, Marsh's mounted detachment rode away from Prairie du Chien and headed towards General Atkinson's army on Rock River. They reached Fort Hamilton during the final stages of the battle of

THE BLACK HAWK WAR

Pecatonica, or Horseshoe Bend, where a band of seventeen Sauk and Foxes was completely annihilated.[15] Not one red man was left to carry the news to their friends.[16] Here Marsh's Sioux found the fresh Sauk trail and hastened to the battlefield, where they fell upon the warm corpses of their old-time enemies, mutilated them with savage ferocity and scalped them with shouts of glee. Holding aloft their bloody trophies, they danced around them in great triumph as if they themselves had achieved the victory.[17] Marsh allowed them to complete their orgy, then with his command retired to Dixon's Ferry.[18]

Thus ended, for the whites, the first decisive victory of the war. In fact, it was its turning point and broke the back of the belligerent Indians. Discouraged and cowed, with dismay in his heart and terror in his ranks, Black Hawk sought safety in flight, hoping to regain the west banks of the Mississippi by a circuitous route through the swampy country around Four Lakes and the Wisconsin River, which he hoped to put between himself and an avenging army of 4,000 whites, ten times stronger than his own.

Marsh and his command took up the pursuit. Finally they came into perilous proximity with the rear guard of the savage Sauk. An engagement seemed imminent, but suddenly the Sioux turned tail and ignominiously fled, leaving Marsh on the field with no command. He tried to overtake and rally them but, oblivious to his orders, they galloped madly on. On June 22 they reached Prairie du Chien and General Street berated them soundly for their cowardly conduct. "You have not hearts to look at the Indians who murdered your families and friends," he thundered. "Go home to your squaws and hoe corn, and never again trouble your great Father with your anxiety

JOHN MARSH, PIONEER

to go to war. Take your canoes and clear yourselves."¹⁹

Of all the Indians which Marsh had led to Illinois, only the Menominee and six Sioux remained in the struggle. The former had not forgotten the massacre of their women and children and were determined to be revenged on the Sauk and Foxes personally before they quit.²⁰ They stayed until the bitter end.²¹

With the flight of his command, Marsh was forced to return to the Prairie. For fifty days he had been in the saddle, with scarcely time to undress in the entire period.²²

But he did not have long to rest. By July 21 Black Hawk's retreat reached Wisconsin Heights. The old Sauk was in a desperate plight. Dodge's Rangers and General Atkinson were in hot pursuit, trying to cut off his escape, and a terrific battle raged in his wake.²³ Street had some important dispatches for Atkinson. He summoned Marsh and told him to deliver them. It was a dangerous mission and required a man of iron nerve, for the river bottom was held by the retreating Sauk and, had they captured him, they would not have hesitated to scalp him.

Marsh knew every inch of the ground intimately. He travelled mostly at night, secreting himself in the undergrowth during the day. He proceeded up the south side of the Wisconsin. At the shot-tower at Helena, some eighty miles above the river's mouth, he overtook Atkinson and delivered his dispatches. By that time Black Hawk had made his escape across the river and Atkinson was making his plans to take up the pursuit.

On July 28 John went with him. By July 29 they were forty miles above the Portage and had progressed six miles on the trail of Black Hawk and hoped to overtake him before he reached the Mississippi.

In spite of his desperate condition, the Hawk eluded his

THE BLACK HAWK WAR

pursuers. Winnieshiek, the Winnebago chief from the village at La Crosse, guided him through the marshes.[24] On August 1 he reached the Mississippi, just below the mouth of Bad Axe River, and immediately began the work of crossing. He felt that if he could only reach the Iowa shore he would be safe.

As Atkinson neared the Mississippi he realized that the only chance he had of preventing Black Hawk's escape again was to get a message to Fort Crawford at Prairie du Chien, warning the garrison of the old Sauk's intentions, and ordering them to take measures to prevent his retreat across the river. He summoned Marsh and entrusted this important dispatch to him. Everything depended on its delivery. It was another hazardous undertaking, for a forty-mile wilderness lay between his position and Prairie du Chien, and Black Hawk and his Indians were in the advance. Under cover of darkness Marsh and a man named Deviese set out on an Indian trail. They moved as silently as possible. When they could no longer find their way they lay down in their tracks and slept till dawn. In the half-light of early morning they were horrified to find fresh tracks in the dew about them. They thought the game was up. They feared they were caught in an ambush. They dared not move. As it grew lighter they discovered that the tracks had been made by deer. They were relieved. Relocating the trail, they pushed on to Fort Crawford, reaching there safely that night, and handed over their dispatches to Captain Loomis, the commandant.[25]

Knowing his influence over the Sioux, Captain Loomis prevailed upon Marsh to go to Wabashaw and enlist his help. They must cut off Black Hawk's retreat. The next morning, John and Deviese set out in the *Warrior* for

Wabashaw's village. When the steamer neared the mouth of the Bad Axe, Black Hawk himself spied them. Eager to give up he rushed to the shore, raised a white flag, and cried aloud in the Winnebago tongue that he and his people wished to surrender. This was the third attempt he made to capitulate.

Those on board chose to believe that the Hawk's white flag and pleas for mercy were a ruse, and replied by raking his ragged ranks with canister.[26] The Hawk responded with a volley of musketry, one white man was wounded, while twenty-three Indians fell. There is no record that Marsh attempted to prevent this useless slaughter.

The *Warrior* was now out of wood and returned to Prairie du Chien for the night. Meanwhile the Sauk proceeded with their heart-breaking retreat. Dawn found them on rafts and in canoes, still trying to reach the Iowa shore. Daylight gave the white sharpshooters a better opportunity to resume the carnage. A few of those in the water reached a willow island in the middle of the stream and, like drowning rats, dragged themselves up the bank. Here they lay—men, women and children—too exhausted to move. Here the steamer *Warrior* again found them, raking them with shot and canister, mangling them where they reposed.

The final stages of the conflict resembled the scenes in a slaughter-house more than a white man's battle. A few Foxes plunged into the river and reached the Iowa shore, where Wabashaw and the Sioux, due to Marsh's efforts, were lined up with tomahawks and war clubs.[27] When the Hawk learned that the whites had instigated this act he exclaimed, "None but cowards would ever have been guilty of such cowardice."[28]

With the close of hostilities,[29] Marsh returned to Prai-

BLACK HAWK.
Courtesy of the University of Virginia.

THE BLACK HAWK WAR

rie du Chien—the annihilation of the Sauk and Foxes had not eased his grief. He was more depressed than ever and so dispirited that it seemed impossible to pull himself together and carry on. Seeing his condition, his friends again advised him to change the scene and go away.[30] He had reached one of those stages in a man's life where everything seems to go wrong. Marguerite was gone beyond recall. Due to the war, his fur trade was ruined; his magisterial duties had involved him unfavorably with the military at Fort Crawford, Major Kearney in particular; and worst of all, his boy, the pride of his life, was in the hands of strangers. All things considered, he determined to leave Prairie du Chien—the spot he had once held to be the most beautiful in the universe. In this state of mind he sent in his resignation as a justice of the peace of Crawford County and disposed of his fur trade. Sometime earlier he had sold his house, lot and merchandise for $1,000 to Peter and Joseph Powell, merchants of St. Louis.[31] Now he was ready to go.

Before he could get away, General Scott with 800 regulars arrived at Prairie du Chien, assumed command of all the forces there, and made arrangements to bring the war to a formal close. Much against the latter's wishes he appointed Marsh a commissioner at the forthcoming negotiations and ordered him to proceed to Rock Island immediately.[32] Marsh demurred; he was anxious to depart; but Scott needed him as an interpreter and reluctantly he postponed his departure. It was then early in August, and before he could leave the Prairie, cholera broke out and Marsh threw himself into the work of helping the sick. It was a harrowing time. Four people died in one house, and one hundred soldiers succumbed at Fort Crawford, in two weeks.[33] As soon thereafter as possible he departed for the treaty grounds.

JOHN MARSH, PIONEER

Before the commissioners could proceed with the treaty, plague broke out at Rock Island and claimed the first victim on August 27. Marsh again went to work. All negotiations ceased for the time.[34] From the soldiers the pest spread to the Indians. So many were affected that it was necessary to dismiss them all until they could be reassembled by special summons.

In the fate of three of them, Marsh must have been particularly interested, for he had played a hand in their present plight. They were three young chiefs whom Wapello had surrendered early in the war as having been involved in the murders of the Menominee at Prairie du Chien. Since then, they had been confined in the military prison at Fort Armstrong awaiting trial. When the cholera broke out, General Scott set them at liberty, telling them to seek safety in the prairies from the pestilence and making them promise to return as soon as they saw a prearranged signal hanging from the limb of a dead tree at an elevated point of the island.

On the subsidence of the pestilence the signal was hung aloft and, true to their parole, the three Sauk chiefs presented themselves for trial. So touched was Scott by their integrity that he appealed to Washington in their behalf. Fortunately his request did not fall on deaf ears, and the three who preferred honored death to dishonored life were set at liberty.[35]

By the middle of September the plague had subsided sufficiently to allow negotiations to resume. Marsh was again summoned, and witnessed the part of the treaty that dealt with the Winnebago, who were punished for their secret aid and sympathy extended to Black Hawk at every stage of the campaign. The council was convened with a gallant show of West Pointers, volunteers and redskins.

THE BLACK HAWK WAR

On the 15th, the treaty was drafted and signed by thirty-nine Indians and twenty-five whites.[36] Among the latter were John Marsh, Captain Ord, Joseph M. Street, John H. Kinzie, Major Henry Dodge, U. S. A., Major O. R. Thompson, U. S. A., and others.[37] By its terms, the Winnebago paid dearly for their sympathetic attitude, losing all their lands south and east of the Wisconsin River and the Fox River of Green Bay.[38]

For his services in attending the Rock Island council, Marsh received the sum of fifty dollars to defray his expenses.[39] Thus ended a conflict that had more to do in shaping the destiny of the Mississippi frontier than any other single event. By the treaty he had witnessed, Marsh saw transferred from the hands of the Indians into those of the whites a slice of territory so vast that several counties were carved out of it and were soon teeming with prosperity and opportunity, from which many of the men by whose side he had bivouacked wrested fame and fortune. Here, too, had it not been for that lone grave on the prairie hillside, he might have remained, reaped his share of the rewards and become the pillar in some Mississippi commonwealth. But that grave, in the mind of many of his friends, marked the pivotal point in his career. The man who turned away from it was entirely different from the youth who had sought adventure in the West some ten years before.

But there was another cause that made his departure less dignified than it would otherwise have been. His love of gold!

During the treaty negotiations it was brought out that at the time Marsh was leading the Sioux against the united Sauk and Fox he was secretly selling guns and ammunition to them from his store at Prairie du Chien.[40]

JOHN MARSH, PIONEER

Immediately a warrant was issued for his arrest; but warned in time, he made his escape in a canoe down the Mississippi. Fear of arrest gave speed to his paddle.

BOOK III

COWHIDE

CHAPTER XXV

ESCAPE TO THE ROCKY MOUNTAINS

1832-1833

BECAUSE of the warrant for his arrest, Marsh did not remain long in St. Louis. At the first opportunity he joined a party of fur traders bound for the Rocky Mountains, and that spring the former influential citizen of Prairie du Chien took the trail with some forty roughshod buckskin-clothed mountaineers. Their pack mules were loaded with scarlet shirts, blankets and gewgaws, which they expected to exchange with the mountain man on the Green, the Bighorn and the Yellowstone. Early in April, mounted on a mule, Marsh left Lexington, Missouri, and headed across the prairies for the Oregon Trail, crossing the Kansas River en route westward. Food was scarce; it was principally hardtack and bacon. Everyone was complaining of the larder long before they reached the buffalo country and the eagerly anticipated haunches of prairie cow. After felling their first buffalo, they roasted the meat and consumed it so greedily that the majority of them were swiftly in the throes of "*le mal de vache*," an intestinal disorder caused by being too gluttonous. It was all in a day's experience to these men of the trail; one day hunger and thirst, the next satiety and excess.

After crossing the South Platte, Marsh and his party pressed forward up the southerly side of the North Platte to Chimney Rock, a conspicuous landmark by the riverside. Here the country was desolate and so thickly set

JOHN MARSH, PIONEER

with prickly pears that they were forced to proceed in single file. On one occasion, when Marsh was riding well in the lead of the rest of the party, his mount, switching its tail to right and left, suddenly lodged a small particle of cactus under its tail. Finding itself badly pricked in this vulnerable spot, the mule kicked and bucked at such a rate that Marsh was unsaddled and thrown flat on his back in the midst of a large clump of the prickly pears. There he lay, as prostrate and motionless as if he had been crucified on the spot. As the slightest movement meant untold torture, he did not dare to budge. Although he was over six feet two inches in his stockings, the length of his limbs was not sufficient to deliver him from his bed of persecution. As his comrades passed, he besought each one for God's sake to help him out of his prickly situation. But all he heard in reply to his entreaties were bursts of laughter from the company as they filed by. Such mirth did his unhappy position excite that not a man came to his rescue until the last one in the rear was reached.[1]

On arriving at the Laramie River, Marsh and his companions found it a boiling torrent. There was no raft and no means of making one. But being in the land of the buffalo, they killed several, sewed the hides together and stretched them over a framework of sticks. Thus, in a so-called "bull boat," they reached the opposite shore. Here for the next five or six days they rested, gave themselves up to the excitement of the chase, and feasted royally on buffalo meat. On the seventh day, they topped off this orgy of flesh with a drunken spree, only sobering up in time to move on to the Sweetwater, which they reached near Independence Rock. The next six days they ascended that stream. On July 2, 1833, they reached the Continental Divide and six days later the appointed rendezvous on

ESCAPE TO THE ROCKY MOUNTAINS

Green River. Here, behind a small stockade, they found Captain Bonneville's men and, four miles further on, an outpost of the American Fur Company. In these congenial surroundings, and aided and abetted by their newfound friends, they set up a tent and abandoned themselves to hunting, drinking and shooting. When the spree abated, trade began, and they did a brisk business in scarlet shirts, tobacco, blankets and other things dear to the hearts of the mountain men and the Indians. In exchange they collected thirty packs of beaver, then proceeded to the Bighorn and the Yellowstone.

It was now toward the end of July and so warm that the men disdained tents and, wrapping themselves in their blankets, slept in the open air. This continued until it was rumored that a mad wolf was about, and that he had bitten several of the trappers and some of the horses in a nearby camp. That night several of Marsh's messmates re-rigged their discarded tent and, as an extra precaution, barricaded the entrance with their pack saddles. The majority, scornful of such measures, threw themselves down under the stars and abandoned themselves to sleep. Soon the camp, except for the loud snores of the tired trappers and a periodical "All's well" from the sentries on guard, was wrapped in silence.

Suddenly, in the late watches of the night, the stillness of the prairie was rent by a solitary cry, "the wolf—the wolf—I'm bitten." Almost immediately the call was taken up from another quarter with a similar complaint, and then another, until the whole camp was in an uproar.

During that night three of Marsh's companions were attacked by the mad wolf. Among them, George Holmes, a young well-educated New Yorker, was bitten badly about the ear and right side of the face. By the time the

JOHN MARSH, PIONEER

trappers were aroused and had their guns in action, the wolf had escaped, but the next night, in spite of all precaution, he returned again and this time bit the largest bull in camp.

About July 24 Marsh's party broke up its Green River camp and moved toward the Bighorn. They now retraversed South Pass to the Sweetwater. This time, on reaching it, they struck-off for Wind River, the main upper reach of the Bighorn. Two days before arriving at the latter place, the wolf-bitten bull commenced to show signs of hydrophobia. He bellowed incessantly, and ran up and down and pawed the earth in apparent anguish.[2] These signs greatly distressed young Holmes. Often he paused to ask his companions if they thought he would go mad. These good fellows, although filled with apprehension for their companion, did their best to reassure him.

But every time the mad animal bellowed, Holmes would stop and anxiously inquire of those about him, "Don't you hear the bull?—he is going mad—I am getting scared."

Each time his companions heard that ominous roar, to them full of menace, they felt worse than Holmes. Two days later, when the bull died, they were still more worried. When Holmes heard what had occurred, he went stark mad. From then on he developed rapidly the symptoms of hydrophobia. Even Marsh, with his knowledge of medicine, could do nothing for him.

Holmes could no longer endure the sight of water. Every time they came to a small stream, he had to be blindfolded and carried across. In the end, naked, alone and crazed, he wandered off into the trackless prairie and was never seen again.

ESCAPE TO THE ROCKY MOUNTAINS

By August 10 Marsh's party were at the Bighorn. Due to the topography of the country they came suddenly upon the river. The opposite bank was red with Indians. By way of greeting they rent the air with terrifying and ear-splitting war-whoops. The trappers were panic-stricken. Before they had a chance to seek safety in flight, the red men threw themselves into the river and headed for them. Marsh and his companions jumped from their saddles. They took up a position behind a clump of cottonwoods, cocked their rifles and waited the order to shoot.[3]

In the face of the oncoming Indians they held their positions like veterans. They were determined to make the redskins pay dearly for their scalps. Word went from mouth to mouth that they were Blackfeet—the most treacherous Indians on the plains. Their hearts sank. In the clutches of those cruel devils they knew that they must fight for their lives. There would be no quarter. In less time than it takes to tell it, the Indians were upon them. One tall scoundrel, in advance of the others, brandished aloft a white flag and made signs not to shoot.

Up then spoke an old trapper in authority: "They are not Blackfeet, they are Crows—there is no danger for our lives—but they are great thieves."[4]

Out from under cover came Marsh and his companions. Their hearts went back to their right places. There was a great shaking of hands, smoking of pipes, and that night about the camp-fires a feast of roast buffalo.

From the Crow camp Marsh's party pushed rapidly to Fort Cass on the Yellowstone, a post two miles below the mouth of the Bighorn, and one of the most dangerous on the Upper Missouri. They found the inmates in a wretched condition; several of their men had been recently killed by the Blackfeet, and the rest were even afraid to go out to chop wood. After a day or two of rest, they moved on to the Missouri—many to return to St. Louis for the winter—but Marsh decided to leave the party and to stay on the Upper Missouri.

CHAPTER XXVI

MERCHANDISING; INDEPENDENCE, MISSOURI
1833

BY November of 1833, Marsh was at Independence—then a thriving settlement on Missouri's western border. It was the jumping-off place of the American frontier, the rendezvous of traders and trappers as well as of all the veriest rogues and scoundrels in America. Here, among the dregs of humanity, Marsh argued that he was comparatively safe. Here no man would care whether he sold firearms to the Indians or not. He established himself as a general merchant;[1] probably on the Square, as all the mercantile establishments were grouped about it. On the southwest corner was the log-cabin store of Samuel C. Owens, one of the first and largest in Independence. On the north side of the Square, near the centre of the block, was the store of Samuel D. Lucas, who dealt primarily in goods designed for the Mexican market. On the same side of the Square was the general store of John O. Agnew. These latter establishments were outfitted from the warehouses of the Amercan Fur Company at St. Louis. Marsh apparently received his supplies from Pennsylvania, or under another name, for there is no record of his account with the fur company. For his 1833 license, as a vendor of merchandise, Marsh paid $15 to John B. Flannery, Collector of Jackson County. His competitors were: Pierre Choteau, Jr., Flournoy and Hickman, John Baird, James and Robert Aull, J. B. O'Toole, Taylor and Duncan, and John O. Agnew.[2] In 1834 his license cost him $19.33 1-3, indicating that he was doing well, and had increased his stock. In August of 1835, Marsh paid $15. From these accounts it appears that he operated a bar and retailed wines and liquors, as well as merchandise.[3]

Independence, at this period, enjoyed a happy situation on a rolling prairie, some three miles from the great bend of the Missouri. It was almost completely surrounded by a great forest and was separated from the river by a veritable jungle of trees, vines and bush. Through this almost impenetrable area the settlers had hacked a rough road to their landing-place on the river. In the centre of the town they had likewise cleared out a village square, some three acres in extent. When Marsh arrived, the latter was still full of the stumps of the great trees that once had graced it. Beyond the trees that encompassed the village like a wall, was the *Unknown*—wide, uncharted prairies, and the limitless American desert. Only one path, not discernible from the heights of Independence, stretched across this solitude—the Santa Fé trail. Near Independence it was deep, black and well-defined; but as it disappeared in the distance, it became as indeterminate as the horizon it approached. Even after ten years' use, it was more of a tradition than an entity; yet men knew that if they could follow its indefinable bounds they would reach the rich marts of Mexico and share its prosperity. They also realized that if their instinct as pathfinders betrayed them, and they lost it, they would find hunger and thirst, wolves and Indians, and a hundred other ways to swift oblivion. The Indians were the terror of the trail,—Comanches, Arapahoes, Pawnees and Apaches. Scarcely a party, great or small, escaped their raids. It was this chance to make or break that appealed to the hardy and encouraged them to make the gamble.

MERCHANDISING

It will thus be seen that, in 1833, Independence was the furthest outpost of American civilization. All points beyond were problematical and enshrouded in mystery and uncertainty. Nevertheless, it was the starting-point for the Arkansas, where the Santa Fé trail divided, one path leading to the Rockies, Oregon and the Pacific, and the other to the Southwest, and the provinces of Northern Mexico. During that period it offered to those of stern fibre the great adventure; but for those of frailer stuff, it promised nothing at all. On that account it attracted the bold and daring of every clime.

Marsh thought enough of Independence and its prospects to invest in his mercantile venture some $3,000, practically all of his Prairie du Chien savings. Here, for three years, on the village Square, he catered to the needs, not only of the community, the trappers and traders, but especially of the Santa Fé freighters; for the caravans that moved up and down the trail between New Mexico and Independence were the breath of existence to the trading community about the Square. The outgoing one left in May, loaded with drygoods, silks, satins, hardware and domestic cottons.[4] When the season came around for the traders to start across the plains, they gave Independence an exceedingly bustling appearance. The streets were alive with horses and men and filled with clouds of dust and droves of flies. Pandemonium reigned. The caravans took their departure to the cracking of whips, the swearing of teamsters and the shouts of roustabouts.[5]

Here, in his store, Marsh came into contact with men from all over the countryside. Here he first met Captain John Sutter, the Swiss adventurer, and numbered among his acquaintances Colonel John Bartleson, Lilburn W. Boggs, former governor of the State, Samuel C. Owens,

JOHN MARSH, PIONEER

B. Barnett, William Hague, Michael Nye, and Elias Burnett.[6] He was doing no doctoring then—that part of his past was seemingly dead; some called him "colonel," others "captain." The Missourians were as careless of titles as they were of lives. They did not know where he had come from, why he was there, or where he was going. They asked no questions. No one ever asked Marsh questions; he was not the type that bred familiarity. He held his own counsel, and silence made him a man of mystery. But, on the future of these neighbors, whose lives he touched so lightly, he was destined to have a marked influence.

By no means did Marsh spend all his time merchandising. He must have had a clerk, as he made frequent expeditions to the fur-trading posts in the Rockies and explored the Upper Missouri.[7] Once, in the spring of 1836, he had such an overpowering longing for a sight of his son, Charles, that he took the chance of arrest and travelled all the way back to the New Salem and Concord settlements of Illinois to see him, and found him, a lad of nine, tall and straight as an arrow, who still looked like the son of his father. Marsh was proud of this clean-limbed and fair-haired boy and was delighted with the progress he had made with Doctor Pantier. Weaned from his French and Indian surroundings, he was now like other frontier boys of his age and, in spite of his foot, was a husky, well-set-up youth, and so appealed to his father that he was loath to give him up.

When it came time to depart, Charles begged to go to the Missouri settlements with him, but Marsh would not listen to his plea and told him that he intended to sell his mercantile business at Independence and go into the far West, perhaps to South America, and that when he succeeded he would come, or send for him, and they would

MERCHANDISING

spend the rest of their lives together. Only partially satisfied, the boy saw his father go.

When Marsh returned to Independence he found that his mercantile establishment was far from flourishing. The year 1835 was one of financial depression in the States. Crumbling banks and failing institutions were the order of the day, and the backwash of this business upheaval was felt on the Missouri. Instead of being able to dispose of his business at a fair figure, it failed completely, and Marsh could not meet his creditors; he lost all his stock, and was practically bankrupt. Except for a little money in the belt about his waist, he was penniless. In addition, he discovered that the military had learned of his presence on the Missouri frontier. He determined that the best way out of his predicament was flight down the Santa Fé trail, and forthwith he departed clandestinely, during the night of June 15, 1835, with two chance acquaintances.

The caravan for that year had already started and was well on its way to Santa Fé, but it was Marsh's opinion that they would overtake it and join it en route. He argued, in his predicament, that the trail, hazardous as it was for three lone men, was safer than Independence, failure and creditors. At least it offered a way out. After twelve years in the wilderness, to return to New England, penniless and a bankrupt, was out of the question. Then there was Charles to consider. They knew nothing of his existence at the old Danvers home. Neither did they know much of their eldest son. Since Marguerite's death, and his departure from Prairie du Chien, Marsh had not written home.

Marsh was then in his thirty-sixth year. Tall, bronzed, well-knit, ready for emergencies, he must have presented a commanding figure as, mounted on his steed *Cherokee*,

JOHN MARSH, PIONEER

he boldly faced the manifold dangers of the Santa Fé trail.

There was no pack animal in his party, but strapped securely in his saddlebags were the few possessions he had brought to the wilderness twelve years before; his Andover and Harvard diplomas, Paine's "Works," Johnson's "Lives of the English Poets," the Hymnal he had used at Andover, the "Odes of Anacreon," and his Bibles, an English and a French one—all, except the latter, reminders of Danvers, Lancaster, Andover, Cambridge, Fort Snelling and Prairie du Chien. The French Bible was the same from which Marguerite had learned to read; Marsh prized it highly and cherished it to the end of his days.

CHAPTER XXVII
FLIGHT DOWN THE SANTA FÉ TRAIL
1835

UNFORTUNATELY, when the caravan left that year, Marsh had had no idea of joining it. By June 15, it was well on its way to Santa Fé. It was his plan to travel fast, mostly at night, to avoid both Indians and heat, to overtake it en route, and then to proceed to Santa Fé under its protection. The few provisions they carried were packed in saddlebags, for the rest they depended on their trusty rifles and the wild game along the way.

When they reached the Indian country they remained close together, for their safety lay in numbers. But presently, by some unrecorded mishap, Marsh became separated from his companions. Almost at once he found himself surrounded by a band of Comanches. Even with his swift-footed horse, escape was impossible, and he was captured. After debating among themselves as to what to do with their captive, the Indians finally decided to take him to their chief's headquarters. This they reached after a long journey. The Indian camp was in an uproar when they arrived. The chief had been wounded in a fight with another desert tribe. An arrow was imbedded in his arm, and the whole area was swollen and painful. In spite of their incantations, none of their medicine men was able to extract it, or even to relieve his condition, and the whole tribe were excited and menacing. When they saw the prisoner, they demanded that he be sacrificed in order to appease the evil spirits which had taken possession of their chief. The career of Marsh was in a fair way to come to an inglorious end when a singular incident occurred and saved his life.

JOHN MARSH, PIONEER

Hearing the hubbub outside his lodge, the old chief sent his granddaughter, a comely young squaw, to find out the cause of the uproar. The maiden was very human, and Marsh was young and handsome. She reported to the chief and interceded for his life.[1] The Comanche ordered Marsh to be brought into his presence. On entering, Marsh saw that the old chief was suffering with his arm; when he was asked if he was a medicine man among his own people, he answered in the affirmative and was ordered to examine the wound of the chief. He found a piece of arrowhead imbedded in the soft tissues under the arm. After making a slight incision, he quickly removed the cause of the trouble, cleaned and dressed the wound and withdrew.

The old chief was soon in good health and very grateful and wanted to do something for Marsh. John expressed a desire to go on to Santa Fé and requested that some warriors be sent with him as guides and protectors, but his request was refused. The chief was no fool and did not propose to lose so valuable an adjunct to his tribe. He was told that he was free to come and go as he chose about the camp, but that if he attempted to escape, he would be put to death. Marsh much preferred life, even among the Indians, to an ignominious end, and promised to make no attempt to get away.

He was given a place in the household of the old chief, who, according to one report, insisted upon his forming an alliance with his granddaughter. At first Marsh refused; he was in no humor for such a connection, but finally he was prevailed upon to accede to the old chief's wishes, and a marriage ceremony, according to tribal customs, is said to have been performed.

Marsh was allowed to keep his horse but, in spite of his

FLIGHT DOWN THE SANTA FÉ TRAIL

new domestic arrangements, never unpacked his saddlebags or gave up the idea of escaping. He was too closely watched to render success possible, so he patiently bided his time, meanwhile cultivating the friendship of the braves and living the life of a medicine man.

Finally, after many days of waiting, his chance came. The Indians subsisted largely on the meat of the buffalo, which were plentiful on all sides. When winter approached, the herds were in the habit of going south into Kansas and the Texas "panhandle," where they remained until spring, when they again migrated to the northern ranges where grass was plentiful. That summer the supply of meat among the Comanches was unusually low, so they decided to go south in search of the animals, hoping to meet them on their way to the summer range. They had to go further than was usual, and in the course of their travels, they approached the old Santa Fé trail.

Late one day, as they were crossing it, they saw a caravan of several wagons with an escort of armed men, a short distance away. When they camped that night, they had a discussion regarding the wisdom of attacking it; but fear of the rifles caused the old chief to veto the proposal. In the morning Marsh asked permission from the chief to go back a short distance in order to gather some herbs to make medicine. The request was granted, though two young braves were ordered to keep a watchful eye on his movements. Away they rode, Marsh astride *Cherokee*, and the Indians mounted on ponies. In spite of their vigilance, as soon as he saw the caravan he put spurs to *Cherokee* and raced across the desert, with his escorts pounding in close pursuit. Their wiry Indian ponies gave Marsh's thoroughbred the race of his life, but he outdistanced them and reached a place of safety.[2]

JOHN MARSH, PIONEER

Marsh accompanied the party, who were traders from old Mexico, into the foothills of the Sangre de Cristo mountains. Finally, one day, they reached the promontory from where New Mexico's ancient capital could be seen. Here they stopped long enough to fire off their guns and furbish up their clothing before descending into the streets of the city.[3]

Santa Fé was a tawny *adobe* town, nestling in the close embrace of carnelian-colored hills. It could boast of an ancient church, a porticoed governor's palace, of green trees and squares of rich fields given over to corn and wheat. With its flat roofs and its warm brown walls, it must have afforded a pleasing prospect as Marsh looked down upon it that summer day of 1835. It proved even pleasanter than it looked, for he remained in the capital many weeks, during which he hobnobbed with the natives, mastered the Spanish tongue, mainly through the help of a Spanish Bible still in existence, and went on long, botanical jaunts with a young Englishman named Langstroth whom he found there.[4]

At Santa Fé Marsh heard much regarding the glories of California. The New Mexican-California trade was at its height, and the latter province was no longer a vague and indefinite myth.

Taos and Santa Fé were the depots for all the trappers of the Southwest. As early as 1826 they had opened the northern trail to California. During the next six years they blazed at least six more over the Sierra Madre.[5] The caravans carried *serapes* and *frezadas* and brought back sleek mules.

The traders traversed the regular route down the Rio del Norte to the Colorado, which they crossed a few miles below the mouth of the Gila, and thence made their way

FLIGHT DOWN THE SANTA FÉ TRAIL

by the Mission San Luis Rey to San Diego and Los Angeles. The last, being the largest community in Alta California, became the central point of the trade.

Marsh took a lively interest in these caravans and in the country that lay beyond the Mojave desert and the Cajon Pass, and he soon gave up his plans for going to South America and turned his eyes toward California instead. There, in a Mexican province, he could start life anew. No one need ever know of Prairie du Chien and his past. He would go to California and forget.

He left Santa Fé late in the fall, with an exploring party.[6] By then he had been in the New Mexican capital three months, long enough for him, with his flair for languages, to master the Spanish tongue. First he went to Chihuahua; thence to Casas Grandes, a place celebrated in the aboriginal history of Mexico, and finally along the River Gila to the Colorado, which he crossed at its junction with the former, near the tides of the gulf, and entered the province of California at its southern part.[7]

Along this route he found extensive ruins and met many Indian tribes. In some districts they were wild and hostile, in others civilized and numerous. Hills and mountains were frequently in sight, but at no time was he forced to ascend a range of them.[8] The country in general was excessively arid; yet many places afforded good pasturage for his horses. There was little water, but he slaked his thirst by cutting open a certain species of cacti. Within was water enough for man and beast. A plant, which he took for acacia, annoyed him. It grew so rank and profuse in one district that he found it necessary to protect both himself and his horse with a kind of armor against its rigid and thorny branches.[9]

CHAPTER XXVIII

FIRST AMERICAN DOCTOR IN CALIFORNIA. EL PUEBLO DE NUESTRA SEÑORA, LA REINA DE LOS ANGELES

1836

WHEN Marsh arrived at Los Angeles in February, 1836, the Pueblo of Our Lady, the Queen of the Angels, was the capital of California.[1]

By this time, California, like the mother country, Mexico, was no longer Spanish dominion. It was a Mexican province, torn from one end to the other by revolt and seething with insurrection against its ever-changing officials. One revolt after another had engaged the public mind since Spain's sovereignty had ended. In the fourteen years since then seven governors had arrived, and as many bloodless *opera bouffe* wars had driven them back to Mexico. Just before Marsh arrived, the best of the seven, Figueroa, had cheated the province of a revolution by dying, and Nicolas Gutierrez, a short, red-headed Spaniard, with a squint in his right eye, which earned him the nickname of *El Tuerto*, had taken his place. Shortly after Marsh's arrival the Americans, under Isaac Graham, a Tennessee trapper, unseated Gutierrez, and set up Juan Bautiste Alvadaro, a native Californian. The Americans were led to believe that Alvadaro favored them and thought that by elevating him to the Governorship he would help them foster a lone-star state.

200

FIRST DOCTOR IN CALIFORNIA

Los Angeles was the storm centre of these revolutions. Most of the plots for the overthrow of one governor and the setting up of another were hatched there. A large and idle population, the members of which squandered their time cleaning muskets, playing the guitar, making love and eating highly seasoned foods, prompted unrest. The ideal *caballero* was a devotee of both Venus and Mars and prepared himself for either by carrying his gun on his back and his guitar across the saddle.

On the whole, the *Pueblo*, as Marsh found it, had a squat appearance as gloomy and melancholy as the catacombs of old Rome. The clay-colored walls with their flat, asphaltum-covered roofs, looked like so many brick kilns, ready for the burning. Not more than five of the adobes were covered with red tile.[2] Because of the constant anarchy, there were but two public buildings, a jail and a church, none fit to house the governor after the city became the capital, and he was forced to live in Monterey. Except the church, Our Lady of the Angels, in the Plaza, all the structures were of a monotonous one-story height —and the church itself had been as flat and forbidding as its neighbors until Henry Fitch of New Bedford, Mass., the young captain of a Boston trading ship, eloped with Josepha Carrillo to South America. He was subsequently condemned by an ecclesiastical court to provide the church at Los Angeles with a belfry and a bell of fifty pounds weight. This was the bell that rang out the masses when Marsh arrived.[3]

Marsh did not wish to stay in Los Angeles; a quieter community with less coming and going would suit him far better. There was always the hazard of meeting old acquaintances in the *Pueblo*. These he wanted to avoid. But he had no choice,—his money was exhausted. Not a cent

JOHN MARSH, PIONEER

was left, and he looked eagerly about for a chance of earning more money.

There was not a doctor, lawyer or teacher in the *Pueblo*. For teachers the Californians had no use. It was sufficient for them that their *padres* could read and write, but they needed a doctor—and this gave Marsh his cue. The repressed desire to be a physician again raised its head and manifested itself.

Every foreigner was required by Mexican law to present himself as soon as possible after arrival before the *ayuntamiento*, and to state his name, age, birthplace, occupation and intentions in the province. Marsh appeared on February 4, 1836. He announced that he was Doctor John Marsh, a physician and surgeon of the United States, and that he wished a license to practise his profession in the *Pueblo*. He was asked for his credentials. Here was a dilemma; he had no medical diploma, so he presented his Harvard B.A. degree, arguing that no one would be able to translate it. He was right. As the document was written in Latin, the illustrious *ayuntamiento* decided that it should be returned to Marsh; that he should be instructed to have it translated into Spanish and then submit it again.[4] As few in the *Pueblo* could read Spanish, much less Latin, no one could be found to make the translation, and it was sent to the Mission San Gabriel Archangel, for the *padres* to translate.[5]

On February 18, 1836, it was still untranslated, and Marsh's career as a physician hung in the balance. But of the session of that day the following record is found: "A petition from foreigner, *Don Juan Marchet* (John Marsh) a native of the United States of the North was read. He asks that this illustrious *ayuntamiento* consider him as having appeared, he declaring his intention of

FIRST DOCTOR IN CALIFORNIA

establishing in this city and also that he is a physician and surgeon. The illustrious *ayuntamiento* decided in conformity with the law of April 14, 1828, art. 3 as follows: 'Record and forward the certified copy solicited, reminding said Marchet that he cannot practise surgery until he has obtained permission from this illustrious *ayuntamiento*.' "[6] The minutes of this meeting were signed by Manuel Requena, Pres., and Tiburcio Tapia, each with his proper rubric attached.[7]

By February 25 his diploma having been translated to the satisfaction of the council, the secretary recorded in the minutes for the day: "A petition from Don Juan Marchet, asking to be permitted to practise his profession, was read. The Illustrious Body decided to give him permission to practise medicine as he had submitted for inspection his diploma which was found to be correct and also for the reason that he would be very useful to the community." Thus the *Pueblo Ayuntamiento* made him a physician, and ever after he styled himself Doctor John Marsh.

Forthwith Marsh set himself up as a physician and surgeon, perhaps in one of the forlorn *adobes* on the *Plaza*, that being the central spot of the *Pueblo*. Here, in a sunbaked house with a dirt floor, windows barred with iron and an entrance protected by a cowhide, we can visualize the first American medical offices in California. As for furniture—if his outfit was anything like the others—it consisted of a bench or two, a table resting on notched supports driven into the earth, a crude couch elevated two or three inches above the ground, filled with rushes and leaves and covered with a bullock hide. Marsh was naturally clever with the scalpel, and he had confidence enough to undertake any kind of surgical case from amputations

JOHN MARSH, PIONEER

to difficult obstetrical problems. In addition, he was provided with a quantity of quinine and could thus treat fevers, ague and chills. He also knew how to vaccinate and had the cowpox to do it with. Smallpox was one of the most wide-spread diseases in the Californias, and he had many such cases.

His practice was by no means limited to Mexicans and Californians. By 1838 the *Pueblo* had a foreign population of about fifty, among them many Yankees.[8] Soon Marsh was very busy. His services were always in demand. First, there was an outbreak of mad dogs and hydrophobia. So great was the menace, that a decree was passed that no man should keep more than two dogs, and that both should be securely tied. The others were poisoned.

There being no laboratories, Pasteur treatments, or aseptic precautions in that distant day, it is difficult to know just how Doctor Marsh handled a case of hydrophobia. But he was well supplied with *aguardiente* (brandy) and quinine—the panacea for all ills—and he probably did not lack for remedies. Besides rabies, there were frequent outbreaks of smallpox, and Marsh was an adept with the lance. In addition, he did considerable obstetrics and achieved quite a success as an accoucheur. The Spanish women propagated as rapidly as the cattle—some were the mothers of thirty—and Marsh was in demand at every birthday party.[9]

For his services, Marsh was paid in cowhides—and this presently caused him no end of embarrassment. There was no gold or currency in the old *Pueblo*. Horses, cattle, tallow and hides—principally the latter—were the usual media of exchange, a fact that disgusted the erstwhile New Englander. Beaver and otter skins brought from two to thirty dollars; a cowhide represented two dollars, and

FIRST DOCTOR IN CALIFORNIA

tallow fifty cents the *arroba*. Think of being paid in cowhides or tallow! After practising less than a year, Marsh complained that his *adobe* looked more like a warehouse than the offices of a physician, and in September, dissatisfied with the results of his professional activities, he sold his fees to a Boston trader for five hundred dollars. Thereupon, he put the gold in his belt and rode north in search of a cattle range.[10]

To find a rancho was more easily said than done. No foreigner could acquire California lands without first being baptized into the Catholic faith. Imagine Marsh being baptized a Roman Catholic! He who once had been on the verge of a Calvinist pulpit. But his church had failed him—he rarely thought about such things any more. If baptism would bring him a rancho, why not? Out of the disappointment over his medical career, his grief over the death of Marguerite, his failure in Missouri, and the chagrin of that warrant for his arrest, emerged not a chastened spirit, but a hardened one. Spiritual values were lost. Material ones asserted themselves. It was no longer a question of what he could do for humanity, but what humanity could do for him. His earlier ambitions that had spurred him on to an education and a medical career were now directed toward monetary gain. Leagues of land, herds of cattle and chests of doubloons absorbed his attention. Great riches would compensate for all his disappointments. Gold became his God.

CHAPTER XXIX

EXPLORATIONS. YERBA BUENA
1836–1837

MEANWHILE Marsh had reached the north,[1] in search of his cattle range. Before settling down in any locality he determined to explore California. In the course of events, he reached the Pueblo of San José, then the largest settlement in northern California. In the vicinity of San José, he met José Noriega, a native of Barcelona, who had arrived in California with the vagabond Cosmopolitan Company, sponsored by Hijar and Padres. Noriega had obtained from José Castro—*gefe politico ad interim*—a grant to a large tract of land, four leagues long and three leagues wide. The tract lay in the San Joaquin Valley, on the northern frontier of California, forty miles beyond the Pueblo of San José. It was surrounded by Indians, the most hostile in California. No man dared to travel there without an armed escort. There was not an American or a foreigner within miles, only a handful of semi-savage Spaniards living on widely separated ranchos who went about day and night, armed to the teeth. So desperate was the reputation of the locality that Noriega was afraid to live there alone and most of the time maintained ten *vaqueros*—and never less than seven—to protect him.[2] The description of that place pleased Marsh. Danger meant isolation and hence solitude, and he knew no fear.

It so happened that Noriega was weary of this dangerous locality. He wanted to sell his land and move to more congenial surroundings in the *Pueblo*. On meeting Marsh,

EXPLORATIONS. YERBA BUENA

he took the doctor to the property in the hope of selling it to him. Marsh was greatly impressed by the surroundings, and wrote to his friend Stearns at Los Angeles, asking him to forward his naturalization papers, which he had filed in Los Angeles in January, 1836, and telling him about the rancho, adding that he was about to be baptized—in order to acquire it.[3] When the papers arrived, he went to the Mission and was baptized a Catholic. Shades of the Reverend Skelton! He took the name of *Juan Maria*—*Maria* for the Virgin Mary—and from then on was called *Don Juan*.

Before buying the rancho, however, Marsh determined to see more of northern California and inveigled Noriega to go with him. The two joined an exploring party bound for Oregon and the Columbia River country. Their route lay through the great interior valleys of the Sacramento and San Joaquin, along the same path that Peter Skeene Ogden, McLeod, Michel Laframboise, Ermetinger, and other Hudson's Bay Company brigades, followed when they came into California to hunt beaver and otter, or to spend the winter at French Camp, not far from Noriega's rancho.

Once when Marsh and his party were traversing the San Joaquin Valley, they stopped on the banks of a river which the Indians in the neighborhood called the Yachekumna. It formed the northern boundary of the territory claimed by the Yacheko tribe, the main rancheria of which occupied the present site of Stockton. Wild grapes grew profusely along its margins and, on that account, the Hudson's Bay Company recorded it on their maps as Wine Creek.[4] Evening was coming on when Marsh's party arrived there and, after crossing the dry bed of the river, they pitched camp and spent the night. Next morning, before the others were up, the *mayordomo* went out to gather wood to cook the breakfast. Almost immediately he rushed back in a great state of excitement, woke up Marsh and the rest of the party, and told them to come out, for they were camping in the midst of a great quantity of human skulls and bones. The men tumbled out of their blankets and discovered that they had been sleeping in a veritable graveyard—skeletons and skulls were strewn in every direction. By chance they had happened on the ancient Indian battleground where the Yachekos and the Siyakumnas under Estanislao had fought a sanguinary conflict. Not knowing this, they imagined the spot had been visited by some great calamity or gigantic epidemic, and they gave the stream the name of *Calaveras,* meaning "skulls." Ever after, in speaking of that locality, Marsh and the members of the party referred to it as *Calaveras,* and they claimed that both the river and county were named from their discovery.[5]

The rainy season was already upon them, and, as the party could scarcely walk owing to the floods, they felled some trees and made dugouts in which to ascend the Sacramento River. While proceeding up the stream, they reached the mouth of a smaller tributary, and ascended it to a place where the whole surface was covered with feathers. From this circumstance they christened the stream *El Rio de las Plumas,* now known as Feather River.[6]

Continuing northward, they presently reached the headwaters of the Sacramento. There they met almost a hundred people from the Columbia, who—though they lived 800 miles distant—regarded themselves as neighbors of those who lived about the Bay of San Francisco.[7]

Late in March, 1837, after wandering about the country for several months and gradually becoming acquainted

A BULL FIGHT AT MISSION DOLORES, HELD AFTER HIGH MASS, IN CELEBRATION OF THE PATRON SAINT, SAN FRANCISCO DE ASIS.

EXPLORATIONS. YERBA BUENA

with it and its inhabitants, Marsh returned to the bay region. He went to Yerba Buena, now San Francisco, and there found everything in a ferment of excitement. Another revolution was fomenting. It was reported that an army from Sonora, estimated at from 200 to 600 men, was on the march—its purpose the conquest and plunder of California. This report filled him with doubt and apprehension.[8] He was well satisfied with northern California and felt he had found the part of the country best adapted to agriculturists from New England, and he wanted to settle there. But he felt it lacked one thing— just and equal laws, and a government that would be paramount and give confidence to the *gente de razon* like himself.

Circumstances such as these determined his program. He wanted a great rancho, cattle, riches and security, but he did not want them if he could not hold them. Influenced by these ambitions, his great desire became the annexation of California to the United States. It was evident to him that the province, rent by revolution and anarchy, was fast drifting to a debacle, and that the Russians, French and English were preparing to seize it. But he was determined that it should belong to his country, and in the events that brought about this result he played no inconspicuous rôle.[9]

When Marsh reached Yerba Buena, the future San Francisco, that village was in its swaddling clothes and far from alluring. It looked like what it was,—a bleak, half-deserted fishing hamlet. It could boast of a well-sheltered cove, in the lee of which an annual fleet of whalers and Boston traders found anchorage. At high tide it had a pretty, crescentic beach, but when the tide was out, an unsightly mudflat occupied the foreground.

JOHN MARSH, PIONEER

The village itself consisted of three buildings: one on the beach, the other two, at quite a distance, occupying one corner of the *plaza*—a sandy stretch of barren soil that three years before had been a potato patch. Beyond, were naked, beetling hills and rounded hummocks of sand, some barren and shifting, others thinly draped with *chaparral* and the creeping herb from which the hamlet took its name. On the outskirts were a few scattered *adobes*. Over a path tracked with the heavy imprint of grizzlies, were the melancholy walls of the Mission of *Nuestra Señora de los Dolores*—Our Lady of Sorrows. It accorded well with its bleak, wind-swept surroundings.

In an opposite direction, along the entrance of the bay, stretched the tumble-down *adobes* of the *presidio*, with rusty, dismounted guns[10] and a tottering flagpole that only periodically displayed the tricolored flag of Mexico.[11] Between these three settlements—mission, *presidio* and cove—was drifting sand, dune on dune, pile on pile, *ad infinitum*.

Of the three buildings Marsh found there, the largest, called the *casa grande*, was occupied by William A. Richardson, a sailor who had "left" his English ship, the *Orion*, at the cove as early as 1822.

Adjoining Richardson's *casa* was the combined store and dwelling of Jacob P. Leese, a native of Ohio, and a partner of Hinckley and Nathan Spear of Monterey.[12] Here Marsh found a lodging and gave a helping hand in Leese's store. His establishment became the rallying point for all the Spanish *hidalgos* and foreigners around the bay and, like the American village store the country over, it became a political centre. Here, seated on kegs and boxes, the settlers discussed the political situation of California and speculated as to whether their land of *Mañana*

EXPLORATIONS. YERBA BUENA

would fall into the lap of Great Britain, Russia, France or the United States. Marsh sat there with the others during the spring and summer of that year, absorbing their talk. He was already playing a telling hand in California's destiny.

All this time Marsh was living with Jacob Leese, sharing with him his *tortillas, frejoles* and *chile con carne*. Once he paid out fifty cents for fresh fish to amplify the family fare, and, incidentally, for his own enjoyment. When he left, after having been entertained, free of charge, the better part of a year, he dunned his host for the fifty cents.[13] Even in this land of prodigality he had not forsaken his frugal New England gods. It was no wonder that the Californians looked on him as penurious.[14]

CHAPTER XXX

CATTLE RANCHING, LOS MEGANOS

1837

EARLY in 1837 Marsh bought Noriega's great rancho in the valley of the San Joaquin. The transaction did not please his cronies on the kegs and crates at Leese's store.

"Too many Indians and horse thieves," some complained.

"They'll kill you and steal all your cattle," declared others. "The land's no good."

"Nothing can be raised in that San Joaquin adobe."

"San Joaquin? Why, that's the end of the world!" added others. "There'll be no settlers there for another generation."

Well might his friends try to dissuade him from buying land on this uninhabited northern frontier, infested by semi-savages and overrun by murderous horse thieves. For all that, the rancho Marsh had selected was romantically situated in a beautiful, though isolated, spot at the base of Mount Diablo.[1] It was, in fact, in the very shadow of that inspiring mountain which the superstitious Mexicans and Indians in the neighborhood held in fear and awe, and avoided because they said it was visited by an extraordinary being in grotesque plumage who masqueraded as the evil spirit of the mountain,[2] and who made his home in the rocky defiles of the summit. Once a detachment of Spanish soldiers who had been sent to rout out the thieves saw this fantastic person. With many a *caramba*, they turned tail and fled, declaring that the mountain was haunted by a

CATTLE RANCHING, LOS MEGANOS

devil, and giving rise to its name, *El Monte del Diablo*.[3] Under the circumstances it is not to be wondered at that Marsh's friends in Yerba Buena were not enthusiastic when they learned that he had bought a rancho in the very shadow of a mountain that was clouded with such a reputation.

His holding was enormous, extending from the base of the mountain to the banks of the San Joaquin River, nine miles distant. Although Noriega had held it for about three years and had built some corrals and outhouses, he had never obtained judicial or actual possession, through the *alcalde*, as was required by Mexican law. But that was not his fault. When he acquired it, Antonio Maria Pico was *alcalde* of the Pueblo of San José, and Noriega repeatedly urged him to go to his rancho and confirm it. As often, Pico gave as an excuse that he dared not go into such hostile country without a military escort, and that he had been unable to obtain one.[4]

When Noriega sold the rancho, Dolores Pacheco was *alcalde*. In order to make the title as perfect as possible for his successor, Noriega urged Pacheco to go to the rancho and give Marsh judicial possession. But Pacheco, too, hesitated, giving as his excuse that he was afraid of the horse thieves, that the danger of travelling into such hostile country was great, and that he could not insure his safety by obtaining a military escort. He, therefore, refused to go. Marsh did not consider that a flaw. Such a reputation would keep these Californians away and leave him in peace, and he bought the rancho late in December, 1837, but, owing to the winter rains, he did not take possession until the following spring.[5] It was late in April, 1838, when he arrived. By that time, the great valley of the San Joaquin, which extended from the Straits of Carquinez almost to the Colorado River, and lay, flat as the palm of the hand, between the snow-capped mountains of the Sierras and the chaparral-clad range of the coast, was one glorious green of waving grain—mile upon mile, and acre upon acre. Not a fence or house, only the trees along the watercourses marred its level expanse. Here and there, peacefully grazing, were bands of wild mustangs and herds of untamed, spotted cattle, sprung from the stock introduced by the mission fathers.[6]

Nature used a lavish palette, especially in spring, in embellishing the *Valle de Los Tulares*, as the Spanish called it. Plumes of yellow mustard were splashed over the landscape, but the general effect was that of an emerald sea. One breath of wind and the wide expanse rippled over all its surface. A heavier breeze and it broke into waves that rolled away to the distant Sierras or was lost in the haze of a horizon. The air was filled with the drone of bees and the call of birds, and was heavy with the fragrance of myriad wild flowers. The one sad note in the beauty of this terrestrial paradise was the continual lament of the doves.

Such was the San Joaquin Valley in the spring of Marsh's arrival, a country to make his pulses thrill, a haven for one who had lost himself in the great world, and who sought to re-find himself amidst scenes of solitude and isolation.

His rancho was a principality, including within its boundaries mountains, vales, springs and streams. A California mustang could hardly traverse it in a day. It was four leagues long and three wide. About forty miles from the Bay of San Francisco, it lay within the area where the San Joaquin and Sacramento Rivers unite to meet the tidewater of the bay.[7] Two miles of its northern boundary

CATTLE RANCHING, LOS MEGANOS

lay along the San Joaquin River, and it took its name—
Los Meganos, meaning "Sand Dunes"—from the low-lying
sand hills which skirted the banks and afforded skulking
grounds for coyotes and jack rabbits, to say nothing of
bears and mountain lions. The rancho was well irrigated
and was traversed by a stream, the *Arroyo de los Pabladons*—"River of the Villages," derived from the thriving
settlements of the Bolgones Indians that once dotted its
banks.

Such an enormous tract of land precluded close neighbors, and, in spite of the romantic surroundings, Marsh
lived a lone and solitary existence. But it was one suited to
the mood of the time. Thirty miles distant was the mission
of *San José*, secularized, but not yet demolished, and then
the most prosperous mission in California. It was the abode
of 2,000 Indians, fifty of whom were weavers; twenty, tan-
ners; thirty, shoemakers; forty, masons; twenty, carpen-
ters; and ten, blacksmiths. Once, when he first arrived, the
doctor saw a hundred Indian ploughmen all at work in one
field, each at his plough.[8] Architecturally, *San José* was
the least pretentious of California's ecclesiastical baronies,
but it could still boast of its reservoirs for irrigation and
its splashing fountain for washing and bathing.[9]

Fifteen miles beyond the mission, but in the same direction, was the Pueblo of San José with a population of some
700, forty of whom were foreigners, mostly Americans and
English. All were housed in *adobe* buildings, or *jacals*,
clustered about a *plaza* where thousands of ground squir-
rels burrowed. Gambling was the order of the day—also
of the night, with men, women and children feverishly
striving for the stakes—which often included even their
shirts. It was a place of sunshine, hospitality, ease, *siestas*,
serenades, *mañana* for work, general *dolce far niente*—and

a lotus-eater's life.[10] Here also was the southern extremity of the Bay of San Francisco, with an *embarcadero* to which Marsh hauled his hides and tallow and received in exchange goods from the Boston ships that anchored there.

Marsh considered every one a neighbor, in old California. Even white-haired McLaughlin, chief factor of the Hudson's Bay Company, was a neighbor in his estimation,[11] although he lived on the distant Columbia. But he had neighbors much nearer than that. In the Napa Valley was that western Enoch Arden,—Yunt; in the Sonoma, General Mariano Guadeloupe Vallejo, Commandante General of the California forces—a proud haughty Castilian, who was virtually ruler of the northern frontier, and in whose presence and before whose Gothic-towered *adobe*, the Californians bared the head and bent the knee in homage. Some thirty miles beyond Sonoma, at Fort Ross, near Bodega Bay, was a Russian peeress—the Baroness Alexandra Rotcheff—born Princess of Gagarin, who had eloped with the man of her choice to preside over the Eagles of the Czar on a wild bit of California coast. Here was an offshoot of the Russian-American Fur Company and a colony of half-breed Slavs who drank *vodka* and raised enough grain to feed the two cows belonging to Ivan Kuprianof, governor at Sitka.

1839 brought Marsh another neighbor, albeit a hundred miles distant, in John F. Sutter, a Swiss adventurer, whom he had known on the Missouri. Their relationship was not always cordial. The doctor twitted his old friend about money matters and some shady transactions on the Missouri, and Sutter retaliated by broadcasting the fact that Marsh was never known as a doctor in Missouri, and that in his opinion he was a fugitive from justice and a "quack."

CATTLE RANCHING, LOS MEGANOS

Marsh's nearest—and only—American neighbor was Robert Livermore, an old sailor, who lived some fifteen miles away, in a pass which still bears his name, leading to the *Mission San José*.[12]

For at least a part of each year Marsh had a brigade of the Hudson's Bay Company for neighbors. They entered the valley in the fall, coming from the Oregon country, and left in the spring, carrying off with them thousands of dollars' worth of pelts and furs.[13] They had little competition until Marsh appeared. The Mexican government could not prevent their coming, and after his arrival he cut into their trade by giving the thirsty trappers *aguardiente* in exchange for their furs. Michel La Framboise was then their leader, and he caused Marsh a good deal of trouble by buying mustangs that the Indians had stolen from his corrals. When this trade became so flagrant that he could no longer endure it, Marsh complained to Monterey, with the result that the authorities placed such a high duty on furs that it was no longer profitable for the Hudson's Bay Company to operate in California.

Except Livermore and the Hudson's Bay brigade, Marsh's only other neighbors were Spanish and Mexican families. The closest of these were the Mesas on *Los Medanos*, which adjoined *Los Meganos* along the river; Mirando Higueroa on the *Canada de los Vaqueros;* Salvio Pacheco on the *Monte del Diablo*, where Concord now stands, and Ygnacio Sebrian, destined to become his archenemy and eventual nemesis, on the *San Miguel* on Walnut Creek. All were then considered adjoining ranchos, but the *haciendas* were ten to fifteen miles distant from his *adobe*, so distant that he could not even see the smoke of their kitchen fires.

JOHN MARSH, PIONEER

It is hard to picture more solitary surroundings than these for a highly educated American, but perhaps it was just the place for a man who had not yet assimilated his disappointments nor adjusted his misanthropy.[14]

Although living at a distance from one another, his neighbors led contented and happy lives, congregating often to celebrate church days, bull-fights, *meriendas* and *fandangos*. They lived in the hospitable splendor of great, bare, earthen-floored red-tiled *adobes*, surrounded by flocks of children, dogs and cattle. The California *caballero* was a centaur—half man and half horse—and rode his mustang from the cradle to the grave. He rarely did anything that could not be accomplished with a lasso and on horseback. If he had a fence to pull up, he first threw his lasso about it, then started his horse in motion; if he had to haul hides from one part of the rancho to another, he threw a lasso about them and proceeded on his way; in capturing a bear, a runaway Indian, a refractory cow, a bandit, the lasso was in requisition, and a horse supplied the power. Years later, under tragic circumstances, Marsh was to be reminded of this custom.

Practically all the clever young Yankees who arrived in California during this period acquired cattle ranches by making advantageous alliances with the daughters of the Vallejos, Carrillos, Lugos, de la Guerras and Estudillos.

Once when the doctor needed cattle, one of his Yankee friends asked him why he didn't "marry some."

"Me, marry a Greaser!" said Marsh with a sneer. "When I marry, it will be to one of my own kind."

Long years afterward when that story was repeated in a crowded court-room at Martinez, it did not make much of an impression.

In the meantime the doctor took a squaw for a mistress.

CALIFORNIANS THROWING THE LASSO.
Mission San José in the distance.

CALIFORNIANS BRANDING CATTLE.
Courtesy of the University of California Extension Division, Department of Visual Instruction.

CATTLE RANCHING, LOS MEGANOS

She served his purposes, endeared him to the Indians and entailed no responsibilities on his part. That fact did not improve his standing among his neighbors. The Californians were very hospitable people; Marsh was not. He did not want visitors; he preferred to be left alone. They always had a bed they were willing to vacate, even for a stranger, but they never had one for Marsh. They called him a miser, and in care-free California that was a crime. They liked joy and happiness, laughter and music. They could not understand his brooding nature. He was too reserved. His sharp business methods were a constant source of irritation. Once, when he hauled some hides into a neighboring Spanish town, there was such a surprising lack of hospitality among the *rancheros* that he was forced to sleep under his cart.[15]

Even the Boston traders complained about him. They termed him a "sharper" and did not like to deal with him because he tried to beat them at their own game and was always postponing payment of what he owed them.

To one and all he was a man of mystery. They knew he had lived in Missouri, and it was commonly understood that he had graduated from the Harvard Medical School. Beyond that, his past was a blank. His career on the Mississippi, Marguerite and Charley were a closed book, at least as far as he was concerned. He never mentioned them. His silence was an offense. Gradually he came to stand apart. Some admired him, others feared him, and some avoided him. To all he was an enigma. However, Vallejo, Czar of the Californias, spoke of him in terms of the highest praise, commending his gratitude and his services as a physician, and only regretted that his taciturn manners, and a youthful disappointment, prevented him from becoming a general favorite.[16]

Marsh found a tribe of Indians—the Bolgones—on the

arroyo when he bought the rancho. They had been there from time immemorial. They were as hairy as Esau, with beards that would do honor to a Turk, and their eyes had a Chinese conformation, showing that some distant sire had been a shipwrecked Mongolian mariner.[17] They were a degraded type of red men. They made him homesick for the Sioux. He missed their proud and haughty bearing, especially when they played the moccasin game and accompanied it by singing precisely the same air as the tribes about Prairie du Chien.[18]

There were about thirty in this tribe when Marsh bought the rancho. They were wild and savage and bore an evil reputation, but they never molested the "Señor Doctor" as they called him, because on various occasions he had treated their Indian women who were suffering from various maladies which their medicine men did not know how to handle.[19] Many of them were sick with malaria, and the doctor wrought such marvellous cures with his quinine that he became almost superhuman in their estimation. So grateful were they, that in return they became his willing serfs, and he enjoyed a life among them not unlike that of a Southern plantation owner.

They helped him to build an *adobe* on the banks of the *arroyo*. It was just across from their village. Then they went to the *Mission San José* and brought him cuttings and helped him to lay out a vineyard. When the vines began to bear, they showed him how to distill *aguardiente*. They also helped him to lay out an orchard of pears, figs, almonds and olives, likewise obtained from the old mission, and they furrowed an enormous field with an iron-shod plough and helped him to plant it in wheat,—the first cereal cultivated within the confines of Contra Costa County.[20] Then the doctor brought some traps from the

CATTLE RANCHING, LOS MEGANOS

Hudson's Bay Company and taught these Indians how to trap for bear and otter. The furs they brought him launched him in the California fur trade. All the doctor gave them in return for this service was a part of their food, some beeves and *frejoles* and a few clothes to cover their loins, but he was kind to them—very kind. They loved him, and he found greater happiness among them than he had known since he left Prairie du Chien.

His *adobe* was a crude affair, of sun-baked walls and thatched roof. Within were four large rooms and an attic.[21] The latter was large enough to accommodate two of his *vaqueros*, who always slept there and acted as his personal bodyguard. He, who had faced the fierce Sauk and Fox and the terrors of the Santa Fé trail, now had a bodyguard! The walls, underneath the eaves, were perforated by loopholes large enough to admit the muzzle of a gun. Through these the doctor and his *vaqueros* often drove away robbers and horse thieves. Thus, in the midst of wild mustangs and degenerate Indians, emerged the first fort in the valley, as well as the first centre of civilization.

One room of the *adobe* had a fireplace, an unusual thing in a climate where all the cooking was done out-of-doors. Marsh, however, used it for other purposes. By the light of blazing pine-knots he lay on the well-beaten floor and reflected and often read all night,—read everything that came to hand, medicine, agriculture, old newspapers and, sometimes in his hunger for matter to peruse, he re-read his Greek and Latin books until he knew long passages by heart. What thoughts assailed him there? Did visions of Marguerite, with his son in her arms, invade his solitude? Or did the Sioux with their bloody trophies file stealthily by?

In another room, on a shelf that ran part way around

JOHN MARSH, PIONEER

the wall, were the books he had brought with him and those he had acquired from sailing ships and men-of-war, chief among which were his Bibles—English, French, and Spanish—stepping-stones to the last-named language, the "Odes of Anacreon," the inevitable Paine's "Works in Verse and Prose," and Johnson's "Lives of the English Poets." Other books found a place on the shelf: a medical book which he had bought from one of the Boston ships, a book on horticulture and several written in Greek and Spanish.

His furniture was meager, a table or two, some benches and a bed,[22] the latter unlike those of his Spanish neighbors—a rude pallet with a hide, stretched across a wooden framework. In one corner was a Chinese camphor-wood chest,—his holy of holies. In it were hidden his deeds to *Los Meganos*, his Phillips-Andover certificate and his Harvard diploma.

Across the entrance to his *adobe*, facing the mountain and an oak grove, was a portico roofed with tules but, like the house proper, floorless. On either side of the door were rude benches, their backs against the wall. Here Marsh used to sit in the long summer twilights that distinguished the San Joaquin Valley, smoking his pipe and drinking his *aguardiente*, and listening to the night-birds and the coyotes. Here he could think of Charley, of Prairie du Chien, or of Danvers. He had written home but once since Marguerite died. He had cut himself off completely, even from his old mother. But through Henry Mellus, of the Boston firm of Bryant and Sturgis, who bought his hides and pelts and supplied him with clothes, his aged parents learned of his whereabouts in California and sent him long, pathetic letters, imploring him to answer. Once his brother Caleb, who had married a sister of the great London banker George Peabody, wrote:

CATTLE RANCHING, LOS MEGANOS

"Could you realize how our dear, old mother yearns after her first-born, even as Jacob of old after his lost and beloved son, you would again return to the arms that first embraced you. Do, my dear brother, gratify your aged mother in particular with a sight of her well-beloved son once more before she dies. At least let her hear from you, should the world frown upon you, should fortune be capricious, here in that loved retreat will always be a shelter, here will hearts always beat in unison with your own."[23]

But he never told them how the world had frowned upon him, or that his past was wormwood.

Whatever may have been his reactions to these letters from home, he did not let his aged mother know that she had a grandson named Charles. His family were still in ignorance of the existence of this youth, but the tenor of those home letters aggravated the yearning he felt to see his motherless boy in Illinois. One night he wrote him, and the next time he was in Monterey he sent money, through a Boston trader, to be forwarded to "Uncle Jimmie." At that time a letter from California had to travel a long way. It had first to go around the horn to Boston, then to be forwarded by a precarious route to the frontier. Charley never received his father's letter or learned that his father had yearned to see him.

Great changes had taken place in Illinois since the doctor left. In 1839 Sangamon County was divided, and the part where "Uncle Jimmie" lived became Menard County. By that time John Marsh was almost forgotten on that frontier. Few of the late comers had ever heard of him, and Charles had given him up for lost and was better known by the name of Pantier than by his own.

CHAPTER XXXI

THE DOCTOR AND THE HORSE THIEVES
1838–1840

AFTER paying Noriega $500 for his rancho, all the money Marsh had saved in Los Angeles was gone. He had an enormous rancho on his hands,[1] fine meadows, ranges and water-courses for grazing—but no cattle. In order to obtain them, he resumed the practice of medicine and surgery. But diseases were not very prevalent in the San Joaquin Valley, and none could be attributed to the influence of the climate. Fever and ague were frequent,[2] but the most common complaint was due to "the knife," having reference to the treachery of the Spaniards, who settled all their differences with the avenging stiletto.[3]

Aided by the knife, chills and fever, smallpox and childbearing, Marsh managed to get a start.[4] He became the first physician in the San Joaquin Valley and remained the only one for many years. His medical fees were paid in cattle, and he demanded big pay for his services.

The cattle ranches were widely separated, and to visit them, Marsh was compelled to travel long distances on horseback—a fact that presently won him distinction among both Indians and Californians.[5] In a short time he gained a reputation as a great physician—the Indians especially having untold faith in his ministrations. Many a poor settler's wife had his aid as she went through "the valley of the shadow," and to many an ailing child he brought comfort and relief.[6]

After General Sutter established his New Helvetia, he

THE DOCTOR AND THE HORSE THIEVES

sent Marsh all the cases he could not himself handle at the fort. The general had a medical book, the directions of which he followed implicitly, and with its help he treated all kinds of diseases; occasionally, however, he encountered one beyond his powers. Such patients he dispatched to Marsh by canoe or mule-litter, and the doctor kept them on his rancho until improvement set in, or until they were cured.[7] All the trappers or hunters in the mountains who were ill or hurt made for Marsh's rancho for treatment.[8] Thus, his *adobe* became a hospital for the whole region. But his practice was by no means confined to his immediate precincts or to the great valley where he lived. His fame as a *medico* spread far beyond, and he was often called to distant points and exacted his fees in cattle. This time cattle were exactly what he wanted.

On one occasion he was called on a consultation and, after examining the patient, prescribed two doses of salts. The result was satisfactory, and the doctor rendered a bill for twenty-five dollars, payable in cattle. On another occasion he was hastily summoned to a woman in labor. She was desperately ill and could not have survived without immediate relief. It was a long journey, and Marsh refused to go unless the husband promised to pay him fifty cows.[9] The terms were accepted, the journey performed, the child delivered, and the grateful father paid him his bill.

Presently cattle bearing the doctor's brand on ear and rump began to make their appearance on the ranges of *Los Meganos*. As the years went by, and his fame increased, and he was forced to make longer and longer journeys to visit the sick, his herds likewise multiplied. When the child of Larkin, United States Consul at Monterey, came down with the smallpox, he went to Monterey,

JOHN MARSH, PIONEER

ninety miles away, to visit her. The child was very ill, but recovered, although she was fearfully pocked.

Once he was called to San José to see Señora Sunol—wife of the *alcalde*. "My wife is very ill," wrote Antonio, her husband. "According to the books, the symptoms which one may recognize seem to be either of dropsy or anasarca. I wish you would be so kind as to come and make her a visit. Come to San José and take horses, as the case is quite urgent. Bring some remedies with you, if you can, as none can be found here."[10]

DOCTOR MARSH'S CATTLE-BRAND
From the records of brands recorded in the County Recorder's Office, Martinez, Contra Costa County, California.
By courtesy of G. T. Barkely, Esq.

For covering such a distance, the doctor charged two or three hundred head of cattle.[11] The greater the distance, the more cows he exacted, but it was generally agreed that he brought comfort and relief to the households he visited. His reputation spread. Cows or no cows, his services were in demand.

Once, Vicente Martinez, who lived at Merced, some ninety miles in the interior, summoned him post haste. "I will pay you whatever you wish, my friend, but come soon," he wrote. Then the distracted husband went on to say that the Señora Guadelupe, his wife, was in labor, that in giving birth to twins, she had been able to bring only one into the world; that twenty-four hours had elapsed and she was suffering intensely, and the second was yet unborn; that he feared it was obstructed; that his midwife, Egisiaca, could not come, and the half-crazed husband implored the doctor to hurry and end Guadelupe's suffering.

THE DOCTOR AND THE HORSE THIEVES

"Hasten! Nothing else is of importance," he concluded.[12] We can imagine the doctor throwing a *serape* over his shoulders, seizing his saddlebag, mounting his swiftest mustang, plunging through the night over unbroken roads to the next rancho, where a change of mustangs was in readiness, and so on down the valley to the distant *adobe* at Merced. But he arrived too late. The Señora was dead.

Again, he was summoned across the bay to Sonoma, to visit one of the Vallejos—possibly the General himself. He was admonished to be at San Leandro, at one o'clock the next afternoon, where he would find a boat in readiness to embark. His brother was very ill, wrote José de Jesus Vallejo of San José, and he begged the doctor to cross the bay with him so that "you may see whether any medicines you can give him will benefit him. . . . Grant me this favor for the sake of humanity," he begged, "and I promise to make good any loss that it may occasion you in your business."[13]

No physician would envy the doctor a trip across San Francisco Bay in an open boat in the foggy month of July, but he went.

Sometimes he encountered medical problems that would have worried a specialist, let alone a general practitioner. Once he was called to see a case of amaurosis—partial or total loss of vision—and was perplexed as to its handling, for he had nothing to read on eye conditions, and had no medicines to treat them. But, hearing that the United States man-of-war, *St. Louis*, with Surgeon B. R. Tinslar on board, was in the harbor at Monterey, he dispatched a note to him, asking for literature on the subject, his opinion, and enough strychnine to handle it.[14] Tinslar's reply must have been a disappointment. "It is difficult to venture an opinion on a case without seeing the subject," he wrote. As for medical books and drugs, he had given his Thatcher as well as all his strychnine to Mr. James Stokes of Monterey.[15]

Like all doctors, Marsh's efforts were not always appreciated. Once he was called a long distance to visit a child suffering from headache. As usual, he went on horseback and on arrival examined the youngster and administered two or three doses of a medicine he carried with him. The child was soon relieved and after a day or two was well, much to the joy of the parents. But when the doctor presented a bill for fifty cows, that was quite another story, and the family was astonished at the size of the fee. They were not wealthy people; they were, in fact, comparatively poor as riches were then computed in California; and, as their herd consisted of only 150 cows, they demurred at parting with a third of them. Marsh, however, was obstinate, pointing out that he had travelled a long distance to see their child, that he had been absent from his rancho for several days, that their youngster was cured, and that he felt he was entitled to the fee.

Still the family was not satisfied, and they cudgelled their brains for means of avoiding payment. Finally they accepted his demands, but, as the doctor had had two shirts washed while stopping there, the mother of the patient decided to charge him twenty-five cows for doing his laundry. Grumbling and dissatisfied, the doctor rounded up his twenty-five cows and departed for the San Joaquin, driving his diminished fee before him.[16]

One day in the fall of the year 1838, Marsh was called to the Pueblo of San José, and left his *adobe* and rancho in the care of his two steady and trustworthy Indians. On his return, before he reached his house, he met his two

THE DOCTOR AND THE HORSE THIEVES

vaqueros flying from the place. They were in great distress and informed him that a band of thieves had entered his *adobe*, broken up his chest, rifled it and lassoed and driven off most of his horses.

On reaching home, Marsh found from the appearance of his *adobe* that the reports were not exaggerated. The camphor-wood chest—the repository of his sacred treasures—was broken open and pilfered. His deeds to *Los Meganos*, his Phillips-Andover certificate, his Harvard diploma, his license to practice medicine and surgery in California, and all his other documents were stolen or destroyed. Scattered on the floor was a pile of torn papers so defaced as to be utterly worthless. In his despair, he tried to put them together, but the pieces were in such a condition that he could not make head or tail of them.

In a towering rage, he mounted his mustang, found the trail of the robbers and followed it until he came to a spring of water, eight miles from his place, where they had encamped for the night. But he had arrived too late. In the mud, trampled under the horses' hoofs, he picked up pieces of his Harvard degree, his license, and, most important of all, his deeds to *Los Meganos*, all intermixed in one unintelligible mass.[17]

He vowed he would chastise the thieves, and with this in view, joined an expedition to punish the outlaws. Mounted on mustangs and armed with rifles, they rode toward the Sierras, located the thieves' lair and attacked it. The Indians were completely overwhelmed, eleven were killed and 500 horses were recovered, many of which bore Marsh's brand. Thus was the loss of his Harvard diploma, that had already caused so much grief, avenged.[18]

Marsh's part in this feat won the Californians' eternal gratitude and pleased Vallejo so much that he reported his

JOHN MARSH, PIONEER

action to Governor Alvarado, calling his attention to the fact that it was to the interest of the government to cement cordial relations between such men and the natives. His Excellency agreed, and he publicly manifested his gratitude to Marsh.[19]

CHAPTER XXXII

TREACHERY. THE GRAHAM AFFAIR
1840

THE longer he remained in California the greater became Marsh's desire to see his rancho American soil. Then and then only would his possessions be safe. Ever since his arrival at *Los Meganos* he had been working toward that end. Russia, England and France were already on the field and contenders for the prize. Many within and without California were for an English protectorate. Rumor had it that the natives had already asked protection of the Russians at Bodega, and even France was flirting with the possibility of ownership. Marsh realized he must work fast.

His plan was a subtle one. Opposed to filibusterism in all its forms, he wanted to create among Californians an overpowering sentiment for the United States, and he felt that the best way to go about this was to encourage emigration and thus create, in peacefully cultivated farms and communities occupied by his countrymen, an overwhelming enthusiasm for American domination.[1] In this way, he argued, the history of Texas would be repeated. For months he had been writing to his old neighbors in Missouri, to Baldridge, Owens, Nye and others, giving them glowing accounts of California, of its climate, crops, fruit-trees, vineyards, commerce, of the ease and joy of its life. He urged them to migrate, the more the merrier, the quicker the better, telling them that cattle were numerous and cheap, that land was plentiful, easy to acquire and to cultivate.

JOHN MARSH, PIONEER

With his mind full of these schemes, one April day, he rode to the *Mission San José* to transact some ordinary business. On arrival there, much to his surprise, he was seized, informed that he was a prisoner;[2] that he was accused of plotting with the Americans to seize California; and that he and they were to be deported to Mexico. He was flabbergasted. Thoughts of his letters to Missouri flashed through his brain, and he feared that they had been seized en route, opened and read. But he held counsel and permitted himself to be cast in the mission's loathsome dungeon, a spot reserved for refractory neophytes. After two days' detention, he was shackled, thrown on a horse and suffered the indignity of having his legs bound together beneath the horse's belly. In this position he was taken to Monterey, in company with two Frenchmen and two Englishmen, and thrown into jail.

Here he found his compatriots in dire straits. All, to the number of a hundred or more, were jammed into a cell eighteen by thirty feet. So closely were they packed together that one had to stand while another slept. The room had no flooring, and the dirt was damp and so muddy that at every shift of position they sank in the oozing mire over their shoe-tops. For ventilation, there was only one closely barred window, and the air was so vile that they took turns at the opening. By the time Marsh arrived the others had been in jail several days. Most of the time they had been without food and drink. In the serving of that, they were forced to submit to every indignity. Once they found the breechclout of the Indian cook in the soup and had the choice of drinking it or going hungry.

Marsh found Graham, the old Tennesseean who had made Alvarado governor, in a pitiable condition. He was cut, bruised and heavily ironed, and had been so severely

TREACHERY. THE GRAHAM AFFAIR

beaten that his spirit was broken by the insults heaped upon him.[3]

It seemed that recently an American, Ambrose G. Tomlinson, better known as "Tom, the Trapper" among the hunting fraternity, had been desperately sick, and it was thought that he was dying.[4] Having recently become a Catholic to marry one Jesus Bernal, his friends sent for a priest so that he might make his final peace with God. Padre Suarez del Real of San Carlos, a dissolute priest, was summoned. The dying man confessed that the Americans were brewing a revolution to overthrow Alvarado and deliver the province to their country, and he denounced Captain Isaac Graham as the arch-conspirator.

Knowledge of the confession and the supposed plot reached the ears of Governor Alvarado, and he was consumed with fear that the power that had made him would likewise destroy him. He was sick and tired of the Americans, anyway. They were omnipresent; they felt that they owned him. When he met them on the street, instead of taking off their hats and saying "Your Excellency," they clapped him on the back and with easy familiarity called him "Bautiste."[5]

Once Graham told him to his face that, had it not been for him, he would never have been governor. It was insufferable. He was weary of such liberties. Because he wanted to be rid of the Americans, he chose to believe that prompt action was necessary. He connived with José Castro, a villain with a lean body and uneasy eyes, to raise a force and arrest all foreigners, from Monterey to San Francisco,[6] and especially Graham. Plans were secretly made for concerted action.

The authorities throughout the province were explicitly

JOHN MARSH, PIONEER

ordered to secure and imprison all Americans and other foreigners on the same day. Many were captured while they slept.

Graham put up such a fight that he was cut and bruised from head to toe. Worst of all, his self-respect was gone. Over and over he looked at his fettered limbs and muttered that he could never be a man again. His pride was crushed.

In this condition Marsh found the old Tennesseean. With him he found many of the men upon whom he had counted to Americanize California, all prisoners and all about to be deported.

It was shameful. Marsh was utterly discouraged. This then was to be the end of him and his plans,—yet, not if he could prevent it. He was a glib talker when occasion demanded. After a few days' incarceration, he talked himself out of jail, but only on parole; he was forbidden to leave the capital.

Before he left, he promised his countrymen to do what he could for them. But liberty proved he was powerless. Their sufferings angered him the more. Nowhere could he escape their cries. Hour after hour he heard their piteous appeals. He could not rest or sleep. All night long, between the breaking surges on the rocks of Puntos Pinos, he could hear their complaints:

"Breathe fast, for God's sake! I must come to the grate soon, or I shall suffocate. Give me water, you merciless devils; give me air, you infernal sons of the Inquisition, or take me out and fire on me."

He soon learned that more than half were too exhausted to speak, some were half-mad, and others in a stupor.[7] He had to listen, but could do nothing. The time of deportation approached.

After thirteen days of torment, Marsh saw his country-

ISAAC GRAHAM.
Courtesy of the California State Library, at Sacramento.

TREACHERY. THE GRAHAM AFFAIR

men marched to the shore, like criminals, between two files of soldiers.[8] Their irons had been taken off to enable them to walk. To this order, Graham and another American were the only exceptions. They were considered too dangerous to be granted any freedom and were carried on the shoulders of Indians, with their chains and fetters still hanging on them.[9]

In their wake, walked three native California women, wives of those about to be deported. With tears and supplications, they implored the guards to release the fathers of their children; but the jailers were deaf to their pleadings and beat them back with their swords. In spite of this rough treatment, they clung desperately to their mates and lifted the chains that were galling their bleeding limbs.[10] At the shore the women were held back, while their men were thrown into boats and rowed to the bark, *Joven Guipuzcoana*—"Maid of Guipuzcoa"—bound for San Blas. As she sailed out of the harbor, the women sank to their knees upon the sand, crying despairingly, "O Mary, Mother of God, pray for us."[11]

This achievement on the beach was followed by a public *Te Deum* on the *plaza*, when thanks were offered up to the Omnipresent Power for saving California from the Americans. Padre Real, in full pontifical robes, performed the high mass, standing near the door of the Governor's dwelling where his *Excellentissimo* could be seen kneeling before the altar, devoutly responding to the prayers for repentance.[12]

The brutal treatment accorded him stirred Marsh to the depths. Never afterwards could he dwell upon his sufferings undisturbed. The mere thought of that time infuriated him. "It may well be believed that feelings were excited," he wrote, "ay, deep and burning feelings, that will not soon be forgotten by the witnesses nor the victims of those horrible acts of injustice and cruelty."[13]

When he returned to the rancho, he filed a complaint at Washington, asking protection for Americans. "The French and English protect their subjects," he wrote, "and are consequently more respected, while our consul at Tepic and the American Minister in Mexico are absolute ciphers. Our government thinks we are better able to take care of ourselves than the people of any other nation, and I am disposed to think there is some truth in the opinion. Be this as it may," he concluded cryptically, "in a year or two more we shall at least be able to protect ourselves in California."[14]

CHAPTER XXXIII

INAUGURATES CALIFORNIA IMMIGRATION

1841

THIS bitter experience only increased Marsh's desire to see California in the Federal Union. He wrote more letters to Missouri, urging his countrymen to come with all speed to California. California's ownership, he declared, was not to be determined by diplomats or explorers, or "manifest destiny," but by settlers in actual possession of the soil. Feverishly he played the Texas game and dispatched his letters by every caravan going east on the Santa Fé Trail.

He thus inaugurated a movement which of itself, under normal conditions, would have led to the acquisition of the province by the United States in the course of a few years without the firing of a gun. Up to that time no one had ever come directly overland to California. But from his knowledge of Bonneville's experiences, Jedediah Smith's, Ogden's and Walker's travels, Marsh had a good idea of the country lying between the Missouri and the Sierras, and he figured out a route which, he said, was direct, with good pasturage and water all the way.[1] He sent copies of this route to Baldridge, Owens and Michael Nye, in Independence, urging them to follow it over the Rockies and Sierras to California, and to come direct to his rancho, where he would take care of them.

When they left Missouri, he directed them to follow the Oregon trail westward to Fort Hall; from there he told

JOHN MARSH, PIONEER

them to locate the Portneuf River, a branch of the Snake in the Upper Shoshone. This stream they were to follow in a southwesterly direction. When they reached the desert, he warned them above everything else to locate Mary's River, a stream that flowed northwesterly, then southwesterly until it disappeared in a lake—also called Mary's—but which had no outlet. From there they were to pursue a southwesterly course to the Snowy Mountains (the Sierras), and pass through a gap where they would find a river flowing to the south. That river, he wrote, emptied into the San Joaquin, and if they followed it, it would bring them into a wide valley of the same name. Sixty miles from the point where that stream emptied into a great bay, they would find his rancho.[2] Among other details he gave them the latitude of San Francisco Bay,[3] and he instructed them explicitly, when inquiring of the Indians for the San Joaquin River to pronounce it as if it were spelled San "Waukeen."[4]

On their arrival in Jackson County, Missouri, these letters caused a great commotion. They were read and re-read wherever men congregated, handed around and published in the village newspapers, from which they were copied by the press up and down the frontier, and set in motion a train of circumstances which were the immediate[5] causes of the first migration to California.[6] In so far as the destiny of the province was concerned, this migration proved to be the trump card. In addition to outlining a route, Marsh's letters contained a glowing description of California, of the climate and its resources, and awakened in Baldridge, and all who received them, a great desire to see the country. Baldridge was so taken with the California idea that he imparted some of his enthusiasm to Colonel J. B. Chiles when the latter returned from the Florida

INAUGURATES CALIFORNIA IMMIGRATION

wars. Together they perfected their plans, called meetings, and formed a company which included John Bartleson, Michael Nye, Charles Hopper, Robert Hickman and others.

Probably the first public meeting was held February 1 at Independence. Fifty-eight then agreed to make the trip to California[7] and unanimously adopted "Marsh's route," as the best by which to cross the Sierras.[8] It was further recommended that all individuals and companies designing to emigrate to California rendezvous at Sapling Grove on the old Sante Fé Trail, on the 10th of the ensuing May. An account of this meeting and its resolutions was copied in papers as far east as New York,[9] with copious editorial comment stating that the object of the migration was to wrest California from Mexico. Excerpts from these statements reached Mexico City long before the Missourians left the Platte, involving them and their sponsor in endless difficulties.

At the last moment, after all plans had been formulated, Baldridge, who was a wheelwright by trade, was detained by some mill contracts,[10] and the project was completed under the direction of Bartleson and Hickman.[11]

In the meantime, Robidaux, a returned California trapper, was rousing the inhabitants of Platte County, Mo., to a similar high pitch of enthusiasm, representing California as a land free of chills and fever, of boundless fertility, perpetual paradise, and perennial spring, whose hillsides were dotted with herds of cattle and wild horses, and in whose valleys oranges and lemons and other semi-tropical fruits bloomed and ripened.

As a result of these stories of Robidaux and the more concrete evidence of Marsh's letters, the Western Emigration Society came into being, and a pledge was drawn up,

JOHN MARSH, PIONEER

to which 500 names were appended, binding the signers to convert their property into emigrant outfits and to meet the Jackson County enthusiasts at the Sapling Grove meeting-place the following day.

When spring arrived the enthusiasm of the would-be emigrants had cooled. Many doubts had arisen,[12] and more particularly, news of the Graham affair had chilled their ardor. As May approached, it was evident that Bartleson could muster only nine of the ninety who had signed at Independence, while one only, John Bidwell, remained of the 500 enthusiasts in Platte County.

These, however, congregated at Sapling Grove and were subsequently joined by others from other localities, so that when the day of departure approached there were some sixty-nine men, women and children anxious to go. Paul Geddes, alias Talbot H. Green, was elected president, John Bidwell, secretary, and John Bartleson, captain. The latter was elected, not as a matter of choice, but of necessity. He and his Jackson County contingency absolutely refused to budge unless he should be made captain, and they had their way, for the others could not afford to give him up, he being in possession of Marsh's letter giving the route.

On May 19, 1841, these "Pilgrims of the Pacific" left Sapling Grove and turned their eager eyes toward California, with no other guide than that letter[13] and with Marsh's rancho as their destination.

At almost exactly the same time that Captain Bartleson began his historic march, news of the expedition reached Mexico City, and General Almonte, Mexican Minister of War, incensed over reports of American annexation, wrote to General Vallejo, ordering him to forbid these immigrants from entering or remaining in the country without

INAUGURATES CALIFORNIA IMMIGRATION

legal passports,[14] and directing him to ascertain what Doctor Marsh meant by inviting such a horde to California.

The emigrants reached the Rockies over the trail Marsh had followed ten years before—up the Platte and its north fork to Fort Laramie, thence by the Sweetwater and through the South Pass to the Great Salt Lake and Bear River Valley.

It was late in August when they reached Soda Springs and Father de Smet and thirty-two of their party left them. Then began the search for Mary's River. Marsh had written that they would be lost if they did not find it. It was well into September before it was located. By then they were almost exhausted, but, choked by the alkali, blinded by the sun's glare and betrayed by the pitiless mirage, they pushed on. It was October when they crossed the Carson and reached the Walker. The latter flowed toward the south, and, because of its direction, they believed they were on the San Joaquin, in accordance with Marsh's letter.[15] But they were doomed to disappointment; the Sierras loomed ahead. It was the middle of October when they began the ascent, and the 18th before they reached the summit and found it deep with snow. They were horrified. Wind roared through the giant trees. Darkness and solitude yawned on every side.[16] They were discouraged. Only the thought of the welcome at Marsh's rancho and the promise of vineyards and plenty sustained them. Then they found a river. It certainly flowed toward the south. It must be the one Marsh had designated, they argued. They decided to follow it; it brought them out into a great valley which was scarred and charred as if by fire. This could not be California. They were looking for scenes of perennial spring, groves of oranges and fields of ripening grain. They stumbled on.

JOHN MARSH, PIONEER

A few days later one of their party met an Indian. He evidently knew Doctor Marsh. He kept repeating "Marsh, —Marsh," and offered to guide them to his rancho. They followed.[17]

CHAPTER XXXIV

FIRST EMIGRANTS ARRIVE AT MARSH'S RANCHO
1841

Two days later, November 4, the emigrants crossed a ford on the San Joaquin River and reached Marsh's rancho at the foot of Mount Diablo. The doctor was delighted to see them. Elias Barnett and Michael Nye brought him letters from his Missouri friends, William Hague,[1] a Santa Fé trader, and Barnett of the firm of Barnett and Sheafe, asking him to write a full description of the country, its soil, climate, timber, water, productions of the province, etc., commercial and mercantile and manufacturing advantages, its population, health and government—promising him that if they could get the assurance they desired, they could bring out 200 to 400 families within three years.

The emigrants were all greatly disappointed in California. It did not look at all as they had pictured it. The great valley was parched and exhausted. Look where they would, there were no signs of perennial spring or of autumnal harvest. They had reached the land of prodigality and paradise, only to find the country in the pangs of thirst—the greatest drought in its history, they were told. There had been no rain for eighteen months; the wheat crop had failed; there was no bread in the country, and everybody was living on meat and *aguardiente!* They were all disillusioned. Reality was entirely different from anticipation. They were but tolerably well pleased with the doctor. They were disappointed with his forlorn es-

JOHN MARSH, PIONEER

tate, his crude *adobe* thatched with tules, his floorless rooms with their meagre furnishings, and they found a squaw presiding over his premises.[2] In the grove of oaks that grew around his *adobe* there was not one tall enough to make a railcut.[3]

On his part, Marsh was delighted with their advent and was very communicative and enthusiastic. Some of the party had known him in Missouri, others knew his acquaintances in Independence. All had a great deal to say.[4] Although his *adobe* was small, he found quarters there for the Kelseys and for Bartleson, Hopper and Chiles. He did not have beds enough, but he provided cowhide to spread upon the floors and others for covering.[5] The rest of the party pitched their tents near by under the oaks and starry sky. That night the doctor killed two shoats, corn-brew flowed freely, and later he opened a barrel of mellow *aguardiente*. He gave the company so much to eat and drink that they became more grateful and began to feel more hopeful about California. The fat pork was especially tempting after having starved on the lean meat of their thin mules. Nor was Marsh yet satisfied; he set his Indian cook grinding wheat and making *tortillas*, and when these were baked, he brought them out to the men under the trees, giving one to each of the party. They were very grateful when they learned he had used his seed wheat, for he had no other.

That night they talked late around their campfire. The doctor was anxious to hear of their trip across the plains, and they were anxious to hear about California and their prospects in the province. The doctor waxed eloquent. He proved a most voluble companion and spared no pains in giving them details. The Missourians listened, open-mouthed. Bidwell was charmed and said he had never lis-

FIRST EMIGRANTS ARRIVE

tened to so clever a linguist or to a man with a better command of English or a wider fund of knowledge.[6] They were all spellbound. They wanted to make him some presents to express their appreciation. But they had no money and, having thrown away everything portable, were almost destitute. Nevertheless, they dug out their few remaining treasures. One gave the doctor cartridges; another, a pound of lead; another, a can of powder; another handed over his butcher knife, and still another surrendered his gun. One even presented a serviceable set of surgical instruments. Marsh was well pleased with their gifts and said that a gun in California was better than money.

Then, picking up his gifts, the doctor bade the weary company good-night. He invited them to help themselves to a beef for breakfast, and indicated the spotted herds that grazed on the nearby plain. He then disappeared behind the walls of his *adobe*, well pleased with the outcome of the letters he had written to Missouri and with his future plans for the destiny of California.

The next morning he was up betimes, but he presently discovered, to his horror, that the Missourians had not only helped themselves to a fine fat steer, but had also slaughtered his best work-oxen.[7] Even though this was probably done by mistake, the doctor's anger was aroused, and he was particularly bitter toward Bidwell. Not realizing what they had done, Bidwell hailed the doctor cheerily. He wished to continue the delightful conversation of the night before and to learn something about Yerba Buena. He approached Marsh, asking him what business was carried on there, and what were the prospects for work. But the doctor was in no humor for conversation. He replied brusquely that the chief occupation was "charging up and down the hills and getting drunk," and he ended the conversation by remarking that his guests had already cost him over one hundred dollars, and that God knew whether he would ever get a *real* in return.

Bidwell reported Marsh's behavior to the others and found that some had already been snubbed in a similar manner. They held a consultation, and all agreed that they would leave as quickly as they could. Some of them left to hunt otter on the San Joaquin, Bidwell remained behind to guard the packs, but the majority went to the Pueblo of San José to obtain passports for all.[8] Before they departed, Marsh promised to write and ask Governor Alvarado to meet them at San José.[9]

Accordingly, on November 5, the doctor wrote Antonio Sunol, sub-prefect of San José, notifying him that thirty-one men and a woman and child from the state of Missouri had arrived at his rancho with the intention of settling in California. He enclosed a complete list of the party, and signed himself with many flourishes, a rubric, and all the grandiloquence of a Spanish grandee—"your servant, John Marsh, who kisses your hands."[10]

The Missourians then started for the Pueblo of San José. When they reached the spot where Coyote Creek crosses the road, three miles from the town, they were met by a party of soldiers under an officer, and were placed under arrest. They were told that a report had preceded them, stating that a large party of Americans had entered the country from the east who were going to start a revolution and take possession of the country.[11]

Fortunately, General Vallejo happened to be at the *Mission San José*.[12] Otherwise, in accordance with orders received from Mexico, they would immediately have been driven back into the Sierras, but he had mercy on them and had them brought before him and demanded an ex-

FIRST EMIGRANTS ARRIVE

planation of their presence in California.[13] One of the men said that they had been invited and urged to come, and to prove his statement produced Marsh's letter. On reading this, the general was very angry. He ordered a horse to be brought and dispatched Nye with a peremptory order for Marsh to present himself "with the greatest possible promptness" before the Commandante-General at the *Mission San José*, and to explain his conduct in inviting such immigration into the country and also to declare their intentions.[14]

Nye travelled rapidly. He was gone a day and a night and returned with Doctor Marsh, and they went together to the general. Marsh could hardly expose his real motives in inviting the Missourians to California and explained the migration as one actuated by peaceable intentions. But the commandante had been warned not to accept this explanation—the original Texas immigrants had used a similar one.[15] Whatever his feelings, Vallejo decided that the only prudent course was to agree to what he had not the force to prevent. Taking Marsh's explanation for what it was worth, he promised to grant the Americans passports, providing the doctor would sign a bond as security for the good behavior of the men he had invited to the province. Marsh demurred at this,[16] but when he heard the Missourians plotting to fight their way out of the calaboose, he determined the only logical thing he could do was to execute a bond.[17] It began: "I, the undersigned doctor of medicine and proprietary citizen settled in this jurisdiction declare: That I constitute myself [etc.] surety for 15 individuals of the expedition from Missouri."[18] Thereafter followed their names. The passports were signed and handed over to Marsh; no charge was made; he started back to his rancho.[19]

JOHN MARSH, PIONEER

Altogether he had been gone three days. Meanwhile the men on the San Joaquin had been called in to await results. They were gathered about the door of his *adobe*, and he said ominously to them: "Now, men, I want you all to come into the house, and I will tell you your fate."[20] They entered, and Marsh announced: "You men that have five dollars can have passports and remain in the country and go where you please." Five dollars! Not one had five dollars! Nine-tenths of them had not a cent! Marsh began telling off the names and as each man's was called, he stepped up, received a passport and settled by giving the equivalent in something. Those unable to produce money or property contributed what they could and gave notes for the balance. Finally, all the names had been called but Bidwell's. Apparently there was no passport for him.[21] Bidwell demanded: "Doctor, have you no passport for me?" Marsh replied, "No, you don't need any," to which Bidwell retorted: "Why? Am I not a man? Don't I look like other people?"[22]

The next morning, although it was raining hard, Bidwell mounted a jaded horse and rode to the *Mission San José* and obtained his passport.

"How much is it?" said Bidwell on departing.

"It costs nothing," replied the prefect.

Bidwell was furious when he recalled that the doctor had charged the others five dollars for theirs. Thoroughly incensed he returned to Marsh's rancho to collect his belongings and depart. Wet, tired and hungry, he arrived and told the doctor he would like to spend the night, for he intended to start for Sutter's Fort the next day. Marsh received him coldly and threw him a piece of dried beef to roast before the campfire, saying his cook was ill. While Bidwell was cooking this meagre meal in the coals, Marsh's

FIRST EMIGRANTS ARRIVE

cook passed, carrying the doctor's supper, which consisted of antelope meat, beans and *tortillas*. Thereupon Bidwell wrote to his friends in Missouri to beware of Marsh; that he was the meanest man in California.[23]

On April 3, 1842, Marsh wrote his parents at Danvers: "A company of about thirty of my old neighbors in Missouri arrived here the first of November last, and some of them are about returning and are the bearers of this. They arrived here directly at my house with no other guide but a letter of mine. From all the numerous letters I have received from various parts of the United States I am satisfied that an immense emigration will soon swarm to this country. I am now fully satisfied that the Anglo-Saxon race of men who inhabit the United States are destined very shortly to occupy this delightful country. A young woman with a little child in her arms came in the company last fall and was about a month in my house. After this, the men ought to be ashamed to think of the difficulties. It is an object I much desire and have long labored for, to have this country inhabited by Americans. It will now soon be realized."[24]

CHAPTER XXXV

BETRAYS MICHELTORENA
1841-1845

THUS Marsh ushered in the period of organized emigration to California. After 1841, Americans arrived thick and fast. Practically all of them, because they were familiar with his Missouri letters, went direct to *Los Meganos*. He was happy. Soon, now, he argued, his rancho would be American soil. Then the worry over its future and his future would be over. He could settle down to a life of ease. *Mañana* at last!

One spring day, Frémont and Kit Carson appeared at Marsh's rancho. They were wearing the Scotch caps of the Hudson's Bay Company. Marsh took them for members of a brigade until they explained who they were. They were going back to Missouri they said; they were in a hurry. The Mexicans were in pursuit, but Marsh persuaded them to wait while he wrote his old mother in Danvers. He might not have another opportunity in months to send a letter. Frémont promised to mail it just as soon as he reached St. Louis.

In the spring of 1845 it was reported that 7,000 persons were at Independence, ready to take the road to Oregon and California. Sometimes these figures were swelled to 10,000—to 20,000, even to 100,000.[1] The great trek to California began. Marsh's propaganda was at flood tide. Wave after wave poured over the Sierras and literally broke at his feet. He saw his dream of an Americanized California materializing. The time to strike was approach-

BETRAYS MICHELTORENA

ing! California would soon be American soil. Then he awoke to reality. Astounding news arrived!

General Manuel Micheltorena landed at San Diego. A new Mexican governor for California! Alvarado was dismissed. Micheltorena was accompanied by an army of convicts. They were naked and filthy and recruited from the vilest jails and prisons in Mexico. Micheltorena was armed with a Mexican decree ordering him to expel all citizens of the United States then in California beyond the frontiers, and empowering him to refuse passports to all future immigrants from that country.[2] It was reported that his army of convicts was expressly selected to deal with the Americans and to save California from the fate of Texas.

On Marsh and other exponents of an Americanized California the news fell like a thunderbolt. After all his work, he was to be driven out of California by a band of cut-throats. But not if he could defeat the plan!

Notwithstanding these reports, Manuel Micheltorena was an imposing person—tall, handsome, of military bearing, and his gray eyes shone with a kindly expression. He was well-read, spoke French fluently, but was addicted to indolence and *mañana*. These were his Achillean spots.

But it was difficult to keep his convicts out of mischief. Micheltorena tried to accomplish this by drilling them all day; it was useless; they committed deviltry all night. Neither life, laundry, kettles, hen-coops, nor the honor of women was safe. Once, in broad daylight, one audacious fellow removed a *serape* from the dignified shoulders of Don Antonio Lugo, one of the notables of the town, as he walked down the street.

The Californians were the first to revolt. They said they preferred the Americans to the Mexican "jailbirds,"

JOHN MARSH, PIONEER

and they complained bitterly that the Mexican government had turned their beautiful province into a Botany Bay. The governor restrained them as best he could, reimbursed their victims out of his own pocket, paying for pots, pans and virtue that had never existed.

At last, Alvarado and Castro seized upon his army as an excuse and started an insurrection to expel it from California. With the help of Captain Weber, an American, they forced the Mexican general to sign the treaty of Santa Teresa, which stipulated that he must deport his mongrel army within three months. Marsh was happy again. He could manage a Castro or an Alvarado, but not a Mexican.

Before the three months expired, the dreaded José Jesus, the terror of the Tulares, came to the governor's aid. Then Isaac Graham, who had returned from banishment, offered help. He wanted revenge on the Californians for his arrest and exile. Captain Sutter promised not only support, but the heads of Castro and Alvarado[3] if the governor would make him another grant.

Thus encouraged by greed and malice, Micheltorena refused to deport his army and set about recruiting a force for resistance. He divided California into nine precincts and ordered the enrollment of all the citizens between the ages of fifteen and sixty years, including Americans and naturalized foreigners, and directed their formation into nine separate companies. Over each he appointed a captain and decreed the men were to be drilled every Sunday and to hold themselves in readiness for active service as *defensores de la patria.*

Over the precinct of the Sacramento and San Joaquin he appointed Sutter, with the title of *Commandante Militar de las fronteras del Norte y encargado de la justicia.*

MANUEL MICHELTORENA, GOVERNOR OF CALIFORNIA IMMEDIATELY PRECEDING PIO PICO.

BETRAYS MICHELTORENA

Thus Marsh fell under the latter's jurisdiction and boiled with indignation. Sutter knew Marsh's sympathies were entirely with the Californians; that he did not want to offend them, and that he hated the Mexicans. With his appointment, Sutter lost no time in letting him know who was in command, and he wrote the doctor to hold himself in readiness for service against the Californians.[4] Marsh was in a dilemma. Matters had taken a turn entirely foreign to his desires. He had devoted his energy to the Americanization of the province and had labored incessantly to keep his countrymen on the good side of the Californians. Now, by an uncontrollable turn of fate, he, and many other Americans in the valley, were aligned against the very men they wished to placate, and with whom their sympathies lay. But he could see no way out, and, in the debacle, he feared he would lose his rancho.

On a day late in December, Salines, one of Sutter's *vaqueros*, appeared at Marsh's door with an official note from General Sutter, ordering him to deliver to the bearer two bullocks and a yoke of oxen, and notifying him that he was landing on the San Joaquin, January 3, 1845. The note was signed, "J. A. Sutter, Commander in Chief of the forces of the River Sacramento."[5]

In the meantime, Sutter organized his forces to march against the Californians under Castro and Alvarado, then encamped near San José. Under his command he had José Jesus and a hundred Indians, armed with bows and arrows and carbines.[6] In addition he had eight or ten artillerymen in charge of a brass field-piece; forty cavalrymen who had deserted General Vallejo; a hundred mounted riflemen, mostly American under Captain Gantt, late of the U. S. A. The balance were infantry. On January 1, 1845,[7] with a force numbering 400, he marched out of the fort, with music playing and colors flying. On January 5 the combined forces pitched their tents under the doctor's oaks.

Soon after his arrival, Sutter sent Sinclair, his aide-de-camp, to Marsh with a note informing him that his commanding officer, General J. A. Sutter, had arrived and requested his immediate attendance at headquarters; also that he was commanded to furnish some serviceable horses, two yoke of oxen, one cart, a part of such medicine as he had on hand, and some ammunition, percussion caps, etc.[8] How the old Swiss must have chuckled when he dispatched that note! On receiving this summons, Marsh's anger knew no bounds, but he hastened to Sutter's camp, where the general ordered him to join his command and march against Castro and Alvarado. Marsh refused, telling Sutter that his sympathies were entirely with the Californians; that they were his friends, and that he would not take up arms against them. Thereupon Sutter retorted that unless he complied with his demands and joined him immediately, he would put him in irons and send him back to the fort, where he could keep company with his friend Weber, who was already in a cell, nursing similar sentiments.

Marsh thought the matter over. He realized that it was monstrous for him and other Americans to fight against the Californians, to antagonize them and to jeopardize their holdings as well as the future of the province, but at the moment there seemed no escape. He then made a desperate resolve: If he refused to march, he would be shut up in a fort on the Sacramento where he could do the Californians no good, but if he went he could do a good deal of damage, one way and another, within the Mexican ranks, and this he decided to do—to betray Micheltorena.

BETRAYS MICHELTORENA

Pretending to have changed his mind and to be friendly with Micheltorena and his cause,[9] he joined Sutter's force. But from the beginning it was with the deliberate intention of breaking down the morale of the Mexican troops from the inside, by persuading the Americans with him not to fight and to desert at the first opportunity. Sutter accepted his decision, but he did not give him a command as he had Gantt or Bidwell and other prominent Americans. Instead, wishing to heap ignominy upon him, he assigned him as a private to the infantry. Marsh was immensely pleased. There he would have a better chance to execute his plans.

On January 6, they left *Los Meganos* and headed south, Sutter astride a prancing horse, Marsh marching in the ranks, preaching treachery at every opportunity. But he had set himself a hard task, for most of the Americans in the force were there for the express purpose of getting grants from Micheltorena.[10] To them, victory meant leagues of California land, and they were much more anxious to obtain a good portion of the province than to have it annexed to the Union. So he had to bide his time and wait.

The rebel army under Castro and Alvarado, ninety strong, were then encamped at the Pueblo of San José, and Sutter determined to march against them and destroy them as quickly as possible. When Alvarado learned that Marsh was a private in the forces advancing against him, he was well pleased, understanding perfectly the circumstances under which he had been forced to act, and believing his sly and sinister influence would disorganize them.[11]

Sutter travelled fast. By the end of the first day he reached Sunol's rancho, ten miles north of the *Mission*

JOHN MARSH, PIONEER

San José—quite a walk for Marsh. The next day Marsh trudged an even greater distance, reaching the *Mission San José* about noon. Before night he was within five miles of the *Pueblo*. Sutter was doomed to disappointment. Castro and Alvarado had escaped and were retreating down the valley. Marsh was delighted. The next morning, before dawn, he was on the march again. It commenced to rain, and the troops began to complain of marching in such weather. Using this opening wedge, Marsh sowed seeds of discord among them, and many of his countrymen, grants or none, felt their ardor cooling under the combined chilling effects of his arguments and of the weather.

Hearing of Sutter's approach, Castro and Alvarado again fled southward, but Micheltorena joined Sutter on the Salinas River. There were now 800 men in pursuit of 100.[12] The odds were too great. Castro and Alvarado retreated toward Los Angeles.

Marsh was still in the ranks, marching now with the convicts, now with the Indians and Americans. Micheltorena's progress was deadly slow. He was ill and physically unable to sit on horseback, and was drawn to the impending carnage stretched at full length in a kind of spring wagon.

The Americans were disheartened at the snail's pace at which they travelled. The cold and wet chilled them to the marrow. The wretched roads were almost impassable for the baggage and munition transports. The troops were discouraged. Their morale sank lower and lower. Marsh watched them shrewdly and, seeing their discontent mounting, planted a sly word here, an insidious remark there, particularly among those who had no real interest in the result. Many of the others he made so dissatisfied

BETRAYS MICHELTORENA

that he reduced them to a state of mind bordering on desertion. Sixteen Americans were captured at the *Mission Buena Ventura*.

There were by that time only fifty foreigners left in the general's forces—just half the original number—but Marsh still had much to do, for the remaining fifty were unwilling to abandon the cause upon which they had embarked, and all still had their eyes on possible grants. In the meantime Castro and Alvarado reached Los Angeles.

CHAPTER XXXVI

TREACHERY. BATTLE OF CAHUENGA
1845

AFTER dark on February 19, Micheltorena and his army arrived at El Encino, in the beautiful San Fernando Valley, only a few miles from Los Angeles.[1] From a hill close by, Marsh could see the camp of Castro and Alvarado. Micheltorena prepared for action. It was a decisive time; Marsh was filled with apprehension. Success for the Mexicans meant the defeat of his plans.

Castro and Alvarado had reached their present position at the southern end of the San Fernando Valley only the day before. They had experienced no trouble in augmenting their force in Los Angeles. Their reports of the convicts and the atrocities they were committing en route enlisted the aid of the entire population, including a great majority of the Americans.[2] Thus Americans in the opposing forces faced each other across the valley.

It was a terrible night in Micheltorena's camp. A war of the elements was raging. Wind was blowing, sand was flying about in clouds, and tents were overturning in the dark. Marsh could not sleep and kept an anxious eye for any emergency. By dawn, all were astir; fife and drum beat "To arms," and Micheltorena's three cannon belched forth. The Californians barked back with their two field-pieces. By sunrise the cannonading ceased. The rival armies moved toward one another. Micheltorena gave orders for the infantry to advance. Marsh moved forward; the artillery brought up the rear; together they marched

BATTLE OF CAHUENGA

eastward up the valley. Castro was advancing toward them. Both armies followed the general course of the Los Angeles River until they approached within cannon range. Then the cannonading began again.

When the firing began, all those left behind in the Pueblo of Los Angeles hurried to the top of a nearby hill. They were highly excited. They had been warned that a hideous fate awaited them at the hands of the Mexican convicts if Castro were defeated. The wind blew from the north; the cannonading was deafening. The women and children fell upon their knees, raised their crucifixes aloft and prayed aloud to the saints to save them.[3]

The bombardment continued all morning. Marsh was relieved to find that it was mostly an artillery duel. The contestants kept themselves well out of musket range. The tide of battle rose and fell with varying success as the day waned. Many trees had their limbs broken, the rabbits were frightened almost to death by the sudden explosions of gunpowder, and a horse on Castro's side had its head blown off.[4] Micheltorena's gunners used grapeshot and fired over a hundred times, while Castro's men resorted to balls, and in some cases, small stones. The first shot from Micheltorena's cannon broke the wheel of one of Castro's guns and scared away the gunners. Then was the time to charge! But bad luck and Marsh's crafty propaganda were pursuing Micheltorena. At this crucial moment the Mexican dragoons wavered, and many of them deserted.

Micheltorena ordered Captain Gantt and the American riflemen to occupy a deep, winding gulch midway between the opposing forces. At the same time, the infantry was directed to approach within rifle range.[5] Again private Marsh advanced. Cannon balls passed over his head, plow-ing up the ground in front of him, and grapeshot whizzed through the air. Marsh was in the fore of these shock troops, and once, when the smoke lifted, he could plainly see that Castro had more Americans with him than Governor Micheltorena. He was surprised, wondering who they were, and where they had come from. He did not remain long in doubt.

During a momentary lull in the battle, he rallied his countrymen and suggested that they make an effort to signal the Americans in the opposing force that they wished to communicate with them. Suiting the action to the word, he signalled, and in answer thirty Americans from the rebel side came over to his.[6] From them Marsh learned for the first time of the arrival of Beckwourth with thirteen rifles,[7] and of *le gros* Fallon's party. Among them, he, and practically every man near him, found some acquaintance. Many had known each other in Missouri. In the excitement of the meeting, of inquiring about friends, and exchanging news, they forgot all about fighting, although cannon-balls and grapeshot were still flying overhead.

Now was Marsh's opportunity. He addressed the Americans in no uncertain terms. He pointed out the fact that if the Americans fought in these factional fights, they would make enemies of both sides, probably lose their ranchos and thus destroy the peaceful settlement of the territory later on.[8] He ended by proposing that they all withdraw, save their strength for a day that was fast approaching, and let the Mexicans fight it out among themselves.

Meantime, Micheltorena gave the order for his mounted riflemen to charge. Captain Gantt and his men did not stir—they were listening to private Marsh's arguments.

BATTLE OF CAHUENGA

Sensing something wrong, Sutter turned to Micheltorena and said: "I'll go and see why Gantt doesn't advance."[9]

Sutter found Gantt and his men calmly balloting as to whether they would fight or desert. Private Marsh was still talking, and, as a result of his entreaties, the Americans withdrew and flatly refused to fight against one another.

Seeing what was in progress, Sutter shouted: "What are you doing here? Why don't you advance?"

Unperturbed, Gantt replied: "We are voting to find out who wants to go with one side and who with the other."

"This is the time to fight, not to vote!" roared Sutter.[10]

Unable to get any satisfaction out of Gantt, and seeing that Marsh had betrayed Micheltorena, Sutter[11] started making his way back to the governor. But presently he found himself surrounded by the Californians. Without a struggle, he surrendered and was taken to Alvarado.[12] Some say that this was exactly what he wanted. But Sutter's grants were lost. Marsh had settled that question.

Micheltorena continued fighting as only a brave man can. As night closed in, the general and his faithful convicts gained a good position on a lofty hill, and they held it gallantly. When the sun rose the next morning, he looked down on yesterday's battlefield and, realizing that the Americans and Sutter had deserted him, and that his supplies were cut off, he raised a white flag. A few days later he was deported to Mexico—betrayed by private Marsh.[13]

CHAPTER XXXVII

MARSH CALLS THE AMERICANS TO ARMS. THE REPUBLIC OF CALIFORNIA

1845

IN this manner Marsh rid California of the last of her Mexican governors.[1] To him belongs the credit of breaking one of the last bonds that bound the province to the mother country. Pio Pico, the new governor and a Californian, was so well pleased with Marsh's accomplishment that he made a contract with him and John Gantt for the capture of the Indian horse thieves who were still making life miserable in the interior valleys,[2] promising to give them in return 500 cattle, and half of all the live stock they might recover.[3] The raid was to start immediately with their return to the north. At the last moment this project failed, for their followers refused to go on so dangerous a mission.

Marsh arrived at *Los Meganos* early in March.[4] There he found a letter from Danvers which had been entrusted to one of Henry Mellus' boats. It brought him bad news: that his mother was dead, and that she had died grieving for her missing son. The letter stated that his family had not heard from him since 1843, at the time the first emigrants returned to Missouri; that ever since then his mother had mourned continuously for him; that a few days before the end she had taken out the packet containing the letters he had written her during the past twenty years and re-read them, one by one, and declared, as she put them away, that her greatest desire was to hold her

PIO PICO, GOVERNOR OF CALIFORNIA AT THE TIME OF ITS ANNEXATION.
From the painting in the possession of the California State Library, at Sacramento.

THE REPUBLIC OF CALIFORNIA

first-born once again in her arms. A few days later she had succumbed suddenly to a heart attack.

Shortly after her burial, a letter arrived addressed to her. It was from Captain Frémont stating that he had been in California, that he had seen her son there, that the latter had written her a letter and entrusted it to him to mail at St. Louis. He added that when he arrived home, he could not find it, that only recently it had turned up again, and that he was enclosing it. It arrived at Danvers almost a year after it was written.[5]

Following his mother's death, Marsh threw himself heart and soul into his plans for the peaceful annexation of California to his country, and for effecting a change of flag without the shedding of blood or the creation of rancor. He had had a taste of politics. He longed for more and desired to manipulate events. All California needed was a leader. Possibly he was that man. He knew that a large majority of the Californians were well disposed toward his countrymen, and that they would hail with delight any change of sovereignty that would insure them peace and prosperity.

Marsh's plan included the union of California and Oregon into one independent nation, extending not only to the Columbia but as far north as the forty-ninth parallel and possibly to the fifty-sixth. Many of the people from the Willamette settlements had already approached him with the idea of uniting with California. During the Micheltorena revolution, some of the most influential Californians had expressed a wish to amalgamate their destinies permanently with those of Oregon.

Nature herself, Marsh said, had clearly indicated such a union, and the rapidly developing course of events rendered it almost inevitable, in spite of the cupidity of

The undersigned in common with all other foreigners with whom they have been able to communicate personally, being very desirous to promote the union and harmony and best interests of all the foreigners, resident in California, have thought that this desirable object can be best attained by a meeting of some individuals from each of the different districts of the northern part of the country. We therefore hereby invite the the persons of foreign birth, whether naturalized or not, to send two or more of their number to represent them in a meeting to be held in the Pueblo de S. José on the 4th day of July next. It is considered to be very desirable that Monterey, Sta Cruz, Yerba-Buena, Sonoma & the district of the Sacramento should be fully represented. In the mean time we think it will be obvious to every man of sense or reflection, that the foreigners ought to carefully to refrain from taking any part either in word or deed in any movement of a political nature that may take place in the country— (amongst Native Mexico.)

Pueblo of St Joseph March 27, 1845

Wm Gulnack
Peter Dourson
John Marshe
Charles M. Weber

THE CALL TO ARMS IN
From the "History of

MARSH'S HANDWRITING
San Joaquin," 1876.

JOHN MARSH, PIONEER

the Hudson's Bay Company and the ambitions and intrigues of the British Government. The capital of this new nation, he said, would be on the Bay of San Francisco, possibly on the site of the village of San José. He predicted that Yerba Buena would become a place of importance; that it would be within the next century one of the great commercial emporii of the world, a centre of all the whaling operations on the Pacific, and the main point of communication between America and Asia.[6] His brain teemed with plans, and he conspired with Captain Weber, a merchant of the Pueblo of San José, with the idea of putting them into effect by organizing the foreigners, particularly the Americans, into a unit that would be of value in days to come. In this frame of mind he wrote out the "Call to Foreigners." On the surface it looked to be a harmless document, but back of its seeming innocence lurked conspiracy and treason—and the "Republic of California."

On March 27, 1845, Marsh and Weber issued their "call" to their followers, inviting all who were living in northern California,—Monterey, Santa Cruz, Yerba Buena, Sonoma, and the District of Sacramento, to assemble at the *Pueblo* on the Fourth of July. The object, as outwardly expressed by the "call," was to promote union among the foreigners and to prevent their taking sides, especially different sides, in California quarrels. In this way they could make their strength felt instead of dividing it against one another.[7]

Thus did Marsh cast the die for the California republic. In addition to the objects outwardly expressed, the "call" had the motive of perfecting a systematic organization, the ultimate effects of which should, when Americans became sufficiently strong in numbers, result in wrest-

THE REPUBLIC OF CALIFORNIA

ing from Mexican control that portion of California lying north and east of the San Joaquin River and north and east of the bays of San Francisco, San Pablo, and Suisun, and make this area, like Texas, an independent state.[8]

Marsh felt that by 1846 plans for the "Republic of California" would be matured sufficiently to proceed. By that time, he claimed, there would be enough American sentiment among native Californians to warrant the revolt, as well as enough Americans in California to authorize the step and back him up in any emergency.[9] Some of the conspirators planned to make Marsh the first governor, or—should a new country result—its first president.[10] That idea was pleasing to the doctor. Governor John Marsh, or better President Marsh! Not bad at all!

CHAPTER XXXVIII

FRÉMONT. COUP D'ÉTAT FAILS

1846

WHILE Marsh and Weber were planning their *coup d'état*, events about them were moving rapidly in another direction; yet, there is no doubt that, had their plans been allowed to mature, they would have succeeded. But James Polk came to the presidency, and all was changed.

He entered the White House with the avowed purpose of annexing California to the Union by purchase, revolt or war. In the critical period he believed to be approaching, he appointed Thomas O. Larkin, a Monterey merchant of New England antecedents, agent, and, later, confidential agent, of his government. One of the first acts carried out by Larkin after his appointment was to make a list of the most prominent men then in California and to send it to President Polk. Among them was Marsh. Of him he wrote that he was a man of talents and possessed more knowledge of California than almost any other, and that he had been engaged in sending the Mexicans to Mexico by apparently being in their favor (having reference to the Micheltorena affair).[1] He would be useful.

Soon after this appointment, Larkin communicated with Marsh, soliciting his aid in acquiring California, in these terms:

"Now you as a settler and extensive landholder in California have a great interest in this stake. The new settlers at the Oregon are running down California while I am

FRÉMONT. COUP D'ÉTAT FAILS

engaged in running it up. They publish in American papers that we have no timber; no rain; that we have to send to Oregon even for flour, and that there are a few drunkards yet left in the Oregon who are going to California to settle, etc.

"I should like to have you . . . come forth into the field and write for the country you intend to live in. You are a good writer, know well the country, its people and resources, its climate, rivers, bays and soil; whether it will grow hemp, cotton, wheat, or corn, wild or cultivated fruit. Do by all means sit down to the task, write everything you can regarding California, and I will have it published in the New York papers. I am so confident of your skill that I assure you your letters will be copied into every paper.[2] . . . Write everything you know respecting English agents or consul control or her projects, all you know respecting the Hudson's Bay Company agents, trading, smuggling in California, aiding revolution, acting for or counteracting the supreme or local government in any way.

"If you will send such papers, and no other person in California is better calculated, I will remit them. . . . Do not let the new settlers in Oregon cry down California. Awake! . . ."

In considering how he could best help California at this stage of events, Marsh thought of his old friend, Lewis Cass, who had been governor of Michigan Territory when he first went to Fort Snelling, and who had befriended him when the machinations of his enemies appeared likely to terminate his career there.

Since that day—some twenty years before—Cass had been going steadily up the political ladder until in 1845 he was at the zenith of his career and one of the most astute politicians in the country. Successively he had been

JOHN MARSH, PIONEER

Minister to France, Democratic nominee in 1844 for the presidency and, since 1845, a member of the United States Senate. In 1846 he was a leader among those demanding the "re-annexation" of all the Oregon country south of 54° 40' or war with England. Marsh had watched his distinguished career with interest. He would be just the one to appeal to. He could do no better for California than to write to his old friend.

Accordingly, on February 1, soon after receiving Larkin's request, he sat down by his open window and wrote Cass a long letter, recalling to his mind that day in his youth at Green Bay, Wis. (in 1825), when the older man advised him to give up New England and turn his face again toward the setting sun, and Marsh reminded him that but for his influence at that crucial time, he would probably be administering pills in some quiet Yankee village instead of growing gray-headed breeding cattle and cultivating grapevines on the shores of the Pacific.

From that introduction, he launched forth into a long and careful description of the resources of the country and, with prophetic touch, indicated that the political futures of California and Oregon were inseparable, and that he believed that their destiny at that very moment was a foregone conclusion. "The natural conformation of the country strongly indicates it; and a sympathy and fellow-feeling in the inhabitants is taking place, which must soon bring about the consummation," he wrote. He then went on to say that the Californians cared as much for the government of Mexico as for that of Japan; that they were as independent of it as Texas and *must ere long* share the same fate; that there were 7,000 persons of Spanish descent, 10,000 civilized or domesticated Indians, 700 Americans, 100 English, Irish and Scotch, about 100

FRÉMONT. COUP D'ÉTAT FAILS

French, Germans and Italians, and probably a million wild, naked, brute Indians in California.

He added that the climate was regular and uniform, that no disease whatever could be attributed to its influence, and, as a proof of the mildness of the winter, he cited the humming-birds. Continuing, he stated that upper California had a gold-mine (this was before the discovery of '48), silver ore and quicksilver, that fertile valleys and rivers and forests abounded, that the Bay of San Francisco was the finest in the world, that California could not remain long under the domination of its present owners, that if it did not come into the possession of the Americans, the English would take it, that a British ship-of-war was lately in California waters, that her officers declared openly that the port of San Francisco would shortly belong to them, that he considered that remark an ebullition of John Bullism, but that the British wanted California and would have it if possible, of that there was no doubt in his mind. And he concluded by hoping that Cass would take an interest in the matter.[3]

Cass did take an interest. He was vitally concerned in Oregon, and he handed over Marsh's letter to the Press. It was copied and recopied all over the country. Eventually it reached President Polk's attention, and, it is claimed, played a conspicuous part in his prosecution of the war with Mexico and in strengthening his decision to wrest California from that country.[4]

While these schemes and intrigues were agitating the doctor, Frémont again appeared in California, first at Fort Sutter, then at Laguna Seco, about thirteen miles from San José. Immediately on Frémont's arrival there, Captain Weber dispatched an express to Marsh, couched in startling words:

JOHN MARSH, PIONEER

"Facts, more terrible than thunder," Marsh read, "lightning, hurricanes, volcanic eruptions! Hear! Hear! Great News! War! War!

"Captain Frémont of the United States Topographical Corps with sixty or more riflemen has fortified himself on the heights between *San Juan* and *Don Joaquin Gomeros' rancho*, the Stars and Stripes flying over their camps. José Castro and two or three hundred Californians with artillery are besieging his position. Captain Graham and sixty or more boys are moving to his rescue. The country is in revolution, Spaniards and foreigners are enlisting under their respective banners, Frémont arrived on Wednesday of last week at *San Juan*. . . . He was ordered by Castro to return to the frontier. He refused, alleging he could not leave the country for two months to come. Their correspondence got warmer every day, and now Castro is in arms to drive Frémont off by force. We send this night a person to Frémont's camp to bring us better information and to know his intentions.

"Please forward the news immediately to the Sacramento and spare no expense.

"I should judge your presence here in the Pueblo would not be amiss. Affairs are becoming serious, and I think I will see the repetition of the Texas history in this country."[5]

Marsh did not at all approve of Frémont's action, but he felt that the great hour had struck; that the moment he had long awaited was at hand. Dispatching Weber's letter to Sutter's Fort to warn the Americans there, he mounted his own mustang and rode rapidly toward San José.

On the way he met Frémont, humbled and humiliated, retreating up the valley, and complaining that he had

FRÉMONT. COUP D'ÉTAT FAILS

waited for Castro as long as he could and had only departed because he did not have men enough to protect his large *caballada* and the property of the United States, and that not one American had come to his assistance. In high dudgeon, Frémont withdrew to the frontier to run, as he told Sutter, the line of the forty-second parallel and to make it so distinct that the citizens of the United States and other foreigners might know when they were in Oregon.[6]

In Frémont's wake came Gillespie, a frenzied Polk envoy, masquerading as an invalid. He was in mad pursuit of the general. He had some important dispatches for him, he claimed. "Where is he?" he vainly queried at Fort Sutter.

The next thing Marsh knew, Frémont was back in the Valley, encamped near the Marysville Buttes. All the time he was gathering men about him, particularly the dregs of Western civilization; all the time he kept moving down the Valley, and all the time he was stirring up a panic among the ranchos. Reports flew thick and fast: Castro was going to drive the Americans out of California; the Consumne Indians were going to burn their crops.[7] Some say the pathfinder instigated these reports—anyhow, he pacified the terrified settlers by assuring them that he would not leave the valley while they were in danger. They gathered that he desired some kind of a revolt and would join any kind they engineered.

At this stage of the game, Frémont bethought himself of Marsh. The general said that the doctor was a man of marked sagacity, that he was favorable to American interests, and that he was likely to be informed of any intended movement by the Californians.[8] He was just the man Frémont needed. Forthwith he dispatched a messenger

JOHN MARSH, PIONEER

to *Los Meganos*, begging Marsh to co-operate with him in the movement he was undertaking.[9]

Marsh refused to return with the messenger. He sent back word that the Californians were his friends, and that he would have nothing whatever to do with Frémont's actions against them.

In the meanwhile Frémont took Sutter's Fort and dispatched some of his followers against Vallejo at Sonoma. There they took the garrison by surprise.[10] One of their number issued a proclamation declaring California independent of Mexico and hoisted aloft a flag showing a grizzly bear upon a white field. The Californians mistook the bruin for a pig.[11]

Marsh received this news through an express from Fort Sutter. It filled him with dismay. Like all old settlers, he was greatly startled by the Sonoma action, and blamed Frémont for putting it in motion, knowing it meant the end of all good feeling between the Californians and the resident Americans. To him, it was ill-timed, ill-advised and inconsistent with the policy which he, Larkin and others had been pursuing and, at best, he considered it a serious blunder and not in line with the President's wishes.

He felt, too, that Frémont should have notified him of the approaching hostilities. For while Frémont and his men could maintain their position, it left him, as well as all Americans about San José and especially farther south, unadvised and unprotected and at the mercy of the infuriated natives.

Realizing the danger of his situation, Marsh mounted his mustang and started for Fort Sutter. There he found General Vallejo already in jail. This insult to the best friend the Americans had among the Californians aroused

FRÉMONT. COUP D'ÉTAT FAILS

his ire the more. During the night of his arrival, an express arrived from Captain Montgomery at Yerba Buena. He brought an American flag and the information that Commodore Sloat had raised one at Monterey, and that another was flying over the custom house at Yerba Buena.

At sunrise the Stars and Stripes were run up over Fort Sutter, and a salute of twenty-one guns shattered all the glass in the establishment.[12] Marsh's wish was fulfilled.

CHAPTER XXXIX

PARK'S BAR
1848

ONE April day in the spring of 1848 a courier swung down from the mountains into the San Joaquin Valley. He was riding like mad and shouting at the top of his voice as he rode.

Settlers at Tuleberg, where Stockton now stands, ran out to meet him, taking their rifles as they ran. They thought the Indians were in his wake, or that the horse thieves were on the rampage again.

The courier dashed into their midst, checking his foaming steed in mid-gallop, held out a small but weighty bag of buckskin and cried: "Gold! Gold! In the Sierras. They have struck gold!" He would have rushed on, had not the bystanders grasped his horse's bridle and plied him with questions.

There followed great excitement as the man told his tale —now familiar to every schoolboy—of how James W. Marshall on January 19 had come upon flakes of scale gold while digging a mill-race at General Sutter's mill on the American River, how he had taken his "find" to Sutter, how the two had kept their secret for weeks until Marshall's men had learned it by staging an independent discovery of their own, and that then the secret was out.

Having finished this recital, the courier put spurs to his horse and disappeared in the direction of Pueblo San José—leaving the bystanders agape in his wake.

PARK'S BAR

Thus the news of gold on the American reached Doctor Marsh. It was a welcome sound.[1]

Gold in the Sierras! He had always been in search of it. At last!

It was April when the courier reached San José. By May, Marsh had organized a company to go to the gold mines and was on his way there with a party consisting of Major Stephen Cooper whom he had known on the Missouri frontier and by whose side he had fought in the Black Hawk War, his son Sarshel, a Contra Costa neighbor Nicolas Hunsacker, and another doctor named Long. Red-shirted, booted, and with pack animals loaded down with picks, shovels and pans, they hurried to the Yuba River. Already there was a mad scramble to the Sierras.

At a place sixteen miles from Marysville, Marsh struck camp and started washing gold from the sands of the Yuba. Almost immediately he found one of the richest bars along the river. From the beginning he cleaned up as much as fifty dollars an hour and was disgusted because he could not do better.

His companions called his discovery "Marsh's Diggings." Not satisfied with his rich returns from the river bottom, the doctor set himself up as an embryo banker and trader as well. Goods brought enormous prices, especially among the Indians, who knew little of the worth of gold dust, but set great value upon beads, bright colors and sugars. Capitalizing his knowledge of the redskins, Marsh laid in a stock dear to their hearts. They would give him a tin cup full of gold dust for the same quantity of glass beads, and would buy sugar weight for weight. He was elated. He had never dreamed of so much gold.

When his supplies were exhausted, he traded them everything he owned, and even the red shirt off his back

JOHN MARSH, PIONEER

went to an Indian for $300 worth of gold dust and nuggets.[2] The color of red was more alluring to the savage eye than the glitter of virgin gold, and the accumulation of wealth was a paramount desire with Marsh, transcending all other aspirations.

Once, while he was working in the river bottom, the doctor spread out his gaudily-colored bandana on a rock and, as he recovered the nuggets from his pan, piled them up in it until he had a sizable mound. On one of his return trips from the river he was horrified to find his handkerchief gone—but the nuggets were there just as he left them—and in the distance he saw an Indian disappearing with his bandana.[3] In addition to what he mined and took in by trading, he bought seventeen pounds of gold, as weighed by steelyards.[4]

Marsh's Diggings were so rich that the argonauts were soon flocking there in hordes and staking out claims all around him. It was disgusting, always competition. Soon the river at that point was lined with red-shirted miners, and a mushroom town—six stores, three hotels, two blacksmith shops, a barber-shop, post-office and a number of saloons with women at the monte tables—had sprung into existence.[5]

The first woman in the Diggings was Mrs. Park. She was the wife of David Park and with her husband had been on her way to the Oregon when they heard of the discovery on the American. Turning aside, they arrived at Marsh's Diggings some six months after the doctor and his company had located it. Their covered wagon was filled with goods intended for the Willamette, and they set up a trading post in opposition to Marsh. While Park spent the day with rocker and pan, his wife presided as clerk over a makeshift store. Her store acquired a reputation.

PARK'S BAR

Marsh's Diggings became Park's Bar. Together the Parks cleaned up over $85,000, but Marsh too was making money hand over fist. He had nothing to complain about. His wildest ambitions were gratified. Soon the unusual physical labor took its price. He was stricken seriously ill, and, gold or no gold, had to return to his rancho,[6] but with dust and nuggets in his saddlebags estimated at $40,000.[7]

The doctor did not know what to do with all his riches. There were no banks or safety-boxes for the deposit of valuables. California was overrun with desperate highwaymen and bandits, who did not hesitate to rifle cabins or throw a lasso about the necks of returning miners, drag them bodily from their horses, stab them to death and rob their saddlebags. Marsh knew all this. Already he had had numerous experiences with these robbers—on eleven distinct occasions they had rifled his *adobe*. Thus on his return with his precious gold dust, he dug a secret *cache*, such as the old fur traders had used in the Rockies, and buried his wealth. With his usual secretiveness, he told no man the whereabouts of this hiding-place.

A great change came over California. The days of *mañana* were gone. The miserable village of Yerba Buena became the white-tented city of San Francisco and bade fair—as Marsh had once prophesied—to become one of the great emporia of the world.[8] The sand dunes disappeared. On them appeared churches, public houses and hundreds of dwellings. Flags from every nation floated over the spars of deserted ships in her bay. Masts were so closely packed together that, in an incredibly short time, the harbor looked like a leafless forest. The bight was piled high with crates and bundles of merchandise.

Tuleberg, a few miles from *Los Meganos*, became

JOHN MARSH, PIONEER

Stockton, the embarking point for the southern mines. Sutter's Fort was swamped under an avalanche of immigrants. Sacramento City became the central point of the northern mining region. San José blossomed out as the capital of the State. Other towns with picturesque names —Rough and Ready, Poverty Flat, Deadman's Bar, Graveyard Cañon, Hang Town, Hell's Delight, Jackass Gulch, Lousy Ravine, Nigger Hill, One Eye, Red Dog, Shirt Tail Cañon, and You Bet—sprang up over night in the mining localities.[9] Marsh was jubilant. More riches poured into his coffers.

This great influx of gold-seekers vastly increased the value of the doctor's 17,000 acres and provided innumerable markets for his cattle and produce. Formerly he had slaughtered his cattle at the yearly *matanza*, for their hides alone, and had been glad enough to receive the two dollars apiece paid by the Boston traders. Now his herds became a gold mine, more valuable than the nuggets he had panned in the waters of the Yuba. The hides were of little value as compared to the meat. No longer did the bones of his herds whiten on the plains of the San Joaquin. Instead, they brought fabulous sums in Sierra mining towns.

A regular shipping establishment grew up around his *embarcadero* on the San Joaquin, which became known far and wide as "Marsh's Landing." Here, by his *rodeo* grounds, he built a slaughterhouse and a smokehouse for curing hams, and imported from the States a one-story-and-a-half dwelling, embellished with a liberal allowance of fretwork. It was brought around the Horn and set up by the river. In it he established as *mayordomo*, John Beener and his pretty Spanish wife.

He then built a pier extending far out into the river,

LOS ANGELES IN 1853.
From an official report of the railroad survey, made to the then Secretary of War, Jefferson Davis.

SAN FRANCISCO IN 1848, AT ABOUT THE TIME OF THE DISCOVERY OF GOLD.

PARK'S BAR

where vessels drawing fifteen feet of water could tie up at any season of the year. Every night one of the steamers plying between San Francisco and Stockton and the southern mines stopped there, left the mail and took a cargo of beeves from his corrals, hams from his smokehouse, grain from his fields, or grapes from his vineyards. Once he received $10,000 for one shipment of cattle, and during 1849, and for several subsequent years, his annual output in cattle and grapes amounted to $20,000.[10]

Thus James Marshall's discovery made Doctor Marsh the wealthy man he had always wanted to be. His ambition for great riches was achieved. Another of his wishes was gratified. The chief difficulty with which he had to contend was the lack of a bank in which to deposit his gold, and his mysterious *cache* grew more and more valuable. As his wealth increased, his reputation for driving close bargains became more widespread than ever. He was feared and hated, cajoled and respected, as the case might demand.

The great trek to California was now in full swing—by land and sea they came, in ox-teams, prairie schooners, on horseback, in steamers, sailboats and tugs—rich men, poor men, beggars, thieves, men of title, men with pasts, doctors, lawyers, artisans—all bent on one object—gold. The rush was unprecedented. By 1849, 5,000 wagons had arrived, with 7,000 more expected, and it was thought that the overland arrivals would reach 40,000 that year.[11]

Among these gold-seekers were many whom Marsh had known elsewhere—in Massachusetts, Minnesota, Wisconsin, Illinois and the Rockies. Among others came S. P. Webb, an old Harvard classmate and once mayor of Salem, Mass.; E. D. Baker, whom he had known at Prairie du Chien; and the Reverend John Cameron, the

JOHN MARSH, PIONEER

Cumberland Presbyterian minister, who, with James Rutledge, had founded the town of New Salem, Ill. and built the sawmill on the Sangamon River where Abraham Lincoln floated his flatboat. The doctor, too, had boarded with Cameron at New Salem. The old minister had known Marguerite and Charles at "Uncle Jimmie's," and now this meeting in California brought back a flood of recollections.

The Reverend Cameron had left Oscaloosa, Iowa, in May of 1849, one of a caravan of forty wagons. Most of the party remained in Salt Lake City, but the old patriarch scaled the Sierras alone and reached the Sacramento Valley the last day of October, 1849.

On his arrival he made his way to *Los Meganos*, and the doctor welcomed him with untold joy. At last he would learn something of Charley. In his enthusiasm he almost embraced the old man. Their last meeting had been at New Salem, when Marsh was visiting his boy at "Uncle Jimmie" Pantier's. The first question he asked him concerned Charley. Cameron recalled the doctor's boy well. But a look of sadness overspread his face as he replied: "Charley Marsh? Charley Pantier, you mean? Why, he died when he was a boy."

CHAPTER XL

WOMEN

1849–1851

AFTER Cameron's departure, the doctor was very lonely.[1] Every one for whom he cared was dead. Now he was a rich man, and he wanted an establishment, a wife and a family. Once, half in jest, half in earnest, he wrote his brother, Caleb, at Lockport, N. Y., and asked him if he thought he could find him a good wife there. Caleb, wholly in earnest, replied that he had found two, either of whom was ready and willing to go to California.[2]

White women were a great curiosity in that country. Among a male population, women of any kind, good or bad, created a sensation. The majority of the first-comers were gaudy bold-faced creatures, recruited from the ranks of the adventuresses, the Mississippi towns being especially generous in their contributions. On arrival, they became decoys or entertainers in the saloons, or were employed as dealers at the monte tables or other games of chance. Anywhere—everywhere, they were paying attractions, drawing big crowds who gathered about to look at them. Good or bad, they received reverent attention, merely because they wore skirts, and the poor, homesick boys spent their last hard-earned nuggets just to be near them. Marsh preferred a squaw to that type.

Once Captain Gantt, Marsh's old friend—who knew that the latter was lonesome—happened to be in the Napa Valley when two young girls, with their father, put in an appearance there. The first thing the captain did when he heard the news was to dispatch a letter to Marsh, in these terms:

"I will attempt, and, I hope, succeed in drawing your attention to a subject of much interest to yourself. Near where I am, at present, resides my old friend Major Stephen Cooper, and I have seen his two daughters, Frances and Susan, both fine-looking girls, particularly Miss Susan, who I think would 'pass muster' both in person and accomplishments. Indeed, although they are from the upper part of Missouri, there is nothing of the 'Ned' about them. Therefore, permit me to take the liberty of advising you to pay a visit to Napa. It is well worth the ride (about seventy-five miles) to see the young ladies, and at the same time you will patronize the 'Horse Dentists' ' ferry.

"I will go with you and introduce you to the family; indeed I have already told Miss Susan I had a beau for her, and that she may expect a visit from you, but Miss Frances said she thought as she was the oldest, she was of course, entitled to the preference; that matter, however, is to be settled among yourselves. Come over to Napa at all events. If the Misses Cooper do not come up to what I have represented them to be, a little further up the valley you will find some girls who play on the violin, and if your organs of tune should predominate at the moment, perhaps they may suit.

"Then there are several long-built widows, some long-sided ones etc., all in the fertile valley of Napa.

"I hope to have the pleasure of seeing you over on this side of the Bay soon. You must not disappoint the young ladies, now I have told them you are coming.

"The girls are impatient, and I will be glad to hear from you."[3]

Marsh did not go on this seventy-five-mile jaunt, but

WOMEN

his reputation as a desirable husband spread over California, and in the course of time reached the ears of another young lady—Abigail Smith Tuck—a "schoolma'am" of Santa Clara.

"Abby," as she had been affectionately known during her seminary days at Northampton, hailed from Chelmsford, Mass., and was a devout Baptist. She was young, tall and good-looking, with cheeks so rosy they might have been called hectic. She sang "like a nightingale" and took the soprano parts in the village choir. In addition, she could play the piano, write music and transcribe it, paint with oils and embroider birds, fruits and flowers of lifelike semblance.

Measles, contracted at Northampton, put a temporary stop to these activities. It left her with an annoying cough. Feeling that she would never get well in New England, she went south, first to North Carolina, then to Georgia. When gold was discovered in California, and the papers were full of commendation of the climate in that earthly paradise, she decided to migrate there. Joining a party of Baptist missionaries, she sailed in June of 1850 from New York and in the fall of the same year passed through the Golden Gate. The Reverend O. C. Wheeler, a Baptist minister of the embryo city, was at the wharf when the missionaries arrived and took them all, including Abby, home with him.[4]

When a select school for young ladies was founded at Santa Clara, near San José, he prevailed upon her to become the principal. Abby went to live at the Santa Clara Hotel with Captain and Mrs. T. N. Appleton, the proprietors.[5] San José was a busy place at that time. It was the capital of the State, and the Legislature was in session. Abby was in great demand, no social affair was complete

JOHN MARSH, PIONEER

without her. Many of the lawmakers were her avowed suitors, and more than one, enamored of her talents and accomplishments, proposed marriage. To all she gave a negative answer, much to the disappointment of the Appletons, who wanted to see their boarder married and settled in the valley. Teasing her one day because she was so particular, her landlord said: "I don't know who will suit you—unless it is Doctor John Marsh."

This mention of Marsh aroused Abby's interest, and she inquired who John Marsh might be. Appleton described him as a mysterious bachelor who lived in the San Joaquin Valley, who read Greek for pleasure and herded cattle for profit, who could converse in every known tongue, including many Indian dialects, who could throw a lasso as well as any *vaquero*, who could outshoot any marksman, but who spent most of his time reading, writing, accumulating wealth, and avoiding his fellow men.

This was enough to arouse the curiosity of any young woman. When Appleton had finished his recital, Abby exclaimed: "He is the very man. I'll set my cap for him and marry him."[6]

After the school term was finished, Mrs. Appleton, whose brother was the Reverend William W. Smith, founder of Antioch, Contra Costa County, proposed that they should take a driving trip through the San Joaquin Valley, and visit him. Antioch was on the San Joaquin River, only two or three miles from Marsh's Landing. This the Appletons well knew, and Abby was easily prevailed upon to go, especially when she learned that the mysterious bachelor lived in the immediate vicinity.

Early in June, with two horses and a wagon, they left Santa Clara for the San Joaquin. The first day they travelled twenty-five miles and reached Livermore's rancho

WOMEN

by nightfall. By sunset the next night they were still far distant from Antioch. Night was coming, and they did not relish the prospect of spending it in an open wagon. Finding themselves within the confines of an immense rancho, they travelled on to the ranch house to inquire the way and were greeted by the doctor himself. He welcomed them warmly, insisting that they put up their team and spend the night as his guests, and putting his *vaqueros* to work cooking a meal before the fire. After dinner they spent a memorable evening about the hearth. The doctor proved a delightful host and regaled them with his many adventures in the old days of California.[7] It was after midnight when they separated for the night.

The next morning at daylight, the doctor roused Captain Appleton and urged him to go with him and look at a trap that had been set some miles from the house to catch a California lion. From the doctor's inquiries, Appleton soon discovered that he was more interested in hearing about Miss Tuck than he was in California lions, although they found one in the trap when they arrived. On their return to the *adobe*, the ladies were waiting for them, and a pot of beans was simmering over the fire. From the first, Abby was interested in her host. Ere long she discovered that he was a Harvard graduate, and had been sixteen years in California, that he had secured enough of this world's goods to be comfortable, and that he was about fifty years old. She noted that he was a little taller than her father, that although he was robust and ruddy, his hair was fringed with gray, that he was very good-looking, although inclined to be portly. She liked his appearance and his manner, and delighted in his conversation. The more she saw of him, the more fascinated she became.[8]

JOHN MARSH, PIONEER

After breakfast the team was brought around, and the doctor accompanied his guests the nine miles across his rancho, to the residence of the Reverend W. W. Smith at Antioch. There he tore himself reluctantly away. He was charmed with Abby and could not get her out of his mind as he rode back to his lonesome *adobe*. She was just the sort of girl he might have known at home. A day or two later he rode to Antioch to call and stayed to supper.[9]

After tea, the doctor and the Reverend Mr. Smith took a walk along the river front. The latter told Marsh that the school-teacher had fallen in love with him. "Tut, tut, tut!" replied the doctor. "I always thought I would like to marry a Massachusetts lady. I don't know why I shouldn't fall in love with her myself."[10]

When he left the next morning, he invited Abby and the Smiths to visit him the following Sunday at the Landing. Before the appointed time he dispatched a *vaquero* with some of his best horses, to guide them. Abby was much delighted with the Landing and took a great liking to Mrs. John Beener, the *mayordomo's* Spanish wife. She was especially interested in the little house that the doctor had brought around the Horn.[11] The afternoon went quickly. When it came time to depart, Mrs. Beener asked Abby to spend a few days with her, and the Smiths returned alone to Antioch.

The following week passed delightfully. Abby and the doctor rode all over the rancho, inspected his immense herds of cattle and horses, his extensive vineyards, and his orchards of pears and figs. He showed her his stables with carriage and harness room, and the stalls for his imported stallions, and the houses he had just completed for his agriculturists. All the time he was regaling her with his past, his years on the Mississippi and his adventures in the Rockies, but for all his frankness on other subjects, he failed to mention the little son he had left in Illinois, or the lonely grave at Prairie du Chien that held Marguerite and her baby.[12]

What girl would not be carried off her feet! Abby acknowledged she was swept off hers. In the happiness that possessed her, she propounded only one question—but that one was paramount; on it she felt everything hinged. One day as they were riding toward the river, she turned to her companion and queried: "Doctor, are you a Christian?"

Marsh hesitated—he, who had once put an emphasis on spiritual things, was embarrassed. After a long silence, he replied: "I hope I am."

"And that is all I can find out," wrote Abby to her father.[13] But so far as Abby was concerned, that was all that was necessary. Under such circumstances a week elapsed, and, as the next Sunday approached, the doctor suggested that the Reverend Mr. Smith and his wife spend another week at the Landing.[14]

They came. It was a beautiful June day, with a blue sky, the air full of the calls of birds. Abby was appealing in her white graduating dress, although a little wistful at times. After a jolly dinner, they adjourned to the sitting-room, and at a signal from the minister, Abby and the doctor stood before him, and he made them man and wife.[15] The brief service completed, the Smiths departed, the doctor went to look at the stock, and Abby found herself alone in the little room under the gingerbread eaves. While she was awaiting his return, she wrote her parents the events of the day. "Pray for us," she concluded, "that we may be as bright and shining lights in the world."

CHAPTER XLI

ABBY

1851-1853

THE first time the doctor went to San Francisco after the wedding, he brought his young bride a beautiful set of pearls fashioned like bunches of grapes. There were long pendants for her ears and a large brooch for her bosom. The miniature leaves and stalks glistened with tiny diamonds.

Abby was divinely happy. "Had I gone the world over," she confided in her home letters, "I could not have found a husband that would have suited me better in every respect." There was but one rift in the lute; again and again she recurred to it; "I hope he is a Christian." While this doubt assailed his bride, the doctor was convinced that the Lord had guided an angel to his door.

Soon after their wedding, the doctor took his young wife to the old *adobe* to live. The dirt floors were the despair of Abby's life, but the romantic situation of her new home appealed to her. She loved the broad brook that ran, deep and still, near the kitchen door. It never failed, and it was always cool and refreshing to drink. Under the oaks and elders that fringed its bank was a favorite spot where she sat and read. Before long she had planted roses, dahlias, cinnamon pinks and peonies along its banks, and was writing to Chelmsford for peach, cherry, and plum stones, apple seeds, and a few ears of sweet and "snap" corn to augment her kitchen garden. Soon she had the garden enclosed with a broad fence, so closely nailed together that no squirrel could penetrate the sacred enclosure. Before

ABBY

long the New England stones came and then sprouted, much to Abby's delight.

But what gave her the keenest pleasure was the vineyard. It almost surrounded the *adobe*, row after row of hardy Isabella and Catawba grapes. They grew, not as they did in New England, over a trellis or arbor, but each vine was pruned like a little tree and had a stake to keep it straight. The vines bore great bunches of delicious purple fruit. The first summer and fall after Abby's coming, the crop was so plenteous that, selling for 87½ cents a pound, it brought $4,000.[1] Most of the grapes were destined for the gold mines. Abby herself packed them in crates, in the long, low packing-room that adjoined the *adobe*. Often, from its door at sunrise, especially in the spring, she could see the gold mines in the Sierras. To her they looked like vast snow-banks reaching to the clouds.[2]

Across the brook were the Indians—a never-failing supply of faithful workers, men, women and children. They still tended the doctor's herds, vineyards and gardens. Not a day passed but two or three of the squaws came to see Abby and to take care of her laundry.[3] They all spoke Spanish, and when the doctor was away on the ranges, as he frequently was for weeks at a time, Abby amused herself by learning the language. She thought it would please the doctor. As the summer ripened into autumn, the Indians suffered greatly from chills and fever. Each morning Abby visited their quarters, with her own hands giving the sick food and medicine. Many would have died without her ministrations. They came to adore "the Lady of the *Adobe*" and brought her presents of wild game and berries.

Sometimes Abby galloped over the ranges by her husband's side. She loved those days in the open. The doctor now ruled over a great principality of 50,000 acres.[4] In his employ, besides the Indians, there were some twenty *vaqueros*, cowboys and herders in charge of his 6,000 cattle, 500 hogs, and his droves of horses, herds of sheep and hundreds of chickens. The doctor took an especial pride in the breed of his horses. To improve the strain, he imported to California at a cost of $800[5] one of the finest studs in the States—a descendant of the famous Tennessee stallion, *Shakespeare*.

The yearly *rodeo* was a thrilling event. Abby never missed an hour of it. She liked to watch the *vaqueros* segregate their cattle from those on the neighboring ranchos. It was exciting to see the cattle thrown and then branded with a red-hot iron. There was an annual increase of between 1,500 and 2,000 calves to the *Los Meganos* herds.

Soon after her arrival, the doctor sold 100 bullocks for $5,000 dollars, and shipped 200 calves to the mines, receiving for each one, according to size, from $30 to $40. In the same market he sold chickens at $2 and $3 each, and for a time received $3 and $4 a dozen for eggs.[6]

Butter was in great demand. The doctor told Abby she could have for pin-money all that she could make and sell. He set aside 150 gentle cows for her. The *vaqueros* milked them. The squaws did the churning. Together they made from fifteen to twenty pounds a week, which sold for one or two dollars a pound in the open market. The entire proceeds found its way to Abby's parents at Chelmsford.[7]

In spite of all this wealth, there were two things that Abby missed, and missed sorely: a church in which to worship, and her father's voice at prayer. She preferred things of the spirit to those of a material nature—God to Mammon. Sundays made her homesick, until she inaugurated Sabbath worship in the *adobe*. Once again the doctor read from his book of Psalms.

ABBY

Business kept the doctor moving. He was often absent, even at night, and Abby was alone with no neighbors but the squaws. She loved it most when a fire crackled on the hearth, and she sewed on tiny white garments while the doctor lay on a nearby sofa reading aloud.

"He prefers to read lying down," she wrote. "When he is at home, he reads more than half the time, sometimes all night. When out of interesting matter, he reads novels."[8]

The doctor disliked to be away at this time, but he had no choice in the matter. He was subjected to many troubles and difficulties, that had been unknown to him before 1849. Squatters were an ever-increasing menace. The loss of his deeds made his hold precarious. He spent months proving his claim before the land commission. He had to assemble witnesses, and these did not always help his cause; one especially, his neighbor, Ygnacio Sebrian, who branded his calves, swore that the bounds of *Los Meganos* were entirely different from what the doctor claimed.[9]

About this time Marsh began to have trouble with his *vaqueros*. With the general increase in prices, they demanded a raise in pay. When this was not readily forthcoming, there was mutiny. Sometimes he did not pay their salaries when they fell due, and for one reason or another postponed payment from month to month. His procrastination bred continual bad feeling. They were like a tinder box, ready for the spark.

Every time the doctor returned from his business trips he brought Abby presents, once a beautiful Spanish *rebozo* of many colors, again a wide silken cape, and once, in February of 1852, three pairs of lamb's-wool booties.[10] He was very proud of that purchase—those little knitted shoes!

In March, just as the leaves were putting forth and

the hills were turning green, a daughter was born. She was a frail infant, with dark blue eyes and fair skin, so fair that her veins showed through. Her hair was almost white, but the doctor wrote to Chelmsford that she was the rarest specimen in the country and the prettiest and smartest child in the world. They called her Alice, and the first thing he did when she was dressed and laid in his arms was to carry her across the brook and exhibit her to the dwellers in the wigwams. The Indians were proud of this little white child, born on their ancient *rancheria*. They appointed themselves her guardians and fairly worshipped her. This brought much joy to her young mother, who had rallied slowly and grew poor and weak from, as she thought, nursing her child. Even the sight of the green hills and the sudden burst of a California spring failed to bring the bloom back to her cheek, or the old elasticity to her limbs.

In addition to his other activities, the doctor was promoting a railroad from the Mississippi to the Pacific. He outlined a description of the route in the *California Star*. The railroad was needed. Besides, it would have made him fabulously rich. He advocated following the trail he had pursued to Santa Fé. That he claimed was the only practical route across the country for a railroad, for there were no mountains to scale, and an easy pass into the San Joaquin Valley. He promised to give the road a right of way through his rancho and to provide a Pacific terminus at the mouth of the San Joaquin.[11]

Abby was tremendously interested in this proposed route that was to skirt their property, but from an entirely different point of view from the doctor's. To her, it was an added link to Massachusetts. In her eagerness to see it completed, she pictured herself as one of the first

THE STONE HOUSE BUILT BY MARSH IN THE EARLY '50s.

The tower fell during the earthquake of 1869. The man in the top hat on the second floor balcony is Charles Marsh. From an old daguerreotype in the possession of Amy Cameron.

passengers. "Oh! Pray for the railroad to be completed," she wrote home. "Then we will have as many apples as we please."[12]

All of the doctor's dreams were coming true. He had wealth, an accomplished wife, a child. Now he must have a home worthy of them and of the richest cattle-baron on the San Joaquin! He told Abby she should have the finest home in California. She selected the site.[13] It was ideal, in the portal of a pretty valley and almost directly opposite the old *adobe*. It commanded a fine sweep of the San Joaquin plain and was shaded by oaks, century old, two of which stood like sentinels near the portal. Construction commenced.

The building was considered an architectural gem. There was nothing in California that approached it in magnificence. It had the manorial proportions of an old English residence—peak roof, seven gables, projecting eaves, arched windows, carved lintels, and a tower sixty-five feet in height dominating the whole. The brick of which it was constructed was burnt on the place. The drab-colored freestone with which it was ornamented was quarried on the property. Abby and the doctor drew the plans for the interior. They had great fun over those plans.

There was a wide hall. It ran from east to west through the house. On one side was a living-room forty feet long, with a white marble mantelpiece and long French windows, and on the other side was a dining-room of ample proportions, with a service section in the wing. Above was a bedroom at the head of the wide stairs and, over the living-room, a suite for Abby and the doctor, one room of which, with mantel and bookcase, was intended for a library. They spent long, happy hours planning the nursery, and the wide portico, supported by beautiful octagonal pillars and inclosed by an elaborately finished balustrade, on which it opened. Here tiny feet could race up and down and be amply guarded.

The closer the stone house came to completion, the nearer the fruit trees came to fruition, the weaker Abby grew. The old cough came back and with it drenching perspirations that consumed her vitality and left her weak and inert upon her bed, often too spent to rise. She felt that it was the nursing that dragged her down, and promptly weaned her baby; still she did not rally. Her thoughts turned sadly upon the future. "I feel how uncertain life is," she wrote. "Even in health we know not when we shall be called to exchange worlds. Oh! Lord prepare me for life or death, is all I ask."[14]

Little Alice was four years old and chattering like a parrot; but her mother could not look at her without misgivings. What would happen if . . . ? She could stand it no longer. Finally, she summoned Mrs. Thompson, who then lived at the Landing, nine miles away. When she arrived, Abby said to her: "I know I shall never get well. I want you to take Alice and love her as your own."

"I don't know that I could," replied she. "I have never been tried that way. Why not send her East?"

"Take her," insisted Abby. "Take her and train her as you would your own. Teach her to be truthful and teach her to pray."

The doctor's heart sank at the proposal. The *adobe* without the baby! It was not to be borne! "Oh! Abby let her stay a little longer," he pleaded. "Leave her with me as long as you can."[15]

By the middle of June the great valley sweltered in its own heat. The grass was burnt to a crisp. The foothills

ABBY

took on a coppery hue. *Los Meganos* was a furnace. Some days the thermometer registered 109 degrees. The parched air exhausted Abby. There was not a breath of wind. The heat sapped the last vestiges of her vitality. Finally, she could no longer write. She was broken—the last tie with Chelmsford was gone.

One day as the doctor bent over her couch, she pressed her pen into his hand and bade him write her parents. He could hardly tranquillize himself for the task, but Abby was determined and already dictating.

He sat down beside her, picked up her pad and wrote mechanically: "To you I must say farewell," she whispered. "Death is about to take one more of your little band and claim her as his own. . . . But do not weep or mourn for me; you know the source from whence to draw consolation. I did hope to see you again in this world, but God has ordered it otherwise. He calls, and I must go. . . . Oh, that I could have you with me! That I could hear your prayers! . . . Feel your sympathies! My strength fails. . . . I can say no more. My weak and trembling hand would fain clasp yours and say, farewell!"[16]

CHAPTER XLII

VIGILANTES
1855

AT dawn of a breathless August morning, Abby breathed her last. She was calm and resigned, even desirous to depart.[1] On the following Sunday they laid her in a redwood coffin. In the cool of the evening, while the Reverend Mr. Brierely spoke the prayers of the dead, they lowered her into a grave, dug in the orchard in the midst of the trees that as seedlings had come from Massachusetts.

Immediately after the funeral, the doctor carried Alice to Mrs. Thompson at the Landing. He could not go back to the *adobe;* not yet at least. "Sadly oppressed and overwhelmed with grief," he took the night-boat for San Francisco.

"I have been for the last two months residing in this city," he wrote to his wife's parents early in the following January, "only going home occasionally. Indeed it seems to me that I have no home now that I have lost my companion, the joy of my life. I now send you a trunk of her clothes, according to her request a few days before she died. . . . It was Abby's repeated request during her last illness that I should marry again . . . but it seems to me almost impossible to comply with it at present. Who is worthy to take her place? If I should find no one here, I may perhaps go East for that purpose."[2]

But the squatters and cattle thieves gave him little time for grief or further uxorial adventures. He was surrounded by thieves and vagabonds, who, like wolves, were ready to tear him to pieces if he allowed his vigilance to relax.[3] His great property was always in jeopardy. The law afforded him scant protection. California jurisprudence, written for a pastoral population of twenty or thirty thousand, could not cope with one of a quarter of a million, a large proportion of whom were ex-jailbirds and criminals of one form or another. Already San Francisco had been burned to the ground three times, but fire had not purified it.

Robbery, murder and theft went on, hand in hand with arson. Judges and police were often in connivance with criminals. Juries were packed and decisions were bought and sold to the highest bidder. No one's property, in or out of San Francisco, was safe. Lawlessness and license reigned uncurbed. Crime of all kinds went unpunished.

Sutter's property on the Sacramento was already overrun by the argonauts and appropriated by land-grabbers. The general was unequal to cope with the situation and was already on the road to ruin. Not so Marsh. He had no intention of being robbed of a property now valued at half a million dollars, that had taken the best years of his life to accumulate.

During the summer of 1852 his troubles with the squatters began. When he thwarted them they threatened to shoot him and his *mayordomo*, Thompson, and to burn down his houses at the Landing. The cattle thieves were even worse. They stole his cows, regardless of brand, and in spite of the guards he had placed about his ranges. The thieves sold their loot in the open market. Once he caught four of them red-handed. He was cool, but decided. They deserved no mercy, he said. He assembled his neighbors, strung up the thieves on a tree and left them hanging as an object lesson.⁴ This incident did not improve his standing among the nefarious.

On another occasion Marsh rode down to the river and found a squatter had already fenced off part of his acres. That was too much. The doctor ordered him to be gone. The squatter was insolent; Marsh was so furious that he drew out his *reata* and threw it dextrously over the offender's head and would have dragged him to death had not the squatter cut the rope and fled. Neither did this episode improve his reputation among evil-doers. They all hated and feared him.

When John Sanders squatted on a generous slice of his acres and contracted with an Irishman to fence it in, the doctor was more cautious, but no less determined.⁵ On his orders, his *mayordomo* tried to eject him, but without success.

Then Gilbert Leonard, another "sand-lapper," as those squatters were sneeringly referred to, "jumped" a big slice of the Landing, claimed it on squatter's rights and defied the efforts of Marsh, Thompson or the courts to oust him.⁶ This time the doctor appealed to the law and instituted a suit against Leonard for forcible entry and detainer. The case was bitterly fought. Marsh had many enemies, and Leonard, many partisans, who threatened to kill the former as well as his *mayordomo*, and to burn down his house. In the end, Leonard was the temporary victor and remained in possession of the land.

Being so far successful, Leonard joined forces with John Osborne. Having successfully acquired the doctor's land, they then began to appropriate his cattle. They drove them into a sequestered nook, corralled and shot them, burned the telltale hides and hoofs, dressed the meat, and sold it in the markets of Stockton and San

VIGILANTES

Francisco, thereby making a good living at the doctor's expense. For this state of affairs there was no redress in the county court-house in Martinez, where the judge had great respect for squatters. Thereupon, the doctor took his troubles to the grand jury, but its members took no cognizance of his complaint. They were nearly all latecomers. They had more sympathy for the squatters than for the holders of grants and argued that the immigrant, after the long perilous trip from the States, was entitled to settle where he saw fit.

Finally, Marsh appealed to Judge Daniel Hunsacker of Martinez, telling him that the squatters were stealing and killing his stock, and that he did not know which way to turn. The judge was powerless. He retorted that if people were killing his own stock, he would call on "Judge Lynch" to remedy the evil.[7] He further assured Marsh that if he needed his services at any time in such an emergency, he was his to command.

The doctor made no reply and departed. The law had become such a farce in California that the people were taking affairs into their own hands. Already the Vigilantes had hung many bad men in San Francisco. It was rumored that a Band of Regulators had been organized in Martinez, the county seat. The ranchers thereabouts had already strung up two cattle thieves—a Frenchman and a Belgian, who had hides in their possession bearing the brands of neighboring farmers.[8]

Having tried all the legitimate channels, Marsh now decided on "Judge Lynch" again. Taking his *mayordomo* with him, he went to Martinez and appealed to one A L. Brown, a blacksmith, who was supposed to be the organizer of the local Regulators.

The doctor took Brown to a room at the Morgan House,

JOHN MARSH, PIONEER

latched the door and drew the curtains behind him.[9] He must be careful. He then enumerated his grievances against Leonard and Osborne; that he had appealed to the grand jury without effect; that there was so much prejudice against him, he could not get justice; that now he was determined to get it, law or no law; that he wanted Brown to organize a body of men to go to his Landing; that he would pay them well and bear all the expenses, and provide the swiftest horses in Martinez for the purpose; that they must go by night, wearing black crêpe masks over their faces; that on arriving at the Landing, they must take the two scoundrels out of their houses, tie them to a tree, administer a hundred lashes to each and order them to leave the country, under penalty of death. If they did not leave immediately, the Regulators were to take the pair out on the Bay in a boat and then scuttle the boat. He warned Brown that he did not want to be known in the affair, as his life was already in jeopardy.[10]

At this juncture, Brown left. He said he wanted to think the matter over and would get in touch with him later. Marsh had appealed to the wrong man.

Outside, Brown met the sheriff and told him the whole occurrence. While Marsh and Thompson awaited his return, Brown went before the grand jury, which happened to be in session at the time, and gave them the gist of the conversation he had just had with the doctor. Forthwith that body found two indictments against the doctor, charging both him and Thompson with "the crime of conspiracy for the purpose of committing assault and battery on one Gilbert Leonard, and one John Osborne, against the peace and dignity of the people of California."

On the 11th of February, 1855, the doctor and his *mayordomo* were arraigned in Judge Nat Wood's court at

VIGILANTES

Martinez. They pleaded not guilty and were acquitted at the first trial; but in the next—although the jury was one of their own selection—the judge turned about, determined to convict them, and gave the jury instructions exactly the opposite to those he had originally given.[11] At first the jurors could not agree, but finally they found "the defendants guilty as charged in the Bill of Indictment and recommended them to the mercy of the Court." Immediately the doctor filed a motion for a new trial, but this was denied. The judge ordered Marsh to stand up and sentenced him to pay a fine of $500, or in default of payment, to "be confined in the county jail for a period of fifty days."[12]

It was infamous. The courts were in cahoots with the criminals.

Marsh had no idea of submitting to such treatment. He hired the best counsel he could find around the Bay and took the case to the Supreme Court, where the decision was reversed on a restatement of the issues.

CHAPTER XLIII

ROBBERS

1856

ONE day Marsh returned to his rancho and found two robbers ransacking his *adobe*. One escaped, but the other he caught, tied him hand and foot and left him on the kitchen floor while his *vaqueros* went to Martinez to get an officer to take him to prison. While he lay there without hat, coat, shoes or stockings, as miserable a specimen of humanity as could well be imagined, the doctor talked to him. "I never heard a fellow speak better Spanish," he afterward wrote. "It was pure Castilian, and after conversing with him nearly an hour, I was inclined to untie him and let the rascal run, for I thought it was a shame to incarcerate a man who spoke such pure Spanish."[1]

A short time afterward, the tables were reversed. Marsh had been riding about his rancho, when his horse stumbled and threw him, spraining his ankle. Being in the neighborhood of the Landing, he managed to reach the Thompsons' door and knocked. There was no response to his summons, and he dragged himself over the threshold and threw himself in great agony upon the floor, trying to pull the boot from his swollen foot. While thus engaged, a party of horsemen rode into the yard and dismounted. Presently the door was thrown open, and a young Spaniard, booted and spurred, stood before him with pistol coolly levelled at his head. Marsh recognized him instantly as Murietta, the bandit, the terror of the mines.

Once, during a temporary absence, the outlaw's young

wife had been grossly mistreated by the miners, and had subsequently died from her injuries. On top of that, his brother, mistaken for a horse thief, had been hanged from a tree. These unprovoked deaths had turned the sober young Mexican into an avenger, and the notches on his pistol were witness to his success. Marsh knew all this, and also that few of Murietta's victims escaped his knife. He was unarmed and unable to stand upon his feet and defend himself. He told this to Murietta in Spanish, but, before he could finish speaking, a cloth was rammed down his throat and his arms and legs were trussed. Then, bound and gagged, they threw him in a corner and rifled his pockets of watch and money.[2]

This occurrence came to Marsh's mind one dark, rainy night late in March, when there came a sudden pounding on the door of the *adobe*. As was his wont, the doctor lay in bed reading, a lamp was burning at his side, and a fire crackled on the hearth in an adjoining room. His Indian boy, Juan, opened the door cautiously, and the doctor looked up from his book. The rain was coming down in torrents, but on his threshold he could see a seedy, hungry-looking man of about thirty years. He stuck his muddy shoe through the aperture so that the door could not be closed in his face. At the same time, the stranger begged in a hoarse voice for a place to spend the night, pleading that he was sick, wet and tired, and wanted to get out of the storm.

"The Señor-Doctor is in there," said Juan, indicating his master's bedroom. "Come in and ask him."

The stranger did so, dripping at every step and leaving little pools of water in his wake.

"What do you want?" asked Marsh, gruffly, suspiciously eyeing the shabby young man before him.

JOHN MARSH, PIONEER

"Can I stay here to-night? I'm tired and want a night's lodging."

"No, sir, you can't remain here to-night," retorted Marsh. "I am building a new house and have thirty mechanics about the place now and cannot accommodate you."

"But, sir, I'm tired and have lost my way. I don't ask for food, though I'm cold and hungry, but I do ask for shelter. I saw a light here and came in." He tottered as he spoke.

"Have you any money?"

"No," said the stranger.

"A man has no business to be travelling here afoot and alone without money."

"I can't help that. I'm tired, and my feet are sore. The great Joaquin plain lies beyond, as I hear, without houses. I don't ask for money, or even for food or a bed. Let me sit down by your fire until daylight."[3]

The doctor eyed the newcomer closely. He looked with disapproval on his miserable, suspicious appearance. But he observed that he looked sick and worn and seemed so weak that he could hardly stand. The stranger continued:

"It's hard to turn a man from your door on a rainy night like this, and it's hard for a man who is sick in a civilized country to have to sleep in the open air. I have come from the States to search for some one I know."

"Well, I've heard that story before, and I can't give you a bed—they're all full. And you can't sleep with me," and he laughed. "But if what you tell me is true, if you're a stranger and have lost your way, I won't turn you out-of-doors. You can sit down by the fire, dry your clothes, and when you are tired, you can lie down upon the floor

ROBBERS

and put your carpet-bag under your head for a pillow."

"Thank you, sir. That's all I require," replied the stranger, and he limped away to the fireplace and slumped down by the hearth, glad to get a shelter, for he had thrown away his blankets when he had found himself unable to carry them farther. He proceeded to warm and dry himself by the fire. The doctor returned to his book. Outside, it was still raining.

After a little, the doctor either came to the end of a chapter or grew tired of reading. He looked up from his page and said:

"You say you landed in San Francisco yesterday?"

"Yes, sir."

"What steamer did you come by?"

"The *Sonora*."[4]

"You say you are from the States—what State?"

"Illinois—from the neighborhood of Springfield."

After a brief pause, the reader looked up again and inquired: "Know any one there named Berry—Reverend John M. Berry?"

"Yes, a Presbyterian minister; he baptized me."

"Know a man named Rutledge?"

"Yes," said the stranger.

"What's your name?"

"Marsh."

The older man sat up in bed. "How do you spell it?"

"M-a-r-s-h, Marsh," he explained.

"Any connection of the Marshes of Jacksonville?"

"No," replied the younger man.

"Been long in Illinois?" persisted the doctor.

"Yes, from the time I was six years old."[5]

"Where were you born?"

"Prairie du Chien."

JOHN MARSH, PIONEER

"Prairie du Chien!" exclaimed the doctor in a loud voice.[6] Then he added: "Come to me closer—I want to look at you."

The stranger pulled himself to his feet and hobbled to his host, who, now greatly agitated, was seated on the edge of the bed.

"Who brought you up?" he demanded.

"James Pantier. A man named James Pantier," faltered the stranger.

Trembling with excitement, his face agitated with emotion, the doctor jumped out of bed, ran and put his hands upon the younger man's head, turning it this way and that and scrutinizing every feature of the face. Then his interest slackened, but he looked at him still.

"You say your name is Marsh—what's your given name?"

"Charles."

"Father and mother dead?"

The stranger was getting tired of this useless interrogation, and replied:

"I don't know."

"Well, tell me their history."

"I have nothing to be ashamed of, but I don't care to give my pedigree to a stranger."

"Tell me, young man," insisted the other. "It may be to your advantage."

Then the stranger began the story of his life, and the older man watched every look and drank in every word, and was presently gasping with excitement.

"I have one more request—and it is a strange one. Show me your foot."

The stranger burst into peals of laughter. "That's a strange thing to ask a man. Which foot?" he countered.

ROBBERS

The doctor winced a little, and then said:

"I have almost forgotten, but I think it is the right one I want to see."

The stranger drew off his boot and sock and showed the doctor a raw and blistered foot. The older man drew it toward him and looked at the toes. He examined them closely. They were webbed to their ends by a strong membrane. As soon as he saw the deformity, the tears ran down his cheeks. He heaved a deep sigh. A load of years of forgetfulness seemed to roll away.

"Old Jimmy Pantier raised you," he said. "Your name is Charles Pantier Marsh. I am your father, and you are my son, my dear son!"

Then the old man, whom *vaqueros* hated, and squatters, horse thieves, cattle stealers and all the semi-savage population of Contra Costa feared and detested, and whom most looked upon as a hard, selfish, intolerant old fellow, fell upon his son's neck and sobbed aloud, even as Israel wept over his long-lost son, Joseph. In broken accents he said:

"Man, you may stay, for you are my son. I supposed you had died a boy!" Calling loudly, "Juan! Juan!" he summoned his servant. "Get a hot supper, Juan, and make up a good bed for my son!"

Food and drink were brought, and the young man strove to eat; he had been hungry enough an hour earlier and could have devoured the crumbs that fell from his father's table, but now the food choked him. Seeing his weakness, fatigue and emotion, his father said, "Come," and half-supporting him, led him to a room where Juan had made up a bed. The boy, clothes and all, sank exhausted upon it, while the doctor pulled off his damp and soggy garments.

JOHN MARSH, PIONEER

But sleep did not come to those tired limbs for many hours. The doctor sat down on the bed while Charles told him that no news had come from him after he left Independence; that they believed he had gone to South America; that when nothing was heard of him, he grew up as one of the Pantier family and in the course of years took their name; that when he reached man's estate "Uncle Jimmie" had given him some hogs and a farm at Petersburg and his niece, Sara, to wed; that they had three children, but that his ruling passion all the time had been to find his father, and that once, after the gold discovery, a returned argonaut had said to him:

"I know a gentleman in California by your name, whom you resemble very much. You look enough like him to be his son."

He had replied: "My father was a physician!"

"The man I know in California was a physician," the argonaut had retorted, "and the more I see of you, the more certain I am that you are his son. You have the same eyes, the same nose, the same carriage."[7]

From then on, Charles added, he wanted to go to California and see if this man were his parent; that his wife would not hear of his leaving his family and going off on so wild a chase as the search for a father who had run away from his country twenty years before; that for twelve months he never spoke to her of his resolve to go, but all the time he was gradually forming his plans; that finally he sold his hogs for $200 and on February 4, 1856, had kissed her good-bye and told her he was going to Petersburg; that en route he sent back word that he was going to California to find his father.

Charles related how he had gone down the Mississippi to New Orleans, sailed for the Isthmus, crossed over, and

ROBBERS

embarked for San Francisco on a steamer called the *Sonora*, and had arrived March 23; that he had slept there one night and set out for Martinez the next day and had spent another night there. Early the next morning he was directed to travel toward Monte Diablo, and had set out to walk the twenty-five miles to his supposed father's house. But his progress was slow, for he was very feeble, having been seasick ever since he left the Mississippi. After he started, it began to rain and continued, harder and harder, as he progressed.

Charles had never seen any mountains around Petersburg, and when, that day, he reached the summit of one and looked over the wide expanse of country, his heart misgave him, and he berated himself for a fool to desert his own blood, his wife and babies, to seek one who had never been much of a father. He had sat down to reflect, and it came to him that there were many Doctor Marshes in the world, and that it was very unlikely that the one he had come so many miles to see would prove his father. He had no money with which to return to Petersburg, and it occurred to him that he might die there on the mountain-top, and his sons would never see or hear of him again, just as he had never again heard of his father.

Then he had burst into tears and, throwing himself face down on the wet ground, had wept like a woman at the folly and cruelty of his conduct. Finally he had realized that he could not remain on the mountain-top; that he might be eaten by grizzly bears or devoured by mountain lions, and he had got up and stumbled down to the valley. When it became dark, the rain had increased, and he could hardly walk. Arriving at a cattle corral, he had decided to lie down and wait till morning, for his strength was gone, and he could not hobble a hundred yards without resting.

JOHN MARSH, PIONEER

The worst of it was he did not know where he was. Fear of nocturnal prowlers had driven him to further exertion, and he had said to himself: "I shall perish if I remain here." Shortly after, passing round a clump of oaks, he saw, a quarter of a mile distant, two houses, both lighted, one with one window, the other with two. He could now no longer stand up and, falling on his hands and knees, had crawled slowly to the larger house and knocked at the door.[8]

When he finished this recital, the old man tore himself away and went to his room. Later, he returned in his night-clothes with a lamp, to satisfy himself again that the strange man was the same person as the prattling, curly-pated boy whom he had left in the Concord settlements of Illinois. Being again assured, he remained standing at the door from ten o'clock until after two, with the lamp in one hand and the latch in the other, talking as fondly as a mother. And the habit, begun the first night, continued nightly thereafter.[9]

The next morning after breakfast, Marsh took his son through the new house, then almost finished, and told him there were thirty mechanics on the rancho rushing the work to completion. He showed him the marble fireplaces, the shelves for his books, and the long French windows disclosing a wide view of mountain and plain and creek. Charles had never seen anything so magnificent. In a secret hiding-place the doctor opened an old iron-bound chest. It was filled to the brim with Spanish doubloons. Charles had never seen so much gold before. His eyes nearly bulged out of their sockets. He had more hidden wealth, his father said. He was afraid of the rickety California banks and had been forced to bury it all. Then he told his son about Abby and Alice, and that he was about

ROBBERS

to marry again and move into the stone house. He promised him that in the spring he would send him back to Petersburg to get his family and bring them to the rancho, and that they could live in the old *adobe*.

Then he had his old wagon brought around and drove Charles to Stockton. On the way, he stopped at Chamberlain's Tavern to water his horse. There were a number of men standing about the bar, and the doctor called them out and one by one introduced them to his son, saying he hadn't seen him for twenty-five years.

"Well," said Chamberlain, regarding the younger man's blue eyes, light hair and robust build, "I should know he was your son. He is a 'chip off the old block.' " And the doctor rode on, stopping to introduce his son to every one he met.[10]

CHAPTER XLIV

HARVEST TIME
1856

IT was 1855. The time for the yearly *rodeo* rolled around. The doctor, as had been his custom for many years, summoned his neighbor, Ygnacio Sebrian, to brand his calves.[1] Ygnacio came, bringing his own crew of *vaqueros* with him. Among them was his brother-in-law, Felipe Morena, a handsome, dark-complexioned, slender youth of nineteen. Down was just appearing on his lips. He had fine, white teeth, a sprightly air, and a cruel smile.[2] With the women he was a great favorite, and they affectionately called him "Nino." Even the *vaqueros* respected him. He was more adept than they with the lasso. It was for him his uncle always called when he had a particularly refractory calf with which to deal. It was Felipe who invariably brought the animal to the ground and to a realization of the situation. He was a valuable adjunct to any crew.

Another of Sebrian's crew was José Antonio Olivas, whom the other *vaqueros* called "Chino," because he had black, kinky hair and a complexion darker than theirs, showing that a negro strain was freely mixed with his Latin blood. He was the boldest rider and best *vaquero* in Contra Costa, and the doctor employed him frequently to break his colts.

Marsh always paid Sebrian twenty-five cents—the customary amount—for each calf he branded; but that year the doctor neglected to make a contract before the *rodeo*

HARVEST TIME

started. When the work was finished, Sebrian announced that his price had gone up, and demanded a dollar for each calf.[3] Marsh, however, refused to be imposed upon, and paid him a sum computed on the old basis. Ygnacio was furious and promptly sued Marsh for the difference —$1,200. The case was tried at Martinez. At the trial the doctor swore he had paid him in full, and proved that twenty-five cents was the amount he had paid him previously—and that every one else paid—and that this was all the job was worth. The verdict was rendered in Marsh's favor.[4]

After the trial, as the doctor came down the court-house steps, elated over his victory, one of his friends stepped up to him and whispered in his ear.

"Marsh, you had better have paid that man what he asked. They'll get you."

"The hell I had," replied Marsh. "I'm in the right, and I *will* have justice."[5]

Sebrian was boiling with rage, as were Felipe Morena and all the servants, *vaqueros* and Mexicans connected with the rancho.[6] They all thirsted for revenge. In his anger, Sebrian offered $500 to any one who would kill the doctor.[7] Nino was listening.

When it came time to pay Olivas, he too demanded an exorbitant sum, much in excess of previous years. Marsh laughed in his face, telling him to accept what was offered or be gone. Olivas swore that he would sue him.

"Sue me?" retorted the doctor with a sneer. "You can't; you're a nigger."[8]

That year's *rodeo* ended in bad blood.

The great stone house was about completed. It was a splendid pile of stone and masonry—a worthy seat for the wealthiest cattle baron in Northern California. The doc-

JOHN MARSH, PIONEER

tor looked at it with pride. There was not another mansion like it in the whole State. It told the world that John Marsh had reached his goal. He was rich and powerful. Where else in the country could be found such cattle, such horses, such vineyards as at *Los Meganos?* He was proud of his accomplishment—from a farm to a rancho—from poverty to riches.

One September night the doctor moved into the room at the head of the stairs. He arranged his books to his liking—Paine's "Works," Johnson's "Lives of the English Poets," the "Odes of Anacreon," a French Bible. Strange, they had been with him from the beginning. They were his oldest friends—often his only ones. They had remained by him through thick and thin, from better to worse, from worse to better. Every night he read a few pages out of one of them. He prized them. He spread out pen, ink and pads on his writing-table. He would do more reading and writing now. He would enjoy life while his cattle multiplied, and the stream of gold flowed in. *Mañana!*

But he had little time for his favorite recreations. The cattle thieves were again at work among his herds. He spent all his spare moments in the turret of his tower, trying to spy them out with a glass. From it, for miles around he could watch his great herds grazing and could have seen any one in the vicinity who might try to drive them off or kill them. But this time he was dealing with a new variety of cattle thief. These were too clever to work under his, or any one else's nose, and for a long time neither he nor his *mayordomo* could discover how his cattle continued to disappear in such wholesale proportions. He then hired a sort of detective—a man named R. M. Fugate—who stationed himself among the tules on the water front.

HARVEST TIME

In the middle of one September night, Fugate saw a sloop come up the river. He saw it moored among the tules, saw three men land, round up a bunch of cattle and drive them on board. The pirate sloop then disappeared silently down the river, and in a short time another took its place, was loaded with cattle and silently sped away. He watched the proceedings long enough, and overheard sufficient of the men's conversation, to learn that the thieves employed three sloops; that they stole the cattle alive, shot them, quartered and salted them down in the hold, then sold them the next day to the markets of San Francisco.

Satisfied that he had discovered the cause of the loss of immense numbers of the doctor's cattle, and convinced that they could catch the thieves in the city, Fugate gave a Mexican boy fifty cents and dispatched him with a note to the doctor.

"We must go to Martinez or Oakland on Tuesday," he wrote, "and may arrive in the city by steamboat before the sloop. I know the names; one man of the gang remains here. Understand, that you must furnish me with say, fifty dollars, and if we arrest them, one hundred dollars for each conviction must be mine."[9] At the end of the letter Fugate appended a postscript: "I promised to treat the young man to grapes, if he bears this to you."

Marsh received Fugate's letter that day, and after reading it, turned to the messenger and said:

"Have you any money?"

"Yes," replied the messenger, "fifty cents which Fugate gave me for bringing this letter to you."

"Well, give it to me," returned Marsh, "and I'll cut you some grapes." And he went to the vineyard and returned with a bag of the luscious fruit.[10]

JOHN MARSH, PIONEER

Marsh accepted Fugate's conditions. Two days later the latter was aboard a steamboat, with a letter in his pocket addressed to the Honorable S. P. Webb, the doctor's lawyer and his Harvard classmate.

"This will be handed to you by Mr. Fugate," wrote Marsh, "who goes to San Francisco for the purpose of causing the arrest of some thieves who have been stealing my cattle on a large scale. Please take him to the chief of police and give him such advice as may be of service to him. I cannot go down tonight because I have important business tomorrow here, but I will endeavor to come down on tomorrow night's boat."[11]

The important business on the next day, which fell upon a September 24, was the sale of some of his cattle to a butcher. His *vaqueros*, among whom happened to be Juan Garcia and Felipe Morena—the two had been to a *fandango* the night before and were still drunk[12]—rounded them up on the *rodeo* grounds for inspection. The butcher selected the steers he wanted and gave Marsh $5,000 in gold—enough to excite the lust of any *vaquero*, Garcia's and Morena's particularly.

After this deal, the doctor returned to the stone house, hid his gold, and made ready to drive to Martinez, intending to take the night-boat from there to San Francisco. He dressed himself very carefully that day and donned his broadcloth coat, his best black satin stock, his whitest linen—and stretched a massive gold chain over his brocaded waistcoat. Humor said that the thought of a waiting bride in San Francisco, a lady of some position in society, the sister of a gentleman who had been mayor of the city, filled his imagination and quickened his pulse.[13] At any rate, he looked particularly fit that afternoon; his fifty-six winters sat lightly upon him, and a stranger

HARVEST TIME

would have taken him for a much younger man. The passage of time had but fringed his hair with gray, and his robust person and ruddy color showed that the hardships of a life of adventure had not impaired his constitution. Virile, broad-chested and muscular, he looked like a well-proportioned English squire off to the chase.

Between twelve and one o'clock he left the rancho in a low Concord buggy, drawn by a bay horse with a great white blaze in its face.[14] Before leaving home, he asked his son to get him some money from his chest, and Charles gave his father some $400 in gold and a bag of silver. In the compartment behind the movable apron back of the seat, he threw a carpet-bag, a loaded cane, and a basket of grapes.

It was a beautiful warm hazy September afternoon. Fields lay fallow. Hay was stacked. Barns were filled with grain; vineyards shorn. It was harvest time. The hills were mellow. The sky was blue. Birds sang. Crickets chirped. The air was aromatic with tarweed. It was a lazy day.

The doctor heaved a great sigh. He would have liked to take it easy, but he must go to San Francisco. He picked up the reins, nodded to his son and was gone. He drove rapidly through the foothills. He must travel fast. A five-hour journey lay ahead of him.

The sun was sinking behind the summit of the coast hills as he left Pacheco, a village distinguished by Pablo Morago's grocery-store and saloon, and emerged upon the plain.[15] On his right was the Suisun Bay, its glassy surface gilded by the reflection of the setting sun, its gentle ripples washing the edge of the tule. On his left arose a range of rounded hills, their slope enriched by the light and shade of many shrub-skirted gulches and ravines.[16]

JOHN MARSH, PIONEER

He passed a point where a spur of the hills ran far into the plain. Here the tide had washed away the tule on the farther side until there was but a narrow space, over which the road passed. Before him was an open area, and at its extreme edge he could see the large white house of Colonel Gift, and a mile and a half beyond, the village of Martinez. He had plenty of time. He slowed up.

Riding toward him from the town he might have seen three Californian *vaqueros,* mounted on mustangs and wearing belts and knives. They were of the ordinary Mexican half-breed type, showing by their dark skins, their black, wiry hair, high cheek-bones, heavy jaws, sullen looks, and low foreheads, the inherited ignorance and revengeful disposition of their breed. Down the hill the three horses clattered, champing their heavy Mexican bits and beating their flanks against the great rowels on the jingling spurs of their riders. The *vaqueros* were shouting at the tops of their voices, swinging their *reatas,* cursing and singing snatches of Mexican songs. The three advanced toward Marsh, and he toward them.

In the middle of the plain, half a mile from the white house, the doctor and the *vaqueros* met. The sun had gone down. The last ray had deserted the highest perch of Mount Diablo. Sombre shades were gathering over the bay and settling on the plain.

Marsh had just emerged from the second of two little gullies, only one of which was bridged, and was passing over a patch of yellow clay. On his right was a ditch, some two or three feet deep and three or four feet wide, and beyond that and rising from its edge was a sod-covered bank. Here the *vaqueros* drew rein. As they met, the eldest of them, the kinky-haired youth, who bore the name of Chino, shouted to the doctor: *"Buenas tardes!"*

HARVEST TIME

"*Buenas tardes,*" replied Marsh, recognizing them as Juan Garcia, Felipe Morena, Sebrian's brother-in-law, and the expert *vaquero*, Olivas.

"Pay me for the two months' work I have done you in breaking colts," sharply demanded Chino. Marsh started to pass on, then thought better of it and drew rein.

"I can't," he replied. "I have no money with me. I'm going to San Francisco. When I return, come to the rancho, and I will pay you."

"Pay the Chino what you owe him," shouted the smooth-faced Nino. "Give the *vaquero* his money, or we'll kill you."[17]

The doctor looked him coolly in the eye, made no response, and drove on. The three *vaqueros* stayed behind, arguing as to what they would do. The money they had seen exchanged at that morning's *rodeo* decided them. They galloped in pursuit of their victim. They would rob him. As they approached his buggy again, Nino took command of the situation and ordered Olivas aside. He had his *reata* in his hand and was swinging it wildly back and forth. Finally he let it fly. The lasso settled neatly about the doctor's shoulders, grew taut about his neck, and the next instant, before he could protect himself, he was jerked over the back of his seat and into the dust.[18] Although momentarily stunned, he was quickly on his feet and drew himself up as if he would overawe them.

"Do you want to kill me!" he shouted.

"No," said Chino.

"Yes," shouted the bloodthirsty Nino. "Yes." At the same time he dismounted and advanced, making a menacing gesture.

"Nino! Nino! Don't do anything!" entreated Chino, who, though willing to commit highway robbery, shrank from anything more drastic.

JOHN MARSH, PIONEER

But the appeal was in vain. The heavy blade of Nino's Mexican knife gleamed for an instant in the twilight. The next second it was buried in the doctor's cheek, ripping it from nose to ear. With his gloved hand, Marsh seized the bare blade and endeavored to wrench it from the assassin's grasp. But Nino drew it dextrously through Marsh's hand, its keen blade cutting through the stout buckskin and severing the tendons of his fingers as it passed. At the same moment, Juan Garcia, who was standing behind the wounded man, buried his stiletto in his back. Then the doctor fought—with blood in his mouth and gushing out of his side—fought hard, fought as only a strong man could fight against three lithe, young Mexicans, all of whom were active as cats and cruel as panthers.

One of them he kicked in the stomach, gaining for himself a momentary respite. Then he grasped Olivas, who stood closest to him, and dealt him a stinging blow that brought him to the ground. Falling upon him, he held him there by his beard and bushy hair, and proceeded to throttle him. Olivas was a child in the powerful grasp of the wounded man. He bellowed in pain as his struggles brought his hair out by the roots.

"Help! Nino! Help!—take him off me," roared the prostrate man.

And Morena came to his assistance. Although he was half-blinded from the blood that poured from the cut in the doctor's face, Chino saw Nino raise his terrible knife and bury it in Marsh's chest.

"Don't," Chino protested. "What are you trying to do?"

The fierce young murderer fairly shouted:

"What! Did you think I would let the old *cabrona* go?" He stabbed him again in the side.

The doctor loosened his grip, and a cry—as if, while

HARVEST TIME

hope and life were ebbing together, he would make one last appeal for mercy—broke from his lips. But there was no room for anything but revenge in the Nino's nature. Again and again he raised his insatiate blade. Again and again he sheathed it to the hilt in his victim's body.

By a supreme effort, Marsh pulled himself away from his assailants, rose to his feet, tottered, regained himself. He drew himself erect. For an instant he stood poised at the edge of the ditch. Then he slumped, sprawled across it, his arms outstretched, one leg caught under him, his blood-stained face upturned to the starlit sky.

Not yet satisfied, Nino again descended upon his victim. He slit the doctor's throat from ear to ear, then turned his pockets inside out.

"The dead tell no tales," he yelled to his companions, as he mounted his mustang and galloped away.

Some time later, the horse with the great white blaze in its face walked into Martinez, the reins dragging in the dust.[19]

CHAPTER XLV

BY THE LAWS OF FRANCE

THE next day they carried the doctor's body back to *Los Meganos* and laid it in the hall of the stone house. During the night a red cross had appeared on some nearby cliffs. It was painted in blood. The *vaqueros* said that it was a warning, and they refused to go near their old master; but the Indians with their blankets over their heads, their faces painted with pitch, crouched at his bier all that day and night. On the second floor, in the room at the head of the stairs, slept the Reverend John McClure of San Francisco. He had come to commit his old friend to the dust. The next evening, in clerical robes, he led the way to the orchard. The Indians carried the doctor's body in an improvised coffin on their shoulders. In their wake came the little Alice; Charles was leading her by the hand.

An uncanny incident happened on the way to the grave. It was due to the lack of proper embalmers. Nevertheless it left a lasting impression on the mourners. The sides of the redwood casket gave way, and by the time the procession reached the spot where Abby was buried, the doctor's body lay on an open litter.

Marsh's death created a great commotion in California. He was one of the State's most eminent men. Too many of her prominent citizens had already fallen by the assassin's hand. San Francisco, dripping with blood, was avenging their murders with the gibbet. Law and order had been defied. Masked *vigilantes* usurped the seats of the inadequate officers of the law. Marsh's murder was the last

BY THE LAWS OF FRANCE

straw to the California governor, J. Neely Johnson, and he issued a proclamation giving a description of the mur-

PROCLAMATION!
ONE THOUSAND DOLLARS
REWARD.

WHEREAS, Information has been received that a murder was committed on the body of Dr. JOHN MARSH, on the evening of the 24th day of September, ultimo, near Martinez, in the County of Contra Costa, and that one of the persons suspected of said murder, namely, FELIPE MORENA, has eluded arrest and is now at large.

NOW THEREFORE, I, J. NEELY JOHNSON, Governor of the State of California, by virtue of the powers vested in me by law, do hereby offer a reward of One Thousand Dollars for the apprehension of the said Felipe Morena, and his safe delivery into the custody of the Sheriff of Contra Costa County.

[SEAL]

WITNESS, my hand, and the Great Seal of State, at Sacramento, this 13th day of October, A. D. 1856.

J. NEELY JOHNSON.

ATTEST: DAVID F. DOUGLASS,
Secretary of State.

DESCRIPTION:

FELIPE MORENA, commonly called NINO, is a native Californian or Mexican, about 19 or 20 years old; has black hair turning inward at the border ends; complexion dark and cloudy; has a thin beard about the upper lip; has fine white teeth; is about 5½ feet high, of rather slender appearance; weighs about 140 pounds; is of lively and sprightly air and action; speaks Spanish rapidly. His mother resides at San Jose, where it is suspected he may be concealed; if not there, he has probably gone to the southern portion of the State.

The following is a description of the Watch on the person of Dr. Marsh at the time of his murder, and which is supposed to be, or to have been, in the possession of Felipe Morena;

Gold Hunting Detached Lever, marked "Cooper, London," No. 20,038.

PROCLAMATION ISSUED BY THE GOVERNOR OF CALIFORNIA, 1856, OFFERING A REWARD FOR THE CAPTURE OF FELIPE MORENA, WHO MURDERED JOHN MARSH

derer, Felipe Morena, and offering a thousand dollars for his capture.

As soon as they heard the news of Marsh's death, Stephen H. Webb, the doctor's lawyer and former Harvard class-

JOHN MARSH, PIONEER

mate, and General James Wilson, of Keene, N. H., went to Martinez to take charge of his estate for the heirs.[1] They knew that he had thousands in gold, estimated to be as much as $50,000, hidden away. They wanted to locate it, but were unable to do so. Under direction of Wilson and Webb, searchers dug for days, turned the brook aside, excavated its bank and the cellar, but without success. Finally they sent for a divining rod, but even that instrument did not disclose the hidden wealth.

Nor could they find a will. The court appointed Captain Swain of Martinez and the doctor's nephew, James, as administrators. The first thing the latter did was to search out Charles.

"Go away," he ordered that young man. "Leave the ranch. You have no business here."

"What do you want to drive him away for," demanded Captain Swain.

"The doctor and his mother were never married," retorted James. "He is a bastard. His mother was a squaw. He has no claim."

Captain Swain did not think it a good policy to quarrel with his associate. He went to Charles and told him to leave the rancho quietly, but not to leave the country.

Alice, the heiress, became a bone of contention. A set of scoundrels applied for her guardianship.[2] The probate judge, a corrupt scamp, appointed a notorious gambler, Bowen, as her legal guardian. His choice created such furor among the respectable element of the county that the judge rescinded it and appointed in his place a Captain and Mrs. Coffin, a pair of sanctimonious hypocrites. Neither Alice nor her father had ever even heard of them. Armed with their papers, they went to Marsh's Landing, and, in spite of her pleadings, took the child away from

BY THE LAWS OF FRANCE

Mrs. Thompson. At their home in Martinez the orphan led a sorry life. From morning until night she worked like a servant, and was forced to wear her guardian's cast-off clothing.[3]

When the final account was settled in the probate office, Captain Swain took Charles to San Francisco and introduced him to Crockett and Page, the heads of an eminent law firm of that city, and explained to them his history. He asked them for what amount they would undertake the young man's case, explaining that if he won he would be entitled to one-half the estate and could pay them handsomely, but that if he lost, they would get nothing, as he had only the clothes he wore.

They consulted a few moments, then replied that they would take the case for $6,000.

"I think that is reasonable," said Captain Swain, "for if he prevails, he will be worth several hundred thousand."

"If what you tell me is true," replied Colonel Crockett, "that Doctor Marsh acknowledged him as his son to everybody in and about Contra Costa County, then there will be no difficulty in the case."

That year Colonel Crockett visited his old home on the Atlantic seaboard. On his return to San Francisco, he went to Prairie du Chien, where he interviewed the old inhabitants and took affidavits of sheriffs and others.

Meanwhile his partner, Mr. Page, had died, and Mr. Crittenden—who was afterwards killed by Mrs. Fair in one of the most famous San Francisco murders—was admitted as his partner.

Charles was anxious that Colonel E. D. Baker should be added to his legal force. He had known him in Illinois, knew his gifts of oratory and knew that he had been the friend of his father, mother and "Uncle Jimmie."

JOHN MARSH, PIONEER

Captain Swain called upon Crockett and Crittenden and made known Charles' desire.

They replied: "We have no occasion for Colonel Baker's services. The case is a good one."

Charles was still persistent, and Captain Swain went a second time, but again the lawyers refused, saying that it would be throwing money away for nothing. Thus Charles failed to retain Colonel Baker, and his services were engaged by the other side.

Charles told Captain Swain about the Reverend John Cameron, the Cumberland Presbyterian minister, who had lived at New Salem, and who had known his father and mother. Charles knew he was in California, he said, because his father had seen him. The captain made inquiries and finally located him at Bodega. He engaged horses, drove to see him and asked him if he knew anything about the case.

"Oh, yes," the Reverend Cameron replied. "I know all about it. I resided near Prairie du Chien when Doctor Marsh lived there, and I knew the little French-Indian girl. I couldn't swear to a marriage, but he lived with her as his wife, and he introduced her to all his friends as his wife. She visited my family at New Salem, and I would not have permitted her to do so if she were not respectable."

"Will you swear to that?" said Captain Swain.

"Certainly."

"Well, say nothing about it until the time arrives and you are wanted."

The case was finally called at Martinez. All Contra Costa turned out, drawn by curiosity, the murder, and by the remarkable circumstances connected with the whole affair. Mr. Crittenden opened his case by putting the Reverend John Cameron on the stand. The latter was so frank, so candid and had such an air of truthfulness in his whole

BY THE LAWS OF FRANCE

story that it made a profound sensation in the courtroom. In simple terms he told the pathetic tale of Marguerite, of her red-headed French-Canadian father, of her full-blooded Sioux mother, and of the coming of John Marsh, a youth of twenty-four, as Indian sub-agent to the Sioux at Fort Snelling.

He spoke of Marguerite's beauty, and of her gentle manners, more French than Indian. He said that Marsh saw her and immediately fell in love with her and taught her to read and write, and to love books; that she was just the reverse of the doctor; that he was rough and brusque, while she was all tenderness and affection; that no one was surprised when he became her lover and either married her or took her under his protection, as was customary in Mississippi communities. Then he went on to say that they were very happy together; that Marguerite was immensely proud of the young Yankee who took such an interest in her development; that, on her part, she strove hard to please him and to improve herself for his sake; that Marsh devoted all his leisure to perfecting her education; that in an incredibly short time she became a cultured woman; that she bore him a son, Charles; that the doctor and Marguerite and her baby had visited him at New Salem; that she was known everywhere as his wife and respected as "Mrs. Marsh"; that she died suddenly during the birth of a second child; that her death had a terrible effect upon the doctor; that he became dispirited and hypochondriac on account of it, and his friends advised him to go away.

As he concluded his testimony, one could have heard a pin drop. Mr. Crittenden arose, carried away by the sympathy of the spectators and by the old minister's story. He said: "I will rest my case here."

Then Colonel Baker stood up, a handsome, dignified,

JOHN MARSH, PIONEER

white-haired person, with a commanding presence. The atmosphere in the courtroom was hostile. The sentiments of the spectators were noticeably on the side of Charles. It was noted that Baker had a file of papers in his hand. The least observant could see that they were yellow with age. He, too, had been busy on the case during the summer. One of his colleagues had been to Danvers, talked with the doctor's old father, John Marsh, Sr., and learned that Marsh's family had never heard of Marguerite or a grandson on the Mississippi. The old man backed up these statements with copious quotations from his son's letters written from the Mississippi frontier some twenty-five years before. These letters he had turned over to the lawyers; they were in Colonel Baker's hand when he arose to refute the testimony of the Reverend John Cameron.

Baker introduced no testimony, but made a speech to the jury, about an hour in duration. In his ardent, silvery voice he began:

"There was no marriage here, gentlemen; there was no marriage here," and amidst a profound silence he paused to allow that fact to sink in. "These letters of John Marsh prove it."

Then, selecting a letter from the top of the sheaf in his hand, he unfolded it and in an impressive voice read the superscription:

"St. Louis, October 9, 1827." At that time, he pointed out, Charles was a baby of twenty months, yet his father under that date wrote to his parents at home: "I have nothing in particular to tell you, but that I enjoy health and happiness. What more does anyone want? I answer: A single man wants a wife; a single woman wants a husband. I for my part expect to want something to the end of my life and never expect to be more contented than I am at present."[4]

BY THE LAWS OF FRANCE

"Does that letter sound," he demanded as he finished reading, "as if the doctor considered himself married?" There was a rustle of uneasiness in the courtroom as he laid the letter aside. Charles, flushed of face, drew himself up in his chair while Baker went on dramatically:

"There was no marriage here, gentlemen," and selecting another time-stained page, he remarked that it was written from Prairie du Chien to the doctor's brother, the Reverend Ezekiel Marsh, at a time when Charles was six years old, and just before Marguerite died in childbirth, and he read: "You inquire if I am married and a number of other questions which seem to have been suggested by some report . . . I have to answer *that I am not married* and am sorry to say that I can see no prospect of it, nor has any material alteration taken place in my affairs."[5]

Charles wilted in his chair, and the Colonel resumed:

"There was no marriage here. Marguerite was not the doctor's wife; she was his mistress. I resided at Prairie du Chien at the time the doctor lived there. I knew Marguerite, the pretty little French-Canadian girl who was under his protection. I knew the old clergyman who has testified here upon the stand. It was usual and customary for young men going from the Atlantic States into these French-Canadian villages, such as Prairie du Chien, to take these beautiful young Canadian girls under their protection. I did it; Mr. Marsh did it; everybody did it."

Charles was upset. Crittenden was disturbed. Baker sat down amid a profound silence. Then Judge McKinstry arose and charged the jury:

"It is of no consequence whether there was a marriage or not," he declared. "If John Marsh lived with this little French-Canadian girl as his wife, and if he introduced her to all his friends and acquaintances as his wife, she

JOHN MARSH, PIONEER

was his wife by the laws of France and by the laws of the United States."

The jury filed out of the room and in half an hour returned a verdict giving Charles half the estate of his father.[6]

CHAPTER XLVI

MARSH'S LIGHT

In spite of the thousand-dollar reward for his capture, Felipe Morena eluded his pursuers and escaped.[1] No one heard of him again. But Charles vowed retaliation and swore that he would never rest until he had brought the murderers of his father to justice.

First he went to Petersburg, collected his wife and family, returned and moved into the great stone house. Then he set to work to track down the assassins. That became his sacred duty. He learned the Spanish language, made friends with the families of the murderers and frequented their ranchos. Once, on a false scent, he went to Mexico. Several times he made fruitless trips up and down California. But he was not discouraged. To expedite the search, he had himself deputized an officer of the law.

Ten years passed. The search went on.

One autumn day, while riding near Visalia, he heard an old Spanish woman say that Olivas was living near Santa Barbara. The man-hunt began again. He took the stage down the coast. At Santa Barbara he learned that a *vaquero* answering Olivas' description was working on the Faxon rancho, eighty miles distant. That night he set out on horseback.

At dawn he arrived before the *adobe* where Olivas was supposedly sleeping. Charles hammered on the door. The man who opened it saw two pistols levelled at his head.

"Hands up, or I fire," ordered Charles.

The man surrendered. It was Olivas.[2]

JOHN MARSH, PIONEER

After a violent tussle, Charles handcuffed him. Then, with the help of Faxon, he threw him on a horse and tied his feet beneath the horse's belly. In this fashion he drove him before him to Santa Barbara and there had him chained to the jail floor until the steamer for San Francisco sailed.

When the ship was well out to sea, Charles removed the chains and handcuffs from his prisoner and told Olivas he could jump overboard if he wanted to. Olivas refused. He preferred to take a chance with the California law.

Finally, Charles arrived with his prisoner at Martinez and had him arraigned before the Grand Jury. Olivas turned state's evidence. He claimed that Ygnacio Sebrian had promised to give him $300 to kill the doctor, and the other two men $100 each. On the strength of this confession, the prisoner was indicted. But the indictment proved defective. The word "was" was omitted in an important sentence. The indictment was declared invalid. Olivas was dismissed.[3]

But Charles was not downhearted. He soon discovered that Felipe Morena was in a little town in Sonora. He went to Mexico. As soon as he arrived he learned that Morena had lately murdered a man and had escaped across the border. Charles figured out that Morena would make tracks for his uncle Ygnacio Sebrian's rancho. He hurried back to California and made for the rancho. But warned of his coming, the murderer again escaped. Charles traced him to Sacramento but lost him in the crowds.

One night he went into a dive on Second Street. There he found his man dancing. Unobserved, Charles crept up behind Morena, held a pistol to his head and demanded his surrender.[4]

CHARLES MARSH.

MARSH'S LIGHT

Morena was tried at Martinez. The jury brought in a verdict of murder in the second degree, and he was sent to San Quentin for life.[5] With his father's death avenged, Charles retired to the great stone house to resume the hunt for the gold his father once had shown him. But he never found it. To this day, so far as any one knows, the treasure's whereabouts remains a mystery.

Twenty-five years passed.

In 1891 Governor Markham pardoned Felipe Morena. He emerged from San Quentin gray-headed. When he appeared in his former haunts, he had an unlimited supply of money. The report became current that he had solved the mystery of the hiding-place of the doctor's wealth. An open pit, recently excavated, was found on the rancho to add credence to the gossip.

As for Alice, she grew to womanhood in the midst of unsympathetic surroundings. At eighteen she came into an immense inheritance. During her minority her fortune had trebled in value. There were more cattle on the ranges of *Los Meganos* than there had been in its earliest glory.

Soon after she came of age, she married W. W. Cameron, the son of the Reverend John Cameron, thus cementing the tie her father had begun at New Salem, Ill. The newlyweds moved to Oakland and set up an extravagant establishment. There were servants, a coachman, carriages, horses, and harness mounted in silver.

Charles moved to Antioch and took on the dignities of a justice of the peace. Towns encroached on the great rancho. Land became more and more valuable. Finally it went out of the Marsh family.

To-day the great holding, the first centre of American civilization in California, is dotted with villages, factory towns and peaceful farms. It is the heart of the most pro-

JOHN MARSH, PIONEER

ductive area in the San Joaquin Valley. Steamboats plow its waterways. A railroad traverses its extent; strange as it may seem, it follows the lines which the doctor once laid down for a railroad.

Only in the little valley at the foot of Mount Diablo is there any reminder of the personality that once presided over this principality. The great stone house is still standing, stark, lonely and uninhabited, a monument to unfulfilled ambitions, a melancholy reminder of hopes never accomplished. No one for whom it was built ever lived in it.

But Mount Diablo again fulfills the purpose to which Marsh dedicated it three-quarters of a century ago. On its summit is a revolving light—a beacon. From dusk to dawn it flashes out its signals to light a pathway for the airmen when they reach the Sierras. It should be called "Marsh's Light," in memory of the man who first used the venerable old mountain as a sign-post to guide American civilization toward the Golden Gate.

APPENDIX

ACKNOWLEDGMENTS

THIS biography of John Marsh is based entirely on source material: on old diaries, journals, faded letters, statements, reminiscences and memoirs found in many quarters: the library at Harvard University; the Minnesota, Wisconsin, and Illinois Historical Society Collections; the Historical, Memorial, and Art Department of Iowa at Des Moines; the Michigan Historical Commission at Lansing; the Jefferson Memorial at St. Louis, Mo.; the files in the Indian Office of the War Department at Washington, D. C.; the Bancroft Library at the University of California; and the California State Library at Sacramento. All these sources have been culled in the interests of John Marsh. All of them have yielded up valuable and, in many instances, hitherto unused material regarding some phase of his career.

It has taken five years to locate, assemble and piece together the material thus collected. Even then it could not have been accomplished without the co-operation and assistance of the overseers of these collections. To them my gratitude is due. In this connection I wish to thank Mr. W. C. Lane, formerly Librarian of Harvard University; Mr. S. E. Morison, Editor of the Tercentennial History of Harvard University; Mr. Solon J. Buck of the Minnesota Historical Society, his aids, the Misses Grace Nute, Livia Apple and especially Bertha Heilbrun; Mr. Joseph Schaefer, Superintendent of the State Historical Society of Wisconsin at Madison, and Miss Annie Nunns, but especially Doctor Louise Phelps Kellogg; Miss Stella Drumm of the Jefferson Memorial at St. Louis, Mo.; Mr. J. Franklin Jameson, Director of the Department of Historical Research of the Carnegie Institution at Washington, D. C.; and Doctor N. D. Mereness, who ferreted out a long list of Marsh documents in the files of the Indian Office of the War Department.

ACKNOWLEDGMENTS

To the Newberry Library at Chicago, Ill., I am indebted for photostatic copies of the manuscript diaries of Henry Snelling describing school-days at old Fort Snelling.

To Thomas P. Reep of Petersburg, Ill., a great Lincoln scholar and author of "Lincoln at New Salem," my debt is a large one. It was Mr. Reep who ran down the Marsh tradition at New Salem, interviewed old settlers and sent me detailed accounts of his researches. To Mr. Reep I am also under obligations for many snapshots of the old Pantier log-cabin and other localities closely connected with the early days and Marsh.

To Robert S. Torrey of Los Angeles, Calif., a great grandson of Doctor James Pantier, a prominent character of this narrative, I am indebted for pictures, manuscript accounts and family letters—all dealing with Marsh's connection with the New Salem and Concord settlements of Illinois.

For Frank E. Stevens' assistance in the Black Hawk War chapter I am most grateful. Mr. Stevens is the author of an authoritative book on the Black Hawk War. He examined my material relating to that section and gave me many valuable suggestions in the preparation of the final manuscript.

The Marsh clan both in Massachusetts and California have been especially co-operative. Through the efforts of Mr. Anson Blake, Secretary of the California Historical Society, I came in touch with Mrs. James Marsh—formerly of Topsfield, Mass., now of Berkeley, Calif.—and from her received valuable family papers, including letters written by John Marsh from Prairie du Chien, Green Bay, St. Louis, etc., but, most important of all, those dealing with the chapters that culminate this biography. Without these letters it would have been impossible to have presented the final episodes in Marsh's career in their entirety. To her I am also indebted for the "Proc-

ACKNOWLEDGMENTS

lamation," a document of considerable historical worth, representing as it does that period when California was dominated by the Vigilantes.

To Ralph Marsh of San Francisco I am grateful for the letters concerning General John Sutter of Fort Sutter fame; and for those documents relating to Doctor Marsh's practice of medicine on the California frontier from 1836 to 1856.

To Harry Marsh of San Francisco thanks are due for the papers and letters dealing with the litigation that tied up the doctor's estate for many years in the California courts. For the Danvers, Mass., part of this biography I am indebted to Miss Florence Mudge, a Marsh connection. She has been indefatigable in rounding up all kinds of interesting family traditions and other material and placing it at my disposal.

My thanks are due above all to the late Mrs. Alice Marsh Cameron and her daughter Miss Amy G. Cameron of Santa Barbara. Without their able assistance and cooperation, John Marsh would never have materialized. From them I received the journals and diaries that John Marsh wrote in Massachusetts. In them was a complete record of his school-days in New England. On their contents was based the "Sheepskin" section of this narrative.

Fortunately Doctor Marsh was a prolific writer. To Miss Cameron I am indebted for many of these manuscripts portraying early Spanish and Mexican days in California. From them the descriptions in the "Cowhide" section are largely drawn. From a longhand manuscript of Mrs. Cameron's I drew descriptions of life at *Los Meganos*, as well as accounts of other stirring events in the days of Doctor Marsh. These documents have been supplemented by letters, statements and interviews, enabling me to round out the picture. In addition to this material, there are the Tuck letters written from the doctor's rancho in the early 'fifties and a mine of information themselves.

ACKNOWLEDGMENTS

My debt to the California State Library at Sacramento is a large one. I wish especially to thank Milton Ferguson, State Librarian, and his assistants, Miss Eudora Garoutte and Miss Caroline Wenzel. All have been generous and helpful to the last degree, especially the last two. The most valuable manuscript collection dealing with Doctor Marsh from birth to the grave is in the archives of the State Library. All these were generously put at my disposal. From them I have drawn copiously and freely.

When words have been put into the mouth of any person who figures in these pages, those words have been quoted from documents. The last chapters of this book are almost entirely written in conversational form. They were not invented. The material was taken almost *verbatim* from the testimony brought out at the several law trials which terminated the doctor's career. All this testimony may be found in the newspaper files housed at the California State Library at Sacramento.

I am indebted to Miss Emily June Ulsh, M. A., University of California, for permission to quote from her master's thesis entitled "Doctor John Marsh, California Pioneer, 1836–1856," which has supplied me with a firm foundation and a ready source of invaluable material.

In conclusion, I wish to express my appreciation to Miss Mary A. Byrne of the San Francisco Public Library.

To my secretary, Mrs. Elizabeth Railsbach, my debt is a large one. She has typed and retyped my manuscript, checked my bibliographies and evinced a cheerful interest in the progress of John Marsh down the frontier.

Even with all these acknowledgments, I am neglecting to mention a source from which I have drawn a large part of my information—that army of old and early settlers whom I have interviewed hither and yon.

GEORGE D. LYMAN.

BIBLIOGRAPHY

CHAPTER I

BIBLIOGRAPHY: JOHN MARSH OF SALEM. 1633

1. *John Marsh of Salem*, Amherst, Mass., 1878, pp. 244–245.
2. *Ibid.*, pp. 10, 248.
3. *Ibid.*, p. 110.
4. Ensign Ezekiel received his commission August 21, 1754, in the 28th year of the reign of His Majesty King George the Second. See *John Marsh of Salem*, p. 109. Also see records at the State House, Massachusetts, vol. 13.
5. Bill of Sale, Caleb Low to John Marsh. Courtesy Jasper Marsh, Danvers.

CHAPTER II

BIBLIOGRAPHY: DANVERS AND FRANKLIN ACADEMY. 1807–1817

1. Slocum, W. A., *History of Contra Costa County, San Francisco*, 1882, pp. 606–607.
2. Cameron, Amy G., statement of.
3. See receipts in possession of Jasper Marsh at Danvers, Mass., dated February 9, 1807, and September 17, 1810.
4. In earlier periods it was customary for male teachers to receive £2 monthly; and females six pence each week. See *John Marsh of Salem*, p. 222.
5. MS. John to father, Andover, September 15, 1815: Marsh Papers, Santa Barbara. "Agreeable with your request I improve this opportunity of informing you that we like our boarding very well, we have two others in the same room with us, James Osgood and John Kimbal. There are likewise boarding at Mr. Abbot's, Dr. Lamson, Mr. Bridges and three girls. We fare as well as we could wish and Mr. and Mrs. Abbot are very obliging.

"The new preceptor is Mr. Rufus P. Hovey, of Haverhill, a classmate of Mr. Richardson. He is very strict in the Academy and keeps excellent order, but I think he is inferior to Mr. Richardson. He advised me to review the arithmetic which I am now doing besides writing, studying grammar and rhetoric. Caleb has begun his manuscript and succeeds well. He also studies grammar and is going to speak in the Academy next Saturday, as it is strictly required of us all. We have enjoyed good health except this morning I have the headache which prevents my going to

BIBLIOGRAPHY

the Academy this afternoon, for which reason I hope you will excuse my bad writing. It is now dinnertime and I must close these few lines with stating that, I am with respect your

Dutiful Son, John Marsh, Jr.

"P.S. We expect to come home in about three weeks."

6. Tapley, H. S., *Chronicles of Danvers, Old Salem Village,* Danvers, 1923, p. 150.

7. See entries Marsh's Journal, February 18, 19, 1817. Possession of author.

CHAPTER III

BIOGRAPHY: LANCASTER ACADEMY. 1817–1818

1. Marsh, John, Journal of. In possession of the author.
2. *Ibid.*

CHAPTER IV

BIBLIOGRAPHY: ANNUAL TRAINING AND DRILLING. 1817–1818.

1. Marsh, John, Journal of, written at Boxford. In possession of the author.

CHAPTER V

BIBLIOGRAPHY: BRIMSTONE HILL. 1818–1819

1. Fuess, Claude M., *An Old New England School,* pp. 187–188.
2. *Ibid.,* New York, 1917, pp. 159–160.
3. *Ibid.,* pp. 173–174.
4. Marsh's Andover Journal, under date of "Sabbath, December 13, 1818."

CHAPTER VI

BIBLIOGRAPHY: HARVARD. 1819–1823

1. Government-ology in Manuscript records of the Class of 1815. For much of this information the author is indebted to S. E. Morison's article on the *Great Rebellion in Harvard College,* Colonial Society of Massachusetts, vol. 27, pp. 37–128.

2. Cameron, Alice Marsh, Santa Barabara, Calif. Statement.

3. Mr. Adams to Kirkland, Washington, May 19, 1823. Harvard Archives.

4. Peabody, Andrew P., *Harvard Reminiscences,* Boston, Mass., 1888.

5. Levi Hedge, College Professor of Logic and Metaphysics.

6. Among those who later defended Thomas Dorr when he was

BIBLIOGRAPHY

generally regarded as an outlaw were his classmate John Preston, then in the New Hampshire Senate, and George Bancroft, a tutor in the college during his senior year. Bancroft's letter on behalf of Dorr was characterized by George Ticknor Curtis as seldom surpassed in "studied insinuation" and "degree of depravity." *The Merits of Thomas W. Dorr and George D. Bancroft*, by a citizen of Massachusetts, Boston, 1845, p. 31.

7. "By Pickering Dodge." (MS. note by John L. Sibley, the Librarian, when this document was received.)

8. "November 4. It appeared that Greenough, a member of the sophomore class, on the evening of the 3rd instant was guilty of an assault upon the windows of a College Officer; wherefore voted, that Greenough be rusticated. It appeared that Marsh was a principal Agent in throwing down heavy balls from the upper story of one of the Colleges, accompanied with a deliberate insult to a College Officer; wherefore voted,—that Marsh be dismissed."—Faculty Records, IX 242. John Greenough of Roxbury returned to the class below and took his degree in 1824. John Marsh of Danvers was readmitted and obtained his degree in course.

9. Morison, S. E., *The Great Rebellion in Harvard College and the Resignation of President Kirkland*, Colonial Society of Massachusetts, vol. 27, pp. 37–128.

10. Frothingham, Octavius Brooks, *George Ripley*, pp. 19–20.

11. MSS. Order of Exercises—Commencement, 27 August, 1823. Harvard Library, Cambridge, Mass.

CHAPTER VII

BIBLIOGRAPHY: MASSACHUSETTS TO FORT ST. ANTHONY. 1823

1. Langham to Taliaferro, August 19, 1826. Taliaferro Papers, Minnesota Historical Collection.

2. Doctor John Dixwell was a practising physician in Boston from about 1804 to his death in 1834. His earlier name was Samuel Hunt, and he was the son of Samuel Hunt, master of the Boston Latin School from 1776 to 1805, and Mary (Dixwell) Hunt, his cousin. Samuel, the son, was admitted to the B. L. S. on March 16, 1784, at the age of 6½ years, and graduated from Harvard College in the class of 1796. He took his degree of B. M. in 1800, and his M. D. in 1811. I find that he was an usher in the B. L. S. in 1801–2; that he was a physician in Boston in 1803; and that he appears in the Boston Directories

BIBLIOGRAPHY

from 1805 to 1834 as "John Dixwell, physician." His descent from John Dixwell, the regicide, through a female line, probably led to his change of name.—Julius H. Tuttle, Massachusetts Historical Society.

3. As to stages, the following entry appears in the *Boston Directory*: "New York commercial mail, by Worcester, Stafford, and Hartford. From Earle's daily at 1 A. M. arrive at 12 night." Probably Marsh went the same way from Worcester to Springfield and so on.—Communication from Julius H. Tuttle, Massachusetts Historical Society. The letters themselves are included in the Marsh Papers, in the possession of Alice Marsh Cameron, Santa Barbara, Calif.

4. William Alexander and John W. Catton were the lieutenants with these recruits. Entry Taliaferro Journals, October 8, 1823.—Minnesota Historical Collections, St. Paul, Minn.

5. It is probable that 203 of these recruits ultimately reached Fort Snelling. In the Taliaferro Journals, under entry of October 8, 1823, the major records: "203 recruits arrived this evening from Boston for the 5th Infantry, etc." This would also give us the date Marsh arrived there.—Minnesota Historical Collections, St. Paul, Minn.

6. Fort St. Anthony was rechristened "Fort Snelling" in 1824 by General Scott, in honor of the colonel of the 5th Infantry.

7. These boatmen were not without tradition. It took a four years' course in wilderness discipline to achieve the title of *voyageur*. During the first three years they were called *mangeurs du lard* or "pork-eaters," or "greenhorns." Having passed the apprenticeship stage, they became *hivernants* or "winterers."

8. Sibley, H. H., Minnesota Historical Collections, vol. VI, p. 265.

9. Marsh Papers, Santa Barbara.

10. Taliaferro Journal, October 8, 1823.—Minnesota Historical Society.

CHAPTER VIII

BIBLIOGRAPHY: FORT ST. ANTHONY, THE SNELLINGS AND TALIAFERRO. INDIAN AGENT OF ST. PETERS. 1823

1. Entry Taliaferro Journal, October 7, 1823: "A canoe arrived from Prairie du Chien this afternoon bringing information of there being *150* recruits at that place bound for this Post." On October 8, 1823, Taliaferro notes "203 recruits arrived this evening from Boston for the 5th Infantry under Lieutenants

BIBLIOGRAPHY

(William) Alexander and (John W.) Cotton."—Minnesota Historical Collections, St. Paul, Minn.

2. Hansen, Marcus L., *Old Fort Snelling*. Iowa City, Iowa, 1918, pp. 27–28.

3. *Ibid.*, p. 81.

4. Ellet, *Pioneer Women of the West*. New York, 1852, pp. 309 and 327.

5. Van Cleve, *Life-long Memories of Fort Snelling*. Minneapolis, Minn., 3d edition, 1895, p. 20.

6. Adams, *Reminiscences*. Minnesota Historical Collections, vol. VI, p. 97.

7. Hansen, *Old Fort Snelling*, p. 67.

8. *Auto-Biography of Major Taliaferro*, Minnesota Historical Collections, vol. VI, p. 199.

9. Hansen, Marcus L., *Old Fort Snelling*, p. 68. Van Cleve, *Life-long Memories of Fort Snelling*, p. 30.

10. For all that, Lawrence Taliaferro was an excellent choice as Indian agent. Although his courage and convictions were adamant, constant friction ultimately wears away stone, and he finally resigned because the government, niggardly in supplies, prevented him from keeping his promises to the Indians, and because he could no longer endure the machinations of the traders. But unlike most other agents he never used his position to fleece or exploit, and his epitaph should be his own autobiographical words: "For more than twenty years an Indian agent and yet an honest man."

11. Hansen, Marcus L., *Old Fort Snelling*, pp. 91–92.

12. Ellet, *Pioneer Women of the West*, p. 327.

13. Minnesota Historical Collections, vol. VI, p. 440.

14. Holcombe, R. I., *Minnesota in Three Centuries*, p. 63.

15. Minnesota Historical Collections, vol. VI, p. 439. It is interesting to note the subsequent career of Nancy McClure. Her own nuptials, when she married Faribault, the son of Jean Baptiste and Pelagie Faribault, were among the picturesque events at the treaty of Traverse des Sioux.

16. Riggs, Stephen R., *Mary and I: Forty Years with the Sioux*. Chicago, 1880, p. 24.

17. Taliaferro Journal, September 19, 1838. Minnesota Historical Collections, St. Paul, Minn.

18. Edward Purcell was born in Virginia, and he was appointed a hospital surgeon's mate on May 2, 1813, which rank he held until April 18, 1818, when he was made a post surgeon.

BIBLIOGRAPHY

There is no indication where he was stationed from 1813 to 1815, but the registers give Fort Gratiot as his post from 1815 to 1818. On July 21, 1818, he was appointed surgeon in the Fifth United States Infantry and he went to Fort Snelling in August of that year. He died at Fort Snelling on January 11, 1825.

19. Slocum, *History of Contra Costa County, California*. San Francisco, 1882, p. 606.

CHAPTER IX

BIBLIOGRAPHY: MINNESOTA'S FIRST SCHOOL. ITS MASTER AND PUPILS. 1823–1825

1. Neill, Edward D., *History of Minnesota from the Earliest French Explorations to the Present Time*. Fourth Edition, Minneapolis, Minn., 1882, p. 89.

Neill, Edward D., *Fort Snelling, Minn., while in command of Colonel Josiah Snelling, Fifth Infantry*. New York, 1888.

Holcombe, *Minnesota in Three Centuries*, vol. II, p. 52.

2. Hansen, Marcus L., *Old Fort Snelling*, p. 75.
3. Van Cleve, *Life-long Memories of Fort Snelling*, p. 38.
4. Upham, Warren, "The Women and Children of Fort St. Anthony," *The Magazine of History*, July, 1915, vol. XXI, pp. 25–39.

Snelling, H. H., *Memories of a Life*. Manuscript, Newberry Library, Chicago, vol. I. Whether or not Joe Snelling was ever one of Marsh's students is questionable. He was about nineteen years old and had lived a varied career before Marsh's advent. According to the Marsh Papers the main reason Colonel Snelling had for importing a Harvard schoolmaster was to provide his own sons with an education and that would include Joe and Henry, as the others at this time were mere infants.

Van Cleve, C. O. C., *Life-long Memories of Fort Snelling*, chapter V.

5. Charlotte Ouisconsin Clark was born at Fort Crawford, Prairie du Chien, July 1, 1819, and lived with her parents at Fort Snelling from 1819 to 1827. She married Lieutenant, afterward Major General, Horatio Phillips Van Cleve, March 22, 1836, and resided at Long Prairie, Minn., 1856–1861, and later in Minneapolis. She died there April 1, 1907.

6. Ellet, *Pioneer Women of the West*, pp. 321–333.
7. Van Cleve, *Life-long Memories of Fort Snelling*, p. 38.
8. Snelling, H. H., *Memories of a Life*. Manuscript, Newberry Library, Chicago, Ill., p. 45.

BIBLIOGRAPHY

9. Van Cleve, *Life-long Memories of Fort Snelling*, p. 149.
10. *Ibid.*, p. 62.
11. Snelling, *Memories of a Life*, p. 75.

In 1834 he was a West Point cadet. One day, during parade, he took an unworthy adversary by the collar and trounced him with a rawhide. For this act, although he offered a manly defense, he was court-martialled and later shipped to Texas, in order to enter the struggle for independence of the Lone Star State. There he became an officer and led his men into victorious action. Years passed and in young manhood he became a trader with the American Fur Company and was stationed among the Blackfeet Indians on the Missouri. Here he married the daughter of a chief of that tribe and had many children by her. At his ranch at Prickly Pear Valley, he lived the life of a monarch, surrounded by his family and retainers. During the Indian outbreak of 1869 he was treacherously murdered by tribesmen whom he had benefacted. He lived and died consistently.—Montana Historical Society Collections, vol. I, p. 84.

12. Snelling, *Memories of a Life*, pp. 2-3.
13. *Ibid.*, pp. 4-5.
14. *Ibid.*, pp. 12-13.

Ellet, *Pioneer Women of the West*, p. 328.

15. Neill, Edward D., *History of Minnesota*, fourth edition, p. 920.
16. Keating, W. H., *Narrative of an Expedition to the Sources of St. Peter's River*, Philadelphia, 1824, vol. I, p. 314.

Upham, "Women and Children of Fort St. Anthony," *The Magazine of History*, vol. XXI, p. 34.

He wrote many sketches and stories of the Sioux about the fort which were generously praised by Catlin, and he is the author of at least one book, *Tales of the Northwest or Sketches of Indian Life and Character by a Resident beyond the Frontiers.* He spoke the Sioux language in its many dialects perfectly, and he understood and appreciated manners and customs of the natives. Subsequently he settled in Boston, where he became editor of the Boston *Herald*. His early demise, in his forty-fourth year, was hastened by intemperance.

17. Van Cleve, *Life-long Memories of Fort Snelling*, pp. 49-50. Mrs. Van Cleve claims these children arrived in the spring; Mrs. Ann Adams, vol. VI, Minnesota Historical Collections, says it was the fall; Henry Hunt Snelling, in *Memories of a Life*, writes they left Pembina in the spring and, as the Selkirk Colony

BIBLIOGRAPHY

was 500 miles from Ft. Snelling, it was undoubtedly late fall before the Tully boys arrived at the fort.

18. Van Cleve, *Life-long Memories of Fort Snelling*, p. 51, gives a different version of this incident. According to her account, the Indians seized the baby, dashing out its brains on the ice.

19. Snelling, H. H., *Memories of a Life*, vol. I, p. 92.

20. *Ibid.*, pp. 76–78.

21. Neill, Edward D., *History of Minnesota*. Minneapolis, Minn., 1882, fourth edition, p. 891.

22. Van Cleve, *Life-long Memories of Fort Snelling*, p. 38.

CHAPTER X

BIBLIOGRAPHY: JOHN MARSH, MAIL CARRIER. 1825

1. Snelling, Taliaferro, July 26, 1825. Taliaferro Papers.

2. Williams, *A History of the City of Saint Paul and of the County of Ramsey*, pp. 44–45.
Minnesota Historical Collections, vol. VII, p. 99.

3. Wisconsin Historical Collections, vol. V, pp. 226-229.

4. This means that ten days after leaving Prairie du Chien he reached the fort, having travelled thirty miles a day.

5. Marsh Papers: There are three groups of these documents in California. The larger group comprises his Massachusetts Diaries, Phillips-Andover Journals, and his letters written from Fort St. Anthony, Minn., Prairie du Chien, Wis., and the rancho *Los Meganos*, California, now in possession of his daughter by his second marriage—Alice Marsh Cameron of Santa Barbara, Calif. The smaller group, comprising letters written by Sutter, Sunol, and other California pioneers to Doctor John Marsh, is in the possession of the latter's great-grandson, Ralph Marsh of San Francisco. The third group, comprising valuable family letters to and from Marsh, is in possession of Mrs. James Marsh, formerly of Topsfield, Mass., now of Berkeley, Calif., and includes the letters that figured in the litigation over his estate.

6. Taliaferro Journal, Tuesday, March 7, 1826:
"Could not influence O'Karpee [the Okh-pee of Marsh's letter] to go express to Prairie du Chien in consequence of Mr. Marsh's conduct to him in February, 1825. Mr. Marsh did not pay him for his services."

BIBLIOGRAPHY

CHAPTER XI

BIBLIOGRAPHY: JOHN MARSH, INDIAN AGENT OF ST. PETERS. 1824–1825

1. *Autobiography of Major Taliaferro,* Minnesota Historical Collections, vol. VI, p. 249.
2. MS. Snelling to Taliaferro, dated Fort St. Anthony, October 19, 1824.—Taliaferro Papers, Minnesota Historical Collections.
3. MS. Marsh to Governor Cass, Detroit, November 20, 1826.—Indian Office, Cass Letter Books (letters received), 1826, No. 2, Washington, D. C.
4. MS. Snelling to Taliaferro, dated October 19, 1824. Taliaferro Papers, Minnesota Historical Collections.
5. MS. Taliaferro to James Barbour, Secretary of War, December 10, 1825.—Indian Office Files, Washington, D. C.
6. MS. Snelling to Taliaferro, Fort St. Anthony, October 19, 1824.—Minnesota Historical Collections, Taliaferro Letter No. 50.
7. Campbell was a half-breed whom Meriwether Lewis had picked up as a boy on the Missouri and taken to St. Louis, from which place, after the death of Lewis, he had drifted to Fort Snelling. At the agency where he was interpreter, his services were indispensable, as he was the master of four languages, and possessed the confidence of all the tribes within 400 miles of the post. He probably also was indispensable to Marsh, for he initiated him into the perplexities of the agency and schooled him in Indian affairs to a proficiency which early distinguished him.
8. Hansen, Marcus, *Old Fort Snelling,* p. 77.
9. Beltrami, J. C., *A Pilgrimage in Europe and America,* vol. II, p. 217.
10. Hansen, Marcus, *Old Fort Snelling,* p. 67.
11. *Ibid.,* p. 107.
12. Folwell, *History of Minnesota,* vol. I, p. 269.
13. MS. Brierge, Bancroft Library.
14. MS. Cameron, Amy G., statement of, Santa Barbara.
15. Sibley, H. H., *Memoir of J. H. Faribault.*—Minnesota Historical Collections, vol. III, pp. 172–173.
16. MS. Brierge, Bancroft Library.
17. *Ibid.*
18. *Ibid.*

BIBLIOGRAPHY

CHAPTER XII

BIBLIOGRAPHY: DEPARTURE AND RETURN. 1825–1826

1. MS. Snelling to Taliaferro, October 19, 1824.—Taliaferro Letter No. 50, Minnesota Historical Collections.
2. MS. Marsh to Cass, November 20, 1826.—Indian Office, Cass Letter Books. (Letters received 1826—No. 2.)
3. MS. Taliaferro to Barbour, December 10, 1825.—Indian Office Files, Washington, D. C.
4. MS. Snelling to Taliaferro, October 19, 1824.—Minnesota Historical Collections.
5. MS. Snelling to Marsh, August 18, 1826.—Indian Office (letters received), Washington, D. C.
6. MS. Snelling to John Marsh, August 18, 1826.—Indian Office Files, Washington, D. C.
7. MS. Snelling to Taliaferro, July 25, 1825.—Taliaferro Papers, Minnesota Historical Society.
8. *Ibid.*
9. Marsh Papers in possession of Alice Marsh Cameron. Marsh in his difficulties with Taliaferro was apparently determined to get in touch with Lewis Cass, Governor of Michigan Territory and superintendent of Indian Affairs, and thus the major's superior.
10. Marsh to Cass, first printed in Contra Costa *Gazette,* December 21, 1867, and reprinted in a number of the California County Histories, notably Elliot's *History Contra Costa County,* pp. 5–6; *History Tulare County,* 1883, pp. 43–46; *History Merced County,* 1881, pp. 35–39. This letter was printed in numerous papers in the eastern States and is said to have stimulated emigration toward California.
11. Lockwood: Wisconsin Historical Collections, vol. II, pp. 169–170.
12. Marsh Papers in possession of Alice Marsh Cameron, Santa Barbara, Calif.
13. *Ibid.*

CHAPTER XIII

BIBLIOGRAPHY: TALIAFERRO'S REVENGE. 1825

1. *Ibid.* A biographer also states that: "In company with Governor Cass and Schoolcraft with whom he was very intimate, he went on horseback to Washington, D. C., remaining several

BIBLIOGRAPHY

months." See sketch of Marsh, by S. P. Webb, his Harvard classmate, in Slocum's *History of Contra Costa County, California*. San Francisco, 1882, p. 606.

2. Taliaferro to Barbour, dated December 10, 1825.—Indian Office Files, Washington, D. C.

3. Cass to Barbour, January 3, 1825.—Indian Office Files, Washington, D. C.

4. Barbour to Marsh, dated January 10, 1826.—Indian Office, Letter Books, vol. II, Washington, D. C.

5. McKenney, Thos. L., to Marsh.—Indian Office, Letter Books, vol. II.

6. Marsh to father, dated January 12, 1826.—Marsh Papers.

7. Snelling to Taliaferro, August 26, 1826.—Taliaferro Papers, Minnesota Historical Collections.

8. "The grand opening of the Erie Canal took place in October, 1825. Packets had been running over the sections already opened for at least two years, 1824 to 1825, but I am unable to find in the local histories any statement as to when the first packet west made the entire route of the Canal. Since in 1825 navigation did not close until December 5, it seems almost certain that there must have been passenger packets the entire length that fall. It should be noted that the terminus for passenger traffic was at Schenectady so as to save the delay incident to the numerous locks around the Cohoes Falls.

"Navigation opened in 1826, April 25, according to the records of the State Engineer's Office, and the letter which you have shows the arrival of Doctor Marsh in Buffalo, April 28. It seems altogether likely, therefore, that when he refers to the first packet, he means the first packet of that year."

Communication from Peter Nelson of the Division of Archives and History, University of the State of New York, Albany, N. Y.

9. Marsh Papers, in possession of Alice Marsh Cameron of Santa Barbara, Calif.

10. *Ibid.*
11. *Ibid.*
12. *Ibid.*

CHAPTER XIV

BIBLIOGRAPHY: MARGUERITE

1. Marsh's letter dated July 14, 1826.—State Library, Sacramento, Calif.

See entries, Taliaferro Journals, February-May, 1826; Drur-

BIBLIOGRAPHY

ries, *Annals of Prairie du Chien,* Madison, 1882, p. 8; Minnesota Historical Collections, vol. II, pp. 106–126.

2. Fairfield, George, in Prairie du Chien *Union,* July 27, 1905; Snelling, Joseph, *Early Days at Prairie du Chien.*—Minnesota Historical Collections, vol. V, pp. 125–129. In practically all the Wisconsin Histories, Methode's murder is placed in 1827. According to Marsh's letters home, it actually occurred in March of 1826, and it was the arrest of these murderers, their incarceration in the jail at Fort Crawford and their transportation to Fort Snelling, with the subsequent report of their murder by the Chippewa, that started Red Bird on the warpath and precipitated the Winnebago outbreak. In a letter, dated August 25, 1926, from Doctor Louise Phelps Kellogg of the Wisconsin Historical Society, she has this to say regarding the Methode murders: "Several years ago I noticed the discrepancy of which you write, and entered on the margin of my copies of the *Collections,* 'Methode was killed in 1826.' The evidence is a letter dated Fort Crawford, July 9, 1826, from Colonel Willoughby Morgan, in which he gives a full account of the murder of the Methode family 'about March 26, last.' Also another letter from John Kinzie to Cass, July 15, 1826, saying the Winnebago murderers have been delivered to the military authorities at Prairie du Chien. These letters are from our own copies of those in the Indian Office files at Washington. So the letter of Marsh corroborates this evidence. Lockwood, of course, wrote from memory, and Dr. Draper, thinking the occurrence connected with the so-called Winnebago War of 1827, misinterpreted the date."

3. Snelling: *Early Prairie du Chien.*—Minnesota Historical Collections, vol. V, p. 127.

4. Snelling to Taliaferro, August 26, 1826.—Taliaferro Papers. Langham to Taliaferro, August 19, 1829.—Taliaferro Papers, St. Paul, Minn.

CHAPTER XV

BIBLIOGRAPHY: PRAIRIE DU CHIEN. 1826

1. Marsh to father, Prairie du Chien, July 14, 1826.—Marsh Papers, Santa Barbara, Calif.

2. Langham to Taliaferro, August 18, 1826.—Taliaferro Papers, Minnesota Historical Collections.

3. Snelling to Marsh, August 18, 1826.—Indian Office Files, Washington, D. C.

4. Marsh to Cass, November 20, 1826.—Indian Office, Cass Letter Books (letters received), 1826, vol. V, p. 2.

BIBLIOGRAPHY

5. Taliaferro to Marsh, September 5, 1826.—Taliaferro Letter Books A, Minnesota Historical Collections.
6. Marsh to father, Prairie du Chien, January 14, 1827.—Alice Marsh Papers.
7. Wisconsin Historical Collections, vol. IX, p. 292. Perhaps Brisbois made some mistakes in his dates but the story belongs to the legends of the Prairie.
8. Drurries: *Annals of Prairie du Chien*, p. 2; Kellogg, L. P.: *The French Régime in Wisconsin and the Northwest*, Madison, 1925, pp. 386–402. The Americans built Fort Shelby in 1814. It was taken by the British and called Fort McKay, evacuated in 1815.
9. Mahan: *Old Fort Crawford and the Frontier*, pp. 127–128.
10. Nicolas Boilvin was born in Canada in 1761; went to St. Genevieve, Mo., about 1795; to Prairie du Chien in 1811, where he was Indian Agent; he aided the Americans in the War of 1812. He was married at St. Louis, 1802, to Helene, daughter of Hyacinth St. Cyr, and by her had two daughters, Catherine and Elizabeth, and two sons, one of whom, Nicolas, went to California and died.
11. Wisconsin Historical Collections, vol. IX, p. 65.
12. Turner: *The Fur Trade in Wisconsin*, p. 93.
13. Wisconsin Historical Collections, vol. IX, p. 300.
14. Their summer villages were on the east side, the most permanent of their habitations were chiefly in the valley of Rock River, in or near the present State of Illinois. On the west side, their villages occupied the lower valleys of the Iowa, Skunk and Des Moines Rivers. See terms of the Treaties of Prairie du Chien in 1825 and 1830, United States Statutes at Large, vol. VII, 1854, p. 272 and p. 328.
15. Atwater: *Tour to Prairie du Chien*, pp. 72–73.
16. Mahan: *Old Fort Crawford and the Frontier*, p. 162.
17. Wisconsin Historical Collections, vol. XII, pp. 220–221.

CHAPTER XVI

BIBLIOGRAPHY: JUSTICE OF THE PEACE. 1826

1. Marsh to father, dated Prairie du Chien, October 6, 1826.—Marsh Papers. Lockwood, Governor of Michigan, Prairie du Chien, January 29, 1830. Michigan Historical Commission, Lansing, Mich.
2. Judge Reaume was commissioned under George III, when

BIBLIOGRAPHY

Great Britain held jurisdiction over the country. After it was given up by the American government and attached to Indiana, he was commissioned by Governor Harrison of Indian Territory, probably soon after the organization of that Territory in 1801. In 1818 Governor Cass of Michigan Territory appointed him one of the associate justices of the court for Brown County. He died in 1822 and was buried at Green Bay.—Wisconsin Historical Collections, vol. II, p. 126.

3. This story is from Lockwood's narrative, Wisconsin Historical Collections, vol. II, p. 170. Judge Lockwood was a justice of the peace of Crawford County at the same time as Marsh. Lockwood did not like Marsh and seems never to have forgotten his resentment.

4. Street to Clark, April 8, 1829.
Street to Eaton, February 22, 1830.—Street Papers, Des Moines, Iowa.

5. It is interesting to note in this particular that Brunet sued Street and Kearney for damages and in due time won his case in the court of Judge James Doty, formerly of Prairie du Chien, who held that he was not "satisfied that it was the intention of the government to guarantee any country to the Indians or protect it from infringements." Eventually Congress passed a bill to relieve Street and Kearney, but the amount was only sufficient to pay judgment and costs. Both defendants were compelled to pay their attorneys' fees out of their own means. See Street to Clark, March 20, 1829.

CHAPTER XVII

BIBLIOGRAPHY: RED BIRD. THE SIOUX' WARNING. 1827

1. Post Returns, Fort Crawford, 1817–1831,—August, 1826, September, 1827, in the Adjutant General's Office, War Department, Washington, D. C.

2. Marsh: Cass, November 20, 1826.—Indian Office, Cass Letter Books (letters received), 1826, No. 2.

3. Cass: McKenney, Detroit, September 22, 1826.—Indian Office (letters received), Washington, D. C.

4. McKenney: Cass, Department of War, October 9, 1826.—Indian Office, Letter Books, vol. 3, Washington, D. C.; also McKenney: William Clark, October 9, 1826.—Indian Office, Letter Books, vol. III.

5. Marsh: father, Prairie du Chien, October 6, 1826.—Marsh Papers.

BIBLIOGRAPHY

6. Marsh: McKenney, July 10, 1827, Des Moines, Iowa: "I had received intelligence from some confidential Indians among the Sioux that the Winnebagoes were about to attack this village and murder all the Americans in it. I immediately sent off expresses in various directions."

See Lockwood's: *Early Times and Events in Wisconsin* in the Wisconsin Historical Collections, vol. II, pp. 156–158; Quaife's: *Chicago and the Old Northwest,* pp. 310–321; McKenney's: *The Winnebago War* in the Wisconsin Historical Collections, vol. V. pp. 148–204; Snelling's: *Early Days at Prairie du Chien and Winnebago Outbreak of 1827,* Wisconsin Historical Collections, vol. V, pp. 143–153.

7. Marsh: Taliaferro, June 26, 1827.—Taliaferro Papers, Minnesota Historical Collections.

8. Marsh: Taliaferro, June 26, 1827.—Minnesota Historical Collections.

Langham: Taliaferro, August 19, 1826.—Taliaferro Papers, Minnesota Historical Collections, St. Paul, Minn.

9. Marsh: Cass, July 4, 1827.—Indian Office, Cass Letter Books (letters received), 1827, No. 2, Washington, D. C.

10. Snelling writes that Red Bird visited Boilvin at this time, but as the latter was already en route to St. Louis, perhaps dead, and as Marsh was acting in his stead at the agency, undoubtedly it was upon him that Red Bird called.—Wisconsin Historical Collections, vol. V, p. 145.

11. Marsh: Cass, July 4, 1827.—Indian Office, Washington, D. C.

Marsh: Clark, June 30, 1827.—Indian Office. (Letters received.)

Marsh: Clark, July 25, 1827.—Indian Office. (Letters received.)

12. Ellet: *Pioneer Women of the West,* p. 328.

CHAPTER XVIII

BIBLIOGRAPHY: MARSH COMMANDS FORT CRAWFORD. 1827

1. Strange as it may seem, this child recovered from her ghastly wounds, grew to womanhood, bore a family and died at an advanced age.

2. Marsh: Cass, July 4, 1827.—Indian Office, Cass Letter Books (letters received), Washington, D. C.

BIBLIOGRAPHY

3. Marsh: McKenney, July 10, 1827.—Historical, Memorial and Art Department, Des Moines, Iowa.
Marsh: Cass, July 4, 1827.—Indian Office Files, Washington, D. C.
4. Lockwood's Narrative.—Wisconsin Historical Collections, vol. II, p. 160.
5. Mahan: *Old Fort Crawford and the Frontier,* pp. 109–110.
6. Cass: Clark, July 21, 1827.
7. Marsh: Clark, June 30, 1827.—Indian Office, Washington, D. C.
8. Marsh: McKenney, Prairie du Chien, July 10, 1827.—Historical, Memorial and Art Department, Des Moines, Iowa.
9. Marsh: Clark, July 20, 1827.—Indian Office, Washington, D. C.
10. Cass: Marsh, July 4, 1827.—Indian Office, Washington, D. C.
11. Taliaferro Journals, entry Monday, July 9, 1827.
12. Cass: Marsh, July 4, 1827.—Indian Office (letters received), Washington, D. C.
13. Marsh: Clark, June 30, 1827.
14. Taliaferro Journals, July 9, 1827.
15. Marsh: McKenney, dated St. Louis, October 5, 1827.—Indian Office, Washington, D. C. (His expense account incurred during the progress of the treaty is still preserved.)
16. Marsh: Cass, July 4, 1827; July 31, 1827.
17. Marsh: Clark, July 20, 1827.—Indian Office, Washington, D. C.
18. McKenney, Thos. L.: *Memoirs Official and Personal,* 1846, vol. I, pp. 81–84.
19. Marsh: Clark, July 20, 1827.
20. Thwaites, Reuben G.: *The Americanization of a French Settlement,* chapter IX, pp. 205–228.—Houghton Mifflin Co., 1908.
21. Quaife: *Chicago and the Old Northwest,* p. 318.
22. Marsh: father, dated Portage of the Ouisconsin and Fox Rivers, September 2, 1827.—Alice Marsh Cameron Papers, Santa Barbara, Calif.
23. Quaife: *Chicago and the Old Northwest,* p. 318.—Wisconsin Historical Collections, vol. V, pp. 178–204.
24. McKenney, *Memoirs,* pp. 107–108.
25. Thwaites claims that this incident, next to the landfall of

BIBLIOGRAPHY

Nicolet in 1634, was the most striking picture in Wisconsin history. See his *The Americanization of a French Settlement*, chapter IX.

CHAPTER XIX

BIBLIOGRAPHY: GAGNIER'S SCALP. 1827–1828

1. Marsh: Cass, November 20, 1826.—Indian Office, Washington, D. C.
2. Atwater, Caleb: *Remarks Made on a Tour to Prairie du Chien*, Columbus, Ohio, 1831, pp. 149–172.
3. Marsh: father, St. Louis, October 9, 1827.—Alice Marsh Cameron Papers, Santa Barbara, Calif.
4. Cass: Barbour, St. Louis, July 12, 1827.—Indian Office (letters received), Washington, D. C.
5. Street: Edwards, Prairie du Chien, December 28, 1827, vol. XI, pp. 362–366.
6. Marsh: father, Prairie du Chien, November 20, 1827.—Alice Marsh Cameron Papers, Santa Barbara, Calif.
7. Pages 10 and 11 of a letter by Joseph M. Street to the Secretary of War, dated November 15, 1827.—Indian Office. (Letters received.)
8. Street: Taliaferro, December 14, 1827.—Taliaferro Papers, St. Paul, Minn.
9. Extract of a letter from Marsh, dated November 19, 1827, Prairie du Chien.—Indian Office (letters received), Washington, D. C.
10. Street: Clark, December 10, 1827, p. 3.—Indian Office (letters received), Washington, D. C.

CHAPTER XX

BIBLIOGRAPHY: MARSH, HENRY DODGE AND THE TREATY OF GREEN BAY. 1828

1. Street: Clark, January 15, 1828, in Pelzer's, Louis: *Henry Dodge*.
Iowa Historical Record, Iowa City, vol. V, October, 1889, No. 4.
2. Pelzer, Louis: *Henry Dodge*, Iowa City, 1911, p. 33.
Street: Taliaferro, January 27, 1828, p. 2.—Taliaferro Papers, Minnesota Historical Collections, St. Paul, Minn.
3. Street: Taliaferro, p. 3, January 27, 1828.
4. Marsh: Street, February 7, 1828, p. 4.

BIBLIOGRAPHY

5. English Prairie. Now Muscoda, northeast corner of Grant County, Wisconsin.
6. Being pages 4, 5 and 6 of Marsh's report to Street, dated Prairie du Chien, February 7, 1828.
7. Marsh: Street, February 7, 1828, pp. 1, 2, 3 and a part of 4.—Indian Office, Washington, D. C.
8. From a speech by Augustus Cæsar Dodge on the Kansas-Nebraska Bill.—Congressional Globe, 1st session, 33d Congress, appendix pp. 375–383.
9. Street: Clark, January 15, 1828.
10. Marsh: father, Prairie du Chien, July 28, 1828.—Alice Marsh Cameron Papers, Santa Barbara, Calif.
11. United States Statutes at Large, Boston, 1854, pp. 315–317; and pp. 320–325. This agreement with the Winnebago was ratified by the U. S. Senate, January 7, 1829.

CHAPTER XXI

BIBLIOGRAPHY: PARTIALITY FOR THE SIOUX. 1828–1829

1. Street: Clark, Prairie du Chien, March 20, 1829.—Indian Office.
2. Street: Clark, March 20, 1829.—Indian Office (letters received), Washington, D. C.
Instructions to Marsh, Street: Taliaferro, January 2, 1829.—Taliaferro Papers, Minnesota Historical Collections, St. Paul, Minn.
3. See entry, Taliaferro Journals, under date February 6, 1829.
4. Taliaferro: Street, February 8, 1829.—Taliaferro Letter Books, Minnesota Historical Collections, St. Paul, Minn.
5. Street: Clark, April 8, 1829.
6. Street: Taliaferro, March 7, 1829.—Taliaferro Papers, Minnesota Historical Collections, St. Paul; Street: Clark, March 20, 1829.
Street: Clark, April 8, 1829.—Indian Office (letters received), Washington, D. C. Marsh's attitude toward the Sioux and Foxes may be better understood by reading M. S. Forsyth to Clark, May 6, 1830, Des Moines, Iowa.
7. Street: Marsh, March 2, 1829.—Street Papers, Des Moines, Iowa.
8. Street: Clark, April 8, 1829.—Indian Office (letters received), Washington, D. C.

BIBLIOGRAPHY

9. Street: Clark, March 20, 1829.—Indian Office (letters received), Washington, D. C.

10. Street's Instructions to Marsh, Prairie du Chien, March 2, 1829; affidavit John Marsh made before Lewis Rause, Justice of the Peace, dated County of Brown, October 6, 1829.—Historical, Memorial and Art Department of Iowa, Des Moines, Iowa.

11. The article from which these quotations were taken appeared in *The Miners' Journal*, Galena, Fever River, April 4, 1829—and was written by Jos. M. Street. See copy of paper in the Chicago Historical Society, Chicago, Ill. A copy of *The Miners' Journal* containing Marsh's original article, March 7, 1829, is not obtainable. Street's letter to Clark—March 20, 1829 —Indian Office (letters received), Washington, D. C., also contains quotations from Marsh's original article.

12. Street: Clark, March 20, 1829.

13. See "N. B.," Street's communication in *The Miners' Journal*, Galena, Fever River, April 4, 1829.—Chicago Historical Society, Chicago, Ill.

14. Communications to the editor of *The Miners' Journal.*— *Miners' Journal*, Galena, Saturday, April 11, 1829.

15. Street: Clark, March 20, 1829.—Indian Office, Washington, D. C.

16. Street: Clark, April 8, 1829.

17. Street: Clark, April 8, 1829.—Indian Office. (Letters received.)

18. Street: Clark, March 20, 1829.

19. Clark: Eaton, St. Louis, May 17, 1829; Clark: Eaton, May 24, 1829.—Indian Office, Washington, D. C.

20. McKenney: Street, Washington, D. C., June 11, 1829.— Indian Office, Letter Books, vol. VI, Street: McKenney, etc.

Street: McKenney, August 12, 1829.—Indian Office. (Letters received.)

21. Volume "A" of Deeds, Office of Register of Deeds, Prairie du Chien, Crawford County, Wisconsin, pp. 189–193. Marsh paid $100 for these premises. See lot 30 on Lucius Lyon's map based on his survey made in July and August, 1828.

CHAPTER XXII

BIBLIOGRAPHY: MARSH BETRAYS THE FOXES, ETC. 1830

1. Stevens, Frank E., *The Black Hawk War*, Chicago, 1903, p. 102.

BIBLIOGRAPHY

Mahan, *Fort Crawford and the Frontier*, p. 152; Lockwood's *Narrative*.—Wisconsin Historical Collections, vol. II, p. 170.

2. Mahan, *Fort Crawford and the Frontier*, p. 152.—Wisconsin Historical Collections, vol. II, pp. 170–171; vol. V, pp. 256–257; vol. IX, pp. 323–326.

Stevens, *The Black Hawk War*, Chicago, 1903, p. 102.

3. Wisconsin Historical Collections, vol. V, p. 257.

4. Wisconsin Historical Collections, vol. IX, pp. 324–326; vol. II, pp. 170–171; vol. V, pp. 256–257.

Taylor to Taliaferro, May 14, 1830.—Taliaferro Papers.

5. Stevens, Frank E., *The Black Hawk War;* communication dated March 22, 1926:

"It is quite natural and under the circumstances quite proper for Marsh to get word to the Sioux that the Sauk and Foxes were coming to Prairie du Chien, especially as Marsh was living with a woman of Sioux extraction. Throughout the border hostilities the Sioux and Menominee were very friendly to the whites; they were friendly too with each other and when the Foxes made raids on the Sioux, which they had done in several instances, naturally the Sioux wanted a chance to hit back (*Lex Talionis*). This visit of the Sauk and Foxes afforded an opportunity and with that friendly feeling which Marsh had for the Sioux he tipped it off to his friends."

6. Taylor to Taliaferro, May 14, 1830.—Taliaferro Papers.

7. United States Statutes at Large, Indian Treaties, Boston, 1854, vol. VII, pp. 272–277.

8. United States Statutes at Large, pp. 328–332.

9. Taliaferro: Clark, July 6, 1831.—State Historical Society of Wisconsin, Street Correspondence.

10. See entry, Taliaferro Journal No. 9, July 16, 1831.—St. Paul. Also Taliaferro: Clark, July 6, 1831.—Taliaferro Papers, Minnesota Historical Collections, St. Paul.

11. Marsh: Street, April 17, 1832.—Street Correspondence, Des Moines, Iowa.

12. Marsh: brother Ezekiel, July 18, 1832.—Marsh Papers.

Ann Crowninshield, daughter of Richard and Ann O'Brien Crowninshield of Danvers, now Peabody, Mass., born January 12, 1807. She was a school-teacher. Dick, her brother, "the terror of Essex County," was an out-and-out scoundrel and would have been hanged for murder if he had not committed suicide by hanging himself in a cell in a Salem jail. It was a famous murder case in which others besides Crowninshield were involved. The gov-

BIBLIOGRAPHY

ernment side of the case was tried by Daniel Webster. It was at the end of his famous speech at this trial that he said "suicide is confession."

13. Taliaferro: Journal, July 3, 1831. St. Paul, Minn.
14. Wisconsin Historical Collections, vol. V, p. 257.
15. Burnett, T. P.: Taliaferro, August 8, 1831.—Taliaferro Papers.

CHAPTER XXIII

BIBLIOGRAPHY: MARGUERITE'S FLIGHT TO ILLINOIS. 1831

1. Early in 1839 the Illinois legislature cut off the north end of Sangamon County and gave it the name of Menard County. In 1836 Abraham Lincoln surveyed and laid out Petersburg, the county seat. The Pantier home fell within the precincts of Menard County.

2. John M. Cameron was born in 1790 in the State of Georgia. He was the son of Thomas and Nancy (Miller) Cameron, his mother being a sister of James Rutledge's wife. Cameron was a millwright by trade, as well as a Cumberland Presbyterian minister. He followed the fortunes of the Rutledge families from Georgia to Tennessee, from there to Kentucky, then to White County, Ill., and from there to the south part of Sangamon County. In 1825 he settled with them in the Concord neighborhood about five miles from Petersburg. In 1828 he moved to New Salem and with James Rutledge built a dam across Sangamon River and erected a grist- and saw-mill combined, which they operated by water-power. During the first year of his life at New Salem, Lincoln boarded for a considerable part of the time at the home of Cameron and they became acquainted and good friends. Cameron was a quiet, sober-minded and rather solemn sort of man, and observed in his household all of the religious forms befitting his cloth. He left New Salem in 1833 or 1834, settled in Iowa and later moved to California where he had charge of a church at Bodega Bay and took a prominent part in the litigation over the Marsh estate. See Reep: *Lincoln at New Salem,* pp. 120–121.

3. Long years after in California, John Marsh's daughter, Alice, married John M. Cameron's son.

4. John Pantier, "Uncle Jimmy," as he was commonly called, was born February 7, 1779. He was one of the first white children born in Kentucky. His father, Philip Pantier, was a com-

BIBLIOGRAPHY

panion of Daniel Boone. From Kentucky he moved to Ohio where he married and where his son, David M. Pantier, was born in 1808. In 1815 he moved with his family to Shawneetown, Ill., and from there he came to what is now Menard County in 1826 and settled in the Concord neighborhood on Sandridge. He bought lots 3 and 4, across the street, west of the Rutledge Inn at New Salem in 1829, but never moved there.

He died January 19, 1859, and is buried beside his wife, Susan Murphy, in a Concord settlement cemetery. His tomb is inscribed, "In life loved, in death lamented." See Reep: *Lincoln at New Salem*, pp. 120-121.

His son, David M. Pantier, married Lizzie, the daughter of Rabut and Nancy Armstrong, in 1829. He was born in Butler County, Ohio, October 16, 1808, and served in the Black Hawk War under Captain Abraham Lincoln.—*History Menard and Mason Counties, Illinois*. Chicago, 1879, p. 748.

The friendship between Lincoln and the Pantiers was extremely close. Much of the material in this chapter is based on several communications from Robert S. Torrey of Los Angeles, great-grandson of Doctor James Pantier. Mr. Torrey has been at great pains to correct the traditions regarding John Marsh, Marguerite, and Charles. For biographical pointers as well as descriptions of the frontier when New Salem and Concord and Sandridge came into being, see Thomas P. Reep's *Lincoln at New Salem*.—The Old Salem Lincoln League, Petersburg, Ill., 1927.

5. "Yarb" is a corruption of the word "herb." Hence he was an herb-doctor.

6. Reep: *Lincoln at New Salem*, pp. 120-121.

7. Torrey, Robert S., Los Angeles, Calif., statement of, November 23, 1925. Mr. Torrey is the great-grandson of Doctor James Pantier of Petersburg, Ill.

8. Torrey, Robert S., statement of. "There were but two roads laid out then [1826], one running from Havana to Springfield, which crossed the Sangamon at Miller's Ferry, fifteen miles south of Havana. This road ran through Salem and Sangamontown."—Onstott's *Pioneers of Mason and Menard*, 1902, p. 248. "Miller's Ferry was once surveyed for a town and was later called Huron." —Onstott, p. 237. "At Athens, a little farther south, was the old Concord Church around which lived James Pantier."—Onstott, p. 246. The doctor was a friend of Lincoln and fought with him in the Black Hawk War.

BIBLIOGRAPHY

9. Brierge Manuscript, Bancroft Collection, Berkeley, Calif., p. 3.
10. Brierge Manuscript, Bancroft Collection, p. 3.
11. Brierge Manuscript, Bancroft Collection, p. 3.

CHAPTER XXIV

BIBLIOGRAPHY: BLACK HAWK WAR. 1832

1. Quaife: *Chicago and the Old Northwest,* p. 323.
Johnson, A. S., *Life of,* p. 33.
Wapello, a Sauk chief, however, delivered three of the sub-chiefs who were incarcerated in the stronghold at Fort Armstrong.
Stevens: *Black Hawk War,* p. 113.
2. Stevens: *Black Hawk War,* p. 114.
3. *Autobiography of Black Hawk,* Cincinnati, 1833, p. 115.
4. Wisconsin Historical Collections, vol. XII, p. 238.
5. *Autobiography of Black Hawk,* p. 119. Stillman's force numbered 341 men.
Black Hawk states that he had 40 followers; Reynolds credits him with not more than 50 or 60; Wisconsin Historical Collections, vol. XII, p. 237, says he had 35, and Quaife: *Chicago and the Old Northwest,* p. 234, writes he had a small number of warriors.
6. Pelzer, Louis: *Henry Dodge,* Iowa City, 1911, p. 51.
7. Stevens: *The Black Hawk War,* chapter XX, p. 139.
8. Atkinson: Street, May 26, 1832.—Wisconsin Historical Collections, vol. II, pp. 255–256.
9. Colonel William S. Hamilton, son of Alexander Hamilton of Revolutionary fame, had "diggings" at Niota, Wis., near Galena.
10. Street: Burnett, Wisconsin Historical Collections, vol. II, p. 256.
11. Neill, E. D.: *History of Minnesota,* Philadelphia, 1858, p. 411.
Holcombe-Return I.: *Minnesota in Three Centuries,* New York, 1908, vol. II, pp. 191–194.
12. Street: Clark, June 7, 1832.—Historical, Memorial and Art Department of Iowa, Street Papers.
13. Wisconsin Historical Collections, vol. II, p. 258.
14. Street: Clark, June 7, 1832.—Historical, Memorial and Art Department of the State of Iowa at Des Moines.

BIBLIOGRAPHY

15. Stevens: *Black Hawk War*, p. 182.
16. Pelzer, Louis: *Henry Dodge*, Iowa City, 1911, pp. 49–66.
17. Neill, E. D.: *The History of Minnesota*, pp. 411–415.
18. In this engagement Lieutenant Charles Bracken, one of the participants, alludes to Marsh as a "colonel."—Wisconsin Historical Collections, vol. II, p. 388.

Again in vol. X, p. 209, Marsh is spoken of as "Colonel of the Rangers," along with Hamilton. The Marsh descendants always understood that their ancestor was an officer in the war. Frank E. Stevens, the greatest living authority of that conflict, doubts whether Marsh held any other command than that of foraging parties.—Communication dated March 22, 1926. For further information on the Sioux in the Black Hawk War, see *Minnesota in Three Centuries*, vol. II, pp. 191–200.

19. A part of General Street's talk to the deserting Sioux as reported in the Galena *Gazette* of July 11, 1832.
20. Street: Taliaferro, June 23, 1832.—Taliaferro Letters, No. 171.
21. Wiconsin Historical Collections, vol. VI, p. 405.

Ibid., vol. X, p. 209.
Ibid., vol. XII, p. 247.

22. Marsh: brother Ezekiel, July 18, 1832.—Marsh Papers.

"You have doubtless heard much of the Indian war in this quarter," he wrote to his brother, "and may probably feel some desire to be assured of my safety. The accounts you see in the public papers are mostly exaggerations. A party of the Sauk and Fox have been at war with the inhabitants of the lead mines and the frontier of Illinois for two or three months. The Indians were first attacked by the whites, but the whites were defeated with considerable loss. The Indians up to this day have been generally victorious although the number of the hostile party does not exceed five hundred, and the whites in the field against them are between three and four thousand. I was sent for by General Atkinson soon after the war began and immediately took the field with about two hundred friendly Indians under my command. I have been about fifty days constantly in the saddle and have scarcely time to undress in all that time. My health was never better."

23. Pelzer: *Henry Dodge*, p. 62.
24. Marsh: Street, July 29, 1832.—Street Papers, Des Moines.
25. Wisconsin Historical Collections, vol. VI, p. 406.
26. *Ibid.*, vol. XII, pp. 257–258; vol. V, pp. 261–264.

BIBLIOGRAPHY

27. Thwaites: *Story of Wisconsin,* p. 190.
Autobiography of Black Hawk, pp. 136-137.
28. Neill, E. D.: *The History of Minnesota,* Philadelphia, 1858, pp. 411-415. Imprisoned first at Fort Crawford, Black Hawk was later taken by Lieutenant Jefferson Davis to Jefferson Barracks and from there to Fortress Monroe. Eventually he was exhibited to throngs of curious people in the eastern States, and obliged to sign articles of perpetual peace, he was finally turned over for safe-keeping to his hated and hating rival, the Fox chief, Keokuk. In 1833 his autobiography was published. He died October 3, 1838, and was buried near where he expired, in the Des Moines River bottom. In 1839 a travelling physician, Doctor Turner of Lexington, rifled his grave and sent the body to St. Louis, where the bones were cleansed and articulated. It was Turner's intention to use them for exhibition purposes. Governor Lucas, then Governor of the Territory of Iowa, demanded their return and receiving them, deposited them in the collections of the Burlington Geological and Historical Society, where they were consumed by fire in 1855. See Stevens: *Black Hawk War,* p. 274.

29. Black Hawk's lament on the occasion of his defeat is worth repeating: "My warriors fell around me; it began to look dismal. I saw my evil day at hand. The sun rose clear on us in the morning, and at night it sunk in a dark cloud, and looked like a ball of fire. This was the last sun that shone on Black Hawk. He is now a prisoner to the white man. But he can stand the torture. He is not afraid of death. He is no coward. Black Hawk is an Indian; he has done nothing of which an Indian need to be ashamed. He has fought the battle of his country against the white men, who came year after year to cheat them and take away their lands. You know the cause of our making war—it is known to all white men—they ought to be ashamed of it. The white men despise the Indians and drive them from their homes. But the Indians are not deceitful. The white men speak bad of the Indian, and look at him spitefully, but the Indian does not tell lies. Indians do not steal. Black Hawk is satisfied. He will go to the world of spirits contented. He has done his duty—his Father will meet him and reward him. The white men do not scalp the head, but they do worse, they poison the heart—it is not pure with them. Farewell to my nation! Farewell to Black Hawk!"

30. Brierge Manuscript.—Bancroft Collection, Berkeley, Calif., p. 3.

BIBLIOGRAPHY

31. Volume "H" of Deeds, Office of Register of Deeds, Prairie du Chien, Crawford County, Wis. From page 392 to middle of page 394.
32. General Winfield Scott arrived at Prairie du Chien August 7, 1832, having been delayed at Detroit and Chicago by cholera. He immediately assumed command of the entire forces and on August 8 mustered the volunteers out of service and on the 10th, aboard the *Warrior*, departed for Rock Island.
33. Wisconsin Historical Collections, vol. V, p. 259.
34. Stevens: *Black Hawk War*, pp. 248–249, Scott's order No. 16, August 8, 1832.
35. Stevens: *Black Hawk War*, p. 249.
Quaife: *Chicago and the Northwest*, pp. 335–336.
36. Pelzer: *Henry Dodge*, p. 71.
37. United States Statutes at Large, vol. VII, p. 373.
38. Koppler's *Indian Affairs, Laws and Treaties*, vol. II, pp. 345–348.
39. See abstract of disbursements by Joseph M. Street, Indian agent at Prairie du Chien, rendered necessary in consequence of the treaty with the Winnebago Indians held at Rock Island, September 15, 1832. Rock Island Treaty expenses, under date of September 3, 1832.—Voucher No. 2, Street Papers, Des Moines, Iowa.
40. Reep, Thomas P., communication from, Petersburg, Ill., dated September 21, 1925.

CHAPTER XXV

BIBLIOGRAPHY: ESCAPE TO THE ROCKY MOUNTAINS. 1832–1833

1. This story of Marsh is narrated by Charles Larpenteur in his *Forty Years a Fur Trader on the Upper Missouri*, New York, 1898, pp. 23–26. Marsh is known to have been in Missouri during this period on his way to the Rockies and was the only known Marsh at that time on the frontier. In the opinion of Miss Drumm of the Missouri Historical Society and of Miss Nute of the Minnesota Historical Society, who examined the original Larpenteur Journal for the present writer, this episode undoubtedly refers to John Marsh.
2. *Ibid.*, p. 41.
3. *Ibid.*, p. 43.
4. *Ibid.*, p. 44.

BIBLIOGRAPHY

CHAPTER XXVI

BIBLIOGRAPHY: MERCHANDISING, INDEPENDENCE, Mo. 1833

1. Jackson County, Missouri.—County Court Minute Book, vol. II, pp. 4–5, under date November 12, 1833.
2. *Ibid.*, p. 63, November, 1834.
3. *Ibid.*, p. 120, August, 1835. "On settlement with John B. Flannery, Collector aforesaid, for November, 1834, Court overdues, following accounts to be certified to Auditor of Public Accounts as having been collected for State purposes prior to first Monday in February, 1835."
4. *History of Jackson County*, pp. 171–173.
5. Waugh, "Desultory Wanderings."—MS., Missouri Historical Society.
6. MS. Hague and Barnett to Marsh, dated Weston, Platte County, Mo., May 18, 1841. Original letter in California State Library.
7. Cameron–Marsh letters, Santa Barbara, Calif.

CHAPTER XXVII

BIBLIOGRAPHY: FLIGHT DOWN THE SANTA FÉ TRAIL. 1835

1. Hulanski, F. J.: *The History of Contra Costa County, California*.
2. "Doctor Marsh: The Story of a Pioneer," Stockton *Daily Evening Record*, February 25, 1919. The same story appears in Hulanski's *History of Contra Costa County*.
3. This was the usual custom for all caravans. See Drumm, Stella, *Down the Santa Fé Trail*, pp. 102–103.
4. Manuscript, Langstroth to Marsh.—Marsh Papers, State Library, Sacramento, Calif.
5. Hill, Joseph J.: *Ewing Young in the Fur Trade of the Far Southwest, 1822–1834*, Eugene, Ore., 1923.
6. Hill, Joseph J.: *The History of Warner's Ranch and Its Environs*, Los Angeles, 1927, pp. 75–101.
Hill, Joseph J.: *Fur Trade of the Far Southwest*, pp. 28–29.
7. Marsh to Cass, dated Farm of Pulpones, February, 1846, *The Overland Monthly*, vol. XV, p. 213.
8. Wilkes' *Narrative*, vol. V, p. 182.

BIBLIOGRAPHY

9. Pickering, Charles, M. D.: *The Races of Man*, London, p. 112. In 1841 Charles Pickering arrived in California with the Wilkes expedition. Marsh told him of his trip down the Santa Fé trail. We can obtain some idea of its interest from the letter Pickering wrote Marsh before his departure.

"San Francisco, Oct. 29th, 1841.
Dear Sir:
"I fully expected the pleasure of seeing you once more, as Capt. Wilkes sent a message two or three times; but by some mishap you probably never received it.—I cannot take leave of you without urging you to write out an account of your tour through New Mexico,—and suggesting that with proper management it might be of considerable benefit to the pocket.

"The country you passed through is of unrivalled interest on this continent—it seems to me that now is the appointed time for the appearance of such a work; when the country in this direction is beginning to excite attention at home, and a stream of Emigration is pointing hitherward.—The general subject too of the history of our Indian tribes, and ancient population of America, Ruins, etc. has become of much more popular interest than in former years.

"Should I happen to be in the United States nothing would give me greater pleasure than to take charge of such a manuscript, to make the best bargain with the Booksellers—or if I am absent my friend *S. George Morton*, M. D. (Arch, near 12th St., Philadelphia) would do everything for you that I could myself; if you write to him and make use of my name.

"I have requested Mr. Hale (of the Expedition) should he arrive here in the spring, to give you a call. He is interested in these subjects.

"An opportunity offering to send to Mazatlan, I have concluded to forward your letter, with those of the Squadron—and should I visit Salem on my return, will make it a point to call on your family.—

"Wishing you health and prosperity, and hoping to meet you ere long in the United States,
I remain,
Your friend
CHARLES PICKERING.

DR. JOHN MARSH
San Joaquin."

(In author's possession.)

BIBLIOGRAPHY

CHAPTER XXVIII

BIBLIOGRAPHY: EL PUEBLO, ETC. 1836

1. *El Pueblo, Los Angeles, before the Railroads,* Los Angeles, 1928.
2. *El Pueblo,* p. 31.
3. Engelhardt: *Fr. Zephyrin,* San Gabriel, Calif., 1927, pp. 164–167; Clarice Garland, Mrs. C. Goodwin of Pasadena, Calif., a descendant of this union, has woven an historical romance about this episode in the lives of her ancestors. See *The Sea King.*
4. Minute Book of Sessions of the Illustrious *Ayuntamiento* of the City of Los Angeles for the year 1836, Session of the 4th day of February, 1836, p. 106, par. 10, Los Angeles City Archives, Translations from the Spanish, vol. 2.
5. Barrows, H. D., "Pioneer Physicians of Los Angeles" in Publications of the Historical Society of Southern California, Part II, vol. I, 1901.
6. Session of the 18th day of February, 1863, vol. II, p. 113, par. 7.
7. See Los Angeles City Archives, Minute Book, etc., Sessions of the 25th of February, 1836, p. 117, par. 3. The only diplomas which Marsh was known to have possessed were his Phillips Andover and Harvard A. B. degrees. It is probable that he submitted these and that the good Padres at the *Mission San Gabriel* did not know the true significance of his Latin degrees. It is also possible that Marsh was provided with a certificate written in Latin saying that he had studied medicine and surgery for such and such a period. Perhaps this was signed by Doctor Purcell at Fort Snelling where for some time he had studied medicine. During this period these medical certificates were quite common in the rural communities of America. Many of their holders subsequently took M. D. degrees at recognized medical schools.
8. "Los Angeles Pioneers of 1836."—Publications Historical Society of Southern California, 1903, p. 80.
9. Willard: *History of Los Angeles,* p. 177.
10. "Some Old Letters."—Publications Historical Society of Southern California, 1902, pp. 251–252.

CHAPTER XXIX

BIBLIOGRAPHY: EXPLORATIONS—YERBA BUENA. 1836–1837

1. "Marsh to Stearns."—Publications Historical Society Southern California, 1902.

BIBLIOGRAPHY

2. José Noriega's deposition Petition No. 213, Supreme Court of the United States Appts. *vs.* Alice Marsh.—State Library, Sacramento, Calif.

3. Publications Historical Society Southern California, 1902, "Some Old Letters, Marsh to Stearns, dated Yerba Buena, March 27, 1837."

4. *History San Joaquin County*, 1879, p. 13.

5. MS. Currey, Judge John, statement by: Incidents in California, Bancroft Library, 1878. Probably Marsh was unaware that Moraga crossed this country in 1809 and, finding the skulls, gave it the obvious name of *Calaveras*. Marsh's and Noriega's discovery is confirmed in Thompson and West's *History San Joaquin County*, 1879, p. 13.

6. Currey MS., Bancroft Library. This river was likewise discovered by Moraga and named by him and his party. Owing to the lack of written reports doubtless Marsh and his friends were unaware of this event.

7. Foster, Stephen C.: "Some Old Letters, Marsh to Stearns, dated Yerba Buena, March 27, 1837."—Annual Publications of the Historical Society of Southern California, 1902, pp. 251–252.

8. Marsh to Stearns, dated Yerba Buena, March 27, 1837.

9. Robinson, A.: *Life in California*, p. 57.

10. California in 1837, diary of Colonel Philip L. Edwards, Sacramento, 1890, pp. 16–17.

11. Wilkes, Charles, U. S. N.: *Narrative of the United States Exploring Expedition*, New York, 1851, vol. V, pp. 152–153.

12. Purdy, Helen Throop: *Portsmouth Square*, California Historical Society, 1924. Tuthill: *History of California*, pp. 289–290.

13. Bidwell, John: *A Journey to California*, p. 31. Bidwell was notoriously antagonistic to Marsh.

14. California in 1837, diary of Colonel Philip L. Edwards, Sacramento, 1890. Edwards found Marsh at Yerba Buena, and the doctor helped him to round up 700 cattle for the settlers on the Willamette.

CHAPTER XXX

BIBLIOGRAPHY: LOS MEGANOS. 1837

1. Smith and Elliott: *History Contra Costa County*, Oakland, 1878, p. 9; Slocum's *History Contra Costa County*, 1882, p. 42.

2. Slocum: *History Contra Costa County*, p. 42.

3. Hittell, T. H.: *History of California*, vol. II, pp. 793–794.

4. Noriega's deposition as to Marsh's grant, Supreme Court

BIBLIOGRAPHY

of the U. S., No. 246, the U. S. Appts. *vs.* Alice Marsh.—State Library, Sacramento.

5. Marsh, John: deposition of, No. 213, S. F., February 25, 1853, Supreme Court of U. S.—State Library, Sacramento.

6. MS. Marsh: The Valley of the San Joaquin. In author's possession.

7. Marsh: Lewis Cass, dated Farm of Pulpones, near San Francisco, Upper California, February, 1846.—*Overland Monthly,* February, 1890.

8. Marsh to Lewis Cass.—*Overland Monthly,* February, 1890, p. 216.

9. Robinson, A.: *Life in California,* pp. 74–76.

10. Kirkman, George Wycherley; Los Angeles *Times,* November 6, 1927.

11. Marsh: Stearns, Yerba Buena, 1837.

12. MS. Sutter: Larkin, November 5, 1845.—Larkin Papers, Bancroft Library.

Bryant, Edwin: *What I Saw in California,* p. 306.

13. Wells, Harry L.: *Great Fur Companies and Their Trapping Expeditions to California,* History Butte Co., California, 1882, vol. I, pp. 94–102.

14. Slocum's *History of Contra Costa County,* San Francisco, 1882, p. 481.

15. Bidwell, John: *A Journey to California,* March 30, 1842, Independence, Mo., pp. 31–32.

16. Sanchez, N. V.: *California and the Californians,* vol. I, p. 421.

17. Smith and Elliott: *History of Contra Costa County,* p. 7.

18. Marsh to Cass, February, 1846.—*Overland Monthly,* February, 1890, p. 216.

19. Vallejo's statement.

20. Marsh to Cass, 1846.

21. Smith, W. W., statement of, Slocum's *History of Contra Costa County,* p. 671.

22. Bryant, Edwin: *What I saw in California,* Philadelphia, 1848, p. 303.

23. MS. Caleb Marsh to John Marsh, February 9, 1838.

MS. Mary Marsh to John Marsh, June 12, 1840, c/o the Brig *Thomas Perkins,* via Sandwich Islands, c/o Henry Mellus. Directed, "Al Sor Don Juan Marsh, San Francisco, Alta California."

BIBLIOGRAPHY

CHAPTER XXXI

BIBLIOGRAPHY: THE DOCTOR AND THE HORSE THIEVES

1. Marsh to Cass, February, 1846.—*Overland Monthly*, February, 1890, p. 214.
2. Bidwell, John: *Journey to California*, p. 27.—Bancroft Library.
3. Bidwell, John: *Journey to California*, p. 31.
4. Wilkes' *Narrative*, vol. V, p. 181.
5. Sanchez, Nellie V.: *California and the Californians*, Chicago, 1926, vol. I, p. 421.
6. Stockton *Daily Evening Herald*. "Doctor Marsh: The Story of a Pioneer," February 15, 1919.
7. MS. Sutter to Marsh, April 2, 1840.—Bolton Collection, University of California.
8. MS. Sutter to Marsh, October 7, 1840.—State Library, Sacramento.
9. Bidwell, John: *A Journey to California*, p. 31.
10. MS. Sunol to Marsh, March 25, 1845.—California State Library, Sacramento.
11. Bidwell, John: Address delivered on November 1, 1897, to the members of the Society of California Pioneers, vol. III, No. 1, p. 16.
12. MS. Martinez to Marsh, Merced, November 3, 1845.—California State Library, Sacramento.
13. Vallejo, José Jesus, to Marsh, San José, July, 1841.—Bolton Collection, University of California. Translated from the Spanish.
14. MS. Tinslar, R. N., to Marsh, U. S. Ship *St. Louis*, Monterey, May 28, 1841.—Author's collection; Bancroft's *California*, vol. IV, p. 86.
15. Lyman, G. D.: "The Scalpel Under Three Flags in California."—*California Historical Quarterly*, vol. IV, No. 2, p. 156.
16. Bidwell, John: *A Journey to California*, Bodega, Port of the Russians, 1842, p. 31.—Bancroft Library.
17. Marsh, John, deposition of, before the Land Grant Commission, No. 213, San Francisco, February 25, 1853.
18. MS. Vallejo, *Historia de California*, vol. IV, 1839–1845; Sanchez: *California and the Californians*, vol. I, p. 422.
19. MS. Vallejo: *Historia de California*, etc. Also see: "John

BIBLIOGRAPHY

Marsh" in the *California Star*, San Francisco, April 10, 1847, signed *Agricola;* MS. Marsh: Horse Thieves, author's possession, *California Star*, April 15, 1846, signed *Agricola*.

CHAPTER XXXII

BIBLIOGRAPHY: THE GRAHAM AFFAIR. 1840

1. Cleland, Robert Glass: "Early Sentiment for the Annexation of California."—Reprint *Southwestern Historical Quarterly*, vol. XVIII, Nos. 1, 2 and 3, p. 19.
2. Marsh: Jones.—*Overland Monthly*, February, 1890, pp. 218–219.
3. MS. Brown: Recollections of Early Events in California, p. 15, Bancroft Library.
4. MS. Meadows, James, statement of, respecting the Graham affair of 1840, pp. 9–12.—Bancroft Library.
Bancroft's *California*, vol. IV, pp. 5–17; vol. V, p. 749.
5. Bancroft's *California*, vol. V, p. 689. MS. Belden, Josiah: Statement of Historical Facts on California.
6. Marsh to Jones, Thomas Ap. Catesby.—*Overland Monthly*, February, 1890.
7. Farnham, J. F.: *The Early Days of California*, Philadelphia, 1869, pp. 57–58.
8. Bancroft says 47, Farnham names about 50, pp. 69–70. See Bancroft, *California*, vol. IV, p. 17.
9. Marsh to Jones.—*Overland*, February, 1890.
10. Farnham, *The Early Days of California*, p. 92.
11. *Ibid.*, p. 92.
12. *Ibid.*, p. 94.
13. Marsh (*Agricola*) "California," No. III, the *California Star*, San Francisco, February 26, 1848, vol. II, No. 8.
14. Marsh to Jones, Thomas Ap. C., November 25, 1842.

CHAPTER XXXIII

BIBLIOGRAPHY: INAUGURATES CALIFORNIA IMMIGRATION. 1841

1. Wilkes' *Narrative*, vol. V, p. 181.
2. MS. Chiles, Col. J. B.: A Visit to California in Early Times, 1878.—Bancroft Library.
3. MS. Chiles.
4. Bidwell: Journal, p. 16.
5. Royce, C. C., Bidwell, p. 14; Cleland, Robert, G.: *A History of California*, New York, 1923, p. 100.

BIBLIOGRAPHY

6. Cleland, Robert G.: "Early Sentiment for Annexation of California," Austin, Texas, n. d., note p. 24.
7. Bancroft's *California*, vol. IV, p. 267.
8. *Colonial Magazine*, vol. V, p. 229–230. This meant the route recommended by Marsh and not the one followed by him to Santa Fé.
9. See the New York *Journal of Commerce*, March 30, 1841.
10. MS. Chiles: Visit to California, p. 2.
11. Niles' Register, vol. LXI, p. 209.
12. MS. Hague and Barnett: Marsh, dated Weston, Platte County, May 18, 1841.—Marsh Papers, State Library, Sacramento, Calif.
13. Marsh to Commodore Thomas Ap. C. Jones. Bidwell, in his Journal, refers several times to this guiding letter, as also does Chiles.
14. Bancroft's *California*, vol. IV, pp. 272–273.
Cleland, "Early Sentiment," etc., p. 26.
15. Marsh to Jones, Comm. T. Ap. C.—*Overland Monthly*, California.
Bidwell: Journal, p. 16.
16. Bidwell, Journal; *Journey to California*.
17. MS. Chiles, J. B.: A Visit to California in Early Times. —Bancroft Library.
Royce, C. C.: *John Bidwell, A Biographical Sketch*, Chic., 1906, p. 37.
MS. Belden, Josiah, statement of, Historical Facts on California, Bancroft Library. Through the Indian, Marsh heard of the plight of the emigrants and sent a *vaquero* with a horse laden with provisions to help them.

CHAPTER XXXIV

BIBLIOGRAPHY: FIRST EMIGRANTS ARRIVE AT MARSH'S RANCHO.
1841

1. MS. Hague and Barnett: Marsh, dated May 18, 1841, Weston, Platte County, Missouri.—Marsh Papers, State Library, Sacramento. Also Marsh to Commander Thomas Ap. C. Jones.
2. MS. Chiles, J. B.: A Visit to California in Early Times, p. 4. Chiles also says that Marsh had several children by her. There is no verification of this statement before or since.
3. Bidwell's *Journey to California*, p. 20.
4. MS. Bidwell, Recollections, p. 73.

BIBLIOGRAPHY

5. Chiles Visit, p. 4.
6. Bidwell: "Address to Pioneers," *Quarterly California Pioneers*, vol. III, No. 1, p. 18.
7. MS. Cameron, Alice Marsh: The Bidwell Affair. In the author's possession.
8. MS. Belden, Josiah, statement of, Historical Facts on California.—Bancroft Library, p. 14.
9. MS. Hopper, Charles: Narrative of a California Pioneer of 1841.—Bancroft Library, p. 3.
10. Vallejo Documents for the History of California, vol. X, 1841, Doc. No. 300.—Bancroft Library. Translated from the Spanish for the thesis of Emily June Ulsh, pp. 86–87.
11. MS. Belden, statement of, p. 14.
12. Bancroft's *California*, vol. IV, p. 275.
13. MS. Hopper, Charles: Narrative of a California Pioneer of 1841, p. 4.
14. The Commandante General to Señor Don J. Marsh, dated November 11, 1841. Vallejo Documents for the History of California, vol. X, 1841, Dec. No. 335.—Bancroft Library. Translated from the Spanish MS. for the thesis of Emily June Ulsh.
15. Cleland, Robert Glass: "Early Sentiment for Annexation of California," p. 26.
16. MS. Hopper's Narrative. Hopper says only five men went to San José. Bidwell claims that fifteen went.
17. MS. Hopper's Narrative of a California Pioneer of 1847.
18. Vallejo Documents for the History of California, dated November 13, 1841, vol. X, 1841, Doc. No. 340.—Bancroft Library. Translated for the thesis of Emily June Ulsh.
19. Bidwell: *Life in California*, Century, 1890, p. 165.
20. *Ibid.*, December, 1890.
21. *Ibid.*, December, 1890, pp. 164–165.
22. Bidwell, John: address of, *Quarterly California Pioneers*, vol. III, No. 1, p. 19.
23. MS. Bidwell, John: California, 1841–1848, an immigrant's recollection of a trip across the Plains, etc.—Bancroft Library, 1877, pp. 77–78.
24. Marsh to father, carried across Plains with Chiles and Hopper party starting east March, 1842.
Hopper Narrative, p. 9, mailed at Independence, September 13, 1842, reaching Danvers early in October.—Marsh Papers.

BIBLIOGRAPHY

CHAPTER XXXV

BIBLIOGRAPHY: BETRAYS MICHELTORENA. 1841–1845

1. Cleland: *A History of California*, p. 118.
2. Bancroft's *California*, vol. IV, p. 380; Cleland: "Early Sentiment for Annexation," etc., Austin, Texas, p. 35.
3. Bancroft's *California*, vol. IV, p. 482.
4. MS. Sutter to Marsh, dated July 21, 1844.—Marsh Letters.
5. MS. Sutter to Marsh, undated.—Marsh Papers.
6. First time in California history that white men had equipped the Indians against men of their own blood.
7. MS. Sutter: Flugge, Salinas, January 12, 1845. De La Guerra, *Documentos para la Historia de California*, Tom. I, No. 2.—Bancroft Library.
8. MS. Sinclair, J., to Marsh, January 5, 1845.—California State Library, Sacramento.
9. MS. Bidwell, John: California, 1841–1848, p. 123.—Bancroft Library.
10. MS. Sutter: Personal Reminiscences, p. 89.—Bancroft Library.
11. Bancroft's *California*, vol. IV, pp. 488–489.
12. Sutter: Personal Reminiscences, p. 93. These figures are probably a gross exaggeration as they do not agree with any authority. See Bancroft: *California*, vol. IV, p. 488. The united force on the Salinas was probably 600; MS. Sutter to Flugge, De La Guerra, *Doc. para la Historia de California*, Tom. I, No. 2.—Bancroft Library.

CHAPTER XXXVI

BIBLIOGRAPHY: TREACHERY—BATTLE OF CAHUENGA. 1845

1. MS. Sutter: Personal Reminiscences, p. 104.
2. Bidwell: California, 1841–48, p. 124.
3. Davis, William Heath: *Sixty Years in California*, San Francisco, 1889, p. 184.
4. Bancroft's *California*, vol. IV, p. 503.
5. MS. Bidwell: California, 1841–48, pp. 125–129.
6. Sutter: Reminiscences, p. 106.
7. Bonner, T. D.: *The Life and Adventures of James P. Beckwourth*, New York, 1856, pp. 469–470.
8. Tinkham, George H.: *California Men and Events*, 1915, p. 50.

BIBLIOGRAPHY

9. Sutter: Personal Reminiscences, pp. 105–108.
10. MS. Sutter: Personal Reminiscences, p. 106.
11. *Ibid.*, p. 89.
12. Bancroft's *California,* vol. IV, p. 508.
13. Larkin, Thomas: "The Prominent Men of California in 1846."—*The Pacific Monthly,* vol. X, No. 4.

CHAPTER XXXVII

BIBLIOGRAPHY: MARSH CALLS THE AMERICANS TO ARMS—
REPUBLIC OF CALIFORNIA. 1845

1. Larkin: Buchanan.—*The Pacific Monthly,* San Francisco, August, 1863, vol. X, No. 4.
2. Marsh y Gantt, Contrato entre el Gab.° Marsh y Gantt. Sabre perseucucion de Ind.ˢ landowner, Appendix, p. 137.
3. Archives of California, Departmental State Papers, vols. V–VI, 1841–1845, pp. 612–613. Translated for the thesis of Emily June Ulsh from the Spanish documents in the Bancroft Library.
4. MS. Sutter to Sunol, June 14, 1845.—State Library, Sacramento.
5. Marsh Papers, Santa Barbara, Calif.
6. MS. Marsh to Larkin, August 12, 1845. Larkin Documents for the History of California, vol. III, 247, p. 4.
7. Bancroft's *California,* vol. IV, p. 599.
8. *History of San Joaquin County, California,* Thompson and West, Oakland, Calif., 1879, pp. 18–19.
9. MS. Farnham, Thos. J., to Marsh, New York, July 6, 1845.
10. MS. Weber to Marsh, March 7, 1846.—Marsh Papers, California State Library, Sacramento.

CHAPTER XXXVIII

BIBLIOGRAPHY: COUP D'ETAT FAILS. 1846

1. Larkin, Thomas: "The Prominent Men of California in 1846." This list was prepared by Larkin during the winter of 1845–46 and sent to James Buchanan, then Secretary of State. —*The Pacific Monthly,* San Francisco, August, 1863, vol. X, No. 4.
2. MS. Larkin to Marsh, July 8, 1845.—Marsh Papers, State Library, Sacramento.

BIBLIOGRAPHY

3. Marsh to Cass, February, 1846.—*Overland Monthly*, February, 1890, pp. 213–216.
4. Hulanski, F. J.: *History Contra Costa County*, Berkeley, 1917, p. 133. Marsh wrote other propaganda letters on California. These were intended for the New Orleans *Picayune* and were signed "Essex"—a Marsh *nom de plume*. After a diligent search of the columns of the *Picayune* we are forced to conclude Marsh's articles were never published there—but his manuscripts remain.
5. MS. Weber to Marsh, March 9, 1846.—Marsh Papers, State Library, Sacramento.
6. MS. Sutter to Marsh, April 3, 1846.—Marsh Papers, State Library, Sacramento.
7. Frémont, John Charles: *Memoirs of My Life*, Chicago and New York, 1883, pp. 503–507.
8. Frémont: *Memoirs*, p. 509.
9. "Frémont's Place in California History."—*Overland Monthly*, December, 1890, p. 579.
10. Shinn, M. W.: "The Bears and the Historians," *Overland*, September, 1890, p. 309; Frémont's *Memoirs*, p. 509.
11. Frémont's *Memoirs*, p. 522. The artist who executed the bear was a nephew of Mrs. Abraham Lincoln.—*Overland*, September, 1890, p. 310.
12. MS. Sutter's Reminiscences, p. 151.—Bancroft's Library, Berkeley, Calif.

CHAPTER XXXIX

BIBLIOGRAPHY: PARK'S BAR. 1849

1. Marsh to Cass.—*Overland*, February, 1890, p. 215.
2. Cameron, Amy G., statement of. In author's possession.
3. *Ibid*.
4. Marsh, L. B.: *The Genealogy of John Marsh of Salem*, p. 225.
5. *History of Yuba County, California*, p. 88.
6. Palmer's *Necrology of Harvard College*, pp. 137–140.
7. San Francisco *Call*, December 9, 1893, p. 3, col. 3.
8. Marsh to Larkin, August 12, 1845.
9. MS. Early Mining Town Names.—State Library, Sacramento.
10. Marsh *Genealogy*, p. 225.
11. *Ibid.*, Marsh to father, September 25, 1849.

BIBLIOGRAPHY

CHAPTER XL

BIBLIOGRAPHY: WOMEN. 1849-1851

1. MS. Cameron, Amy G., statement of. Miss Cameron is a granddaughter of Doctor John Marsh and the Reverend John Cameron.
2. MS. Caleb Marsh to John, dated Lockport, 1849.—Marsh Papers.
3. MS. Gantt to Marsh, Napa Valley, August 22, 1847.—Marsh Papers, State Library.
4. Tuck Letters.—Marsh Papers, Santa Barbara.
5. MS. Tuck Letters, Santa Clara, November 27, 1850.
6. MS. Appleton, John N., to Alice Marsh Cameron, Fresno, June 11, 1886.—Marsh Papers.
7. MS. Appleton to Alice Marsh Cameron.—Marsh Papers, Santa Barbara.
8. MS. Tuck Letters, Santa Barbara.
9. MS. Tuck Letters, Abby, to My very dear Parents, July 14, 1851.—Marsh Papers, Santa Barbara.
10. MS. Cameron-Marsh Papers, Santa Barbara.
11. This house was afterward moved to Boobar Street, Antioch.
12. MS. Tuck Letters, Santa Barbara.
13. MS. Abby to parents, July 14, 1851.
14. MS. Smith, W. W., to Alice Marsh Cameron, Antioch, April 13, 1876.
15. MS. Abby Tuck Letters.—Marsh Papers, Santa Barbara.

CHAPTER XLI

BIBLIOGRAPHY: ABBY. 1851-1853

1. MS. Abby to parents, October 19, 1851.—Tuck Papers, Santa Barbara, Calif.
2. MS. Abby to parents, dated May 16, 1852.—Tuck Papers, Santa Barbara, Calif.
3. MS. Tuck Letters, May 16, 1852.
4. Palmer's *Necrology of Harvard College*, pp. 137-140.
5. Slocum: *History of Contra Costa County*, p. 616.
6. MS. Tuck Letters, September 26, 1852, Santa Barbara.
7. MS. Appleton, John W., to Cameron, Fresno, June 11, 1886.—Marsh Papers, Santa Barbara.

BIBLIOGRAPHY

8. MS. Tuck Letters, September 26, 1852, and April 12, 1854, Santa Barbara.

9. Hoffman, Odgen: *Report of Land Cases determined in the United States District Court for the Northern District of California, San Francisco.* N. Herbert, 1862, vol. I, pp. 301–305.

10. MS. Bill of Sale.—Marsh Papers, Santa Barbara.

11. Project for a railroad, May 6, 1847.—*California Star,* vol. I, No. 18. Strange as it may seem, the route he indicated was afterward followed by the Sante Fé.

12. MS. Tuck Papers, October 22, 1853.

13. *Ibid.,* September 11, 1853.

14. MS. Tuck Letters, March 10, 1855, Santa Barbara.

15. MS. Tuck Papers, Santa Barbara.

16. MS. Marsh to Tuck, June 13–18, 1855.—Tuck Papers, Santa Barbara.

CHAPTER XLII

BIBLIOGRAPHY: VIGILANTES. 1855

1. MS. Marsh to Tuck, August, 1855.

2. *Ibid.,* January 3, 1856.

3. MS. Tuck Papers, October 21, 1854.

4. MS. Marsh: Tuck, September 26, 1852; April 18, 1853.—Marsh Letters, Santa Barbara.

5. Hulanski, p. 121.

6. Hulanski: *History Contra Costa County,* p. 119.

7. Statement of evidence. Appeal of Case of People vs. Marsh and Thompson, County Court, Contra Costa County, 15th Judicial District Court, Martinez.

8. Bancroft's *Popular Tribunals,* vol. I, pp. 541–542.

9. Communication, Office County Clerk, Contra Costa County, July 31, 1925.

10. Brown's testimony before People v. Marsh and Thompson, Court House, Martinez.

11. The People of the State of California against John Marsh and Samuel Thompson in the Court of Sessions of the County of Contra Costa, State of California, at the February Term, A. D. 1855, Court House, Martinez.

12. MS. Curry, Judge John, statement of.—Bancroft Library, pp. 2–5.

BIBLIOGRAPHY

CHAPTER XLIII
BIBLIOGRAPHY: ROBBERS. 1856

1. MS. Brierge, The Story of Doctor Marsh, p. 2.
2. Cameron, Amy G., statement of, Santa Barbara, Calif.; Brewer, William H.: Letter No. 49, June 1, 1862, Yale Press, 1930.
3. Brewer, Letter No. 49. Yale Press, 1930.
4. Cameron, Alice M., statement of.
According to the Brierge MS., p. 6, the steamer was the *Uncle Sam*.
5. MS. Brierge, p. 6.
6. MS. Brewer, Letter No. 49, June 1, 1862.
7. MS. Brierge, p. 4.
8. S. F. *Evening Bulletin*, November 29, 1867, p. 3, cols. 5–6.
9. *Ibid*.
Sacramento *Daily Union*, December 4, 1867, p. 4, col. 2.
10. MS. Brierge, The Story of Doctor Marsh, p. 6–7.

CHAPTER XLIV
BIBLIOGRAPHY: HARVEST TIME. 1856

1. Contra Costa *Gazette*, November 29, 1867, p. 3, cols. 5–6.
2. MS. Governor's Proclamation; Description of Felipe Morena. In author's possession.
3. The San Francisco *Examiner*, December 8, 1893, "The Story of an Old Crime."
4. Oakland *Tribune*, December 16, 1891, "Will He Get Out? Felipe Morena Recommended for Pardon."
5. Cameron, Amy G., statement, dated May 27, 1928.
6. MS. Curry, John, Judge, statement, pp. 3–4.
7. Oakland *Tribune*, December 16, 1891, *Ibid*.
8. The Marsh Murder Case, Sacramento *Daily Union*, November 28, 1867.
9. MS. Fugate to Marsh, September 21, 1856.—Marsh Papers, Santa Barbara.
10. Brown, Elam, statement of, Martinez, Calif.
11. MS. Marsh to Webb, September 23, 1856.—Marsh Papers, Santa Barbara.
12. MS. Brierge, p. 11.
13. San Francisco *Bulletin*, November 29, 1867, p. 3, col. 6.

BIBLIOGRAPHY

14. *Ibid.,* November 29, 1867, p. 3, cols. 5–6.
15. Stockton *Daily Union,* November 27, 1867.
16. San Francisco *Bulletin,* November 29, 1867, p. 3, cols. 5–6.
17. *Ibid.*
18. Curry, Judge John: "Story of an Old Crime," San Francisco *Examiner,* December 8, 1893.
19. Sacramento *Daily Union,* November 27, 1867, p. 1, cols. 4–5.

CHAPTER XLV

BIBLIOGRAPHY: BY THE LAWS OF FRANCE. 1856

1. MS. Brierge, p. 7.
2. MS. James Marsh to father, October 5, 1856.
3. Cameron, Amy G., statement of.
4. Marsh to father, St. Louis, October 9, 1827.—James Marsh Papers, Berkeley, Calif.
5. Marsh to brother Ezekiel, July 18, 1832.—James Marsh Papers, Berkeley, Calif.
6. MS. Brierge, The Story of Doctor Marsh, pp. 8–11.—Bancroft Library.

CHAPTER XLVI

BIBLIOGRAPHY: MARSH'S LIGHT

1. Contra Costa *Gazette,* November 30, 1867.
2. Sacramento *Daily Union,* November 27, 1867, p. 4, col. 3.
3. Curry, Judge John: "Story of an Old Crime," San Francisco *Examiner,* December 8, 1893.
4. *Ibid.*
Also Charles' story of the capture of the murderers of Doctor John Marsh, as taken down by Alice Marsh Cameron, Santa Barbara.
5. MS. Brierge, p. 11.
Guinn, J. M.: *History of the State of California,* n. d., vol. II, p. 670.
Contra Costa *Gazette,* Pacheco, Calif., December 8, 1866, p. 2, col. 2.

INDEX

INDEX

Abbot's, Mrs., boarding house, 10
Acacia plants, 199
Adams, John, Preceptor of Phillips Academy, 25-27
Adams, John, classmate of John Marsh's, 35
Adams, John Quincy, 36, 92-94
Agnew, John O., 189
Almonte, General, 240
Alvadaro, Juan Bautiste, 200; commends Marsh, 230; treachery of, 233-235; dismissed, 251; Mexicans march against, 252-257, 258-261
American Fur Company, 52, 57, 77, 104, 185, 189
American River, 276, 277
Andover Hill, 26
Antioch, 286, 335
Antoine, 161
Apaches, the, 190
Appleton, Captain and Mrs., 285-287
Arapahoes, the, 190
Arkansas, the, 191
Arnold, Benedict, 7
Arroyo de los Pabladons, 215
Atkinson, Brigadier-General, 126, 128, 168; and Black Hawk war, 169 ff., 174
Atwater, Caleb, 133
Aull, James and Robert, 189
Ayuntamiento, Pueblo, 202, 203

Bad Axe River, 175, 176
Baird, John, 189
Baker, E. D., 281, 327-330
Baker's Island, 8
Baldridge, 237-239
Barbour, James, 90, 92, 93, 134
Barnett, B., 192
Barnett, Elias, 243
Bartleson, John, 191; his expedition to California, 239-241
Beaumont, William, 109
Beckwourth, 260
Beener, John, 280
Beener, Mrs. John, 288
Bernal, Jesus, 233
Berry, John M., 167, 307

Bidwell, John, 240, 244-246, 248
Bighorn, the, 185, 186, 187
Black Dog's village, 72
Blackfeet, 187, 188
Black Hawk, 110, 122, 168; war of, 155, 169 ff.; retaliation of, 159; flight of, 173
Boggs, Lilburn W., 191
Boilvin, Nicolas, 93, 98, 109, 112, 113, 127, 134
Boilvins, the, 87
Bolgones, the, 215, 219
Bonneville's men, Captain, 185
Boston, viewed from Charlestown, 14
Bowen, 326
Boxford, 23
Brierely, Reverend Mr., 298
"Brimstone Hill," 26
Broken Face, 153
Brown, A. L., 301, 302
Brown, Polly, *see* Marsh
Brunet, Jean, 114
Brunet, John, 151
Bryant and Sturgis, 222
Buena Ventura, Mission, 257
Bunker Hill, 14
Burnett, Elias, 170, 171, 192
Burridge, 15
Butte des Morts, 126, 127

Caballero, the California, 218
Cacti, 199
Cahuenga, Battle of, 258-261
Calaveras, 208
California, lead fever compared to gold rush of, 137; Marsh hears of glories of, 198, 199; in 1836, 200 ff.; Marsh first American doctor in, 203-205; landowners required to be Catholics, 205; Marsh's part in annexation to U. S., 209, 231, 237 ff., 250 ff., 263 ff., 268 ff.; Bartleson's expedition to, 240-242; their disappointment in, 243; American emigration to, after 1841, 250; Micheltorena revolution, 251 ff., 258 ff.; Pio Pico governor of, 262; plan for union of Oregon and, 263; Republic of, 263-267; Polk's

INDEX

determination to annex, 268; Frémont's action in, 271 ff.; annexation, 275; gold discovered in, 276 ff.; lawlessness in, 301, 324
"Call to Foreigners," 264–266
Calvert, Charles, 35
Calvinists, 26
Cambridge, 14
Cameron, John M., 162, 281, 328
Cameron, W. W., 335
Canada de los Vaqueros, 217
Caravans, 198, 199
Cardinal, Jean Marie, 107
Cardinal, Mme., 107, 108
Carrillo, Josepha, 201
Carroll, Charles, 35
Carson, Frémont and Kit, 250
Carter, Major, 15
Casas Grandes, 199
Cass, Lewis, 83; settles Marsh's difficulties in Taliaferro affair, 85, 86, 92; and Marsh go to Washington, 87, 89; entertains Marsh, 96; and Indian uprisings, 123–127; appointed commissioner to Indian council, 143; his success since 1825, 269, 270; interest in California and Oregon, 269–271
Cassville, 106
Castro, José, 206, 233; Micheltorena marches against, 252–257, 258–261; besieges Frémont, 272, 273
Catholics, Roman, landowners of California required to be, 205
Chambers, Talbot, 108
Chamberlain's Tavern, 313
Chandler's, Mrs., boarding house, 29
Charlestown, 14
Cherokee, 193, 197
Chihuahua, 199
Chiles, J. B., 238, 244
Chimney Rock, 183
Chino, *see* José Antonio Olivas
Chippewa, hostile message sent to Sioux, 147
Cholera, at Prairie du Chien, 177
Choteau, Pierre, Jr., 189
Chouteau, C., 144
Clark, Charlotte Ouisconsin, 61, 62, 64, 66
Clark, General, 123, 147, 150, 151
Clark, Malcolm, 62, 64
Cloudman, 72
Coffin, Captain and Mrs., 326

Colas, 107
Comanches, the, 190; Marsh captured by, 195
Concord, 217
Consumnes, the, 273
Continental Divide, 184
Cooper, Frances, 284
Cooper, Sarshel, 277
Cooper, Stephen, 277, 284
Cooper, Susan, 284
Corn's, Mrs., boarding house, 25
Corumna the Lame, 139
Cosmopolitan Company, 206
Crawford County, 112
Crittenden, Mr., 327, 328
Crockett, Colonel, 327, 328
Crowninshield, Ann, 156, 157
Crows, 187
Curwen, Justice, 7

Danvers, 11–13, 41, 42, 94, 95
Davis, Isaac, 15, 17
Davis, Jefferson, 109
Decouteaux, Marguerite, 329 ff.; Marsh first meets, 78; Marsh educates, 79, 80; approaching motherhood, 83–85, 87; son born, 98; Marsh returns to, 99; Sioux warning to, 118; helps defend Fort Crawford, 124; and Chippewa message, 147; Marsh's partiality for Sioux blamed to, 151; flight of, 161 ff.; escapes from Pantier's, 165, 166; birth of daughter, 167; death of, 167
Dennegri, Gaspard, 11
Denny, St. Clair, 59
Detroit, 52
Deviese, 175
Dewey, Mr., 29
Dixon's Ferry, 173
Dixwell, John, 43, 50
Doan, 29
Dodge, Henry, 128, 179; and Indian lead lands, 139–143
Dodge's Rangers, 174
Dodgeville, 140
Dorr, Thomas W., 35, 36, 45
Dousman, Colonel, 113
Downing, Professor, 40
Dunbar, 41

Eaton, John H., 151
Eaton, Reverend Mr., 23

388

INDEX

El Encino, 258
"Elazeph," L'Arc, 118
Emerson, 19
England, contending for California, 231
English Prairie, 140
Epes, Larnard, 5
Ermetinger, 207
Essex Coffee House, 8
Estanislao, 208

Fair, Mrs., 327
Fallon's Party, 260
Faribault, Jean Baptiste, 78
Faxon, 333, 334
Fay, Mr., 96
Feather River, 208
Felton, Mary, 9
Fever River, mining at, 106, 107, 116, 125
Figueroa, 200
Fitch, Henry, 201
Flannery, John B., 189
Fletcher, 15
Flournoy and Hickman, 189
Forsyth, R. A., 144
Fort Cass, 187
Fort Crawford, 175; flooded, 98; threatened attack, 98, 99, 115; described, 108; Marsh commands, 123 ff.; cholera at, 77
Fort Hall, 237
Fort Hamilton, 172
Fort Nicholas, founded, 108
Fort Ross, 216
Fort St. Anthony, 43, 49, 55–71, 72 ff.
Fort Snelling, 103, 108, 115
Fort Sutter, 271, 274
Fort Winnebago, 132
Fowle, Major, 142
Foxes, the, 110; murder and abduction of Sioux by, 145; massacre of, 152–154; territory ceded by, 155; their hostility to Marsh, 155 ff.
France, contending for California, 231
Franklin Academy, 10
Frémont, Captain, 263, 271 ff.
French, at Green Bay, 52, 53
Frigate, R. M., 316

Gagnier, Mme., 120, 121
Gagnier, Registre, 120, 122; scalp of, 137, 138
Gaines, Edmund P., 158

Galena, 125; Rangers, 128; *Journal*, 149
Gantt, John, 253, 259–262, 283
Garcia, Juan, 318, 321, 322
Geddes, Paul, 240
Gift, Colonel, 320
Gillespie, 273
Gloucester, serpent in harbor of, 8
Gold, discovery of, 276 ff.
Graham, Isaac, 200, 272; denounced as conspirator, 232–235; offers help against Californians, 252
Gratiot, Henry, 144
Green, Talbot H., *see* Paul Geddes
Green Bay, 51–53, 105; treaty of, 144
Green River, camp on, 185, 186
Greenough, 41
Gutierrez, Nicholas, 200

Hague, William, 192, 243
Hamilton, James W., 62, 170
Harvard University, 34–45
Haskell, Charles T., 38
Hastings, John, 9
Haven, 15
Hawthorne, Justice, 7
Hayward, James, 40, 41
Helena, 174
Henry Clay, 96
Hickman, Robert, 239
Higueroa, Mirando, 217
Hijar and Padres, 206
Hollis, stone step split, 41
Holmes, George, 185, 186
Hopper, Charles, 239, 244
Horseshoe Bend, 173
Hovey, Rufus P., 10
Hudson's Bay Company, 77, 207, 217, 266
Hunsacker, Daniel, 301
Hunsacker, Nicolas, 277
Hunter, Lieutenant, 64

Inches, Henderson, 35
Independence (Mo.), 189 ff.; emigrants to California from, 239, 250
Indians, near Fort St. Anthony, 58–60, 72; attack on Tullys, 64, 65; Marsh in camp of, 69; quarrel with smugglers, 70; half-breed girl, 77; massacres, 98; near Prairie du Chien, 109–111; disturbances of, 115 ff., 122 ff., 152–154, 157 ff., 169 ff.; councils of, 127, 155; leaders in uprising surrendered, 128–132; lead

INDEX

lands of, 137, 139 ff.; treaties with, 155, 178, 179; set free at outbreak of cholera, 178; on Santa Fé trail, 190; give equal weight in gold for beads, etc., 277, 278
Ipswich Road, Marsh homestead on, 5, 7

Jesus, José, 252
Johnson, J. Neely, Proclamation issued by, 325
Johnston, Albert Sidney, 109
Joven Guipuzcoana, 235
Juan, 305

Kearney, Stephen Watts, 109, 114, 177
Kelseys, the, 244
Keokuk, 110
Kettle, Fox chief, 153
Kickapoos, the, 158
Kinzie, John H., 144, 179
Kirkland, John Thornton, 34, 35, 49
Kuprianof, Ivan, 216

L'Arc, 72, 110, 171
La Framboise, Michel, 207, 217
Laguna Seca, 271
Lancaster Academy, 13, 14 ff.
Langstroth, 198
Laramie River, 184
Larkin, Thomas O., 225, 268
Lead, Winnebago lands, 137, 139 ff.
Leese, Jacob P., 210, 211
Leonard, Gilbert, 300, 302
Lexington, 14
Lincoln, Abraham, 162, 282
Lincoln, Maria, 15, 18, 19
Lipkap, Solomon, 63, 120, 121, 122
Little Six, village of, 72
Livermore, Robert, 217
Lockwood, Judge, 117, 123, 124
Lockwood, Mrs., 120
Long, Doctor, 277
Loomis, Captain, 175
Los Angeles, 199-201
Los Medanos, 217
Los Meganos, 215, 224 ff., 290 ff., 316
Lucas, Samuel D., 189
Lugo, Antonio, 251
Lunt, William P., 35

Mackinac, 52
Mackinaw, 105
Manza-ku-to, 59
Markham, Governor, 335

Marsh, Alice, 294, 296, 298, 324, 326, 335
Marsh, Caleb, 9, 95, 96, 222, 283
Marsh, Charles, 101, 133, 151, 319; webbed toes, 100, 164, 309; father sees him growing into a savage, 156, 164; Pantier's care of, 161 ff.; Lincoln's interest in, 162; baptized, 167; at nine years, 192; father visits, 192; becomes known by name of Pantier, 223; death reported, 282; visits father, 305 ff.; at father's burial, 324; gets share of father's estate, 326 ff.; moves into father's home, 333; vows retaliation for father's death, 333
Marsh, Ezekiel, 5
Marsh, Ezekiel, Jr., 5
Marsh, John (of Salem), landing of, 3, 4; marriage, 4; children, 4, 5
Marsh, John (son of John Marsh of Salem), 5
Marsh, John (son of Ezekiel Marsh), 5
Marsh, John (grandson of Ezekiel Marsh), 6
Marsh, Rev. John, 35
Marsh, John (great-grandson of Ezekiel Marsh), birth, 6; boyhood, 7-10; education, 9-11, 15 ff., 23-45; teaches in Danvers, 12, 13, 42; at Lancaster, 14-21; fruit pilfering, 17, 18; first love affairs, 18-20; health, 17, 31, 32, 70, 96, 97, 136, 279; determines to enter ministry, 21; evades military training, 22-24; goes to Boxford, 23; a rolling stone, 25, 43; at Phillips Academy, 25-33; at Harvard, 34-45; dismissed from college, 41; determines to be physician, 42; returns to college, 42; tutor at Fort St. Anthony, 43, 49, 55 ff., 61 ff.; trip West, 50-54; takes Harvard diploma West, 49, 50, 194; letters home, 50, 51, 69-71, 83, 87, 88, 89, 93-95, 101, 104, 105, 127, 129, 133-136, 143, 249; description of, 56; opens post school, 61 ff.; mail carrier, 68-71; his relations with the Sioux, 69, 72 ff., 110, 111, 145-151, 168; substitute Indian Agent at St. Peters, 74 ff.; and Marguerite Decouteaux, 78-80; quarrels with the Taliaferros, 73, 81-86, 89-94, 102, 103; letters to Cass, 86, 116, 270,

390

INDEX

271; Indian sub-agent at Prairie du Chien, 86, 92, 93; goes to Washington with Cass, 87, 89; charge filed against, 90, 91; meets President Adams, 93, 94; visits parents in Danvers, 94, 95; visits Cass, 96; returns to Marguerite, 99; birth of son, 100, 101; made Justice of Peace, 112–114; and Winnebago war, 118–132; compiles Indian dictionary, 79, 133; writes grammar, 133; goes to St. Louis, 133; his desire to be Agent, 134, 135; recovers Gagnier's scalp, 138; sent to Indian lead lands, 140–142; rescues Sioux captives, 145; carries Chippewa message to Sioux, 147; arrests poachers on Winnebagoes, 148; Street's complaint against, 147, 150, 151; article claimed to have been written by, 149, 150; loses Indian agency and opens store, 151; sells ammunition to Indians, 151, 179; betrays Foxes to Sioux, 152; gets contract to build blacksmith shop, 155; hostility of whites and Foxes toward, 155 ff.; rumors of his marriage reach Danvers, 156, 157; his fears for Marguerite and boy, 157, 158, 161; leaves them with Pantier, 161–164; grief over Marguerite's death, 167, 179; melancholy, 168, 176, 177; in Black Hawk war, 168, 169 ff.; prepares to leave Prairie du Chien, 177; commissioner at negotiations for Indian treaty, 177–179; helps sick, 177, 178; his love of gold, 179, 205, 211, 277, 278, 281; warrant for arrest, 180, 183; escapes to Rocky Mountains, 180, 183–188; merchant in Independence, 189–193; visits son at Pantier's, 192; flees down Santa Fé trail, 193, 194; possessions taken to wilderness, 194; captured by Comanches, 195 ff.; his escape, 197, 198; reported marriage to Comanche, 196, 197; goes to California, 198–201; becomes doctor, 202–205, 224 ff.; in search of cattle range, 205, 206 ff.; baptized a Catholic, 207; his part in annexation of California to U. S., 209–211, 231, 237 ff., 250 ff., 263 ff., 268 ff.; his ranch in San Joaquin valley, 212 ff., 224, 290 ff.; unpopularity, 219, 281, 300; squaw mistress, 217; and the Bolgones, 220; letters from home, 222, 223, 262; longs to see son, 223, 282; obtains cattle for medical services, 224 ff.; his cattle brand, 226; robbed, 229, 299 ff., 304, 316; arrested for plotting to annex California to U. S., 232 ff.; his delight at arrival of Bartleson's expedition, 244; gifts to, 245; called on to explain presence of Missourians, 247; his treatment of Bidwell, 245, 248, 249; betrays Micheltorena, 254–257, 258–261; mother's death, 262; his plans for Republic of California, 263–267; refuses to join Frémont, 274; discovers gold, 277; his shipping establishment, 280, 281; news of death of his son, 282; and Abigail Tuck, 285–289; marriage, 289; employees, 292, 293; birth of daughter, 294; promotes railroad, 294, 295; new home, 295, 312, 315, 316; wife's death, 297, 298; trouble with squatters, 298 ff.; indictment against, 302, 303; son appears to, 305–313; contemplates second marriage, 313, 318; sued by Sebrian, 315; books cherished by, 194, 316; starts for San Francisco, 318 ff.; murdered, 321–323; burial, 324; estate of, 326 ff., 335, 336
Marsh, Polly Brown, 6, 9
Marsh, Susanna (Skelton), 3–5
Marsh, Zachariah, 4
Marsh's Diggings, 277 ff.
Marsh's Landing, 295
Marshall, James W., 276
Martinez, Guadelupe, 226
Martinez, Vicente, 226
Mary and John, 3
Mary's River, 238, 241
Massacres, Indian, 98
McClure, James, 59, 60
McClure, John, 324
McClure, Nancy, 60
McKenney, T. L., 92, 128, 130, 131
McKinstry, Judge, 331
McLaughlin, 216
McLeod, 207
McNair, Thomas, 117, 123
Mdewakantons, the, 76
Mellus, Henry, 222
Ménard, Pierre, 143

391

INDEX

Menard County, 223
Mendota, 57
Menominee, enlisted by Marsh, 124; join Sioux in attack on Foxes, 152, 153; massacre of, 159; and Black Hawk war, 169 ff.
Mesas, the, 217
Methode, M., 98
Mexico, hears rumors of attempt to wrest California from, 239 ff.; sends new governor to California, 251
Micheltorena, Manuel, 251-257, 258-261
Miller's Ferry, 165
Miner's Journal, 149
Mining, at Fever River, 106, 107, 116, 125; gold, 276 ff.; towns, 280
Minnesota, first school, 61-67
Mississippi, the, 53
Missourian expedition, to California, 240 ff.
Monterey, 275
Montgomery, Captain, 275
Morago, Pablo, 319
Morena, Felipe, 314, 318; murders John Marsh, 321-323; proclamation offering reward for capture of, 325; Charles Marsh's retaliation, 333-335; pardoned by Markham, 335
Morgan, Willoughby, 109
Morgan, warrior of the Fox, 110, 145
Mount Diablo, 212, 213, 336
Murietta, 304, 305

Napa, 283, 284
Neponset Hotel, 38
New Helvetia, 224
New Salem, 161
Newhall, David, 12, 13, 25
Niagara Falls, 51
Nichols, Andrew, 13, 40
Nino, *see* Felipe Morena
Noriega, José, 206, 213
North Andover, 10
Nourse, Jonathan, 12, 13
Nourse, Rebecca, 7
Nuestra Señora de los Dolores, see Our Lady of Sorrows
Nye, Michael, 192, 237, 239, 243, 247

Oakland, 335
Ogden, Peter Skeene, 207
Okh-pee, 68, 71

Olivas, José Antonio, 314, 321, 322, 333
Ord, Captain, 179
Oregon, plan for union of California and, 263
Oregon Trail, 183
Orion, the, 210
Osborne, John, 300, 302
Osgood, Doctor, 24
O'Toole, J. B., 189
Ottawas, the, 158
Our Lady of the Angels, 200, 201
Our Lady of Sorrows, 210
Owens, Samuel C., 189, 191, 237

Pacheco, Dolores, 213
Pacheco, Salvio, 217, 319
Page, Mr., 327
Pantier, James, 162, 163, 308; care of Marsh's son, 161 ff., 192; quarters of, 165
Paquette, Pierre, 144
Park, David, 278
Park, Mrs. David, 278
Park's Bar, 279
Parker, Chief Justice, 11
Pawnees, the, 190
Peabody, George, 222
Pecatonica, 173
Phillips Academy, 25-33
Phillips, Henry, 11, 32
Pickering, Charles, 35
Pico, Antonio Maria, 213
Pico, Pio, 262
Piermosky, 153
Plague, at Rock Island, 178
Platte County, California emigrant enthusiasts in, 239, 240
Polk, James, 268, 271
Portage, the, 126, 128
Porter, Ebenezer, 28, 30
Portneuf River, 238
Pottawatomies, the, 158
Powell, Peter and Joseph, 177
Prairie Aux Ailes, 170
Prairie du Chien, 52, 53; Marsh appointed sub-agent at, 86, 92, 93; flood and massacre at, 98; compared to Fort Snelling, 103; described, 104; history of, 105 ff.; deserted, 116, 117; warned of danger from Indians, 118, 119; defended, 122 ff.; cholera at, 177
Prairie du Pierreaux, 152

INDEX

Pratte, Miss, 81
Proctor, John W., 13, 14
Purcell, Edward, 60, 65
Pygmalion, 80

Real, Suarez del, 233, 235
Reaume, Charles, 113
Rebellion, at Harvard, 44
Red Bird, 99, 109, 110, 126; in Indian uprising, 117 ff.; surrendered by Winnebagoes, 128-132
Religion, in 19th century, 26, 27
"Remarks made On a Tour to Prairie du Chien," 133
Requena, Manuel, 203
Reynolds, John, Governor of Illinois, 158, 159, 169
Richardson, William A., 210
Ripley, George, 35, 36, 45
Robidaux, 239
Robinson, John P., 35
Rock Island, Indian council at, 177-179; plague at, 178
Rock River, 168, 169 ff.
Rodeo, the yearly, 292, 314
Roebuck Tavern, 11
Rolette, "King," 103, 115
Rotcheff, Baroness Alexandra, 216
Roy, Benjamin, 113
"Rudiments of the Grammar of the Sioux Language," 133
Russia, contending for California, 231
Russian-American Fur Company, 216
Rutledge, Ann, 162
Rutledge, James, 162, 282

Sabins, Pliney, 148
Sacramento City, 280
Sacramento River, 208
St. Louis, 227
St. Peters, Sioux agency of, 73-77
Salem, 3-5, 8
Salines, 253
San Francisco, 209-211, 279
San Joaquin, valley of, 212 ff.
San José, 206, 215, 246, 280, 285
San Miguel, 217
Sanders, John, 300
Sandridge, 161, 162
Santa Fé trail, 190
Santa Fé, 198
Santa Teresa, treaty of, 252
Sapa, Ampata, 79
Sapling Grove, 239

Saukenuk, 158
Sauks, the, 110; in mines, 116; territory ceded by, 155; war against whites, 170; set free at outbreak of cholera, 178
Schoolcraft, 85, 86
Scott, General Winfield, 63, 177, 178
Sebrian, Ygnacio, 217, 293, 314, 334
Serpent, in harbor of Gloucester, 8
Shadecker, Barbara Ann, 55
Shakespeare, stallion, 292
Shakopee, 72
Sierra Madre, 198
Sierras, gold discovered in, 276 ff.
Sinclair, aide-de-camp to Sutter, 254
Sioux, the, Marsh's relations with, 69, 72, 110, 111; the agency, 73 ff.; described, 76; warning to Winnebagoes, 117; warning to Marguerite, 118; Marsh's partiality for, 145-151; Marsh betrays Foxes to, 152; territory ceded by, 155; and Black Hawk war, 169 ff.; recruited by Marsh, 170; flight of, 173
Sissetons, 64, 65, 71, 76
Siyakumnas, the, 208
Skelton, Samuel, 3-6, 35
Skelton, Susanna, *see* Marsh
Slavs, colony of, 216
Sloat, Commodore, 275
Smallpox, 204
Smet, Father de, 241
Smith, William W., 286, 288, 289
Snelling, Abigail Hunt, 55-57
Snelling, Henry, 55, 62
Snelling, James, 55
Snelling, Joseph, 56, 62-64
Snelling, Colonel Josiah, 43, 57; described, 57; defends Marsh, 73; appoints Marsh agent, 74; his part in Taliaferro-Marsh quarrel, 73, 82, 83, 90, 91; reinforces Fort Crawford, 99; letter of refutation to Marsh, 102
Snelling, Mary, 55, 62
Song, to Kirkland, 35; Harvard class, 38-40
Sonora, the, 307, 311
South Church of Danvers, 10
Spear, Hinckley and Nathan, 210
Squatters, 298 ff.
Stearns, of Los Angeles, 207
Stevens, Samuel H., 35
Stewart, Mr., 28
Stillman, Isaiah, 169

393

INDEX

Stockton, 207, 276, 280
Stokes, James, 228
Stone, D., 12
Street, Joseph Montfort, Indian agent, 114, 135, 136; and Winnebagoes, 139 ff., 148; at news of murder of Sioux, 145, 146; complained of Marsh's partiality to Sioux, 147, 150, 151; arranges conference of Sauk and Foxes, 152; sends relief to Atkinson, 169, 170; commends Marsh, 172; sends despatches to Atkinson, 174; signs Indian treaty, 179
Suisun Bay, 319
Sunol, Antonio, 246
Sunol, Señora, 226
Sutter, John, 191, 216, 224, 252 ff., 261, 299
Sutter's Fort, 280
Swain, Captain, 326, 327
Sweetwater, the, 184, 186
Sycamore Creek, 169.

Taliaferro, Laurence, 58, 73; quarrel with Marsh, 81–86, 89–91, 94, 102, 103; Marsh warns of Indian attack, 118, 119; commends Marsh, 147
Taliaferro, Muscoe, 58, 73
Taos, 198
Tapia, Tiburcio, 203
Taylor, Zachary, 109
Taylor and Duncan, 189
Tetons, the, 76
Thayer, C., 17
Thayer, Nathaniel, 16
Thompson, Mrs., 296, 298
Tinslar, B. R., 227
Tomlinson, Ambrose G., 233
Tuck, Abigail Smith, 285–289; marriage to Marsh, 289; at Los Meganos, 290–297; death of, 297, 298
Tucker, C. C., 15
Tuleberg, 276, 279
Tully, Andrew, 62, 64, 65
Tully, John, 62, 64–66

Union Osgood, 8
University Hall, 37, 40

Valle de Los Tulares, 214
Vallejo, José de Jesus, 227
Vallejo, Mariano Guadeloupe, 216, 219, 229, 240; and Missourian immigrants, 246, 247; in jail, 274

Wabashaw, 99, 110, 175, 176
Wabashaw (village), 155, 156, 170
Wahpekutes, the, 76
Wahpetons, the, 76 ff.
Walker, Reverend M., 10, 13, 22
Walker, the, 241
Wa-man-goos-ga-ra-ha, 98
Wapello, 178
Warrior, 175, 176
Waugh-ha-ta-kau, 170
We-Kau, 119–121; surrendered by Winnebagoes, 128–132
Webb, Stephen H., 35, 325, 326
Webb, S. P., 281, 318
Weber, Captain, 252, 254, 266, 271, 272
Western Emigration Society, 239
Wheat, first grown in Contra Costa County, 220
Wheeler, O. C., 285
Wheelock, Luther, 15
Whistler, William, 128, 130–132
Whiting, Caroline Lee, 19
Whitings, the, 15
Whitney, Daniel, 91
Wilcox, Captain, 99
Williams, Thomas, 12
Wilson, James, 326
Wind River, 186
Wine Creek, 207
Winnebagoes, 99, 107, 109, 115 ff.; war with, 115–132; law of retaliation, 117 ff.; council at Butte des Morts, 126 ff.; surrender Red Bird and We-Kau, 128–132; Marsh recruits, 170; lands lost by treaty, 179
Winnieshiek, 170, 175
Winona, 79
Winona (Minn.), 170
Winthrop, John, 7
Wisconsin Heights, 174
Wolf, mad, 185, 186
Women, in California, 283 ff.
Woodbury, James Trask, 35

Yachekos, the, 207, 208
Yachekumna, the, 207
Yanktons, the, 76
Yerba Buena, *see* San Francisco
Yuba River, 277
Yunt, 216

ACKNOWLEDGEMENTS

THE EDITOR acknowledges the following individuals and organizations for making this edition possible:

- Argonaut Book Shop, San Francisco (http://Argonaut bookshop.com) for providing the first edition with dust jacket of John Marsh, Pioneer, that was used as the basis for this reprinting. What would society do without Robert D. Haines, Jr. and the longest open antiquarian book shop in San Francisco? Thank you ♥
- Marcy Protteau, copy editor extraordinaire, for her editing abilities and services.
- Hilda Yee, for patiently scanning every page of the book for this facsimile edition.
- Dorothy De Mare, for checking facts and reviewing new content.
- Leigh McLellan, for sharing her talent for graphic design.

ABOUT THE JOHN MARSH HISTORIC TRUST

THE GREAT STONE HOUSE built by Dr. John Marsh, when restored to its original 1856 character, will be majestic in its beauty and provide an important cultural resource for California. The new Marsh Creek State Historic Park is located 50 miles east of San Francisco in Brentwood, eastern Contra Costa County. Once the park is open to the public, it will be multifaceted and provide for a wide range of activities, with the House serving as a centerpiece and constant reminder of the unique history of the site. The John Marsh Historic Trust is dedicated to restoring the historic home in cooperation with the State of California, the City of Brentwood, Native Americans, and regional recreational and cultural interests.

The Stone House, an adobe, and Rancho los Megaños together represent a link between earlier historic sites such as Sutter's Fort, the Bidwell mansion, the Thomas Larkin adobe, the Vallejo adobe, and other significant houses built in California in the 1800s. The Stone House will be the focal point and symbol of early California history that will bring the entire park site to life, remind us of our local history, and teach us about the dynamics of California's early years.

Additionally, the recent discovery near the House of prehistoric remains dating back more than 8,000 years provides the additional opportunity to honor, preserve, and learn about the Native American people who lived on this land. The work of the archeologists is not complete at this time, but we are committed to supporting the development of these significant discoveries as part of the new historic park's overall goal of honoring the contribution of all Americans to the heritage of California.

First, however, we have to "SAVE THE JOHN MARSH HOUSE!" The John Marsh Historic Trust is nonprofit organization incorporated in 1994 and qualified under IRS code section 501(c)3. The specific purpose of this organization is to foster the preservation and restoration of the John Marsh Stone House and surrounding site. We need your support to preserve the remarkable history attributed to pioneers Dr. John Marsh and his wife Abigail, and to share that history with California residents and visitors alike. Your monetary donation of any amount is gratefully acknowledged and is deductible to the extent allowed by law.

The John Marsh Historic Trust
P.O. BOX 1682
Brentwood, CA 94513
Phone: 925-679-5811
Email: Information@JohnMarshHouse.com
Website: http://JohnMarshHouse.com

ABOUT THE TYPE

THE TEXT TYPE of the original book is likely a version of Scotch Roman. A nearly identical typeface is shown in *Printing Types, Vol. II* on page 194, "333. Modern Face Types: Alexander Wilson & Son's Specimen Glasgow, 1833." (Daniel Updike, Dover Publications, Inc., New York. Original printed 1937, reprinted 1980)

SCOTCH ROMAN

Scotch Roman designs were first cut by Richard Austin sometime before 1833 and cast by the Scottish typefounder Alexander Wilson and Son in Glasgow (estab. 1744). Type designer unknown. The Scotch Roman font has wide proportions, bracketed serifs, and large, strong capitals. —*adobe.com*

Alexander Wilson (1714–1786), a surgeon, typefounder, astronomer, mathematician, and meteorologist, was chair of practical astronomy at the University of Glasgow. —*wikipedia*

FOR THE NEW TEXT of the front and back matter, I chose Baskerville MT as being the most compatible of the typefaces in my collection in both style and historical period.

BASKERVILLE

British printer John Baskerville created this typeface in about 1752. He was much admired by Benjamin Franklin who popularized Baskerville's work in the Colonies, making the Baskerville typeface one of the official typefaces of the Federal government after the Revolution. The Monotype Design studio modeled its version on the *Comoediae* printed by Baskerville in 1772. It is a cleaner typeface than the original—the design streamlined the rougher characteristics in Baskerville's work, giving Monotype Baskerville a finer, more modern edge. —*Monotype Imaging*

Leigh McLellan Design

THE AUTHOR OF
JOHN MARSH, PIONEER

DR. GEORGE DUNLAP LYMAN, a distinguished child specialist of San Francisco, owns the best private collection of Californiana, numbering between six and seven thousand volumes. It is probably surpassed by only two public collections — the Huntington and the Bancroft.

He is the chief of the pediatric clinic in St. Luke's Hospital, San Francisco; a lecturer on pediatrics at the Stanford University Medical School; and has a large and important private practice. He has frequently written on medical subjects and also upon medical history in California. He is a director of the California Historical Society, and he belongs to a variety of clubs — including the Bohemian.

George Dunlap Lyman

Among his ancestors is Richard Lyman, progenitor of the family in America, who arrived from England in 1631 and helped to found Hartford, Connecticut. Dr. Lyman's father was a mining engineer; the author of the present volume was born at Virginia City, Nevada, December 12, 1882. He graduated from Stanford University in 1905, and received his M.D. from Columbia University in 1909. After travel in the Orient and Far East he did post-graduate work at Bellevue Hospital, New York City, graduating in 1911. Whereupon he married — in San Francisco. From 1912 until 1914 he travelled and studied in Europe, especially in Munich, and also in Berlin, where he was an externe of the Waissen Haus. In 1914 he began practising in San Francisco, specializing in pediatrics.

CHARLES SCRIBNER'S SONS

Back of dust jacket, first edition, 1930

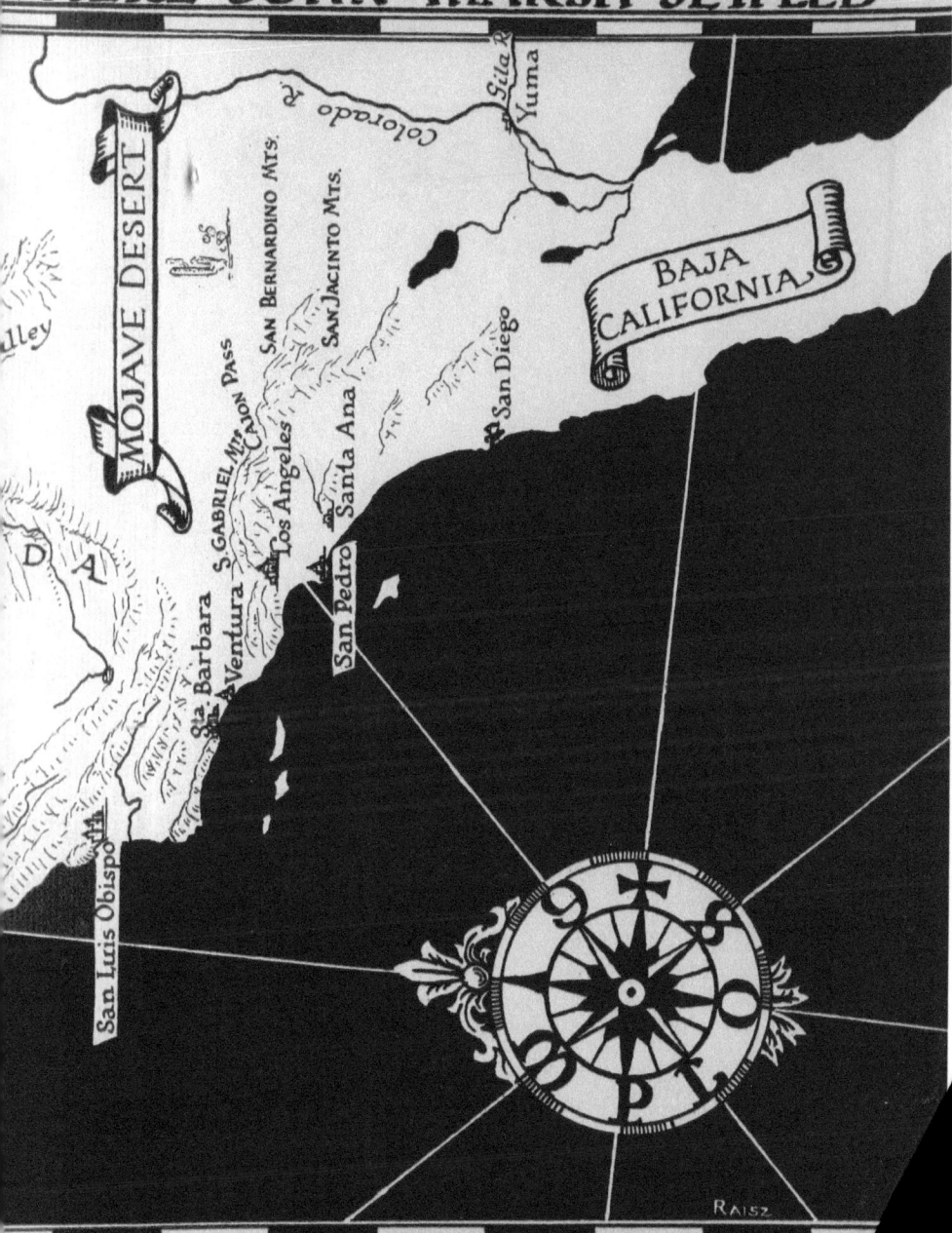